SOUTHERN AFRICA
The Continuing Crisis

CONTENTS

PREFACE TO THE SECOND EDITION

The rapidity with which changes have been occurring in Southern Africa, and the large demand for the first edition of this volume, have led us to do an update in order to take into account important new developments. There is a major revision of the Zimbabwe chapter because of the end of the guerrilla war and the coming of independence, and substantial updating in the South African one, especially on the position of black unions and constitutional innovations. Changes have also been made in the chapters entitled "Zambia," "Botswana," "Economic Patterns in the New Southern African Balance," and "United States Policy toward South Africa," and minor ones elsewhere.

To deal with the ever increasing international interaction in the Southern African region as a whole and with individual states we have also edited a new volume entitled *International Politics in Southern Africa*. This collected work deals with Soviet, Cuban, Chinese, American, Western European, Middle Eastern, and African policies in the region, as well as the evolution of counter regional groupings and the role of national and international aid.

We would like to express our appreciation to the African Studies Program at Indiana University, to Susan Myers, Susan Domowitz, Chloe Ann Miller, and Sue Hanson.

We hope that this updating of *Southern Africa: The Continuing Crisis* and the new companion volume, *International Politics in Southern Africa*, will help those concerned with the area to better understand its problems and possibilities.

INTRODUCTION:
The Continuing Crisis

The area dealt with in this book, the Southern–Central African quadrant, is of special significance today both because it holds possibilities of great power confrontations and because more than any place else in the world it is torn by that most explosive of all issues: black-white conflict for power. American concern derives not only from the United States' own racial history but also from its long and close economic ties with dominant white minorities in the quadrant. Under the Carter administration, the American commitment to human rights and majority rule was articulated clearly in relation to the region. But the Reagan administration, with its global approach to East-West issues, stresses the importance of the rich mineral resources and vital strategic location of South Africa, and warns against undermining the control of its numerous and entrenched white minority.

The authors in this book perceive its purpose to be to analyze the historical, political, economic, and social factors that have molded and are molding the policies of the countries discussed. But none sees any particular country in isolation. On the contrary, all are aware that there are certain common historical, political, and geographical characteristics within the region that cause constant interaction: in particular population movements, including labor migration, financial and economic linkages, and potential for future cooperation. While individual case studies note the historic dominance of South Africa in the region, the independence of Zimbabwe in 1980 following that of Mozambique and Angola limits its earlier political and strategic influence. While in the interests of keeping the book within manageable limits we have decided to concentrate particular attention on nine countries of the quadrant (South Africa, Zimbabwe, Zambia, Angola, Mozambique, Namibia, Botswana, Lesotho, and Swaziland), we are well aware that Tanzania, Zaïre, and Malawi may also be considered part of the Southern–Central African quadrant, and their role is referred to in several chapters.

These countries are distinguished from most of their neighbors to the north, in what is known as Black Africa, by their experience of substantial permanent white settlement. White settlement in the quadrant has varied widely, however, from the long-established white presence in South Africa dating back to 1652 to the much later and lesser colonization of areas to its north, such as Southern Rhodesia, now Zimbabwe, where whites first settled in 1890, and Northern Rhodesia, now Zambia. Various justifications have been articulated by whites at different periods in order to justify their dominance: the Portuguese fiction of assimilation and overseas provinces; the Central African notion of "partnership"; and the South African concepts of apartheid, of separate development, and, today, of pluralism. In all instances the central dilemma has been the same, that of entrenching white privilege while at the same time attempting to meet growing African demands.

The size of the white presence has been the conditioning factor in achieving the transfer of control from the colonial hands to local majorities during the past two decades. Tanzania became independent in 1961, earlier than its East African neighbor, Kenya, which suffered black-white conflict on its way to independence. Although bitter at the time, Kenya's internal conflict was far less prolonged than that between the Portuguese and their colonial territories: Guinea Bissau, Angola, and Mozambique.

In April 1974 an army coup in Lisbon opened the way to conceding independence and majority rule to all three of the Portuguese African territories. The Portuguese military were weary of the fighting that had gone on for more than a decade within these territories. Many observers, including Henry Kissinger, secretary of state under Presidents Nixon and Ford, had previously argued that if change were to come in Southern Africa, it would be through the white regimes. In response to the now notorious secret NSSM 39 (National Security Study Memorandum), Kissinger and President Nixon had agreed in 1969 to "tilt" American policies toward the white regimes in control in Southern Africa: South Africa, Rhodesia, and the Portuguese—who still dominated Angola and Mozambique. When they were proved wrong in 1974, international politics entered the region in earnest and, as individual chapters will illustrate, never left it.

International politics frequently fuel the racial issues that so seriously complicate the achievement of peaceful settlements in long-disturbed territories. The most obvious racial tension is between black and white, but there are also and sometimes even more bitter conflicts between rival African nationalist groups. In South Africa, and to some degree in Zambia, there are strains between Africans and Asians. Southern African politics are complex and often confusing, and simple plans for settling racial issues, like the homeland policy in South Africa, and the attempted internal settlement in Rhodesia, have been fraught with complications.

While there has never been any formal white alliance, certain solidarities used to prevail between the countries in the southern tier. In 1967 Minister of Defense P.W. Botha wrote, "True friends need no signed treaties. South Africa has an interest in what is happening in Angola, Rhodesia and Mozambique . . ." (*News from South Africa*, August 1967). On the African side, recently independent countries in the region, in particular the front-line states, became the promoters and in part the launching pads for pressing the political claims of black majorities. With the coming of independence to Angola, Mozambique, and Zimbabwe, the way has been opening to independence for Namibia and finally for basic political change in South Africa.

Economic factors may override political or racial antagonisms in particular situations. Mozambique, with its strongly Marxist ideology, and the South African regime have maintained their mutually advantageous economic ties. But the similarity of political goals of the presidents of the front-line states— Tanzania, Zambia, Angola, Mozambique, and Botswana—and now Zimbabwe —have created still closer common policies in the interest of promoting the transfer of power in Namibia. They have supported peaceful arrangements where they feel these offer realistic possibilities of a genuine transfer of power to the majority; where this is not the case they contribute their limited resources to the use of force to create such conditions.

Although the Southern–Central African quadrant includes a host of tension points, some of them between African-controlled states, it also offers many possibilities of rewarding cooperative arrangements, as Kenneth Grundy's chapter makes clear. The Cabora Bassa dam, with its immense power potential, could benefit more countries than South Africa and Mozambique, while the dam on the Cunene River in Angola is essential for irrigation in Namibia. Zambia and Zimbabwe share power from the Kariba dam. A common electric grid throughout the region could be a genuine future possibility. Moreover, migration of labor has always occurred within the region. The adverse stereotype attached to this process, particularly in South Africa, might be changed if movement were allowed to flow more freely between as well as within countries. Trade and finance still move more freely throughout the region than current antagonisms would lead one to anticipate. It is mainly political barriers that hamper cooperative planning and activities, so it is politics with which this book is necessarily chiefly concerned.

We see the current situation in Southern Africa as a prolonged turning point in its history. This turning point may lead to a radical reordering of political forces and political power or perhaps to a termination of an existing political order. Crisis politics rarely imply speedy resolutions. If there is no foreseeable resolution of the current crisis, it will continue, for it is the outgrowth of an unacceptable situation that too many people are determined to change regardless of how long it takes and what suffering may be entailed.

In the meantime the region remains in a state of tension, with trade restricted, border incidents, frequent disputes, and countries polarizing into hostile, armed confrontations. As Namibia moves toward satisfying resolutions, if it does, pressures will intensify on the white regime in South Africa, which is the strongest, most heavily armed, and most integrated into the Western economic system of any country or area in the quadrant. American policies will be one of the major factors that will tilt these varied situations one way or another.

Apart from conflict, which has been endemic in the whole region, particular countries may be in a state of *internal* crisis that may or may not be a direct result of the regional conflict. We do not see Botswana, Swaziland, or Lesotho, or for that matter Mozambique, in a current state of internal crisis, though the latter's economic situation is under severe strain. But Mozambique is in the process of consolidating its political institutions and appears to be approaching a stable political culture. Angola, on the other hand, has not yet reached this point and remains in a state of continuing internal crisis. Zambia may be close to internal crisis because its government is being severely challenged due to the fall in the price of copper, weak political institutions, and inefficient administration. Thus the liberation struggle, the coming of independence, and the regional interactions all pose different types of crisis.

In analyzing Southern Africa, we, the editors and the authors, accept certain common values. We favor whatever advances individual countries make toward nonracial government and majority rule. We hope this goal will be achieved through a process of peaceful change in which ruling white minorities participate. Although we recognize the existence of continuing white intransigence in South Africa, we also believe that it is possible for ruling whites gradually to yield their privileged positions, particularly if they recognize that the alternative may be prolonged warfare.

We have long been impressed by the persistent efforts of Africans in South Africa to mobilize peacefully and to seek change through nonviolent means. Younger Africans in South Africa and increasing numbers of its rural as well as urban Africans may not continue nonviolent policies, particularly if conflict persists and even intensifies on that country's borders. While we are primarily committed to analysis, we recognize our concomitant responsibility to point out the dangers of intensified confrontations, locally, nationally, and internationally. We share the fear that such confrontations may become ever more likely the longer the effective sharing of power is withheld.

We are not unaware that there are other scholars and analysts who hold different views and aims than we do. We believe our readers should weigh and balance for themselves these varied positions, and our bibliography includes books and periodicals designed to make this possible. What is vital is that maximum attention be given to an area of great importance not only to the United States and its Western allies, but also to millions of human beings throughout Southern Africa. Their destinies will inevitably be affected by Western policies, just as we will be affected by what happens to them.

GWENDOLEN M. CARTER
PATRICK O'MEARA

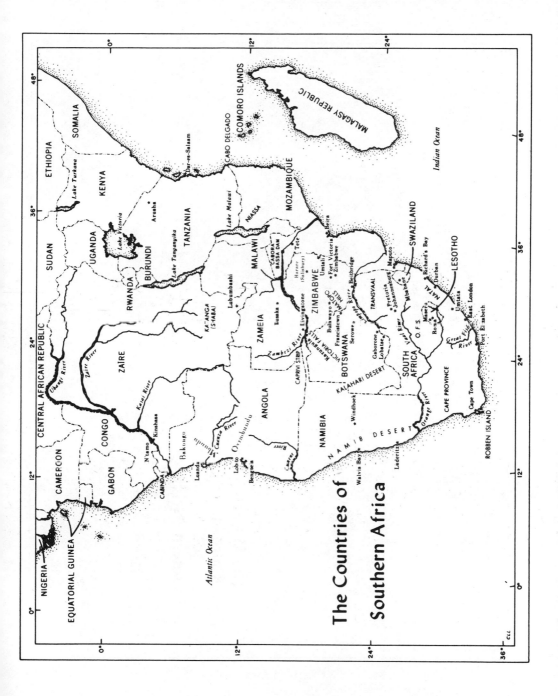

The Countries of
Southern Africa

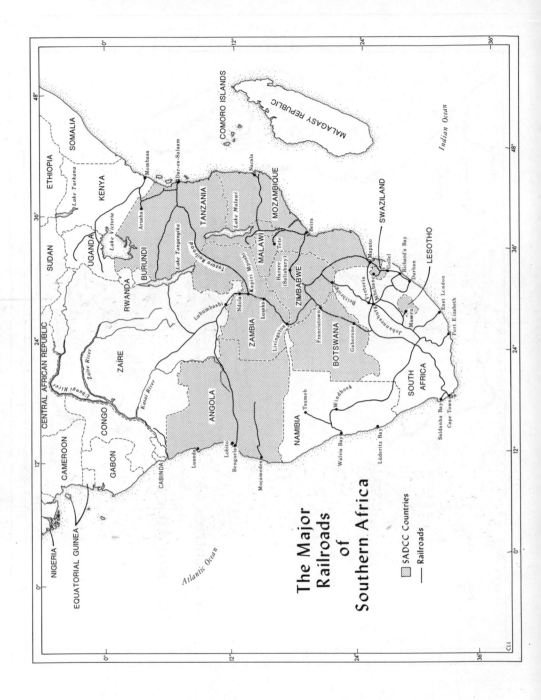

The Major
Railroads
of
Southern Africa

SADCC Countries
Railroads

1.

International Rivalries in the Southern African Conflict

Colin Legum

Four major forces—the West, the Soviet bloc, China, and the Third World —are engaged at different levels in the struggle to achieve a new political and economic equilibrium in Southern Africa. The Third World, the Soviet Union, and China share the common objective of ending white power in the sub-continent, but they are often divided over the means to achieve this end. The Soviet Union and China do not agree on tactics and means of influence within the Third World, and these rivalries are increasingly noticeable within Southern Africa. The West is torn between defense of its long-established interests in that area and its fear that failure to achieve satisfying transitions of power within the "white redoubt" will lead to intensified black-white conflict. Third World countries, and in particular the African-controlled states bordering those parts of Southern Africa still under white minority control, are un-divided in their aim of aiding their fellow Africans to achieve full political rights within their own countries. But their policies are inevitably affected by their perspective on how best to achieve this objective and by their own interests.

The Communist powers—the U.S.S.R. and China—have no interest of their own to defend in Southern Africa; they therefore stand to gain by commit-ting themselves fully to the cause of those challenging the present status quo in the region. Their situation is completely different from that of the Western powers, which see the region's centuries-old power system under serious chal-lenge. Although the Western powers have long ago lost the political hegemony they held over the subcontinent ever since the first Portuguese navigators landed there toward the close of the fifteenth century, they retain considerable economic and strategic interests in the area, as well as a measure of political influence. Just how much political clout they can deliver is a subject of controversy.

The challenge the Western powers now face comes primarily from the Africans, not from the Communist world. The African challengers seek the support of dependable allies to assist them in their struggle to achieve majority rule in the Republic of South Africa as well as in Namibia (South West Africa). Until the early 1970s the Africans had continued to put their hopes in being able to persuade the Western nations to use their political, economic, and military leverage against Portuguese colonialism and the minority regimes of Rhodesia and South Africa to facilitate a peaceful transition to majority rule. While most Africans have not yet finally despaired of getting Western cooperation—because of the West's own interests—they nevertheless no longer feel able to rely on the democracies.

Already, some African leaders and movements have taken up the option of entering into an alliance with either the Soviet bloc or China, thereby inevitably heightening the level of international involvement in the local power struggles. Their decision to take up this option is not primarily based on ideology but was made entirely for pragmatic reasons. A major contributory factor to this changing attitude was the experience of the anti-Portuguese liberation movements. These had found Lisbon's NATO allies not only unwilling to support their liberation struggle, but actually siding with the Caetano regime; by the time Portuguese colonialism finally collapsed in 1974, the three successful liberation movements (Frelimo in Mozambique, PAIGC in Guinea-Bissau and Cape Verde, and the MPLA in Angola) were thoroughly indebted to the Soviet Bloc and China for supporting what they had come to see as a fight against "Western imperialism." The long armed struggle and the close links established with the Communist world resulted in a Marxist-Leninist leadership gaining control over the liberation movements, which enabled it to stamp its ideology on Angola and Mozambique after independence.

But even though the Western powers had lost their political and economic initiative in Angola and Mozambique, they did not for a number of reasons altogether lose their political influence. Not even the new Marxist-Leninist regimes wanted to rely exclusively on their Communist allies since, like most Third World countries, they aspire to maintain a nonaligned foreign policy. They accept that their impoverished countries stand to gain from Western economic assistance and trade. In fact, Western economic aid to and trade with Mozambique and Angola since independence has been greater than that provided by the Soviet bloc. They also recognized the important role the Western powers could play in producing change in Rhodesia and Namibia, although they remain skeptical about their policies toward South Africa. Thus, the presidents of Angola and Mozambique elected to join with the presidents of Tanzania, Zambia, and Botswana in the alliance of front-line African states and cooperate in the negotiations with the Western powers over Rhodesia and Namibia. Finally, the support given by the Nordic countries (especially Sweden) to the anti-Portuguese liberation struggles has kept open important bridges to the West.

Western policies in Southern Africa were radically rethought after the collapse of Portuguese colonialism and, particularly, after the successful Russian/Cuban military intervention in Angola. The main lessons taught by the Angola experience were that if similar defeats were to be avoided in Rhodesia, Namibia, and South Africa, Western policies must be harmonized with dominant African interests. It was recognized that the first major breakthrough achieved by the Communists on Southern Africa's periphery was due to mistaken Western policies, not to any African preference for the Communist world. Western policymakers began to understand—as the Russians and Chinese already knew—that the world balance of power depends largely upon the sympathy of Third World nations.

However, it has not proved easy to adjust Western policies to this new understanding because of the complex nature of the West's historic connections with the dominant interests in the region. These links have acquired a number of important characteristics. First, there is a natural sense of kinship with the local white communities, who mostly originate from Western Europe. Second, the West shares considerable interests—notably economic and defense—with these white minorities who exercised such control over the region. Therefore, the relationship had developed into an almost exclusive alliance between the West and the white minority regimes, which has made Southern Africa a virtual "outpost of the West." The Africans certainly still see it as such. In their eyes it has always seemed possible for the major Western powers to determine policy in the area. Naturally this is an oversimplification of the real nature of the relationship that exists between the white regimes and the metropolitan powers, notably Britain.

While the local white communities have always seen themselves as forming an integral part of the Western world, they have also held strong views about the nature of that relationship. As far back as the late eighteenth century, the Boers in the old Cape of Good Hope had rebelled against the then Dutch rule—inspired partly by the American Revolution. Like other settler communities in the old empires, they wished to rule themselves and to decide their own way of life. Their anticolonial stand long predates that of modern black nationalism. The South African war (1899–1902), fought by the Boers to resist British imperialism, ended in the independence of South Africa. The Act of Union of 1910 transferred effective political and military power to the white minority, while the Act of Self-Government for Rhodesia in 1923 gave its white minority virtual control over the country's internal affairs.

This process of self-determination was carried farther by two crucial developments that brought the local white communities into conflict with major Western policies. The first was the election in 1948 of an Afrikaner nationalist government in South Africa committed to a policy of apartheid. This policy, designed to entrench white political rule in a major area of the African continent, ran directly against the policies on which the major European colonial powers had embarked at that precise time of granting independence to the millions of colored peoples in their empires. The Afrikaner nationalists' sharp deviation from current Western thinking brought white South Africa into direct conflict with the new British interest in developing a multiracial Commonwealth of Nations, and resulted in South Africa's exclusion from Commonwealth in 1961. The second development was the white Rhodesians' unilateral act of independence (UDI) in 1965—a direct challenge to Britain's policy of encouraging black majority rule for its self-governing colony.

Both the election of an apartheid regime in South Africa and UDI in Rhodesia were manifestations of the determination by white minority communities to defend a status quo based on white supremacy—in direct defiance of the growing groundswell of black nationalism and of post-imperial Western policies. These heresies in an "outpost of the West" raised serious problems for Britain and its Western allies. Having surrendered their colonial powers to local white minorities, the British could only effectively check these developments by using military force (in the case of Rhodesia) or by resorting to economic sanctions. Domestic British considerations ruled out the use of force in Rhodesia, and it was hardly practical in the case of South Africa since it would mean a second, and even more serious, Anglo-Boer war. Although sanctions were imposed against Rhodesia, Western (not just British) opinion was against using this economic weapon against South Africa—except for an arms embargo.

This reluctance to support sanctions against South Africa pinpoints the dilemma facing Western policymakers. It is the dilemma of all trading and investor countries faced with a conflict between economic and political interests. Where does the balance of interest lie? South Africa is not just a major Western trading partner; it is also the West's major source of strategically important resources, as is shown in the table on page 7.

South Africa's total international trade in 1977 stood at $7,536 million, the bulk of it with Western Europe, North America, and Japan. The table on page 8 shows South Africa's major trading partners.

British investments in South Africa were $9.5 billion in 1977, half of all the foreign investment in the Republic. United States investments were worth $1.665 billions, this being 40 percent of its total investment in Africa.

These figures explain why South Africa remains a major economic interest to its trading partners—quite apart from its military-strategic interest in the balance of world power, especially in the area of ocean politics. So long as there were no other challenging national interests, the Western nations could simply foster their profitable economic relations with the Republic, irrespec-

Table 1

South African Mineral Production, 1976 (as percentage of total Western
world and total world production)

	Western world rank	Western world production %	World rank	World production %
Platinum group metals	1	86	1	48
Gold	1	75	1	59
Vanadium	1	58	1	46
Chrome ore	1	41	2	26
Manganese ore	1	40	2	24
Andalusite group metals	1	30	1	30
Antimony	1	33	1	22
Vermiculite	2	39	—	—
Diamonds	2	23	3	18
Asbestos	2	18	3	9
Uranium (U_3O_8)	3	13	4	9
Coal	5	6	8	3
Phosphate	5	2	7	1
Fluorspar	7	6	10	5
Nickel	7	3	9	3
Copper	8	3	10	2
Iron ore	10	2	12	1
Tin	10	2	12	1
Silver	13	1	16	1
Zinc	15	2	21	1
Lead	36	0.05	46	0.03

Source: SA Department of Mines; Financial Mail, May 20, 1977.

tive of its political system. Western policies, until the mid-1970s—the Angola episode—were ambiguous. They supported African majority rule and joined other nations in strongly condemning apartheid and UDI; they urged, implored, and warned the regimes of South Africa and Rhodesia to yield to the "winds of change"; but they nevertheless continued to expand their economic stake in the apartheid Republic. They voted at the U.N. for resolutions demanding Namibia's independence, and at the same time actually enlarged their economic interests in that territory. They applied quiet diplomatic pressures on the Lisbon regime to abandon their colonial wars in Africa, but they continued to buttress Portugal as a member of NATO.

Like Micawber, they hoped that something would turn up to save them from making painful choices about South Africa. Their hope, in fact, was that the pressures of black opposition and of international opinion (as well as sanctions against the Smith regime) would result in the Rhodesian, South African, and Portuguese regimes accepting the need to use the time still available to them to begin to change courses by planning for a peaceful

Table 2

Direction of South African Trade (millions of U.S. dollars)

	1975	1976	1977 (Jan.-June)
Major Purchasers			
United Kingdom	1,255.0	1,146.6	773.0
United States	589.7	526.8	378.9
Japan	664.9	592.0	327.1
Africa, not specified	573.1	521.1	291.5
West Germany	601.8	543.8	264.5
Belgium	162.4	224.7	119.8
France	155.6	170.6	108.0
Italy	124.8	165.1	97.0
Asia, not specified	105.9	113.4	84.7
Netherlands	120.3	143.6	78.0
Total (including others)	8,864.8	7,874.1	4,594.5
Major Suppliers			
United States	1,340.8	1,458.2	616.9
West Germany	1,409.2	1,217.5	513.8
United Kingdom	1,493.9	1,185.3	488.2
Japan	840.3	690.5	330.9
Africa, not specified	344.3	356.3	175.3
France	335.4	294.7	150.4
Italy	275.9	243.7	92.4
Netherlands	192.5	170.4	70.6
Switzerland	192.5	142.4	67.8
Asia, not specified	105.5	133.7	59.7
Total (including others)	7,591.2	6,769.4	2,941.4

Source: IMF, Direction of Trade.

transition to majority rule. In the end, something did "turn up"—but it was not what the West had bargained for. In fact, four things "turned up" that forced the West to rethink their policies.

The most traumatic of these developments was the arrival in Angola of a Russian and Cuban military presence in 1974–75, right on the doorstep of Namibia and South Africa. Hardly less important was the practical demonstration of a successful African armed struggle in Mozambique as well as Angola, helped mainly by the Communist nations. Guerrillas had, meanwhile, also begun to operate more effectively against Namibia and Rhodesia. Inside South Africa itself the façade of stability was pierced by the evidence of black urban discontent, brought into the open by the students' demonstrations in Soweto in 1976 and by the rise of the Black Consciousness movement, symbolized by its martyr, Steve Biko. Suddenly, the seemingly impregnable "white bastion" in Southern Africa began to look much less secure than had previously been supposed. The argument that time was on the side of a low-key, pragmatic, and ambiguous Western policy was no longer tenable.

Another significant development was the emergence of Nigeria as a more important trading partner of Britain and other European countries even than South Africa; and the new determination of the Nigerian regime to throw its weight fully behind the "African Revolution" by announcing that foreign firms would have to choose in the future between doing business with them or with South Africa.

The first initiative in launching a new Western policy toward Southern Africa was announced by the United States in a speech delivered by Secretary of State Henry Kissinger in Lusaka in April 1976. He declared:

> I have come to Africa because in so many ways the challenges of Africa are the challenges of the modern era. Morally and politically, the drama of national independence in Africa over the last generation has transformed international affairs.

The significance of his Lusaka speech was that it completely reversed previous policy by putting the United States firmly on the side of black majority rule throughout Southern Africa. If the reason for Kissinger's *volte face*—a straight reaction to the Russian/Cuban intervention in Angola—was American self-interest, this does not alter the importance of the new thrust given to American policy, which has been pursued with greater vigor, and more constructively, by the new Carter administration since 1977.

Carter's decision to send Vice-President Walter Mondale to a meeting in Vienna with South Africa's prime minister, John Vorster, in May 1977 was the most significant of five steps taken in the last two decades by Western leaders in evolving a new attitude toward South Africa. The other four steps were: Harold Macmillan's "Wind of Change" speech in Cape Town in 1960; South Africa's exclusion from the Commonwealth in 1961; support by most Western countries for the Security Council's arms embargo in 1966; and Kissinger's Lusaka speech in 1976. A sixth major step only came later, when all the Western nations backed a U.N. *mandatory* arms embargo against South Africa in late 1977.

The message delivered in Vienna on behalf of President Carter was that white South Africa could expect no support from the U.S. unless there was progress on "majority rule for Rhodesia and Namibia, and a progressive transformation of South Africa's society to the same end." Mondale made it clear that the U.S. did not expect changes to come overnight but that steps should be taken toward the ultimate goal of a democratic society. The decisive change in Washington's position was marked by Mondale's carefully worded warning: "We hope that South Africa will carefully review the implications of our policy and the changed circumstances which it creates. We hope that South Africans will not rely on any illusions that the U.S. will in the end intervene to save South Africa from the policies it is pursuing, for we will not do so." In other words, if South Africa ever found itself in a military conflict with Africans—even if they had Communist support—the U.S. would not intervene militarily to defend apartheid. Prime Minister Vorster correctly interpreted this message to mean the beginning of South Africa's isolation within the Western community: their heresy of apartheid had become intolerable.

British policy shifted in line with Washington's after David Owen became foreign secretary early in 1977. Britain, he said, could no longer continue to pursue its former policy of "contradictions and inconsistencies" which had characterized its African position; implacable opposition to racialism in all forms was "not only a moral obligation: it is the assertion of our national interest. We must make it unequivocally clear that we are now committed to doing everything possible to enable Africans to win their legitimate rights in South Africa."

It is this recognition of where the *national interest* lies that reveals the basic change that has begun to emerge in Western policies. Owen—supported by the chancellor of the exchequer, Denis Healey, and by other British ministers—began to place increasing emphasis on the fact that British trade with Nigeria had grown to twice that of trade with South Africa. Although Owen warned that Britain's economic links with South Africa could not be cut overnight, he stressed that with the passage of time the balance of advantage, overall, must "increasingly lie with black Africa."

This balance of advantage also got a new tilt in Western Europe after 1976. Nine members of the European Economic Community (EEC) began to coordinate their policies toward South Africa and Rhodesia on a number of issues, for example over Namibia and over a code of conduct of EEC firms in South Africa. They also began a study of contingency plans for selective sanctions against the Pretoria regime. It is significant that France, Europe's maverick, joined in this collective stand by the Community toward Southern Africa. The French took a particularly hard line against the Pretoria regime because of its plans to carry out nuclear tests in the Kalahari. And at long last they joined in voting to make the arms embargo against South Africa mandatory in 1977. The West Germans, too, began to shift more clearly away from their careful reluctance to do anything that might affect their trade with South Africa.

This hardening of the European community's attitude toward South Africa and the winding down of France's military connection with Pretoria were not immediately matched by Israel's policies. Under Golda Meir's regime, Israel had been careful to distance itself from Pretoria; but with the beginning of General Y. Rabin's administration and especially under Menachem Begin economic and military cooperation between the two countries increased. Israel needed strategic minerals and other resources available in South Africa, as well as greater trade; South Africa was eager to acquire Israeli military technology. This peculiar relationship between the Jewish State and the apartheid Republic drew little public protest from Israelis, who had come to feel themselves increasingly isolated in the United Nations after the massive break of diplomatic relations by virtually all the countries in Africa in late 1973. They also bitterly resented the U.N. General Assembly vote equating Zionism with racism and apartheid. However, Israel has agreed to observe the U.N.'s mandatory arms embargo against South Africa.

This reevaluation of their policies by the Western nations, which only began in real earnest in 1975, has so far produced three significant changes. The first is that they no longer see their role in Southern Africa as doing the minimum necessary to placate critical African attitudes or to salve their own moral conscience. They have come increasingly to accept that their own long-term national interests require an active commitment to help produce meaningful change within a relatively short period. Although there are still important disagreements about how much time remains, there is no longer any serious debate among Western policymakers about whether any form of apartheid, or separate development, can succeed, nor about the chances of South Africa's present political system surviving. There is now a more realistic understanding about Western interests as well as about the future of the Republic. The second change is that a consensus has begun to develop within the Western community about the nature of the crisis in South Africa and about the possible need for interventionist policies. Thus, Western official opinion—as distinct from public opinion—has become less polarized than it was in the 1960s. The third change is that all the Western nations now accept that their best course of action lies in seeking the cooperation of the effective (not just the "moderate" or "pro-Western") African leaders. There is also a greater readiness to acknowledge the need to consult with Africans and to take fully into account their wishes.

These changed perceptions can be seen in the approach of the two Western initiatives over Rhodesia and Namibia. Both were developed in close consultation with the leadership of the five front-line states—Tanzania, Zambia, Mozambique, Angola, and Botswana—as well as with Nigeria. One striking result of this new approach has been the willingness of the leaders of all these countries to work with the Western nations notwithstanding the strong hostility of the Soviet bloc (though not of the Chinese). There was some initial hesitation on the part of President Agostinho Neto of Angola (though not of President Samora Machel of Mozambique) about accepting the role of the Americans, in tandem with the British, in developing their joint Rhodesian initiative; however, the dominant African forces (guided largely by the head of the front-line presidents, Julius Nyerere of Tanzania) have given strong encouragement to the American role for the muscle it can provide to Britain's negotiating strength.

The Western initiative over Namibia has been even more remarkable than it was over Rhodesia. It brought together all the Western members of the

Security Council (the United States, Britain, France, West Germany, and Canada) under an American head. Its initial success depended on a concerted Western démarche on Pretoria to get it to agree to suspend the internal settlement worked out by the Turnhalle conference. The strong backing given by President Neto to this initiative had been especially striking; in fact he had played a decisive role in helping to bring the reluctant SWAPO leadership to accept the Western proposals for a negotiated settlement. Finally, the initiative has also closely involved the Nigerians.

Whatever their final outcome, these two initiatives on Rhodesia and Namibia have demonstrated the opportunities for confident Western and African cooperation in achieving agreed objectives. They also show that, given a choice, even the most radical of the African leaders stand ready to cooperate with the West in finding agreed settlements for the conflicts in Southern Africa.

The Soviet role in the region has changed considerably since the success of Russia's joint intervention with the Cubans in Angola—a success which showed that Soviet military power now makes it possible for Moscow to intervene in conflicts in the most distant parts of the world. Angola also demonstrated the political advantage to the Soviets of having the Cubans as their allies in African situations, because of the greater acceptability of a small Third World revolutionary country and because of the combat role of Cuban troops. Despite the Soviets' power, they could not have provided the kind of ground support needed by the MPLA forces—nor for that matter, to the Ethiopians in Ogaden—without the use of foreign combat troops. The fact that many Cubans are not white has also been a considerable asset to the Soviets in the African situation.

A few months before his sudden removal from office, President Podgorny surveyed Southern Africa in a speech in Maputo in March 1977.

Is it not symbolic that your frontiers with Rhodesia and the Republic of South Africa are now not only state frontiers but also class frontiers? From Mozambique and Angola is blowing a wind of freedom which inspires the patriots of all southern Africa. The USSR's attitude on the question of southern Africa is plain: we call for the immediate granting of the inalienable rights of the southern African peoples to self-determination; for the liquidation of apartheid and racism in the South African Republic; for the latter's immediate withdrawal from Namibia, and for the unconditional and full transfer of full power to the people of Zimbabwe. The road which the peoples will take to the solution of these tasks is their affair. Depending on the situation and the conditions obtaining, they will choose one or another means of struggle. Of course, a peaceful political solution of all problems would be desirable. But since the rights of the oppressed peoples of Zimbabwe, Namibia and the South African Republic are being ignored, their desire to have recourse to armed struggle is entirely understandable. The Western Press is at present trying to scare the world with such a prospect. What is one to say about this? Just this: hand over power, gentlemen, to the majority of the population—that is, to the Africans in the person of their genuine representatives—and have done with the policy of apartheid. Then the problem will be solved.

The U.S.S.R. now has two Treaties of Friendship in or on the periphery of Southern Africa: with Mozambique and with Angola. Both include Soviet commitments to come to their aid if required to do so in the event of military attacks on their borders. This part of the two agreements is similar to that invoked by the Ethiopian military regime to defend its Ogaden province against Somali incursions.

The U.S.S.R.'s three declared objectives in Southern Africa are to establish friendly relations with the front-line states, to help strengthen the liberation movements, and to assist in seeing the removal of the "outposts of imperialism" and of the stranglehold of the "imperialist transnational corporations." As a rival superpower, the U.S.S.R. is obviously interested in helping to remove American and other "NATO imperialist" influences in the subcontinent; but Moscow also has a major interest in diminishing China's influence in the area as part of its worldwide rivalry with Peking.

Sino-Soviet rivalry is a key factor in the internationalization of the conflicts in Southern Africa. It was a major reason for the Russian/Cuban military intervention in Angola. Today Moscow can rely on President Neto's MPLA regime faithfully to follow its line on Chinese "revisionism." President Machel's regime has also forged close ties with Moscow, even though Frelimo had received most of its foreign support from Peking throughout its long liberation struggle. China withdrew its ambassador from Maputo for a short period because of Mozambique's growing relations with Moscow; it objected particularly to the Treaty of Friendship with the U.S.S.R. President Machel, however, has worked hard to repair his broken fences with the Chinese.

Sino-Soviet rivalry is especially sharp over the liberation movements. The Kremlin's policy toward these movements was described by Aleksey Nikolayev in a radio Moscow broadcast on May 30, 1977:

A basic characteristic of Soviet help should be underlined. By giving disinterested support to all those fighting against national and social oppression and against capitalist exploitation, the USSR has, contrary to what Rhodesian and South African ministers say, never helped any nationalist movements, that is, any splittist groups. Using the pretext of struggle for national independence, the leaders of those movements are in fact seeking to obtain advantages for themselves and for the imperialist monopolies which are behind them.' He identified the 'splittists' in Angola as Unita, FNLA and FLEC, and added: 'The MPLA alone embodied the interests of the whole nation, and it was this movement which was given the wide support of the socialist countries, above all the Soviet Union and Cuba. In Southern Africa, the USSR supports Swapo in Namibia. In SA, the USSR supports the ANC which operates in alliance with the South African Communist Party. In Zimbabwe, the USSR supports those forces which would not let themselves be influenced by national differences existing between the Shona and the Matebele peoples, and which are now fighting for the liberation of the country from the racist and imperialist rule. This is the core of the Soviet policy towards the national liberation movements. It is totally different from the policy pursued by the imperialist forces which, as Nikolai Podgorny said at a dinner given in honour of the Ethiopian delegation, use a whole series of manoeuvres which are as old as imperialism itself, namely exacerbation of national antagonisms, provocation, blackmail and pitting peoples and countries against one another.

Although Nikolayev failed to mention the Zimbabwe African People's Union (ZAPU) by name, Moscow's support went to Joshua Nkomo's wing of the Patriotic Front. The Soviet definition of "splittists" applies to any movement of which Moscow disapproves, either because it is a rival to groups supported by the Soviet bloc or because its leaders look mainly to Peking for their support. Thus, in Moscow's eyes, the "splittists" were the Zimbabwe African National Union (ZANU), led by Robert Mugabe; the Pan Africanist Congress of South Africa (PAC); and the two Angolan movements—Jonas Savimbi's UNITA and Holden Roberto's FNLA. In the latter two cases the Soviet view is reconcilable with a view that movements in opposition to an established African regime (however it came to power) are divisive; but this hardly applied in the case of ZANU or PAC.

The alliance between the ANC and the South African Communist Party (SACP) that Nikolayev emphasized is now standard practice. Hardly any mention is made of the ANC by the Soviet press or radio without reference to its alliance with the SACP. In 1978 Moscow embarked on a new policy of supporting an alliance of Communist and Workers' Parties of Tropical and Southern Africa. Following the first meeting of this new group in August 1978, *Tass* published its manifesto entitled "For Freedom and Independence for National Renaissance and Social Progress of the Peoples of Tropical and South Africa." Oddly enough, the *Tass* report, as broadcast by Moscow radio on August 26, 1978, supplied no details about either the parties that had drawn up this document or the venue of their meeting. Their statement, according to the *Tass* report, takes a particularly strong line against the role of both NATO and the Chinese:

> The Chinese leadership is more and more often acting in league with imperialism, is pursuing a policy directed at undermining and weakening the struggle for national independence, peace, democracy, social progress and socialism in Africa and throughout the world. Since the imperialist Powers and their allies in Africa are doing their utmost to destabilize the countries of socialist and anti-imperialist orientation, full support for and defence of these States is a sacred internationalist and patriotic duty of all Africa's progressive forces.
> We call upon all fighters against imperialism and racialism, democrats, patriots and revolutionaries of our long-suffering continent to strengthen

their unity in order to put an end, once and for all, to racialist and colonialist rule in Southern Africa. We are calling upon them to give material, moral and political aid to the genuine revolutionary forces headed by the African National Congress and the South African Communist Party, SWAPO (Namibia) and the Zimbabwe Patriotic Front.

It is necessary to wage a principled struggle against all forms of chauvinism, anti-communism, anti-Sovietism and Maoism, to deepen the alliance with the socialist community, particularly with the Soviet Union, to strengthen the internationalist solidarity of the working class, of democratic and peace-loving forces all over the world.

African communists solemnly declare that they are an inseparable part of the international workers, communist and national liberation movements. They are sincere friends of the Soviet Union and the other countries of the socialist community, of all States of socialist orientation, of the peoples waging anti-imperialist struggle and upholding the cause of freedom and independence. They have been, and will always be, active fighters for the firm and indestructible alliance of the liberation movement of Africa with the socialist world, with the international working class, the communist and national-liberation movement in all continents.

China's most important link in Southern Africa is with ZANU. Its guerrilla forces had been trained by the Chinese for more than a decade. Robert Mugabe insists that ZANU's policy is dictated by "Marxist-Leninism of Maoist Thought."

As during the Angolan crisis in 1974–75, Peking continues to see the Soviets' role in Southern Africa as another stage in their pursuit of "world hegemony." The Chinese position was set forth in the *Peking Review* on January 6, 1978:

What deserves attention is the Soviet stock trick of division and disintegration, a trick it played in Angola and is playing in Southern Africa. It is sowing dissension among the Front-line countries, infiltrating into the liberation movement to split it by supporting one faction and attacking another, and waiting for an opportunity to stir up another fratricidal war among the Africans. Thanks to the lesson of Angola, the people in Southern Africa are fully aware of the consequences of Soviet interference in their liberation struggle. Therefore, they have time and again reaffirmed that the destiny of Southern Africa must be placed in the hands of the people there. Robert Mugabe, a leader of the Zimbabwe Patriotic Front, said: "We will not call in anyone; we flatly refuse to let those who give us help make themselves our masters." A leader of the Pan-Africanist Congress of Azania said: "The Soviet Union pays lip service to supporting the national liberation movements in Africa. Its real aim is to split them. We will never allow the Angola incident to be repeated in Azania," he declared. In the past year, the Southern African people have closely combined the struggle against racism with that against hegemonism, refusing to be taken in by the Soviet Union in its southward offensive and severely punishing the racist regimes. This is bringing about a new situation both in the armed struggle and in the mass movement.

Playing with fire in the heartland of Africa, the Soviet Union has wilder ambitions than the old-line colonialists. Its strategic goal is to grab the whole of Africa and threaten Western Europe by cutting the African continent right in the middle to facilitate its southward invasion and to isolate and encircle the independent African countries. . . . The new tsars are more crafty than their old colonialist predecessors. They drove mercenaries to the front as cannon-fodder while they themselves remained behind the scenes. Soviet armed invasion of Zaire through mercenaries aroused the African people to action against their common enemy. To fight against aggression, they formed a joint armed force which, in 80 days of bloody fighting, badly battered the Soviet-armed mercenaries and sent them fleeing helter-skelter. Experience of this war against Soviet mercenary invasion opened a new way for the African people to fight future Soviet aggression. The Soviet-paid mercenaries looked powerful when they temporarily succeeded in their armed intervention in Angola in 1976. But their repression and persecution of the masses incurred bitter hatred, and the Angolan people rose in opposition. Guerrilla activity all over Angola has set the mercenaries on tenterhooks.

Summing Up

All the major powers are now actively engaged in the struggles between the white minority regimes and their black nationalist challengers in Southern Africa, with none wishing to be seen as an ally of the former. But while the Communist powers (the U.S.S.R. and China) give their full backing to an armed struggle by the black liberation forces, the Western nations continue to oppose the use of violence as the only means of achieving majority rule. The majority of the African states take an intermediate position, preferring peaceful settlements but unsure whether Western commitments to these objectives are likely to be resolute enough to compel the white regimes, especially South Africa, to change course. In the absence of clear evidence about the chances of achieving negotiated settlements, the Organization of African Unity is committed to helping the liberation movements develop their capacity to wage armed struggles.

Meanwhile, the level of international involvement has continued to increase with the escalation of violence and has contributed toward increasing the military capacity of both sides in the Southern African conflict.

The Western nations, who have traditionally dominated the area, continue to pursue two objectives: to defuse violence and to encourage the white minority regimes to accept the inevitability of change and to prepare for an orderly transition to majority rule. The West, having surrendered effective power to the local white communities a long time ago, still relies only on its political influence to achieve these objectives. Mainly because of substantial economic and other interests in the area, but also because they remain unsure about the effectiveness of the economic weapon, the Western community has remained reluctant to join in the growing demand for sanctions against South Africa. However, its members have begun to distance themselves from the apartheid regime by declaring themselves in favor of democratic rule; and they now stand ready to consider the possibility of gradual disengagement.

In the meantime, the Western nations are engaged in a new form of diplomacy; this requires close collaboration with the leadership of independent African states to develop initiatives to promote negotiated settlements in Namibia and South Africa.

The local black nationalist forces and their African backers continue to look on South Africa as an "outpost of the West" and to believe that it is both possible and necessary for the major Western powers to commit themselves fully to dislodging the apartheid regime. Failing a total Western commitment, the African challengers insist that they will, if necessary, turn to the Communist world to destroy the apartheid system. The first steps toward developing closer military cooperation have already been taken.

The Communist powers—both the Soviet bloc and China—believe that even if the Western initiative were to succeed in Namibia, the interests of "the imperialists" will not allow them to abandon white South Africa. They therefore expect that the armed struggle and other revolutionary tactics will become increasingly important, and they stand ready to increase their military and economic support to such an armed struggle.

The Soviets are not only interested in seeing majority rule come to Southern Africa: they want to ensure that the "revolutionary struggle" is led by a Marxist vanguard, as happened in Angola and Mozambique. For this purpose they have encouraged an alliance between the black nationalists and the Communists, with the latter assuming the vanguard role. This policy has already begun to take root in the alliance between the ANC and the South African Communist Party. This has produced some tensions within the ANC itself. However, in the absence of effective Western policy, the black nationalist forces have no alternative but to accept the assistance of either Moscow or Peking. Moscow's condition for its support is that the nationalists must enter into an alliance with Communists, or "workers' parties," sympathetic to Russia and antipathetic to Peking.

Sino-Soviet rivalry has become a serious divisive force within the liberation movements and among their supporters in the rest of the continent. Thus, the local struggle for power has acquired two international dimensions: rivalry for influence and control between the Western and Communist powers, and rivalry between the two world Communist capitals.

2.

Zimbabwe: The Politics
of Independence

Patrick O'Meara

In his address to the nation on the eve of Zimbabwe's independence, Robert Mugabe said, "Tomorrow we shall be celebrating the historic national event which our people have striven for nearly a century to achieve. Our people, young and old, men and women, black and white, living and dead, are on this occasion being brought together in a new form of national unity that makes them all Zimbabweans."[1]

At midnight on the next day, April 17, 1980, a new independent nation, the Republic of Zimbabwe, came into being, after ceremonies in which Lord Soames, the last British governor, formally handed over his responsibilities. White rule thus came to an end after a bitter and protracted guerrilla war, and Rhodesia was replaced by the new nation of Zimbabwe.

Robert Mugabe went on to say, "Independence will bestow on us a new personality, a new sovereignty, a new future and perspective, and indeed, a new history and a new past."[2] What is the promise of this new nation and what historical factors have led to its coming into existence?

Since 1890 a small body of whites, never totaling more than 5% of the population, had controlled this large and well-endowed country. Rhodesian society was polarized between a dominant white minority and an African majority that was virtually excluded from effective political participation. For whites, Rhodesia proved to be a country of privilege and ease, while for Africans it was one of subservience and frustration. White settlers replaced African institutions with those of a modern state in which Africans provided cheap labor and were separated from the white farms and urban centers either in reserves or in segregated townships.

The Rhodesian government issued a unilateral declaration of independence (UDI) on November 11, 1965, because Great Britain refused to grant it

18

independence until significant political rights, leading to ultimate majority rule, were extended to Africans. But UDI never received international recognition, not even from South Africa, and the government was beleaguered by sanctions organized by the United Nations at Britain's request and by demands for an acceptable constitutional settlement. Above all, Rhodesia was beset by escalating nationalist guerrilla warfare to bring about majority rule.

Africans had never been reconciled to their subordinate position in a country in which they are the overwhelming majority. From the 1920s African nationalist movements unsuccessfully attempted to secure changes in discriminatory legislation, to obtain better allocation of land, and to gain a fair share of an economy designed by the dominant white minority. But it was not until the Portuguese coup in April 1974, and the ensuing independence of Mozambique and Angola, that nationalist pressures in the form of guerrilla raids from both Mozambique and Zambia placed white supremacy in jeopardy. Thereafter the major obstacle to the achievement of a settlement was the central contradiction of providing opportunities for full African political participation while safeguarding entrenched white interests.

How did a small white population remain in power for so long? By what means did it exclude Africans? How did Africans respond to their predicament? At what point and under what conditions was Rhodesia transformed into the independent nation of Zimbabwe? The answers to these questions must be sought in the course of the nationalist struggle, as well as in the fuller historical context.

Part of that history is embedded in the Zimbabwe ruins near Fort Victoria, whose size and form indicate a high level of African civilization. It is not without reason that the two major African nationalist movements in Rhodesia named themselves Zimbabwe African People's Union (ZAPU) and Zimbabwe African National Union (ZANU), and that Africans have chosen the name Zimbabwe for their country. The whites, in contrast, named the land they entered in 1890 after Cecil Rhodes, then prime minister of the Cape and an economic and political entrepreneur in Southern Africa.

The distinction between these two names* is itself a commentary on the history of the country from the first white presence in 1890 until independence in 1980. With the coming of independence it is to be hoped that in the new nation of Zimbabwe regional, ethnic and racial differences will diminish in importance. As the country moves into the new phase of its history it will face new problems of national integration and political and economic development. To some extent Zimbabwe's past will still determine how it grapples with the future.

* Until Northern Rhodesia became independent in 1964 (as Zambia) the country's legal name was Southern Rhodesia. After 1964 the accepted practice became to refer to it as Rhodesia. During the interim government of Bishop Abel Muzorewa, the name Zimbabwe/Rhodesia was used and upon independence this was changed to Zimbabwe.

The Arrival of the Whites

Cecil Rhodes first began to make plans for opening up the region in 1878, but he did not feel it was time for him to act until 1888, after Portugal's claim in 1887 to all of the interior between Angola and Mozambique. He was motivated by a combination of personal gain, the advancement of the British empire, and the pressures of the Portuguese. Rhodes's agents immediately attempted to obtain treaties from Lobengula, the king of the Ndebele, one of the major ethnic groups in the area. The Rudd mineral concession granted by Lobengula in 1888, though later repudiated by him, gave Rhodes a monopoly of the mineral rights in Lobengula's kingdom. A year later Cecil Rhodes and his associates obtained a royal charter to form the British South Africa Company (BSA). The charter authorized the company "to settle and administer [an area] immediately to the north of the South African Republic and west of the Portuguese Dominions." A deeply disturbed Lobengula wrote to Queen Victoria on August 10, 1889: "The white people are troubling much about gold. If you have heard that I have given my whole country to Rhodes, it is not my words. I have not done so, Rhodes wants to take my country by strength."

In 1890 a pioneer column consisting of two hundred settlers and five hundred police reached the site of the future capital of Rhodesia, Fort Salisbury. This occupation by white settlers marks the beginning of the period of sustained conflict between black and white. The Ndebele rebelled against white rule and were defeated in 1893. In 1896 they rebelled again and were once again defeated. Lobengula had fled after the first defeat and subsequently died; to prevent the reemergence of a strong centralized Ndebele state the company refused to recognize any successor in his place. Acting independently of the Ndebele, the Shona, the most numerous ethnic group in the area, also rebelled and were defeated between 1896 and 1897. By 1904 there were 12,000 settlers in Rhodesia and by 1911, 24,000—most of whom were primarily engaged in one form of agriculture or another. For the first fifteen years of its rule the British South Africa Company expected that enough gold would be found to justify its large investment for administration and development. But the company had overestimated the wealth of central Africa, which was far from being a second great gold reef like the Witwatersrand in South Africa, and obtained little profit from its struggling settlement. In addition there were frequent disputes with the settlers, who felt that their interests were kept secondary to company profits. Nonetheless, when the twenty-five-year term of the British South Africa Company's charter expired in 1914, the settlers chose to support the continuation of charter rule for another ten years rather than to join the newly established Union of South Africa or to press for self-government.

In 1921 a royal commission, the Buxton Commission, was appointed to look into the possibility of responsible government and a new constitution for Rhodesia. It suggested that a referendum should be held among the whites on whether there should be continuation of British South Africa Company rule, union with South Africa, or self-government. There was much to be said for the incorporation of Southern Rhodesia into the Union of South Africa. Rhodesia had been colonized from the south; both shared the same legal system based on Roman-Dutch law; and there was a continuous railway line between the two countries. Fearing too close an alliance with the Afrikaners of South Africa, a small majority of the whites, 59.4 percent of a total of 14,763 votes, favored self-government.

Company rule was dissolved and Rhodesia was formally annexed to the British Crown. From this point on, its constitutional status was the ambiguous one of a self-governing colony, governed in effect by a white minority. This was an exceptional position in that the government functioned in a virtually independent fashion, controlling its own police force, army, and air force.

Although under the 1923 constitution Britain retained a veto over openly discriminatory legislation, this power was in fact never exercised. But the existence of British reserve powers maintained the common electoral roll limited by property qualifications and preserved limited individual freedoms in Rhodesia.

The character of white society had been shaped by several factors: the settlers' struggle against a hostile environment; their conflict with the Ndebele and Shona; their fight for political self-determination; and the fact that unlike Kenya, for example, African interests were not to be primary in the development of the area. The early conflict situation was replaced by a form of paternalism in which the African was invariably the servant rather than the master, the employee rather than the employer, and thus Rhodesia could be referred to as a composite society only in economic terms.

Although Rhodesia decided not to join South Africa in 1923, South African influences have been important. Afrikaners became a unified and significant pressure group in a predominantly English-speaking country, and they were strongly opposed to policies of African advancement.

By the late 1930s, Godfrey Huggins (later Lord Malvern) and his United Party, which ruled from 1933 to 1956, had evolved a "double pyramid" policy that stressed the separate development of whites and blacks, who were to have an ultimate meeting at a distant future on the national level. By the late 1940s, Huggins had moved away from the "double pyramid" policy although many of its principles continued to mold Rhodesian thought and political action. In pursuance of this policy the government established separate areas for development of the different racial groups. The Land Apportionment Act

of 1930 (recommended by the Morris Carter Commission) excluded Africans
from permanent rights to land in European areas and reserved less than half
of the colony's land for Africans. The 1923 constitution had set aside close
to twenty-one million acres for African use and occupation; the most favorable land was set aside for white use. The Industrial Conciliation Act of 1934
created a color bar to entering skilled employment.

The Central African Federation

As early as 1924 the possibility of some form of political union between
Northern and Southern Rhodesia and Nyasaland had been discussed. It was
felt that association would not only bring together cheap labor from Nyasaland, minerals from Northern Rhodesia, and technical skill and capital from
Southern Rhodesia, but that it would also consolidate the small white populations in these countries. The Hilton-Young Commission of 1929 that
investigated the possibility of closer relations stressed, however, "the paramountcy of native interests." A conference held between Northern and
Southern Rhodesia at Victoria Falls in 1935 requested the appointment of a
commission to study the possibility of amalgamation "in principle," but
despite serious consideration no action was taken on the matter because the
conference felt that the discriminatory policies of Southern Rhodesia would
clash with Britain's commitment to Africans in Northern Rhodesia and
Nyasaland.

Shortly before the end of World War II, Huggins once again took up the
idea of federation. Despite opposition to amalgamation by white Southern
Rhodesians, who feared that the greatly increased proportion of Africans to
whites in such a federation might bring about "the Gold Coast ideas" of
African domination, there had been a subtle change in white Rhodesian thinking. Economic development and urbanization made complete separation less
attractive for Rhodesians. The growing interdependence of black and white
necessarily modified the "two-pyramid" scheme. In essence, while political
control had to remain in white hands, black-white interaction on an economic
and a limited social level was acceptable.

The Central African Federation came into being in 1953 as a result of
urging by whites in both Southern and Northern Rhodesia and the compliance of the British Conservative government. But as the decade moved on,
the rate of progress toward multiracialism both in the Federation and in
Southern Rhodesia became an issue of concern to the latter's whites. The key
word in the political vocabulary of the Federation was "partnership." For the
British government it implied ultimate equality for the Africans. For Huggins, who called it "a very blessed word," it was the "partnership of the
[black] horse and the [white] rider." For most Africans it meant a still
uncertain future.

The Issue of the Franchise in Southern Rhodesia

In the Southern Rhodesian political sphere, Huggins' move into federal politics in 1953 resulted in the election of a new prime minister, Garfield Todd, a former missionary from New Zealand. The Southern Rhodesian political system had been white-dominated from 1924 to 1957 and was primarily concerned with the interests of the white minority. In terms of party politics, Southern Rhodesia was clearly a one-party system. Todd introduced limited reforms while prime minister. In particular in 1956 he appointed Sir Robert Tredgold to head a commission to reconsider the question of franchise rights, a key issue for political power. In 1958 Todd supported a revised franchise that involved the voter registration of all male Africans with ten years of education.

When Southern Rhodesia had been granted a form of representative government in 1898, Proclamation 17 contained the color-blind franchise taken from the Cape under which the same qualifications applied equally to white and black. In practice the qualifications excluded most Africans. By 1911 there were only fifty-one Africans on the voters' roll. In 1912 the qualifications were raised: a voter had to fill out the whole claim form himself and, if asked to do so, had to write fifty words of English dictation. The minimum property ownership was raised to £150 and the minimum annual wage to £100. The 1923 constitution made no changes in the franchise. In 1928, however, the dictation clause was removed, possibly because of the increase in the number of white immigrants from Europe, but the financial restrictions were sufficient to exclude most Africans. In 1951 the means requirement was increased to an income of £240 per annum and occupation of property valued at not less than £500. The prospective voter also had to be able to complete and sign the necessary forms and speak and write in English.

Partly because of the revised franchise, though more specifically because of personality differences with his cabinet, Todd was replaced by Sir Edgar Whitehead after a special party congress in February 1958. Todd remains a controversial figure in Rhodesian politics; while he tried to introduce some significant reforms, he was at the same time responsible for repressive legislation such as the Public Order Act. Sir Edgar Whitehead became prime minister of Rhodesia at the time when the federal structure was breaking up.

In 1961 Whitehead introduced a new constitution for Rhodesia. It was proposed in an effort to appease African discontent and in an attempt to clarify Rhodesia's constitutional problems. The 1961 constitution introduced a dual-roll voting system instead of a common roll. Voters with higher qualifications were placed on an A roll and those with lower qualifications went on a B roll. Most whites were on the A roll but the majority of Africans were eligible only for the B roll. Franchise proposals formulated on numerous occasions, such as these A and B voters' rolls, with differing weight attached to

African and white votes cast, were either efforts to appease Britain or to pacify African discontent and always fell far short of providing full African political participation.

African Nationalist Responses

African nationalist movements had long operated within the political system and tried to bring about reforms on a constitutional basis. However, since the white establishment was reluctant to broaden its bases of support so as to include Africans, a rigid and permanent dichotomy developed over time. Not only was the white power structure unwilling to permit increased African participation, but it also limited channels of protest and opportunities for political mobilization. Ultimately, therefore, the nationalists moved outside of what they saw as a restricted political system.

One of the earliest African organizations, the Rhodesian Native Association (RNA), concentrated its activities in Mashonaland. It operated on behalf of an educated elite, and it was concerned with constitutional politics. Indeed, in 1920 even the chief native commissioner saw it as a "reputable organization." The RNA was concerned with obtaining "certificates of exemption" to free educated Africans from the operation of the pass laws, which obligated all male Africans over the age of fourteen to carry registration certificates, and it also planned to send a delegation to interview General J. C. Smuts, the prime minister of South Africa, and to oppose the incorporation of Rhodesia into the Union; its leaders were anxious to see a continued British presence and were against links with South Africa.

Like the RNA, the Rhodesia Bantu Voters' Association (RBVA), founded in July 1923 under the chairmanship of Ernest Dube, saw itself operating in order to change rather than to supplant the political system. These associations were run by and appealed to the new African elite, who were greatly concerned to gain from the whites social recognition as "advanced natives" in contrast to the "uneducated masses."

In the 1940s African nationalist activities began to take the form of party politics for the first time; the Reverend T. D. Samkange assumed the leadership of what has now come to be known as "the old ANC"—the old African National Congress—which sought the repeal of discriminatory legislation, such as the pass laws, but had limited success in achieving its ends.

In the early 1950s powerful labor movements dominated African politics, especially the Reformed Industrial Council of Unions (RICU) under the leadership of Charles Mzingeli. Joshua Nkomo, currently the leader of ZAPU, was at the time general secretary of another union, the Railway African Workers' Union. The African Teachers' Association had members such as Ndabaningi Sithole, who was to become the original leader of ZANU, Robert Mugabe, currently the president of ZANU, and Leopold Takawira. Ultimately the union movements failed because the white power structure refused to participate in any form of bargaining with them and used force whenever they felt the movements were going beyond defined limits.

In August 1955 the Youth League (YL) was established by Edson Sithole, with James Chikerema as president. At first it planned to infiltrate secretly into urban and rural areas, but George Nyandoro of the Capricorn Africa Society advocated mass activities to bring pressure on the government. A mass bus boycott in Harare Township in Salisbury was successful. On September 12, 1957, the leaders of the Youth League called a meeting of organized African political groups. As a result of this meeting, a new African National Congress (ANC) was born under the leadership of Joshua Nkomo. It emphasized a nonracial political philosophy and white Rhodesians were welcome to join. The ANC operated in both urban and rural areas and was particularly successful in mobilizing African farmers in 1959 against the Native Land Husbandry Act in what it referred to as "Operation Sunrise." The act ran contrary to the concept of communal ownership and to the status of cattle within traditional society.

Sir Edgar Whitehead banned the ANC in February 1959 because of its potentially strong rural base. The ANC had provided a means of political expression and marked the beginning of a process of mass political education for Rhodesian Africans. Sir Edgar Whitehead maintained that while he could imagine an African political party that showed no trace of extremism, he felt as soon as it became nationalist it would almost inevitably become militant.

On January 1, 1960, Michael Mawema formed the National Democratic Party (NDP); it was essentially the ANC under a new name. According to Mawema, the NDP sought majority rule, higher wages for Africans, land for people displaced by the Native Land Husbandry Act, facilities for the education of African children, and better housing in the urban areas. The NDP had to operate under severe disadvantages: its members were forbidden to organize in the rural areas, mass meetings were discouraged by different municipalities, members of the executive were harassed by both the police and the provisions of the Law and Order (Maintenance) Act. African leaders were beginning to realize that none of the reforms for which they were pressing, particularly majority rule, could be achieved without real political power and that as long as the white minority had control of the sources of power, they could not achieve their ends. In December 1961 the National Democratic Party was reorganized as the Zimbabwe African People's Union (ZAPU) under the leadership of Joshua Nkomo.

The Breakup of the Federation

In 1960 the Monckton Commission held that no form of association between the three territories was likely to succeed unless Rhodesia was willing to make drastic changes in its racial policies. The recommendation of the Monckton Commission was simply that Rhodesia was to put its constitutional house in order before the dissolution of the federation. The right-wing Dominion Party in Rhodesia rejected further black-white compromises and renewed its demands for secession from the federation and for Dominion status, essentially independence, for Rhodesia alone.

Meetings between the Rhodesian government, the British government, and the nationalists took place in February 1961. At first they resulted in an agreement on the new constitutional proposals, but after consulting with members of the National Democratic Party executive, Joshua Nkomo, its leader, withdrew his support and the NDP decided not to participate in the October election. The nationalists felt that the 1961 constitution, with its emphasis on income and educational franchise qualifications, made it impossible for Africans to achieve majority rule for a great number of years, if ever; only about 608,000 of Southern Rhodesia's approximately 3,970,000 Africans were in paid employment in 1963, even less than the 622,000 in mid-1962. The average African wage in 1964 was $315 a year, while the average white wage was approximately $3,300. Current average earnings for whites are $9,240 and for Africans, $830.

The Dominion Party, at this time led by William Harper, saw itself as a white party holding back the African threat. Several African states were becoming independent and white refugees were entering Rhodesia from the Congo. Thus the Dominion Party felt that the future of white civilization depended on the result of the 1961 referendum. Harper was particularly opposed to the presence of African members in the Rhodesian Parliament and the possibility of African cabinet ministers. Sir Edgar Whitehead had proposed that if he won the election, there would be one African cabinet minister, and by the following election, possibly between three and six such ministers. Harper maintained that "to have Africans in this House at this stage is going to damage the structure of European tenure in this country. Whether one likes it or not, European tenure is sensitive to the fact that the African has not proved his case to take part in the administration of the country as a whole." Harper thus voiced the more obvious aspects of Rhodesian intolerance. Whitehead's UFP lost the 1962 election because of the controversy surrounding the new constitution and because of African opposition to the proposals.

In 1963 the Rhodesian Front Party (RF) came to power. This was the year of the breakup of the Central African Federation, and the grant of independence to Nyasaland (as Malawi) and Northern Rhodesia (as Zambia) was soon to be made. The ideology of the Rhodesian Front Party made any form of direct cooperation with black governments impossible. It also saw itself holding the line against "communist infiltration" down the African continent. Southern Rhodesia had benefited considerably from the federation, but the costs for the continued alliance were considered too high, leaving aside the question of whether or not the new black governments themselves wanted to continue the federation. The breakup resulted in Southern Rhodesia's receiving many of the benefits of the federation; for example, all federal military equipment was allocated to it. The demise of the federation ushered in the new era of white extremism in Rhodesia.

Rhodesia's Bid for Independence

One of the first acts of the new Rhodesian prime minister, Winston Field, was to take up negotiations with the British on the future status of Rhodesia and in particular on the question of independence. British conditions for granting independence were based on the NIBMAR Principles: No Independence Before Majority African Rule—which were to become the stumbling block to all future negotiations. They included the principle of unimpeded progress toward majority rule, guarantees against retrogressive amendments to the constitution to retard African advancement, an increase in African political representation, and an end to racial discrimination.

Within the year Winston Field had been eased out as prime minister. In a prepared statement Field said that "serious disagreements had arisen" and Ian Smith was in power, summoning the "Spirit of '96"—1896, the year in which the pioneers had defeated the Ndebele. The main obstacle to independence was the British Labour government, which had been elected in October 1964. White Rhodesians had long been suspicious of the British Labour Party, particularly because in the 1930s Labour had fostered the concept of "the paramountcy of native interests," which Rhodesians regarded as a betrayal. With Smith as prime minister, a unilateral declaration of independence became a definite possibility. There were many, including Sir Edgar Whitehead, who were alarmed at the prospect of such a drastic step and who stressed the economic isolation that might follow such a declaration; even South Africa cautioned against UDI.

A referendum on the question of a declaration of independence based on the 1961 constitution gave Ian Smith a majority of 89 percent, and in a general election in May 1965 the Rhodesian Front Party won all fifty A-roll seats. White opposition parties, such as the Rhodesia Party and later the Centre Party, were only to play a minor role in Rhodesian politics. Smith now had a solid public support for leverage in negotiating with Britain. Following the 1965 election Whitehead's party was eliminated. However, Africans elected to the Legislative Assembly on the B roll came together to form the United People's Party—thirteen parliamentarians elected with a total of less than eight hundred votes.

With the backing of a party highly organized at the grass-roots level, which had won national elections in 1962 and in 1965, Ian Smith felt confident in pursuing a UDI. He rejected the British NIBMAR Principles and emphatically stated that Rhodesia was unwilling to accept the principle of unimpeded progress toward majority rule. On November 11, 1965, the Rhodesian government declared itself independent instead of Britain conceding independence to the country in the customary way.

Britain's immediate response to the UDI was to declare the Rhodesian actions void, and the foreign secretary, Michael Stewart, flew to New York on November 12, the day after UDI, and addressed the Security Council. The Council decided to condemn UDI. It called on states not to recognize the illegal Smith regime, and it required all member states to impose selective economic sanctions that prohibited investment in or transfer of funds to Rhodesia.

Britain incorrectly assumed that there would be significant internal opposition among both Africans and whites toward the Rhodesian Front Party and a UDI, and that sanctions would force white Rhodesians to accept British terms for independence. The immediate effect of sanctions on Rhodesia caused a lack of oil, financial difficulties as a result of foreign exchange controls, restrictions on imports, and travel difficulties for Rhodesian citizens; tobacco was, perhaps, the hardest hit industry.

In efforts to resolve the Rhodesian crisis, Harold Wilson met Ian Smith in 1966 on the H.M.S. *Tiger* and again in 1968 on the H.M.S. *Fearless*. Although the two prime ministers arrived at working documents, the constitutional crisis was not settled. It appeared that Smith's mandate to negotiate was limited, and once he referred the proposals back to the Rhodesian Front, they were rejected even though the terms of the agreement by no means sought majority rule but were variations on the 1961 constitution. It is now apparent that in these efforts Smith was playing a diplomatic game in order to buy time.

A new constitution, accepted in a referendum in June 1969 with 54,724 votes in favor and 20,776 against, reinforced a segregated society in which the possibility of majority rule was all but eliminated. On March 1, 1970, Rhodesia declared itself a republic, claiming to end its "80-year link with the British Crown." The Land Tenure Act of 1969 redivided Rhodesia into two parts: 45 million acres for Africans and 45 million for whites. The 1961 constitution had set up tribal trust lands which expanded the reserves by 19 million acres. By the end of 1966, tribal trust lands were 40,020,000 acres of a total Rhodesian area of 96,600,000 acres.

Under the 1969 constitution ten chiefs were elected by the National Council of Chiefs to the Rhodesian Senate. The chiefs have mainly provided some legitimacy for the preexisting government policy or served in ceremonial roles. Although chiefs differ in power, influence, and authority, it can be said that Rhodesian chiefs rarely tend to be political or social innovators; that they owe their allegiance to the white power structure which ratifies their appointments and pays their salaries; and that they have alienated large numbers of their traditional supporters.

ZAPU versus ZANU: The Nationalists Split

While white politicians were seeking to perpetuate white rule, the African nationalists were seriously divided. Shortly after the banning of ZAPU in 1963, Nkomo decided that because of increasing limitations placed on nationalist activities a government-in-exile would be more effective, and he therefore moved the ZAPU executive to Dar es Salaam. This move antagonized some members of the party executive who felt that the struggle should be in Rhodesia. In July leaflets were circulated in Highfield suggesting the need for a new party. On August 9, 1963, Ndabaningi Sithole announced the formation of the Zimbabwe African National Union (ZANU) and was joined by Leopold Takawira, Morton Malianga, Robert Mugabe, and others. ZANU's aims included the establishment of a nationalist, democratic, socialist, and Pan-Africanist republic; adult suffrage; repeal of all color discrimination and repressive laws; national control of all land with the government as the people's trustee; amnesty for all political prisoners; free health service and unemployment relief; and compulsory secondary education to the level of form two.

ZANU attracted African intellectuals and aimed at "a grass-roots alliance organization of peasants, peasant farmers, businessmen, students, the chiefs and headmen and the professional men and women." Nkomo, nevertheless, still retained mass support because of his remarkable ability to reorganize ZAPU (the permanent staff of ZAPU remained loyal to him) and on his ability to draw large crowds of followers. The intensity and depth of ethnic divisions is hard to gauge; the executives of both organizations were not strictly divided along ethnic lines, but constituencies tend toward such a division. Further, as part of their policy of divide and rule, white Rhodesians have deliberately promoted the dangers of ethnic conflict. Distrust does exist between ethnic groups, but it is simply not comparable to the Nigerian situation, which resulted in the Biafran civil war. Many ZAPU supporters were concerned about the split because they felt that African unity was essential, and they tried to avoid this first major division in African politics. Although the split was based on tactical and personality differences, it also marked the beginning of a new phase; the key issues of where the struggle was to be waged (whether within Rhodesia or from outside), the quality of leadership, and the nature of ideology, can be seen as a prelude to subsequent guerrilla activities. The tensions between ZANU and ZAPU continued when these organizations were forced to operate from outside of Rhodesia despite several efforts to bring them together.

In November 1963 Nkomo was banned from attending all meetings for three months and the People's Caretaker Council (PCC), which was a short-term replacement for ZAPU, was banned from organizing meetings. In February 1964 more than one hundred nationalists were restricted to Wha Wha. In March the Law and Order (Maintenance) Act was amended so as to extend detention without trial from ninety days to one year. In April, shortly after Ian Smith became prime minister, Nkomo, Msika, and Josiah Chinamano of the PCC executive were restricted to a remote area, Gonakudzingwa. Subsequently other leaders of both the PCC and ZANU were placed in restriction or detention. Lusaka now became the base from which the PCC and ZANU began to plan and execute guerrilla activities.

From 1965 some Africans participated in parliamentary opposition parties such as the United People's Party, the National People's Union, and the Centre Party. They operated strictly within the political system and their members were rejected by the nationalists.

In 1971 the Front for the Liberation of Zimbabwe (FROLIZI) was formed in an effort to inspire the young with a new spirit of resistance and to form a new military fighting force. The executive of FROLIZI included Shelton Siwela, James Chikerema, George Nyandoro, and Nathan Shamuyarira. FROLIZI supporters were to be absorbed into ZAPU, and later many of its leaders backed the Muzorewa wing of the African National Council.

A new generation of Africans eager to shift the emphasis from the political sphere to guerrilla warfare was becoming involved. With a predominantly Shona membership, ZANU operated in an area where it was possible for guerrillas to hide in the villages and merge into the local environment. In 1973 there were successful combined efforts by ZANU and Frelimo (Front for the Liberation of Mozambique), especially in the northeastern part of the country.

The Pearce Commission and the African National Council

By the end of 1971 Rhodesia had survived six years of UDI. It had a declining export market, a shortage of skilled labor, and a dearth of foreign exchange. The presence of a Conservative government in Britain led to a new round of negotiations with a British representative, Lord Goodman. In addition, in 1971 the Byrd amendment permitted the United States to resume the importation of chrome, regarded as a strategic mineral despite a stockpile of 1.3 million tons. This was approved in the United States Senate and later in the House of Representatives. The United States thus broke the sanctions imposed by the U.N. Security Council in 1965, albeit on a limited basis, thereby giving the Rhodesian government the right to claim a breakthrough in sanctions at a strategic time in negotiations with Britain.

The agreement worked out by Lord Goodman and ratified by Sir Alec Douglas-Home included, on paper, electoral arrangements to produce an

African parliamentary majority in the distant future. Rhodesia had to declare its intention to make progress toward ending racial discrimination and to accept a new declaration guaranteeing individual rights and freedoms. The proposals provided a complicated formula for a gradual increase in African political involvement and opened the way for a possible African government at some far distant future date. In December 1971 the British House of Commons approved the government's plan for a settlement in Rhodesia by a vote of 297 to 269. Sir Alec Douglas-Home told the House that "in conscience" he did not believe "better terms could have been negotiated" because he felt that "Britain's influence was running out." The terms were only in the form of a proposal, and everything now depended on the findings of a commission headed by Lord Pearce, formed to test opinion on the plan.

Analysis of the terms of the 1971 proposals indicated a considerable willingness on Great Britain's part to compromise. The proposed terms were far from the guarantees of the relatively liberal 1961 constitution, which permitted whites and blacks to register on a common roll under the same financial and educational qualifications and which promised eventual majority rule. Indeed, the accepted formula left the white government with considerable influence over African representatives, particularly since two of every four African seats were to go to traditional chiefs. The major concession Ian Smith made was to abandon his public commitment that Africans would never achieve more than parity in representation in Parliament, although this was to be at a distant time, and to allow at least some African voters to be registered on a common voters' roll with whites.

The presence of the Pearce Commission in Rhodesia in the early part of 1972 precipitated significant African political activity. African distrust and suspicion erupted because of the impending settlement; many Africans realized that a "yes" vote would lead to the entrenchment of the Smith regime and would end Britain's involvement in Rhodesian politics.

The African National Council (ANC) was formed in 1971 to mobilize African opposition to the proposals of the Pearce Commission. Bishop Abel Muzorewa, a bishop of the Methodist Church in Rhodesia, maintained that Great Britain was now merely consulting African opinion in order to give some form of respectability to an already concluded deal. The bishop pointed out that the founding of the organization was a result of spontaneous African concern in both urban and rural areas following the publication of the White Paper on the Pearce Commission. Its primary thrust was to organize strong opposition to the Pearce Commission: "The Constitutional provisions are so full of reservations and escape clauses, the declaration of rights are so open to abuse, as to render the document meaningless. For every right there is a restriction which renders it void. The road to majority rule is boobytrapped every inch of the way."

The ANC of the 1950s had been an important mass movement, and the naming of the African National Council (ANC) was a conscious effort to recall the unified nationalist thrust before the split between ZANU and ZAPU. The ANC rejected a settlement with Britain on the proposed terms, attempted to fuse the followers of the two former nationalist organizations that were still operating outside the country, and planned to operate in both rural and urban areas to obtain African trade union support and the support of the African Christian churches in opposing it.

Active participants in the ANC included several prominent African nationalists such as Eddison Zvobgo, formerly a member of ZANU; Edson Sithole, formerly a member of the ZANU executive; Josiah Chinamano, a former member of the ZAPU executive and a close adviser of Nkomo; and Michael Mawema and Simon Moyo, former members of ZANU.

The Pearce Commission Report, released in May 1972, gave a clear "no" vote to the settlement proposals. Lord Pearce and the commissioners concluded that neither intimidation nor ignorance had made it impossible for Africans to form a judgment on the acceptability of the proposals. The commission reported that it was satisfied that the proposals were fully and properly explained to the people of Rhodesia and that those who gave an opinion had understood the terms well enough to enable them to pass judgment. From this point there was a recognition by African leaders that they were now an important and active political force in Rhodesia; Bishop Muzorewa emphasized that this was the first time in ten years that Africans had actively participated in the Rhodesian political process. Furthermore, the commission stated that far from being a country of placid politics, Rhodesia was in fact "alive with political activity at the grass roots."

In December 1974 the African National Council (ANC) became the umbrella organization for ZANU and ZAPU under the leadership of Bishop Muzorewa. ZANU, which was then under the leadership of the Reverend Ndabaningi Sithole, had received assistance from the Chinese, the Organization of African Unity, and Third World countries and was in the forefront of guerrilla activities; the Russians have supported ZAPU since before the split with ZANU. The Reverend Sithole was expelled as leader of ZANU in 1976 but remained on the executive of the external wing of the ANC. Robert Mugabe emerged as the effective leader of ZANU.

A new era in nationalist Rhodesian politics opened in December 1974, when Nkomo, Sithole, and Muzorewa met with Ian Smith in a railway carriage on the bridge across the Zambezi, which links Rhodesia and Zambia. The nationalists entered the carriage from the Zambia end, and Smith and his party entered from the Rhodesian side. South Africa, keenly aware that the white redoubt was crumbling, had begun to play a bigger role in the Rhodesian issue, as had also the four front-line presidents of Tanzania, Zambia, Mozambique, and Botswana. Because of South African pressures Sithole had been released from prison and Nkomo from detention. Prime Minister Vorster had negotiated with President Kaunda to bring the meeting about; however, because of nationalist divisions and Smith's intransigence, the talks were unsuccessful. In September 1975 Nkomo's uneasy alliance with Muzorewa ended when Nkomo tried to take over the leadership of the ANC. Robert Mugabe, who had opposed ZANU joining the ANC in 1974, left Rhodesia for Mozambique in 1975 and after establishing close ties with the guerrillas became a spokesman for their operations.

New constitutional talks between the Rhodesian government and the Nkomo faction of the ANC, which began in December 1975, broke down in March 1976. Joshua Nkomo insisted on majority rule within a year or two, while the Smith proposals would have delayed this for ten to fifteen years. On March 20 Smith called for the British government once again to play a role in constitutional negotiations. However, he rejected subsequent British proposals for legitimizing Rhodesia's independence based on African majority rule. The British plan, announced by Foreign Secretary James Callaghan, called for African rule within two years, aid for whites who wanted to resettle, and British help in drafting an election plan to precede formal independence.

Changes in United States Foreign Policy to Southern Africa

Direct American involvement in the Rhodesian crisis must be seen in conjunction with the active, although at that time still secret, U.S. role in backing anti-MPLA forces in Angola (see Angola chapter). Coupled with South Africa's invasion of Angola, the arrival in the fall of 1975 of Soviet arms and Cuban forces in Angola led to increased concern with Southern Africa by the United States secretary of state. In March 1976 Henry Kissinger warned Cuba against possible intervention in Rhodesia. In April, in an important policy statement issued in Lusaka, Zambia, he said that the United States was wholly committed to a rapid, just, and African solution in Rhodesia. This marked a crucial shift in United States policy from option two of National Security Study Memorandum 39. Included in his ten-point program was an endorsement of British proposals for majority rule and the transfer of political power to Africans within two years. Kissinger also said that he would ask South Africa to use its influence to promote a negotiated settlement. In addition he promised that the Ford administration would again urge Congress to repeal the Byrd amendment. Kissinger emphasized that the United States had no plans to give military aid to the African nationalists but that help would be given to neighboring countries whose economies would suffer if they enforced U.N. sanctions. American travelers were warned against entering Rhodesia because the United States government would not be in a position to guarantee protection, and remaining U.S. businesses in Rhodesia were urged to end their operations. He also stated that educational, technical, and economic assistance would be given to an independent Zimbabwe.

While in Africa the secretary of state met with two of the five front-line presidents, Julius Nyerere of Tanzania and Kenneth Kaunda of Zambia, and also with Joshua Nkomo. Bishop Muzorewa of the ANC, however, refused to meet him. The secretary of state met with South African Prime Minister John Vorster in West Germany, June 23 and 24, and again in Zurich, Switzerland, September 4 and 5, in a continuing effort to resolve the Rhodesian and the Namibian crises. Kissinger described the U.S. involvement in these talks as an effort to avoid racial war in Southern Africa. Among the issues discussed was a plan that would provide economic compensation for whites who wanted to leave Rhodesia after a settlement and higher economic incentives for those who chose to stay after independence. The largest part of the proposed fund, which was to be internationally raised and guaranteed, was intended to provide new capital investment to rebuild the Rhodesian economy. A "safety net" plan (guaranteeing white pensions and floor prices for land) had been instituted in Kenya under which 30,000 whites out of a total of 65,000 left the country by December 1963. The guaranteeing of white pensions came under severe African criticism because they saw it as a reward for whites.

As a result of the meeting in Pretoria between Smith and Kissinger and the combined United States and South African pressures, Prime Minister Smith announced in September 1976 that Rhodesia would yield power to its African majority within two years. An interim government would be established and a new constitution would be written and details would be worked out for the transition to African rule. After consulting together on the plan the presidents of the front-line states rejected several of its terms. Indeed, it became readily apparent that Kissinger had made a tactical error by not fully informing them of crucial details such as the white control of the key ministries of Defense and Law and Order. Furthermore, the nationalists maintained that they had never seen the agreement but that Kissinger had merely discussed it with the front-line presidents. Kissinger subsequently acknowledged that there was confusion because of the number of parties and delegations involved. Subsequently, the British foreign secretary, Anthony Crosland, said that his government had agreed to convene a conference outside of Rhodesia, which it was hoped would lead to the establishment of a transitional government and which would be followed by a second phase that would involve the writing of a new constitution. Once a new constitution was in effect, international sanctions would be lifted. The conference was convened on October 28, 1976, in Geneva.

Joint United States and South Africa Pressures on Ian Smith

Smith's motivation in agreeing to majority rule within two years was difficult to determine, particularly since he had so frequently stated that there would be no majority rule in his lifetime. On one level he might have been attempting to buy time. The rainy season in Rhodesia from October to March has always proved to be an optimal period for guerrilla activities, and in 1976 it might have been decisive. Indeed, Kissinger is said to have shown Ian Smith three separate U.S. intelligence reports which indicated the weakness of the Rhodesian position and to have stated firmly that Rhodesia could not look to the United States and South Africa for support. Smith might also have gambled that divisions between the nationalists would lead to the collapse of the Geneva talks, as had happened with the 1974 Victoria Falls talks, or that there might be an African unwillingess to make concessions, as with Nkomo in 1975–76. Uneasy alliances between the nationalists had broken up before, and this would be yet another victory for Smith's politics of delay and division. Over the years Smith had acquired a reputation for backing out of agreements: for example, the *Tiger* talks in 1966 and the *Fearless* talks in 1968.

On the other hand, the balance of power in Southern Africa had shifted decisively against Rhodesia with the independence of Mozambique. Rhodesia was indeed a country at war, with very little hope of ultimate victory. It was suffering from depletion of foreign exchange and from white emigration. Smith might have hoped to shape the situation sufficiently to ensure that a moderate African regime would come into power. For whatever his purposes, he agreed to a new round of talks but insisted that the package deal with the secretary of state had to be fully adhered to. While there was some white backlash in Rhodesia (especially from conservatives to the right of the Rhodesian Front, from those who had lost members of their families or received injuries, and from last-ditchers imbued with a sense of white machismo), most whites recognized that there was a need for settlement.

South Africa continued to play a pivotal role in all negotiations. When the white redoubt ceased to have relevance with the coming of independence to Mozambique and Angola, South Africa, the richest and most powerful nation of the redoubt, was not only vulnerable but also aware of its vulnerability. Rhodesia was almost totally dependent on South Africa for trans-shipment of its export and imports and for military supplies. The South African government was also not eager to become involved in an unpopular and drawn-out guerrilla war in Rhodesia which ultimately could involve international sanctions and further confrontation with other African nations. And South Africa was growing increasingly disenchanted with the illegal status of its neighbor.

South Africa also hoped that resolution of the problems of Rhodesia and Namibia would move world attention from the area. To this end, it withdrew its paramilitary support from Rhodesia in July 1975 and made it increasingly difficult for Rhodesian exports and imports to move through its already crowded port facilities. Rhodesians who wanted to emigrate to South Africa found many delays and obstacles placed in their way.

The 1976 Geneva Meetings

Nkomo and Mugabe, with the urging of the front-line states, formed a "patriotic front" before the Geneva meetings and agreed on a joint platform between ZANU and ZAPU. They saw Smith as the common enemy and regarded themselves as political opponents able to unite for a common purpose. Sithole was invited to Geneva and subsequently appeared but was an outside figure without any real base of support. Bishop Muzorewa had a strong and influential delegation and appeared to have popular support in the Rhodesian urban area but not guerrilla backing. The nationalists rejected the Kissinger package and insisted that they should deal directly with Britain, the colonial power, rather than with Ian Smith. They were unwilling to compromise on the question of the key ministries and they considered the two-year transitional period too long.

A suggested nationalist formula for the transition period in Rhodesia included a British high commissioner to head the transitional government and control of the ministries of Law and Order and Defense. In Mozambique the transitional government had been led by a Portuguese governor-general and Joachim Chissano, and there were joint Frelimo-Portuguese army commands. Britain was not eager to get involved in disputes that might develop between the movements, but it was open to the possibility of a joint Commonwealth force.

Rhodesia: The Continuing Crisis

The year 1976 was marked by the escalation of guerrilla activities in rural areas, by attacks in white urban areas, and by pressures for settlement from the United States and South Africa with the effective backing of Britain and the other eight nations of the European community. The front-line presidents of Tanzania, Mozambique, Zambia, Botswana, and Angola also played a forceful role in fostering guerrilla activities and in delicate diplomatic negotiations. Guerrilla activity, which had centered on the northeastern part of Rhodesia, spread to the southeastern part of the country and along the border with Mozambique. It also became apparent that Zambia was permitting guerrillas to operate along its border with Rhodesia, and numerous instances of guerrilla activity in the south and west of the country indicated that the war zone had also spread to these areas.

Britain's and the United States' attempts in 1977 to find a settlement acceptable to all sides for transition to majority rule in Rhodesia met with little success. The British-chaired Geneva talks between the predominantly white Rhodesian government and black nationalist leaders became deadlocked and were adjourned on December 14, 1976, after the conference failed to reach an agreement on means or a timetable for instituting majority rule. A compromise British proposal that would have provided for majority rule within fourteen months was put forth in January in an attempt to resume the Geneva conference, but Smith announced on January 24, 1977, that his government had rejected the proposal.

Still another plan for majority rule was brought to Rhodesia by British Foreign Secretary David Owen, who visited Salisbury on April 15–16, 1977. Owen's proposals called for a constitutional conference, cosponsored by the United States and Great Britain, that would draw up a majority-rule constitution and organize elections. If agreement on a constitution was reached, Smith was to resign and a caretaker government was to supervise the elections. The proposal, aimed at a peaceful transfer to majority rule by 1978, also included the setting up of an international development fund for Rhodesia.

On July 18 Smith rejected the settlement, declaring that several elements of the plan, and especially the goal of a constitution based on "one man, one vote," did not contain adequate safeguards for Rhodesia's whites. At the same time, he announced parliamentary elections for August 31 and presented a plan for an internal solution with a constitution to be drawn up by a broadly based congress of whites and "moderate" Africans. Whites were to retain a veto power in any new parliament. In July 1977 Ndabaningi Sithole's detention order was revoked and he returned to Salisbury. Sithole's return led to further speculation about the internal settlement.

The August 31 elections strengthened Smith's authority in negotiations on Rhodesia's future, as his Rhodesian Front Party captured all of the fifty parliamentary seats reserved for whites (sixteen additional seats are reserved for Africans). The Rhodesian Front Party had been opposed in eighteen constituencies by the more liberal National Unifying Force and in forty-six constituencies by the more conservative Rhodesian Action Party. The RAP had been formed primarily by RFP members expelled from the ruling party following their opposition to a program presented to Parliament by Smith on February 23. The program included some easing of race laws and the opening up for purchase by Africans of agricultural land previously reserved for whites. Those who opposed what they saw as Smith's moderate position included the former defense minister Reg Cowper, the RF chairman Des Frost, and a deputy minister, Ted Sutton-Pryce.

The Anglo-American Plan

Immediately after the August 31 elections, Britain and the United States presented the Smith government with yet another plan for the transfer of power to the black majority. Andrew Young, the U.S. Ambassador to the United Nations, and Foreign Secretary Owen jointly presented the new proposal to Smith at a September 1 meeting in Salisbury.

The Anglo-American plan called for the immediate resignation of the Rhodesian government and the appointment of a British administrator for a six-month transitional period. In essence, the plan would return Rhodesia to a state of temporary colonial rule from which a resident commissioner, Field Marshall Lord Carver, would then lead it to independence by due process. Under the plan both the Rhodesian armed forces and the guerrillas were to be disbanded and an independent peace-keeping force under General Prem Chand, a special United Nations representative, was to be set up. Both the British and the Americans considered this essential in order to guarantee a free, impartially supervised election before independence. The resident commissioner was to prepare an electoral roll for an election based on one man, one vote and a constitution for an independent Zimbabwe which would provide for a democratically elected government and a Bill of Rights on the basis of the Universal Declaration of Human Rights. A development fund of between $1 and $2 billion would become available to the new government at independence which would be subscribed to by Britain (15 percent), by the United States (40 percent), and by other countries such as Canada.

On September 21, Prime Minister Smith condemned this latest Anglo-American initiative, calling it "an attempt to appease the Russian-oriented terrorists operating out of Zambia and Mozambique." At the same time, however, he said that his government had "genuinely come to the conclusion that we've got to get away from discrimination based on color" and that Rhodesia would "try to choose our future government on merit, irrespective of color." The Patriotic Front also requested that it should be given immediate power and independence and that the time for an election would be after independence.

While the Patriotic Front approved of the fact that the plan called for Smith to surrender power, for elections based on one man, one vote, and for an orderly transition, they nonetheless considered that the proposals had serious limitations. They particularly opposed the wide powers given to Lord Carver and the requirement that the guerrilla forces be disbanded. In addition, the Front was concerned that the bureaucracy, the paramilitary forces, the high court, and the subordinate courts would all be under Lord Carver's control. In short, their position was that the plan seemed overly concerned with the interests they opposed. In response to David Owen's statement that the "hot war" had to be stopped, they were skeptical about the United Nations' ability in peace-keeping. As for power being concentrated in Lord Carver's hands, the Patriotic Front felt that the transition period should be one in which Zimbabweans would take up leadership.

The Anglo-American proposals were discussed with the Patriotic Front leaders in Malta in February 1978 by David Owen and Andrew Young. While there was some degree of compromise, fundamental disagreement remained on the questions of where power should lie in the transitional period and who should control law and order. Britain shifted its position on the role of Lord Carver and accepted that he should work with a governing council during the transitional period, but it did not accept the restricted role that the Patriotic Front envisaged for him. Under the Anglo-American plan he was to be the supreme power in the country for the period of transition. The Patriotic Front, however, saw him rather as one member among several of the Zimbabwe governing council, which would also include members of the Front. The Front also remained opposed to the idea of a U.N. peace-keeping force.

Internal Settlement

Seizing the initiative, Ian Smith signed an agreement on March 3, 1978, with Bishop Muzorewa of the United African National Council (UANC), Ndabaningi Sithole of the African National Council, and Chief Jeremiah Chirau, a former senator whom Smith appointed as an African member of the Cabinet in 1976 and who founded the Zimbabwe United People's Organization (ZUPO) in 1976, which, as with the Anglo-American plan, sought to bring majority rule to Rhodesia by December 1, 1978. Pressure from both South Africa and the United States, the intensification of the guerrilla war, and Rhodesia's adverse economic position were all contributory factors that led Smith to take this step.

The constitutional agreement gave Rhodesian whites protective guarantees and parliamentary representation for ten years. Under the agreement, also known as the internal settlement, Parliament was to consist of 100 seats, 72 of which were to be reserved for Africans and 28 for whites. Twenty of the white seats were on a separate voters' roll, and eight were to be elected by African and white voters on a common roll. Thus, whites would be in a position to block any constitutional changes for the next ten years. Minority safeguards were also entrenched in the constitution and could not be changed without a two-thirds parliamentary majority. The settlement also provided for an independent judiciary and a Bill of Rights that could be contested in the courts. Item 5 of the agreement stated that the public service, police, defense forces, and prison service were to be maintained "on a high state of efficiency and free from political interference."

While it was claimed that majority rule was provided for on the basis of one man, one vote, this was simply not the case, because two voters' rolls were established rather than an unqualified universal suffrage and whites had the power to block legislation. In many ways the settlement provided whites with a form of African rule which would enable them to survive as a privileged group and which they hoped would ultimately lead to the end of the guerrilla war. It should not be forgotten that the Rhodesian Front initiated the process and that it was pursued under the leadership of Ian Smith.

The internal settlement provided for an executive council for the transitional period composed of Ian Smith and the three African leaders. Under the arrangement each would take a turn in presiding as chairman of the council. Thus, on paper with the swearing-in of the African leaders on March 21, Smith became one of a council of four that would rule Rhodesia until December 31, 1978. Later this date was extended to April 1979. In addition to the executive council there was to be a ministerial council composed of equal members of African and white ministers.

The internal settlement has been the source of considerable ambiguity and confusion. Was it indeed a significant move by Ian Smith toward majority rule? Should it be accorded international recognition in the hope of making the internal settlement effective? Were the British and Americans correct in their assumption that it had little chance of success as long as it did not include at least a substantial representation from the Patriotic Front? Clearly, thus far the internal settlement has not won the support of the rural population nor has it accorded effective political influence to those African leaders participating in its arrangements. Indeed, the settlement has been breaking down on the administrative level, where, for example, joint African cabinet members such as Byron Hove had not been given anticipated responsibility in shaping policy.

African Cabinet Ministers in the Interim Government

The African ministers were nominated by the heads of the delegations involved in the negotiation, and the white ministers were nominated by Ian Smith. The African cabinet ministers reflected the wide range of political interests and perspectives of the principal negotiators. Bishop Muzorewa's candidates for ministerial positions included Ernest Bulle as minister of Finance, Commerce and Industry, James Chikerema as minister of Transport, Power, Mines, Roads, and Road Traffic and Posts, and Byron Hove as minister of Justice, Law and Order and Public Service. Bulle had been a lecturer at the University of Rhodesia, where he taught Ndebele. Chikerema had been involved in nationalist politics from 1957, when he was vice-president of the Youth League and with George Nyandoro had been responsible for Nkomo becoming president of the ANC. Later he founded Frolizi and in 1971 joined the Bishop as second in command of the African National Council. Chikerema's involvement with the Bishop was said to be tense. Byron Hove was a practicing barrister in England when he was called back to Rhodesia by the Bishop. In 1964 he was elected student president of the University College of Rhodesia and Nyasaland, and he was also detained with hundreds of other nationalists at Gonakudzinqwa. Between 1973 and 1976 he had worked at the OAU headquarters in Addis Ababa. Sithole's candidates included Dr. Elliot Gabellah, who had studied in the United States and at one time had been vice-president of the Bishop's United African National Council, from which he resigned in 1977 because he felt the Bishop lacked leadership and because of a conflict with Chikerema. Subsequently he was appointed second vice-president of the Sithole faction of the ANC. Chief Chirau's appointees included Chief Ndiweni, a former member of the Rhodesian Senate, and Gibson Magaromombe, a sports writer.

The transitional government was authorized to bring about a cease-fire and to deal with the composition of the Rhodesian military forces. It was also to deal with the release of detainees, the holding of elections, and the drafting of a new constitution. Of the 100 detainees released from WhaWha detention camp in April 1978, 66 said they were followers of Bishop Sithole, 30 were Nkomo supporters, and 3 were Mugabe followers. In early May the bans against ZAPU and ZANU were lifted.

The British foreign secretary, Dr. David Owen, had at first maintained that although the settlement was an important first step, there was much farther to go. But the official United States view, expressed in a speech to the U.N. Security Council by Ambassador Andrew Young on March 14, 1978, maintained that since the internal settlement did not include all nationalist leaders it could divide rather than unify the people of Zimbabwe. Furthermore, he charged that the Salisbury plan produced a transitional arrangement of shared responsibility that would allow Smith to hold effective power and to wield a veto. Young also expressed concern that there was no provision for international outside supervision to insure the fairness and impartiality of an election, as there was under the Anglo-American plan, and that the internal agreement was an unsatisfactory guarantor of the rights of all Zimbabweans because it relied on the Rhodesian army rather than on a U.N. peace-keeping force. Finally, under the Salisbury constitution, changes of all entrenched clauses could come about only during a period of ten years, with the concurrence of all African members and six of the white members of Parliament. There was also no guarantee that this provision would not carry over after the initial ten-year period.

Immediately after the announcement of the internal settlement, Nkomo and Mugabe ruled out any talks with those who had signed the agreement. In substantive terms it was unacceptable to the Patriotic Front because of the white blocking vote, because it preserved the existing structure of the state with black leaders simply taking over some of the apparatus and because of the extensive guarantees extended to whites. In practical terms and ideologically, the settlement was far from the Patriotic Front's position. The governing process was unaltered, whites continued in a privileged position, land was not redistributed, dependence on South Africa remained, and the judiciary and bureaucreacy continued in their current forms.

The Patriotic Front made it quite clear that it had two important options. First, it could use its guerrilla forces to disrupt any elections proposed by the interim government and it would continue to escalate the war. Second, it could call on the Cubans and the Russians for more active support. This latter tactic in effect would turn the situation into a civil war. While the Patriotic Front has had many internal differences, it was united in its rejection of the settlement.

As far as South Africa was concerned it was clear that a settlement of this sort was in its best interests, and the South Africans impressed on the Bishop that he could rely heavily on their good will if he became the head of the first black government after December 1978.

Wide differences continued after the April 14–15 meetings in Dar es Salaam, at which the United States secretary of state, Cyrus Vance, and David Owen participated. However, at this meeting Tanzanian President Nyerere and other front-line representatives tried to get the Patriotic Front to moderate its position. The Anglo-American plan had in many ways begun to look more attractive to the front-line presidents because the moves to an internal settlement within Rhodesia excluded the guerrillas and because there was the possibility of a bitter and protracted war with major-power involvement. There were also signs that some of the front-line state presidents were becoming impatient with the Patriotic Front's adamant demand to be given a dominant position in Rhodesia before elections.

On April 28 the transitional government dismissed Byron R. Hove, joint minister of justice on the ministerial council. Hove, whose duties included the supervision of the police courts and prisons, had been extremely critical of discriminatory legislation and practices. Almost immediately after taking office he made a number of speeches in which he maintained that adjustments were needed to give Africans fairer treatment from the police and judiciary. In the past the police and judiciary had enthusiastically enforced racially discriminatory legislation, and he now called for positive discrimination in favor of Africans. Hove also said that in his own ministry he found only two blacks in responsible positions and that in Rhodesia as a whole 12,000 white civil servants earned $58 million while 27,000 African civil servants earned $12 million. He also noted that there were few blacks in the higher ranks of the police force and none in the judiciary.

Fully recognizing the crucial significance of Hove's approach, the transitional government, chaired at the time by Chief Chirau, dismissed Hove after he refused to retract his criticisms. Ian Smith had been annoyed by Hove's comments and after his dismissal said that he had been "put in his place." Hove's remarks had obviously angered white Rhodesians, who feared a threat to existing "standards." At first Hove's dismissal appeared to have the approval of Bishop Muzorewa since it was announced by the executive council on which he had a veto. However, several hours after the dismissal was announced, the Bishop issued a statement indicating that he knew nothing about the decision and that Hove's dismissal could be disastrous to the survival of the interim government. The Bishop also threatened to renounce the internal agreement unless Hove was reinstated. Muzorewa's withdrawal would have threatened the interim government not only because of his widespread support but also because his resignation would have questioned even further the validity of the agreement. On May 14, after a lengthy debate with members of his party, the Bishop decided not to withdraw. The Bishop was clearly biding his time until the end of the year, when he hoped to sweep the election and take full power. Hove's dismissal highlights divisions between the African leaders.

With the appointment of black cabinet ministers and the acceptance of majority rule as a principle, the internal settlement marked a new stage in Rhodesian politics. It went beyond the 1961 constitution and closely approximated the terms specified to Ian Smith by Henry Kissinger in 1976. But Ian Smith's concessions were the result of a devastating guerrilla war and of Rhodesia's deteriorating economic position. Its success depended on whether the settlement was able to attract country-wide support and achieve a cease-fire.

In 1978 the Patriotic Front wanted a settlement on its own terms rather than a partial one based on white interests. Without the involvement of either Mugabe or Nkomo, the internal settlement was clearly not a final settlement. It was valuable in that it formally introduced into the political arena ideas of universal suffrage and of majority rule. It thus represented a significant move toward one of the NIMBAR principles, but it failed in that it does not involve all Rhodesians in the process of testing its acceptability. This was precisely why the Anglo-American initiative had set such a high priority on achieving a cease-fire that would create the environment in which a convincing test of Rhodesian opinion would be possible.

Indeed, achieving a cease-fire proved to be one of the major problems faced by the interim government. It mounted an unsuccessful campaign to "win the hearts and minds" of the liberation force, planning "free entry zones" on the borders for those who wanted to return in peace. But without a cease-fire there could be no international move to remove sanctions or to extend any legitimacy to the settlement. A government headed only by the Bishop could not be accorded any degree of international legitimacy and demonstrated little capacity for the efficient governing of the country. UDI simply continued with economic and political problems passed from white hands to those of conservative Africans. The new regime continued the fight against the guerrillas, now in the form of an open civil war between Africans, with one side possibly backed by whites (although their full loyalty to a black regime was problematical), and another by Cubans and Russians or Chinese.

The Guerrilla Forces

In November of 1975 an eighteen-member Joint Military Command was set up which attempted to coordinate the separate guerrilla activities of ZANU and ZAPU into a new organization, ZIPRA (Zimbabwe People's Army). The biggest faction of guerrillas was from ZANU, and at that time they outnumbered ZAPU forces by possibly as many as ten to one. However, severe clashes occurred between ZANU and ZAPU guerrillas in the training camps, and the ZAPU forces withdrew. Attempts again made in February 1978 to establish a Joint Command were unsuccessful. Thus, in practice, ZANLA referred to ZANU's forces and ZIPRA referred to ZAPU's. ZAPU guerrillas were mainly Ndebele, and most were trained in Zambia by Cubans. The ZIPRA forces did not engage in major guerrilla activities and hence their losses were far smaller than those of ZANLA. While there were guerrilla units within ZIPRA it was substantially being trained as a regular force. ZAPU had a wider ethnic base than ZANU, whose much larger numbers tended to be predominantly Shona-speaking. Clan differences among the Shonas were more significant in the liberation period than the major ethnic divisions between Shona and Ndebele. The Karanga are the largest Shona group and make up almost 25% of the total African population. Other Shona groups are the Zezuru, who make up 21% of the population, the Manyikas at 11%, the Ndau at 6%, the Kerekore at 5%, and the Kalangas at 3%. Within ZANLA quarrels between Karangas and Manyikas were intense and in 1975 resulted in the assassination of Herbert Chitepo. The late Josiah Tongogara and other guerrilla leaders, nearly all Karangas, were arrested and imprisoned in Lusaka for the assassination of Chitepo. ZANU leaders included Solomon Mutuswa (Rex) Nhongo, formerly of ZAPU, and Tongogara, who was trained in China, fought with Frelimo forces in the late 1960s, and became supreme military commander of ZANU forces. He died in a car accident in Mozambique shortly before independence. Robert Mugabe, a former member of the ANC executive and general secretary of ZANU, began to appear as one of the few political leaders trusted by the guerrillas. After the Geneva talks had broken down, Tongogara and Mugabe consolidated their political-military positions of leadership. In contrast, Nkomo was both political and military leader of ZAPU-ZIPRA.

Effects of the Guerrilla War on Rhodesia

By 1978 as the war was reaching its peak, conscription for whites was at its maximum. White males between 18 and 25 were liable for national service for 18 months (extended from 12 months in 1976), but in fact they were called up virtually continuously.

Rhodesian security forces had a total potential strength well over 100,000, not including volunteers and mercenaries from Britain, the United States, and Europe. The call-ups had a disruptive effect on the economy and caused many white Rhodesians to question whether Rhodesian society justified such a sacrifice.

In 1978 the government established a fourth battalion of the Rhodesian African Rifles (in 1976 there were two), bringing the total number of African troops to 4,000. This figure excluded nearly 6,000 African policemen and Africans in the Selous Scouts, a special anti-guerrilla unit. Attempts were being made to desegregate training facilities, and some Africans were promoted to the rank of lieutenant.

The war was now costing the Rhodesian government over $1 million a day in direct outlay and millions more in lost production—an important factor in a country already battling trade embargoes, sanctions, conscription, and losses in formerly productive white farming areas now part of the war zone.

Although the whites, numbering 268,000 in 1978, were strained by the war, the 6.4 million Africans suffered far more. A report of the Rhodesian Catholic Commission for Justice and Peace estimated that more than half a million Africans had been forcibly removed from their homes and placed in one of nearly two hundred "protected villages" or forty "consolidated villages." Some protected villages were set up in 1974, and more were established with the increase in the number of guerrillas crossing the Mozambique border. The Rhodesian government claimed that these stockaded villages with their strict curfew laws, registration of all persons over the age of thirteen, and control of everyone entering or leaving the camps protected Africans from guerrilla attacks. However, the government's main purpose was to prevent guerrillas from gaining a foothold among the African people and to separate them from vital bases of support, since many rural Africans had provided them with food, supplies, cover, and even new recruits. The International Committee of Justice maintained that the villages were overcrowded, had poor sanitation facilities, were disruptive of traditional African culture, and were breeding great discontent.

Although no part of the country was under the total control of the guerrillas in 1978, civil administration was breaking down in some rural areas and tax collection was becoming difficult. In June 1978 the Ministry of Education announced that almost 750 schools in the rural areas had been forced to close and that 63 schools had been burned down. More than 250,000 African school children were affected by the closings.

By mid-1978 there were signs that the internal settlement was not working and that rather than leading to an end of the guerrilla war it was helping to intensify it. Six months after the agreement had been signed, casualty figures in the war had almost doubled, the Rhodesian military command was growing alarmed at the course of the w r, there was no hope of the internal settlement receiving any international recognition, and sanctions remained in effect. At this point Ian Smith bypassed Muzorewa, Sithole, and Chirau and attended a secret meeting in Zambia on August 14 with Joshua Nkomo, President Kaunda, and Brigadier Joseph Garba, former commissioner of external affairs of Nigeria, a sure indication that the internal settlement had failed. It also marked the involvement of Nigeria in the Rhodesian-Zimbabwean struggle.

Smith offered Nkomo the chair of the four-member executive council until elections could be held. In return ZAPU was to agree to a cease-fire. Nkomo maintained that his condition for a return was the complete dismantling of the existing government and the assumption of power by the Patriotic Front. Nkomo had not told Robert Mugabe about the meeting, and President Kaunda had not discussed it with the other front-line presidents. Six days after it had taken place Mugabe heard about the meeting while he was on a visit to Nigeria and immediately returned to Lusaka with Brigadier Garba to see Nkomo. He then went to Mozambique and Tanzania with the brigadier to discuss the situation with Nyerere and Machel. The front-line presidents, meeting on September 1, made it clear that they were opposed to Nkomo's acting alone and because Nkomo had acted independently in attending the meeting, there were severe repercussions for the unity of the Patriotic Front once that information became public.

Settlement—The Lancaster House Conference

Although the Conservatives won the May 1979 British general election, Prime Minister Margaret Thatcher was persuaded to change her pre-election position to recognize the Muzorewa interim government. She had been influenced against such recognition by the active efforts of the Commonwealth prime ministers meeting in Lusaka. This made possible the Lancaster House Conference, which convened on September 10, 1979. Bishop Muzorewa and the Patriotic Front each sent 12 delegates to the conference at which a draft constitution was vigorously debated. Under the constitution that was finally ratified, the Zimbabwean House of Assembly consisted of 80 members elected on a common African roll and 20 seats reserved on a separate white roll until 1987. The Senate consisted of 10 members elected by the white members of the House of Assembly, 14 elected by the African members, 10 elected by the

Council of Chiefs, and 6 appointed by the president on the advice of the prime minister.

On November 12, 1979, the Southern Rhodesia Act formally ending the illegal declaration of independence and restoring legality to Rhodesia was passed by the British House of Commons. This act provided that a British governor would go to Salisbury to supervise the transition to independence. On December 1, 1979, the Rhodesian parliament itself passed the constitution of Zimbabwe-Rhodesia Amendment Act by which Zimbabwe-Rhodesia became subject to British control.

On December 12, 1979, the newly appointed British governor, Lord Soames, arrived in Salisbury and on December 21, a cease-fire stopped guerrilla movements across the border. Hostilities formally came to an end on December 28. The guerrillas were permitted to keep their weapons but were massed at 16 assembly points, under the supervision of a 1,000-member British and Commonwealth force.

In the election on February 19, 1980, for the 20 white roll seats (these included Asians and so-called coloreds), only six seats were contested and these were won by Rhodesian Front candidates. They were unopposed in the remaining 14. Thus all the twenty white roll seats were won by the RF.

The common roll election, in which all African Rhodesian citizens or residents over 18 could vote, was held over a period of three days, February 27, 28, and 29, 1980. The country was divided into eight electoral districts based on the number of potential voters. As a safeguard against intimidation at the polls, five hundred British police were brought to the country and in addition a 63-member Commonwealth group acted as observers to determine whether the election was fair and free. Their subsequent report affirmed that it was.

Joshua Nkomo's ZAPU chose to contest the February 1980 election with a separate party, the Patriotic Front (PF). ZANU campaigned under its own name and Bishop Muzorewa's UNAC was a third contestant. The British anticipated that Nkomo and Muzorewa together would win a majority, but enormous support for ZANU, particularly in Shona areas, resulted in a decisive victory for Mugabe.

On March 4, the Registrar of Elections announced that ZANU had won 57 of the 80 black seats in the 100-member House of Assembly with 63% of the valid votes cast; Nkomo's PF won 20 seats with 24% of the vote. His support came mainly from the Matabeleland North and Matabeleland South electoral districts, which were predominantly Ndebele.

Bishop Muzorewa's United African National Congress received only 8% of the votes cast and three seats in the House of Assembly, though, less than a year before, his party had won 64% of the votes in the election for an internal settlement which was never recognized internationally.

Mugabe's overwhelming victory meant that the uncertainty of an indecisive election result was avoided. The overwhelming ZANU victory formally marked the end of hostilities and excluded the possibility of the guerrilla conflict continuing in any form.

With the attainment of independence Mugabe's government faced a number of vital national concerns and problems. These included: the forming of a government; demobilization of the guerrilla forces; resettlement of those uprooted by the war; reallocation of land; social and political change; the predicament of the whites; and relations with South Africa. On a more positive level, in the year immediately after independence with the lifting of sanctions Zimbabwe showed a growth rate of 9%.

The Cabinet

Robert Mugabe's first cabinet was clearly one which aimed at national reconciliation. After the election Mugabe and Nkomo had reunited to form the ZANU-PF coalition government and controlled 77 of the black seats in the 100-member House of Assembly. Joshua Nkomo was given the important ministry of Home Affairs which controlled the police.

Dennis Norman, who became Minister of Agriculture, had never previously held a political office but had been a former president of the white Commercial Farmers' Association and had advised a settlement with the guerrillas. David Smith, who was appointed Minister of Commerce, had been Deputy Prime Minister in Ian Smith's last cabinet, had resigned from the Rhodesian Front Party, and also favored a settlement with the guerrillas.

The cabinet also reflected a balance among the dominant Shona clans with 10 ministers who were Karangas, 10 Zezurus, and 7 Manyikas. The cabinet also included an ideological balance between radical and conservative members such as Simon Muzenda, Deputy Prime Minister and Minister of Foreign Affairs, and more radical and belligerent personalities such as Edgar Tekere, Minister of Manpower Planning and Development. Other key cabinet ministers included Bernard Chidzero as Minister of Economic Planning, Nathan Shamuyarira as Minister of Information and Tourism, Eddison Zvogbo, Minister of Local Government and Housing, Dzingai Mutumbuka, Minister of Education and Culture, and Kumbirai Kangai (who expertly handled the Minimum Wage Bill), Minister of Labor and Social Welfare.

In a cabinet reshuffle in January 1981, Edgar Tekere, who had been tried for murdering a white farm manager, was dropped and Joshua Nkomo was initially moved from Home Affairs Ministry (from which his control of the police had already been removed) to the less powerful position of Public Service Minister. This reduction in Nkomo's power, visibility, and stature threatened the viability of the coalition and caused further mistrust of the government among Nkomo's Ndebele supporters. Quickly assessing the risks involved, Mugabe later in the month changed Nkomo's appointment to minister without portfolio (with some responsibility for defense and public service), thereby averting a crisis which could have destroyed the ZANU-PF coalition. Nkomo had found his demotion totally unacceptable even though in exchange the PF had been offered an additional cabinet seat as well as a deputy ministerial appointment. Nkomo was satisfied with his new appointment and actively set about trying to reconcile Shona differences particularly in Ndebele strongholds.

To this point Mugabe had repaid prominent ZANU followers who supported him during the years of the liberation struggle. It was now up to his appointees to prove their ability to administer complicated modern bureaucracies. He was well aware that if they were not up to the task there were many capable and eager Zimbabweans waiting to step into these positions.

The Tekere Case

The trial (and subsequent acquittal in December 1980) of Edgar Tekere, Secretary-General of the ZANU-PF party and Minister of Manpower, Planning, and Development, the third most powerful position in the coalition cabinet, in connection with the August 1980 killing of a 68-year-old white farm manager, Gerald Adams, was Mugabe's first serious crisis. However, he successfully used the event to affirm his commitment to due process of law and at the same time withstood demands from the far left of the party for Tekere's immediate release.

In some ways the Tekere case could not have come at a better time for Mugabe. Tekere's outspoken and rash attacks on Joshua Nkomo and his party had run contrary to Mugabe's commitment to reconciliation. Tekere's emphasis on radical change for Zimbabwe had alarmed whites in the country and foreign investors. Despite his long friendship with Tekere, Mugabe, a dedicated and punctilious leader, was becoming increasingly irritated with Tekere's flamboyant style and with his cavalier attitude toward the running of his ministry. Mugabe had made efforts to curtail Tekere prior to the murder, but it was only after the event that a chastened Tekere seems to have been silenced.

The Army

Soon after independence, Robert Mugabe called upon Lt. General Peter Walls, former commander of the Rhodesian Combined Operations, to create a unified national army which would bring together ZANLA and ZIPRA guerrillas and the former Rhodesian security forces. From that time an active effort was made to establish such a united national army. Walls was subsequently exiled from Zimbabwe because of rash comments he made while on a visit to Britain regarding the legitimacy of the 1980 election and the possibility of a white *coup d'état* in the period immediately prior to independence. A revolving team of 150 British military experts were called in and given responsibility for training the army.

In August 1981 Mugabe appointed a white general, Alexander Maclean, as supreme commander of Zimbabwe's military forces. Lt. General Rex Nhongo, former commander of ZANLA, was named commander of the Army and Lt. General Lookout Maksuku, who headed ZIPRA, was appointed his deputy. At the same time, eight of the ten white army commanders and deputy commanders were removed for reassignment. The appointment of Maclean allayed white fears to some extent. Prior to his appointment, there had been a joint high command of the guerrilla movements and the army headed by the Minister of State overseeing army matters.

Following a state visit in August 1981 to North Korea, which Mugabe perceived as a non-aligned nation, more than 100 North Korean soldiers arrived in Zimbabwe, presumably to train a special unit of between 4,000 and 5,000 men. The unit was to fight along the Mozambique border against the South African–backed National Resistance Movement which was challenging the Samora Machel regime in Mozambique. Joshua Nkomo expressed the fear that this unit might become Mugabe's private army. Zimbabwe is ultimately to have an army of between 30,000 and 40,000 men, considerably smaller than ones in other parts of Africa. The new army will absorb at least one-third of the guerrillas who fought in the war and 10,000 African soldiers from the former Rhodesian Army. The creation of such an integrated and unified force will undoubtedly help to stabilize the political situation. Many of the former white officers have resigned or retired and at least 30% of the 2,000 white regulars have also left. Within the next few years the number of whites in the military will be even further diminished, particularly since white conscription has now ended. In addition special units such as the Selous Scouts that played a prominent role in fighting the guerrillas have been disbanded.

In the Bulawayo violence in November 1980 between the Zimbabwe National Liberation Army (ZANLA) and the Zimbabwe People's Revolutionary Army (ZIPRA) guerrillas, one of the integrated national army battalions demonstrated no partisan bias and operated as a unit in an effort to reestablish order. Unfortunately, in the clashes which took place in February 1981 and which resulted in 375 deaths this was not the case and order had to be restored by white officers and former Rhodesian African Rifles. Subsequently the major step was taken of disarming all the guerrillas.

The situation has begun to stabilize. Mugabe's land policy and the resettlement of the guerrillas are connected issues, particularly since maintaining the guerrillas (each is paid $100 a month) now takes 20% of the Zimbabwean budget. The allocation of parcels of land to the guerrillas will be one form of compensation and a number of them will be guaranteed employment

in the rural sector, working on farms, clearing land, or engaging in rural reconstruction or agricultural projects. Because some guerrillas are unwilling to go into the rural areas larger numbers will have to be incorporated into the unified Zimbabwean army, even if this necessitates allotting substantial budgetary rescources to an area that is not really essential for Zimbabwe's long-term growth and well-being. Ultimately, demobilization is a sensitive but short range problem which is a characteristic of a society in transition.

Land Reform

Land reform and resettlement is the biggest issue for the Mugabe government. The guerrilla war was fought over land and political freedom and the Mugabe government must provide tangible evidence of improved conditions. Under white rule, land was almost equally divided between whites and over six million Africans; nearly all the best land was held by some 6,000 white farmers, many of whom still cultivate over 37 million acres and account for over 60% of Zimbabwe's agricultural exports. Three-fifths of the African population live in the scattered Tribal Trust Lands under subsistence conditions, with an average annual income of $200.

The Tribal Trust areas, many of which were devastated during the war, currently carry three times as many people as they are able to support. There has long been overgrazing and overuse of land in conjunction with overpopulation and the situation was worsened by the two-year drought in 1979–1980, that forced the country to import maize from South Africa for food supplies. In 1981, however, there was an abundant harvest that met all local food needs and provided a surplus for export.

The land problem was discussed at the Lancaster House Conference and the participants, including the present government, accepted the situation that if the government expropriated land, the owners would be compensated in convertible foreign currency. The white farm areas grow maize, sugar, tobacco, cotton, beef, citrus fruits, tea, and coffee. With the export of specialized commodities and of minerals, these provide the government with essential foreign currency. The most arable white farm lands are controlled by white commercial farmers, or large foreign- or Zimbabwean-controlled corporations. Thus the government has to balance demands for the redistribution of white-owned lands to relieve pressure in the Tribal Trust Lands with the continuing need for white farmers, whose productivity is essential to feed the population and to earn foreign exchange.

Over the next few years, in addition to resettling peasants on adequate-sized plots, the government may stimulate some cooperatives which would raise essential crops. Experiments in other parts of Africa, such as Tanzania and Zambia, with state farms or state cooperatives have seldom been success-

ful and, considering the individualistic emphasis of Zimbabwean peasant farmers, the future of such ventures would not be assured.

Immediate Social and Ideological Changes

Mugabe's first-hand experiences with the severe dislocations following independence in Mozambique convinced him to opt for a mixed economy in Zimbabwe, to avoid a white exodus, and to favor overseas investment and capital. However, he remains deeply committed to a more equitable distribution of land, better living conditions, health care, and education for Africans, all of which he sees best expressed in a form of African socialism.

Robert Mugabe and his government have the power and popular support to bring about radical changes, but they have been cautious in doing so. Mugabe has shown restraint in restructuring Zimbabwe. He has promised an indigenous form of socialism, but at the same time he has encouraged Western investment. Mugabe guaranteed that all investments would be safe and that, within the limits of exchange control regulations, profits could be remitted abroad on condition that corporations included some local control, paid fair wages, and allowed unions to exist.

So far, socialist labor policies have not gone any further than minimum wage legislation affecting both agricultural and industrial wages, a "workers charter" specifying conditions of work for laborers, and Workers Councils, to improve management and labor relations. In addition, a free health service was introduced for all who earned less than $100.00 per month.

In the year following independence, secondary school enrollments open to all who could qualify, increased from 70,000 to 90,000 students, while 100,000 more primary school children were receiving the newly free education.

The immediate economic objectives of the government included improving the agricultural sector, which was central to the country's economic and political stability, and creating jobs for the more than 150,000 workers who enter the market each year.

Mugabe and his government envisage Zimbabwe evolving as a mix between state and private enterprise. He has persistently emphasized this view, claiming that individualism and free enterprise are a part of Zimbabwe's inheritance. The only requirement that Mugabe placed on free enterprise was that its activities, besides providing a profit return to investors, should also contribute to the realization of Zimbabwe's socialist development.

On the whole, the Mugabe government has demonstrated a pragmatic approach to dealing with international investment. It appears unlikely that it will take radical expropriatory action, but steps will be taken to maintain some equity control and the government might seek to develop some scheme of sharing profits with workers. The vital need to inspire international in-

vestment will limit the speed with which the government will move to implement such controls.

The Riddell Commission—A Challenge for Zimbabwe's Future

The Riddell Commission of inquiry into incomes, prices, and conditions of service released in June 1981 put forward fundamental changes in the Zimbabwean economy in order to adjust income inequities and alleviate poverty. It called for higher minimum wages over a three-year period until 90% of the poverty datum-line was reached, increased taxes on corporations and the rich, and more land and credit for peasant farmers. For the higher-paid Zimbabwean employees, paid more than $29,000 a year, it suggested that there should be no income increases but only cost of living adjustments. Ultimately some of the findings of the Commission might become law. While its suggestions might redress some of the inequities existing, there is a danger that at the same time its more extreme positions might curb individual initiative essential for substantial economic growth and development. The government remains anxious to attract foreign investment and will thus avoid the more extreme ideas expressed by the commission. In addition, the 1981–82 budget presented by Minister of Finance Enos Nkala increased taxation in order to support Zimbabwe's new social programs. Zimbabwe also had a budget deficit of $700 million which had to be met by foreign borrowing and the country had a rapidly increasing inflation rate of about 15% per annum.

ZIMCORD—Strong International Support for Zimbabwe

In March 1981 the Zimbabwe Conference on Reconstruction and Development (ZIMCORD) took place with representatives attending from more than 30 countries and a dozen international organizations. The basic purpose of the conference was to obtain aid for reconstruction and development projects. Before the conference, Zimbabwe had been given pledges for $500 million; a further $1.3 billion was promised during the conference. Half of the total of $1.8 billion was in the form of grants and the rest as loans. Because of ZIMCORD, Zimbabwe should be able to engage in rural development projects, land resettlement, and housing programs. The enthusiasm of the donors and the magnitude of the support indicate a clear awareness of Zimbabwe's economic promise in farming, mining, and manufacturing, and in its ability to become self-supporting once it has recovered from the ravages of the war. Zimbabwe gives every indication of developing into a stable and important nation which will contribute to the general stability of the Southern African region and this support was an international vote of confidence in its future.

Whites

Zimbabwe needs to keep its skilled white population from emigrating. The sudden loss of large numbers of whites would discourage foreign companies from investing in Zimbabwe, and the loss of business and investment would lead to extensive African unemployment. Mugabe is fully cognizant of the far-reaching consequences of such a departure.

The government is particularly concerned about the departure of skilled white workers. There are now significant numbers of vacancies for skilled workers in mechanical, motor electrical, and construction fields and the government is trying to keep more of them from leaving the country. Africans are now eligible for apprenticeship training, and an international effort will also be made to hire replacements; Indian and Pakistani mechanics have already begun to work in some skilled positions.

Emigrants thus far mainly include blue-collar workers, those threatened by Africanization, and those with a limited stake in the future of the country. Whites in the business sector and white commercial farmers have in most cases chosen to stay, either because they have given a vote of confidence to Mugabe or because they do not wish to abandon their assets. As long as Mugabe remains prime minister and maintains his current moderate and flexible stance this vital sector of the white population will remain, particularly since the government has made it more difficult for them to emigrate by placing restrictions on what they can take with them.

In April 1981 Andre Holland announced the formation of a new political party, the Democratic Party, which aimed to be more cooperative with the prime minister. Holland was at one time a Rhodesian Front cabinet minister. Such a move was particularly important because by 1987 the 20 reserved white seats will no longer exist and he thus proposed that whites should begin to identify with African political structures. However, there was little demonstrable interest by the white population in shifting its loyalties from the RF, now renamed the Republican Front Party. On the positive side, some whites were beginning to draw a distinction between the rhetoric of a few cabinet ministers and the government's actual restraint in economic and social policies. Perhaps over time whites will make further readjustments.

South Africa

Despite its financial support for Bishop Muzorewa in the 1980 election, South Africa at first seemed to realize that Mugabe was the key to stability for the region. Mugabe's willingness to maintain and encourage mutual trade and transport links (on which Zimbabwe was highly dependent) and his determination to prevent Zimbabwe becoming a launching point for the liberation of South Africa helped to consolidate the working relationship. Full diplomatic ties were broken and visas were required by both countries, but South Africa still maintained an active trade mission in Salisbury.

By mid-1981, South Africa began to use some of its leverage over Zimbabwe in an effort to prevent the Mugabe government from giving tangible support to the South African liberation movements. It cancelled the 16-year preferential trade agreement first established with Rhodesia. Because of South Africa's actions, Zimbabwe began to face a transportation crisis and a severe shortage of diesel fuel. In May South Africa withdrew 25 locomotives which had been on loan and this removal, plus the loss of white skilled maintenance workers and the unavailability of diesel fuel, caused significant problems. Agricultural export products and general imports and exports were stalled, which in turn adversely affected Zimbabwe's already precarious balance of payment situation. Zimbabwe will be taking delivery of new locomotives from the United States in 1982 and this should improve the situation.

South Africa also refused to renew work permits on expiration for 20,000 Zimbabweans working in South Africa for the period since 1958. The loss of remittance of salaries by these workers, plus their potential unemployment once they return to Zimbabwe, will cause further dislocation to the economy.

South Africa appears to have overresponded to the threat of guerrilla incursions from Zimbabwe and to the need to assert its regional hegemony and in so doing threatens the stability of Zimbabwe which is so vital for the general security of the region.

Events in the black South African urban areas will play an important role in the future of the Zimbabwe-South Africa political and economic involvement. Substantial black urban discontent countered by white police and military repression would force Zimbabwe to play a more active role in the liberation of South Africa. In addition, Mugabe has expressed serious concern about South African incursions into Angola. Such incursions into Zimbabwe would rupture the existing relationship and South African liberation movements would then receive greater support from Mugabe.

For the moment both sides continue to find some form of cooperation advantageous. In particular, Zimbabwe needs links with South Africa, especially for trade and transport.

Prospects for the Future

In the long run, in an effort to articulate and centralize development goals as well as to satisfy radical pressures from within his party, Mugabe might choose to establish a one-party ZANU state. Such a move might increase political unrest unless a majority of key ZAPU supporters have by that time become tacit supporters of ZANU or have been incorporated into the ruling elite of ZANU and no longer give allegiance to ZAPU. At the very least, strong assurances would have to be given to Nkomo supporters and to whites remaining in Zimbabwe.

The firing of Joshua Nkomo and three other cabinet ministers in February 1982 on the accusation that Nkomo had concealed substantial caches of arms in different parts of the country as part of a plan for a take-over of Zimbabwe opened the way for future conflict and instability, even though the PF as a party had, for the moment, decided to remain in the coalition.

The new nation of Zimbabwe is now a reality after years of white rule and a violent and protracted war. Time will be needed for indigenous political policies and institutions to develop and take root. Zimbabwe gives every indication of becoming a significant regional, African, and international power. However, a precipitous move toward a one-party state, the predominance of the military in domestic politics, the splintering of the military along ZANLA-ZIPRA lines, or the humiliation of Nkomo could result in upheavals that will stifle Zimbabwe's growth and development and intimidate foreign investors.

3.

Mozambique:
The Politics of Liberation
Tony Hodges

After its independence in 1975, Mozambique was slowly sucked into a state of war with the white Rhodesian regime on its western border. A base for thousands of Zimbabwean freedom fighters, it became a major arena in that regime's counter-insurgency offensives. Guerrilla camps, Zimbabwean refugee settlements, communications lines, and other economic installations became repeated targets for raiding Rhodesian planes and troops.

As Marcelino dos Santos, Mozambique's minister of economic development and planning, noted in a speech to the United Nations Security Council on June 28, 1977: "From small incursions lasting a few hours and never involving more than fifty men, the army of the outlaw Salisbury regime has begun to launch massive, large-scale attacks with well-defined objectives. Besides the systematic murder of the civilian population, the invader's objectives have come to include vital points of our economic and social infrastructure."

Mozambique's fate was thus closely intertwined with the future of Zimbabwe. Not only was transition to majority rule a precondition for the restoration of peace on Mozambique's western frontier, but traditional economic links between the two countries remained suspended, to Mozambique's detriment, until effective white rule ended in Salisbury.

The intensification of the Zimbabwean nationalist struggle in its last two to three years was itself partly a consequence of the example set to Zimbabwean blacks by the victory of Mozambique's own accession to independence on June 25, 1975. This achievement followed eleven years of guerrilla warfare organized by the *Frente de Libertaçao de Moçambique* (Frelimo), ending Portuguese rule almost five centuries after the famed

Portuguese navigator Vasco da Gama dropped anchor in Mozambican waters in March 1498. The Mozambican people's conquest of independence after years of bitter struggle sent shock waves throughout the rest of white-ruled Southern Africa—proving, as it did to Africans, that determined struggle (in Mozambique's case, against 60,000 Portuguese troops) could in the long run put an end to the colonial subjugation of their countries.

A History of Colonial Oppression

For the first four centuries after da Gama's arrival in 1498, Portugal's presence in the area now known as Mozambique had been sporadic and limited to isolated settlements. Portugal did not start conquering the interior in a serious way until the end of the nineteenth century—in response to the territorial ambitions of its European rivals and after the demarcation of Mozambique's present borders at the Congress of Berlin in 1884–85. Most of southern Mozambique was effectively conquered by the end of the century after a series of wars against the indigenous peoples in the 1890s, but Cabo Delgado and Niassa escaped Portuguese occupation until 1908–12. Even then, African resistance did not stop, as was testified by a major rebellion in 1917 in the northwestern province of Tete.

Portuguese rule was brutal in the extreme. In the early years the African population was scarred by the horrors of slavery and slave-trading. Slavery was abolished in the second half of the nineteenth century, but its place was taken by a system of forced labor. All *indigenas* (natives) were subject to the colonial authorities' draconian labor laws, which allowed the state to impress Africans into involuntary work on behalf of settlers or the government. As the Labor Regulation of 1899 put it: "All natives of Portuguese overseas provinces are subject to the moral and legal obligation of attempting to obtain through work the means that they lack to subsist and to better their social condition. They have full liberty to choose the method of fulfilling this obligation, but if they do not fulfill it, public authority may force a fulfillment." Despite paper reforms, forced-labor practices continued at least until the 1960s.

The only Africans who were exempted from the labor laws were the so-called *assimilados* (assimilated). They were very few in number (only about five thousand in 1950) and achieved their status by proving their ability to speak and write Portuguese and to earn a relatively high income, the tokens of assimilation into Portuguese "civilization." The *assimilado* notion was based on the derogatory idea that "civilization" involved the rejection of all things African and the absorption of Portuguese culture and language. Eduardo Mondlane, Frelimo's first president, judged that: "The most that the *assimilado* system even sets out to do is to create a few 'honorary whites.' "

Mozambique was looked on by Portugal as both a source of cheap material imports and a market for its exports. Most of Mozambique's agricultural exports were compulsorily sold to Portugal at prices fixed below the world-market rates. In the north, African farmers were forced to grow cotton for export to the detriment of the cultivation of food crops. At the same time, a highly protective tariff and foreign-exchange system was in force to ensure that Portuguese industries provided both investment and consumption goods to Mozambique. Another major objective of policy was to build up the main ports in Mozambique—Lourenço Marques (renamed Maputo in February 1976) and Beira—as key outlets for exports from the interior. Lourenço Marques became a major port for traffic from the Transvaal in South Africa and also served the mining and sugar industries of Swaziland. Beira developed as an export outlet for Southern Rhodesia, Northern Rhodesia (now Zambia), and Nyasaland (now Malawi).

But, while Lourenço Marques and Beira were built up into modern cities (and in consequence became major tourist attractions for white South Africans and Rhodesians) and white-owned export-crop plantations were encouraged by the colonial regime, almost no resources were directed to developing agricultural production and raising the standard of living in the subsistence sector, on which 90 percent of the population depended. The failure to develop Mozambique and to provide local employment forced many Mozambicans to migrate to South Africa and Rhodesia to work in mines and farms. The migrant labor system became a major source of foreign exchange for metropolitan Portugal and made Mozambique exceptionally dependent on its neighbors.

For decades, almost nothing was done to provide education and medical facilities for Africans, especially those living in the countryside. In 1964–65, for example, only 636 (8 percent) of the 7,827 students in academic secondary schools were Africans. Of the 321 students at university level that year, exactly four were African. On Mozambique's accession to independence, 85 percent of the population was illiterate.

In addition, like metropolitan Portugal, Mozambique was a thoroughgoing police state until the downfall of the Salazarist regime in April 1974. There was no freedom of speech, press, or assembly. Opposition political parties and trade unions were illegal. Strikes were banned. Mozambican society was permeated with agents of the PIDE, the Salazarist secret police, and scores of oppositionists were incarcerated—and often brutally tortured —in the regime's jails. African protest and unrest were suppressed vigorously and often bloodily. Thus, about six hundred unarmed peasants were killed during the demonstration at Mueda in Cabo Delgado on June 16, 1960, according to the eye-witness account of Alberto Chipande, today Mozambique's minister of national defense. Coming at a time when the "winds of change" were already blowing strongly elsewhere in Africa, the Mueda massacre jolted Mozambique's small but growing African intelligentsia and led swiftly to the formation of Mozambique's first modern nationalist organizations.

Between 1960 and 1962 Mozambican exiles formed political parties abroad: the Uniao Nacional Democrática de Moçambique (UDENAMO), the Mozambique African National Union (MANU), and the Uniao Africana de Moçambique Independente (UNAMI). On June 25, 1962, these groups came together at a conference in Dar es Salaam, Tanzania, to found Frelimo, with Eduardo Mondlane (previously a professor of anthropology at Syracuse University in the United States and a United Nations official) as the movement's first president. Frelimo's long guerrilla war against the Portuguese occupiers began two years later. On September 25, 1964, Frelimo proclaimed a "general insurrection" of the Mozambican people. In fact, about two hundred and fifty guerrillas moved across the border to launch the movement's long rural guerrilla campaign. The guerrillas were increasingly successful, held down ever-larger numbers of Portuguese troops, and in 1968 spread the war to Tete province, a rich farming area astride the Zambezi River.

Rather than concede independence, the Portuguese government decided to step up its repression in a bid to crush the guerrilla movement. On February 3, 1969, the Portuguese succeeded in assassinating Mondlane with a parcel bomb in Dar es Salaam. In the wartorn North the Portuguese employed mass terror methods against African villagers, falsely believing that this would intimidate rural Africans into withdrawing support from the freedom fighters. Foreign missionaries sent word of the atrocities to the outside world, finally prompting the United Nations to appoint a Commission of Inquiry into Mozambique massacres, which revealed in December 1974 that at least one thousand were tortured or massacred during mass killings by Portuguese troops at Wiriyamu and other villages in 1971 and 1972. At the same time, hundreds of thousands of Africans from the Northern provinces were forcibly evicted from their villages by Portuguese troops to remove them from contact with the guerrillas and to relocate them in *aldeamentos* (strategic hamlets).

Despite Portugal's use of sophisticated military equipment and methods of mass terror, the nationalists' tenacity and determination slowly began to give them the military edge over their Portuguese adversaries. At the end of 1973 the guerrilla war spread dramatically southward into the strategic central province of Manica e Sofala, heralding a new stage of the war in which the country's rail links with Rhodesia and Malawi came under incessant attack and the fighting reached within fifty miles of Beira, the country's second-largest city. Frelimo's offensive in Manica e Sofala had a strong psychological impact on the settler community and revealed that Portugal's plans to contain the guerrillas in the North had dismally failed.

The scale of the fighting in Manica e Sofala was such by early 1974 that railway lines in the province were attacked on over thirty separate occasions in the first four months of the year. The Portuguese military position was so serious by March 1974 that Lisbon decided to airlift ten thousand more troops to the country that month to join the sixty thousand already there.

It was Portugal's string of military setbacks in Mozambique in 1973–74 that finally convinced important sections of the Portuguese establishment and military hierarchy that a political solution was urgently required to the crises in Mozambique, Angola, and Guinea-Bissau (where over one hundred and fifty thousand troops had by then been committed). To this end, the officers of the *Movimento das Forças Armada* (MFA) overthrew the Salazarist regime of Marcello Caetano in the Lisbon coup of April 25, 1974. Nevertheless, the coup did not bring an immediate Portuguese withdrawal from Mozambique. On the contrary, Portugal's new president, General António de Spínola, believed at first that he could negotiate a compromise settlement that fell short of full independence. Vice-President Costa Gomes spelled out the government's policy on May 11, 1974, at a press conference in Lourenço Marques. A referendum, he said, would be held in which the Mozambican people would "be able to choose between one extreme of complete independence and another extreme of total integration." He said that he favored a balance between these extremes "within the great Portuguese community" and threatened that, if Frelimo did not accept the government's plans, "the army will have no choice but to go on with the fight and possibly intensify it."

But the tide of liberation was flowing too fast for Spínola's policies to stand much chance of success. "Any attempt to elude the real problem," Frelimo stated on April 28, "will only lead to new and equally avoidable sacrifices. The way to solve the problem is clear: recognition of the Mozambican people's right to independence." Rejecting Portuguese proposals for a referendum, Frelimo's president, Samora Machel, said on June 13: "You can't ask a slave if he wants to be free, particularly if the slave happens to be in full revolt."

The result of Spínola's referendum policy was the continuation of the war. It spread south of Beira for the first time when traffic on the main Beira-Lourenço Marques road was ambushed on May 9. Frelimo used more and more sophisticated weaponry, including SAM-7 ground-to-air missiles, one of which hit a DC-3 transport plane carrying seven foreign military attachés in May. Yet another blow to the Portuguese war effort came on July 1, when Frelimo announced the opening of a new military front in the province of Zambezia, which was soon engulfed in war, culminating in Frelimo seizing the town of Morrumbala on July 21. Most significant of all, perhaps, there now set in an almost total collapse of the Portuguese troop morale. Black troops began to desert the Portuguese armed forces, and in

July a company of Portuguese troops based at Macossa drew up a manifesto supporting Frelimo signed by the entire company, including its officer and three sergeants.

While the Portuguese war effort was bordering on total collapse, the Mozambican economy was hit by a rash of strikes in the cities, as workers moved to take advantage of the liberalization that followed the April 25 coup. Most of these strikes, which started in the Beira docks in May and spread to almost all industries in the following three months, were held to win wage increases, though a few were aimed at removing racist supervisors, foremen, and managers. The Lourenço Marques docks were the scene of the most serious labor dispute when four thousand dockers walked off the job for several weeks, causing losses of twenty million escudos before they returned to work on August 3. Up to eighty ships were held up while waiting to unload at the strikebound quayside, and the port remained congested for months after the strike.

Meanwhile, in the countryside Africans started seizing cattle from European farmers and invading their properties. Rural unrest reached its height on August 10, when a semi-insurrection occurred in the area of António Enes, near Nampula. António Enes itself was virtually sacked as thousands of Africans, driven to revolt by low wages, scarcity of necessities, and price rises, invaded European and Asian properties and stores. Cotton and sisal plantations were burnt and hundreds of whites and Asians fled to Nampula.

The nationalists' steady advances on the battlefield, the collapse of the Portuguese troops' will to fight, the spreading rural unrest, the wave of urban strikes, and the deepening economic crisis forced Portugal's new government to rethink its strategy. On July 27 Spínola abandoned his insistence on a referendum and publicly announced for the first time his "recognition of the rights of the inhabitants of Portugal's overseas territories to self-determination, including the immediate recognition of their right to independence." In short, Portugal's rulers had concluded that their interests—and, indeed, those of the West in general—could only now be defended by negotiating a smooth and stable transfer of power to Frelimo.

To this end, Machel and the Portuguese Foreign Minister Mário Soares met in Lusaka to hammer out a settlement. Two days later they signed the Lusaka Accords, which outlined a series of steps for the progressive transfer of powers to Frelimo, culminating in formal independence on June 25, 1975. During the interim period the country would be administered by a "transitional government" composed of nine ministers, three appointed by Portugal and six by Frelimo. An immediate ceasefire was called and a Joint Military Commission set up, with equal numbers of Portuguese and Frelimo representatives, to supervise its implementation.

The agreement in Lusaka was immediately challenged by right-wing settlers in Mozambique. On September 7, the same day as the accords were signed, a group calling itself the Free Mozambique Movement seized the buildings of the Rádio Clube de Moçambique and other strategic installations in Lourenço Marques, appealing to Mozambicans to "remain Portuguese, and to fight against all people who betray Mozambique and want to trample on the Portuguese flag." The insurgents broke their way into the Machava jail and released scores of imprisoned PIDE agents and officers.

Despite Portugal's agreement with Frelimo, Portuguese troops did little to stop the rebels' action. But Africans' response to the settlers' attempted putsch was swift and massive, despite appeals from Frelimo leaders that the suppression of the white rebels should be left to Frelimo and Portuguese troops. Lourenço Marques was paralyzed by a general strike on September 9. By the next day Africans had thrown up barricades on all the capital's access roads to prevent arms reaching the rebels. White property and stores were attacked and burned. The dramatic scale and depth of this uprising by the African populace in the capital's suburbs and shantytowns were enough to convince the white rebels to abandon their stand. Portuguese troops and police allowed them to leave their occupied buildings without a shot being fired or any arrests being made. In contrast, the Portuguese government decided to put down the black uprising by force. The Portuguese High Command met in emergency session while troops were sent into the shantytowns. Up to a hundred were killed, almost all Africans.

A little over a week later on September 20 the transitional government was sworn into office, with Joaquim Chissano, a top Frelimo leader, as the country's new prime minister, and Rear-Admiral Vitor Crespo the last Portuguese high commissioner. Frelimo's president, Samora Machel, remained outside the country until the following May. During the transitional period Portugal kept several thousand troops in Mozambique to ensure a stable transfer of power. They were progressively withdrawn, the last units leaving the country on June 24, 1975. The next day the Portuguese flag was hauled down for the last time. Direct colonial rule had finally ended and Machel became Mozambique's first president.

Frelimo's Reform Program

The characteristic policies of the Frelimo regime were introduced almost immediately after independence. The first session of the Council of Ministers, July 9–25, 1975, adopted a series of decrees to make education, medical care, and other facilities more accessible to the majority of Mozambicans. On July 24, to a crowd of 150,000 in Maputo, Machel announced major extensions of state control that took effect from August 1. All private schools, including those owned by the missions, were taken over by the state, and the school curriculum was overhauled to teach Mozambicans more about their own history and culture (instead of Portugal's, as in the past). Private law practices were integrated into a state legal service, and private medical practice was abolished. Private funeral firms were outlawed and a state funeral organization established. The most far reaching measures appeared to be the nationalization of land and the abolition of private rent collection.

A particular objective of the new government was to make education and health care more accessible to the rural population, which had been virtually ignored during most of the colonial era. In 1975 a massive literacy campaign began to tackle the country's very high illiteracy rate. By January 1977 the number of secondary schools had tripled, from 33 at the time of independence to 99, and by August 1977 the number of primary school pupils had risen from 695,885 to 1.3 million. In the field of health, the country's first nationwide vaccination campaign against smallpox, tuberculosis, and measles was launched on June 14, 1976, and, by September 1977 more than 4 million people (out of a total population of 9.4 million) had been vaccinated. Then, on November 1, 1977, a Socialisation of Health bill made most medical facilities free for the first time.

The government also moved on retailing facilities and housing. It set up a state retailing organization, the *Empresa das Lojas do Povo* (People's Shops Enterprise), to provide a commercial network of "people's shops" selling essential goods to the population at controlled prices. A particularly interesting part of its reform program was the adoption of a decree on February 3, 1976, that regulated rights to housing that was designed to move homeless families into housing abandoned by the settlers. Rents, which were to be payable to the state, were staggered according to family income as well as size of home. But the decree was not remarkably radical. Not only was each family guaranteed possession of its own home (article 1), but each family was granted the right to maintain an additional house or flat in the countryside or by the sea (article 13), a measure clearly designed to defend the interests of the wealthiest sector of the community.

Nationalization and Labor Policies

According to article 14 of the Constitution of the People's Republic of Mozambique, approved by the Frelimo Central Committee on June 20, 1975, "foreign capital shall be authorised to operate within the framework of the State's economic policy." In the first year and a half of independence, the government restricted nationalization to the take-over of a number of small, Portuguese-owned companies and farms which had in any case already been abandoned by their owners and managers during the settler exodus that accompanied Portugal's withdrawal from the country. (The Portuguese community, which numbered some 280,000 in early 1974, was down to 80,000 by independence and only about 10,000 by 1978.) In 1977 a series of more important nationalization measures began. On January 11 the three main private insurance companies were merged into a new state-owned insurance company, Emose. On May 2 the Sonarep oil refinery at Matola, near Maputo, which is Mozambique's most important secondary industrial installation, was nationalized, and a state petroleum company, Petromoc, was founded. However, compensation was promised to Sonarep's owners (the Portuguese financial group *Bulhosa*), the Portuguese oil company Sacor, and the *Compagnie Française des Petroles.* Finally, on January 4, 1978, the government nationalized five of the country's six private commercial banks and set up a second state bank, the People's Development Bank. Once again, though, compensation was promised, while one private bank, the *Banco Standard Totta de Mocambique,* which is owned by the British banking group Standard Chartered and the Portuguese *Banco Totta e Acores,* is being allowed to remain in business.

Significantly, the government issued a decree (law 17/77) in May 1977 under which (article 12) it lifted the blanket ban on profit repatriation imposed by the Portuguese colonial administration in 1972. This move was obviously designed to attract foreign investors, and later in the year, in October, the minister of industry, Mário Machungo, met a half-dozen American business executives during a visit to the U.S. to discuss investment possibilities for American firms in his country. This evolution has been in line with the economic policies adopted at Frelimo's Third Congress, which qualified its decision to "develop and consolidate the role of the state in the economy" by allowing some private capitalist enterprises and investment on condition that they accord with the government's broad economic goals and priorities.

In those firms that have been nationalized, the workers have not been directly involved in decision-making. The government's practice has been to appoint administrators from above to run these businesses; and in some cases this has led to resentment from the workers in the affected firms. A noteworthy example is what happened at the *Companhia Industrial de Fundiçao e Laminagem* (CIFEL), Mozambique's only smelting and metal-rolling business, which was set up in 1955 in Maputo and today employs four hundred workers. CIFEL was owned by the Portuguese conglomerate *Champalimaud* and was one of the many businesses abandoned during the 1975 settler exodus. The Mozambique government had no choice but to take over the firm, and it named two administrators to run the plant. According to the Maputo daily *Notícias,* the CIFEL workers have complained since the government takeover that the appointed administrators have been "bureaucratic" and "distant from the rank-and-file" and have maintained "unalterable and bourgeois" work methods. *Notícias* reported that the workers at CIFEL felt that the company was still a "capitalist enterprise." One worker reportedly said: "The administration has the power to make decisions and they're the bosses. Can't we who produce the wealth give our opinion on problems? Our work here is just to produce, produce, produce."

Another revealing indication of the authoritarian administrative structure set up in the nationalized industries is given by a report broadcast by Radio Maputo on October 13, 1976, of a meeting of Frelimo activist groups in Maputo, where Machel personally outlined how production targets would be set and achieved. Machel said that each sector would be given weekly, monthly, quarterly, and half-yearly targets and that each sector would be held collectively accountable for the accomplishment of its set tasks. Frelimo activist groups in factories were told to hold monthly meetings with the administrative committees of their firms and then report back to the work force, informing them of the subjects discussed with the administrators.

At the same time, Frelimo curtailed the right to strike as part of its program to impose austerity measures, raise productivity, and combat what it calls "egotism" and "colonial mentality." On September 20, 1974, in a message relayed to the inauguration ceremony of the transitional government, Machel said that "at this stage in the life of our country there is no more room for strikes." The clamp-down on strikes came in the wake of a massive strike wave that swept through Mozambican industries after the downfall of the Caetano regime. To carry through its no-strike policy, Frelimo had also to curb the activities of the rank-and-file "workers' commissions," which had sprung up after the April 1974 Lisbon coup and which played a major part in the strike wave. But, as late as October 1976, workers' go-slows and lack of cooperation seemed still to be giving Frelimo trouble. "There are workers," Machel complained in a speech broadcast on October 13, "who are still trying to resolve their problems in the way that they learned at the time of the provisional government, at the time of the so-called workers' commissions. These workers are staging silent strikes. They are deliberately causing a fall in production." Since then, the government has been championing the slogan "Generalised Political and Organizational Offensive on the Production Front" and has set up "production councils" in factories to raise workers' productivity.

The Nature of the Frelimo Government

"With the Proclamation of the People's Republic of Mozambique on June 25, 1975," an editorial in the Independence Day issue of Frelimo's *Mozambique Revolution* stated, "the revolutionary process in our country entered a new phase, the phase of People's Democracy, during which the lessons of the liberated zones during ten years of armed struggle will be applied at the level of the nation. We are now engaged in the task of destroying all vestiges of the colonial-capitalist State, an instrument of exploitation and oppression, and establishing a People's State which serves the interests of the working masses. This phase will be a period of intense struggle."

But it was not until its Third Congress, held in Maputo on February 3–7, 1977, that Frelimo formally declared its adherence to Marxism-Leninism and announced plans to build a vanguard party of workers and peasants. "The hard class battles," proclaimed the new Frelimo program adopted by the congress, "demand that the working class, closely allied with the peasantry, its fundamental ally, and with the progressive elements of the other labouring classes, organise itself into a vanguard party, guided by the scientific ideology of the proletariat—Marxism-Leninism." Since the Congress, the use of Marxist phraseology has remained the order of the day in official circles. "The fight of the workers of our country is a fight against the capitalists," dos Santos declared over Mozambican radio in August 1977. "Our objectives are clear: destroy capitalism in our country and create socialism."

But two facts stand out in contrast to the regime's official rhetoric. First, as we have seen, despite talk of "destroying all vestiges of the colonial-capitalist state," there are limits to Frelimo's nationalization program, and the government continues to guarantee a significant place for investment by western multinational companies. Second, despite claims that it is building "People's Democratic Power," the Frelimo regime has excluded the mass of the population, including the workers, from participating in effective political decision-making, has suppressed most democratic rights and civil liberties, and has in practice erected an authoritarian one-party state.

Creating a One-Party State

Since its entry into the transitional government Frelimo has sought to consolidate its political supremacy by erecting a one-party state. All opposing political groups are now illegal, and the constitution accords Frelimo the status of a state institution in its own right. All governmental bodies are subordinate to Frelimo. Thus, article 3 of the constitution states that "the People's Republic of Mozambique will be guided by the political line defined by Frelimo, which is the leader of the State and of society. Frelimo will establish the basic political policy of the State, so as to ensure the conformity of the policy of the State with the interests of the people."

After its accession to power, however, Frelimo had to consolidate the movement's structure in the areas outside the wartime liberated zones of Niassa, Cabo Delgado, and Tete. In the central and southern parts of the country (and, above all, in the cities), where Portuguese repression had barred the creation of a strong party apparatus, Frelimo had to build up an organization virtually from scratch after the signing of the Lusaka Accords. In these areas Frelimo at first discouraged the formation of local party units (*circulos*) and instead organized preparatory *grupos dinamizadores* (dynamization groups), with leaders appointed from above by Frelimo. The groups were designed to inculcate and spread Frelimo's political line and to prepare the way for the establishment of Frelimo circulos. The function of the *grupos dinamizadores* was clearly revealed in a major discussion of these bodies at the first national conference of Frelimo district committees, held at Mocuba in Zambézia on February 16–21, 1975. This conference decided that "it is premature to transform the *grupos dinamizadores* into *circulos* because people's power is not yet sufficiently solidly rooted among the masses" and because "there exist in these groups reactionary and opportunist infiltrated elements," including members of "phantom organisations" (illegal anti-Frelimo parties), people "compromised with capitalism," ex-members of the PIDE, smugglers, racists, tribalists, prostitutes, and provokers of strikes. "It is necessary," the conference agreed, "to proceed to a campaign of purification in the ranks of the *grupos dinamizadores*, to discover, denounce and expel the elements which have infiltrated into them."

By 1977, however, the Frelimo leadership felt that sufficient groundwork had been laid to start organizing local party units throughout the country. The norms for admitting new members were set by the Third Congress. The Congress decided that this new phase of party organizing would be a slow and carefully nurtured process and that the party would remain a small, streamlined organization, in marked contrast to the type of mass-membership parties common in African one-party states. The *grupos dinamizadores* would remain meanwhile as more broadly based formations to transmit party decisions to the masses. "In the suburbs," Marcelino dos Santos explained in August 1977, "the residents' organisation will be the *grupo dinamizador,* that is to say that even when the party cells are formed in the suburbs, the *grupos dinamizadores* will remain. They are the mass organisations in the suburbs."

Article 37 of the Constitution states that "the People's Assembly is the supreme organ of the state." But during the first two years of independence this body was appointed[1] rather than elected. The first nationwide elections were held at the end of 1977.

The reason for the delay was that Frelimo wanted first to solidly implant its organization throughout the country. At a session held on August 28–29, 1977, the Frelimo Central Committee decided that this groundwork had been laid. It approved a draft electoral law which was ratified on September 1 by the country's makeshift nominated People's Assembly. This law set the stage for elections at five levels: for members of local assemblies September 25–November 13, 1977; for district and city assemblies by November 27; and for ten provincial assemblies and the national People's Assembly by December 4.

In a speech opening the August 28–29 Central Committee meeting, President Machel claimed that the elections would be "fundamental steps for the building of democratic people's power at the level of the whole country" and that the assemblies would "guarantee the organised participation of the masses in the leadership of the state." Reality was somewhat different. First, the elections were held under the Constitution's one-party system. "The list of candidates will be proposed by the Frelimo committee at the appropriate level or, in districts, towns and localities where there are no party committees, by the *grupo dinamizador*," the electoral law stipulated.

This meant that voters did not have a real choice, though some party candidates were not elected because they failed to gain 50 percent positive votes. Second, there was universal suffrage only at the local level. At higher levels a system of indirect election was used. For example, article 24 of the electoral law laid down that "the provincial assemblies elect the deputies to the People's Assembly." Even city assemblies were not elected by universal suffrage.[2]

The national People's Assembly was elected on December 4, 1977, when the ten provincial assemblies adopted a 226-member slate nominated by the Frelimo Central Committee. In reality, however, the People's Assembly has little power. It meets for only a few days a year and is therefore basically a rubber-stamp body for approval of decisions already made by the government. The real power is held by the members of Frelimo's Central Committee. Moreover, there is little opportunity for Frelimo's rank-and-file members to control decision-making within the party. Frelimo has held only three congresses since its founding in 1962. The political line and instructions issued by the movement's top leaders are transmitted downward through successive tiers of party committees at provincial, district, and local levels.

The party is also flanked by other "mass organizations," all of them tightly controlled by the state. They include the *Organizaçao da Juventude de Mocambique* (OJM—Mozambique Youth Organization), which was founded at a congress in Maputo on November 28, 1977, and the long-standing *Organizaçao das Mulheres de Mocambique* (OMM—Mozambique's Women's Organization). Independent trade unions are illegal.

The press too has been marshaled behind the regime. The newspapers and broadcasts are carefully supervised by the government, and in August 1975 Machel warned journalists that they would be "exposed" if they "serve individual interests and support deviations from the party line."

The government has been especially careful to keep a close political watch over the army, the Popular Forces for the Liberation of Mozambique (FPLM). In March 1977 several high-ranking army officers were arrested on charges of "causing a separation between the population and the armed forces," and on June 29, 1977, a political commissariat was set up to exercise political control over the military.

In addition, the regime has equipped itself with a repressive apparatus to curb dissent. On October 13, 1975, the Government set up the *Serviço Nacional de Segurança Popular* (SNASP—the National Service of People's

Security) with sweeping powers to "detect, neutralise and combat all forms of subversion, sabotage and acts directed against the People's Power and its representatives, against the national economy or against the objectives of the People's Republic of Mozambique." Its director, who is answerable to the president, may decide whether anyone arrested should be "given over to the competent police authority, sent to court or to camps for re-education." Two weeks after SNASP's formation, on the night of October 30–31, 1975, more than three thousand people were arrested in Maputo, Beira, Nampula, Xai-Xai, and Chimoio. Many detainees have been sent to *Centros de Descoloni-zacao Mental* (Mental Decolonization Centers) for "re-education." The two major camps are at Inhassune, north of Maputo, and at Dondo, near Beira.

Opposition to Frelimo

Frelimo came to power in 1974–75 on a crest of popularity, credited by the great majority of the population as the movement that had led the long, bitter struggle for national independence. And, though Frelimo believes that a tough one-party system is needed to prevent potential opposition at a time when economic conditions are rough for most Mozambicans, the existing opposition groups, which are right-wing, appear to be very weak, largely because their leaders, most of whom are in jail, discredited themselves by supporting the unsuccessful white settler putsch in September 1974 on the eve of Frelimo's accession to power. Their unpopularity has been accentuated by the support they receive from the Rhodesian regime's misnamed "Voice of Free Africa," which is popularly known in Mozambique as *Radio Kizumba* ("Radio Hyena"). No group that appears to be associated with Salisbury could be expected to get much of a hearing from Mozambicans, whatever the economic situation, at a time of constant and often bloody Rhodesian border incursions. Immediately after independence the Frelimo government had also to keep on guard against reactionary settler groups like the Free Mozambique Movement and the *Dragoes da Morte* (Dragons of Death). Right-wing groups were believed responsible, for example, for attacks against railway trains on February 19 and March 29, 1975. The latter caused eighty-one deaths and £700,000 ($1,680,000) worth of damage. In September 1975 pencil-bombs were discovered in Maputo.

Several white opponents of the transition to independence were deported, both during the transitional government's term of office and after independence. In October 1975, to cite just one example, Frelimo deported Rogério de Canha e Sa, an ex-governor of Vila Pery district, after he had expressed a hostile attitude to black rule in the country. Other settler opponents of Frelimo were detained. They were believed to number about two hundred in the early months of 1976. In June, however, they were all released and deported after discussions in Rome between Mozambique's foreign minister, Joaquim Chissano, and the Portuguese foreign minister, Melo Antunes.

Finally, on March 16, 1977, the Maputo government decided to expel several thousand of the remaining Portuguese nationals, in order, in spite of inevitable economic losses, to rid itself once and for all of what it considered to be a politically unreliable layer of the population.

The Frelimo regime has also kept on guard against supporters of the so-called "phantom parties," small African anti-Frelimo groups that were banned after Frelimo's entry into the transitional government. The better-known of these very small groups had included the *Comité Revolucionário de Moçambique* (Coremo—Mozambique Revolutionary Committee), led by Paulo José Gumane, and the *Grupo Unido de Mocambique* (Gumo—United Group of Mozambique), which had been founded in 1973 by Joana Simiao. Although Gumo was dissolved by Frelimo supporters in June–July 1974, Simiao set up another small group on August 13: the *Frente Comum de Moçambique* (Frecomo—Common Front of Mozambique). On August 24 Frecomo fused with four other anti-Frelimo groups, including Coremo, to form the *Partido de Coligaçao Nacional* (PCN—National Coalition Party). The PCN called for a referendum on the country's future (in line with Spinolist policy), sought to prevent Portugal from hammering out a deal with Frelimo over the PCN's head, and then, after the signing of the Lusaka Accords, backed the September 1974 settler putsch attempt, thereby losing what little African support it had previously enjoyed.

Several hundred supporters of the PCN were imprisoned by the transitional government. They included Paulo Gumane, Joana Simiao, Uria Simango, and Lázaro Kavandame. Two hundred and thirty-nine of these prisoners were presented to the press by Frelimo on March 16, 1975, and three hundred and sixty were displayed to the press on April 21, 1975. Kavandame, however, reportedly escaped from detention and, early in 1976, set up an underground opposition group called the Cabo Delgado Front. Its aim is supposedly to "liberate" the province of Cabo Delgado, an area populated by the Makonde ethnic group. There is no evidence to suggest that the group has posed a serious threat to Frelimo, though it is true that reference to its existence has been made by the Mozambique authorities. In February 1976 Radio Maputo reported that a political commissar at Montepuez had been dismissed for "supporting enemy reactionaries of the Cabo Delgado Front."

On July 25, 1976, another underground group was allegedly formed: the United Democratic Front of Mozambique (Fumo). Under the leadership of Dr. Domingos Arouca, a lawyer who once supported Frelimo, Fumo adopted a program at its founding meeting at Mocuba. This document proposed the reintegration of Mozambique into Portugal as a federal republic, a pro-Western policy supporting free enterprise, and respect for "the ethnic and tribal realities." In 1977 Fumo changed its name to the Mozambican National Resistance Army (ERNM) and claimed that it had the allegiance of six former Frelimo guerrilla commanders. But there has been no evidence that the ERNM or another group called the *Partido Revolucionário de Moçambique* (PRM—Mozambique Revolutionary Party), which is said to have some supporters in Niassa and Tete, constitute any more of a threat to President Machel than the Cabo Delgado Front.

However, the harsh economic conditions in the country have posed the government with political problems of another sort. After independence Frelimo launched a tough austerity program and a drive for increased productivity by industrial workers. The government has held out little prospect of an improvement of living standards and has urged workers to work harder.

This program appears to have been met with widespread ill-feeling by Mozambicans, especially those in the cities who had engaged in the 1974 strike wave and had expected independence to bring improvements in their standard of living. Above all, as the CIFEL example cited above suggests, workers' hostility to government policies seems to have flowed at least partly from resentment at the way in which these policies have been imposed from above without any democratic involvement in decision-making.

Though Frelimo was successful, by and large, in halting the massive strike wave that swept Mozambique after the April 1974 Lisbon coup, Frelimo representatives had to travel to Moatize in Tete in February 1975 to persuade striking coal-miners to return to work. On September 25, 1975, Machel complained that "in a bid to hinder the realisation of the people's aspirations, the enemy resorted to disorganising production, by instigating disinterest in work and, when possible, even by paralysing work through counterrevolutionary strikes."

The government austerity program aroused considerable discontent in the FPLM, forcing the government to summon a meeting of 350 FPLM cadres on December 10–13, 1975, which, with Machel himself present, warned against "enemy infiltration" into the armed forces and ordered all FPLM units to spend at least twelve hours a week studying Frelimo's political line and engaging in self-criticism sessions. After the meeting, several hundred FPLM soldiers were arrested, an inquiry was opened, and some of those detained were accused of subversion. A few days later, on December 17, four hundred soldiers in an FPLM detachment at Machava, on the outskirts of Maputo, staged an ill-prepared rebellion and tried to march to the center of Maputo. By the next morning they had been routed by troops loyal to the government. Nevertheless, the rebellion showed the depth of discontent among FPLM troops, some of them hardened veterans of the liberation war.

At the end of 1976 the Frelimo regime was still meeting opposition to its austerity and production drives from urban workers. A special meeting of Frelimo activist groups was held in Maputo in October to discuss the problem, and Machel's speech to the meeting was broadcast to the nation on October 13 by Radio Maputo. He implored, "Increase production; increase productivity—that must be our task. Demonstrations have never been organized to increase production. We must stage demonstrations to increase production, to increase productivity. This is our task." Machel also accused some workers of "anti-white racism." "There are people," Machel said, "who do not accept the authority of bosses, just because they are white. Isn't that so? Ideological diarrhoea; ideological confusion. . . ."

The Frelimo regime has also faced problems from rebellious students. On February 16, 1978, Machel launched a blistering attack on what he called the "crises of authority in the schools." He claimed that in 1977 "the enemy openly launched himself at the schools in an effort to fill influential positions and inject his venom." He accused some students of tuning in to Radio Kizumba and said, "Some individuals bring to school magazines which are financed and paid for by the enemy. They are paid to do so. That is why they spread this propaganda. They are *agents provocateurs.*" In fact, there are almost no pro-Rhodesian students in Mozambique, but it has become rather common for the government to attempt to discredit dissidents by falsely pinning a pro-Rhodesian label on them. In his speech Machel declared the biggest problem to be that "at the school level, we have not yet succeeded in implanting the party properly." He ended with a tough warning: "Look here. From today, no pupil should turn up at school wearing a beard. No pupil should turn up at school with long hair. No girl student should turn up at school with uncombed hair or wearing a head-scarf. We shall take some drastic steps against some older pupils. They will be expelled and sent to re-education camps."

Finally, while no clear-cut political divisions have emerged (at least in public) within Frelimo, the movement's leadership has felt it necessary since independence to launch repeated purges in the party and the *grupos dinamizadores.* This has been part of Frelimo's drive to consolidate its structures in the country, impose its unpopular austerity and productivity drives, and build a disciplined, monolithic party. A swift succession of purges in 1975 and 1976 indicated that criticism and expressions of discontent continued to present problems for the regime. In March 1977 the party announced that it had expelled three of its officials in Limpopo because they had "slandered party and government structures, spread rumours and confusion, sabotaged machinery and indulged in indiscipline and systematic refusal to work. These individuals, who also incited their fellows to strike, were handed over to the authorities." The deputy secretary of the *grupo dinamizador* in Changolane, Gaza, was expelled and sent to a re-education camp in July; and in the following September there was a purge of the *grupo dinamizador* in Kissima-jula, Nacala, with the head of its propaganda section "sent to a re-education camp where he will be submitted to a process of rehabilitation."

However, despite all these conflicts and challenges, the Frelimo regime has not faced the type of really serious internal threats that have confronted the MPLA government since the end of the Angolan civil war. Unlike Angola, there have been no deeply rooted rival nationalist movements, no serious guerrilla insurgencies, and no dramatic internal split within the ruling party comparable to the May 1977 coup attempt in Luanda.

Nonalignment

The Frelimo regime has charted a pragmatic, nonaligned foreign policy since independence. "The party," resolved the Third Congress, "stands for the establishment of relations of friendship and cooperation by the People's Republic of Mozambique with all states independent of their social and political regimes." The government has not allowed any foreign powers to set up military bases on its territory, and it has declared its support for the demilitarization of the Indian Ocean. As article 24 of the Constitution affirms, "The People's Republic of Mozambique defends the principle of turning the Indian Ocean into a non-nuclear zone of peace." The point was repeated by Foreign Minister Chissano in a speech to the United Nations General Assembly on October 6, 1975: "We are of the view that the Indian Ocean should constitute a denuclearised zone, free of military and naval bases and fleets."

Nonalignment denotes for Frelimo (like other Third World nationalist regimes) a policy of seeking wide-ranging international relations, with a view to extending the country's range of potential trading partners and sources of economic aid. In other words, freed from the special trading and other constraints imposed under colonial rule, Mozambique's new rulers are trying to increase their room for economic maneuver by diversifying the country's international connections. In fact, however, Mozambique's primary economic links are still of necessity with the apartheid regime in South Africa. The Mozambican government has tried to cement friendly relations and get assistance from any country willing to cooperate—from the Soviet bloc, China, Arab oil-producers, and the major capitalist countries. It has succeeded in establishing bases for cooperation with numerous Western governments that denied Frelimo aid during the war for independence and gave valuable support to the Portuguese. While it retains close ties with most noncapitalist countries, especially the Soviet Union and Cuba, most of its aid has come from Western countries that are keen to cultivate relations with Maputo to further their diplomatic initiatives in Southern Africa to secure an orderly transfer of power in Rhodesia.

Even before independence the British minister for overseas development, Judith Hart, held talks with Frelimo leaders in Dar es Salaam in May 1975 and promised substantial aid to Mozambique after independence. In 1976 Britain offered a £10 million loan to assist energy and road construction projects, and on October 18, 1977, Hart signed an agreement to provide an additional £5 million, interest-free loan for the purchase of British goods.

Though the United States was not invited to Mozambique's independence celebration in June 1975, the U.S. assistant secretary of state for Africa, Donald Easum, had met Machel as early as October 1974 and announced that the United States was "looking forward to a cooperative relationship with the new Mozambique." On September 23, 1975, the American secretary of state, Henry Kissinger, met Chissano in New York and signed a joint communique establishing diplomatic relations. In particular Kissinger saw that the United States needed to cultivate close ties with Frelimo as part of the American effort to further a negotiated settlement of the Rhodesian crisis. To this end Kissinger offered $12.5 million of aid for Mozambique in a major speech in Lusaka on April 27, 1976, that outlined American policies in Southern Africa. Though the aid package roused conservative opposition in the United States Senate, the Ford Administration finally signed an aid agreement in Maputo on September 29 that totaled over $9 million. Since taking office in 1977, the Carter administration has pursued an essentially similar policy. On October 4, 1977, Carter and Machel, at a meeting in Washington, announced a "new era" in Mozambican-American relations, and the following December U.S. representatives in Maputo signed an agreement to provide $8.7 million worth of food aid.

By far the most important aid-donor, however, is Sweden, which gave Frelimo some backing during its war against Portugal. In March 1976 the Swedish minister of development paid a ten-day visit to Mozambique, during which he signed an agreement to provide $45 million over three years to build a dam on the Sabie River. Sweden also agreed to build a power station at Quelimane. In April 1976 Swedish technicians visited timber plantations in the Chimoio region with a view to developing a pulp and paper factory and also visited various sites with mineral deposits.

In coordination with the other Scandinavian countries, Sweden decided to launch a massive agricultural aid program in 1977. The Nordic Council of Ministers agreed to commit £50 million to a three-year program (1978–80) that will assist twenty-six projects in agriculture, fishing, and forestry and will employ at least one hundred Scandinavian experts in the country. One Scandinavian official in Maputo said that the program was "the biggest Nordic support to any country in the history of Nordic aid."

While welcoming these overtures from the capitalist world, the Frelimo government has also found it in its interest to maintain cordial relations with China and the Soviet Union, the two countries that gave Frelimo its greatest military aid during the liberation war. Again, it has done so as a nonaligned, Third World nationalist regime, not as a "satellite" of the U.S.S.R. or China. Though Frelimo ritualistically describes the Soviet Union as the "liberated zone of humanity," Chissano pointedly stated at a Soviet embassy reception in Maputo in October 1975 that outside help during the liberation war did not give any country the right to dictate policy to Mozambique. Mozambique's new rulers have sought economic aid from both China and the Soviet Union. Thus, they have steered clear of embroilment in the Sino-Soviet conflict.

On February 25, 1975, Machel led a Frelimo delegation to Peking to start a seventeen-day tour of China and North Korea. Both countries promised aid, China announcing that it would provide a massive $57 million interest-free loan. During the Angolan civil war, however, China's star waned in Maputo because Peking's obsession with the supposedly "hegemonist" designs of "Soviet social-imperialism" led to its refusal to back the MPLA against the South African troops that invaded Angola in 1975. Frelimo, which feels far more threatened by the forces of white racism in Southern Africa than by the "new tsars" in Moscow, disapproved of Peking's stance, but relations were not broken and Mozambique's desire to receive aid from China soon led to new contacts. Marcelino dos Santos paid a five-day visit to Peking in September 1977 to reset Sino-Mozambican relations on a cordial footing.

The Soviet Union, however, followed up China's Angolan debacle by redoubling its assistance to the Frelimo government. A series of meetings in Moscow in 1976 culminated in May when Machel and Soviet leaders signed agreements covering aid in commerce, education, sea transport, fishing, air transport, and public health. Then, on March 31, 1977, a Soviet-Mozambican Treaty of Friendship and Cooperation was signed during a state visit to Mozambique by Nicolai Podgorny, then Soviet president. Two clauses of the treaty were seen as having special significance in view of the escalating confrontation with Rhodesia on Mozambique's western frontier. Article 4 stated that "in the interests of reinforcing the defense potentials of the high contracting parties, they will continue developing cooperation in the military sphere on the basis of appropriate agreements." And article 9 stated that "if situations arise that threaten peace or break peace, the high contracting parties will immediately get into contact with each other to coordinate their positions in the interests of eliminating the arising threat or restoring peace."

Ironically, however, the Soviet Union has actually provided very little military aid to Mozambique. To date, the U.S.S.R. has shown more enthusiasm for providing the Ethiopian *Dergue* with a military arsenal to crush the Somalis and the Eritrean nationalist insurgents than to send the helicopters, jets, and missiles needed by Mozambique to fend off attacking Rhodesian army and air force units.

"The biggest surprise here," reported David Ottaway from Maputo in the

December 12, 1977, *International Herald Tribune*, "is that there is no evidence that the Soviet Union has given Mozambique the military wherewithal to defend itself. Western correspondents visiting here during the latest Rhodesian incursion, late last month, were amazed to discover how lightly the country's borders and the guerrilla camps are defended against the Rhodesians. It appears that Mozambique has little or no air-defence system, something that is vitally needed to counter raiding Rhodesian jets and helicopter gunships. Mozambican and western diplomatic sources say that the Russians have so far provided this war-battered nation with mostly obsolete weapons such as T-34 tanks and MiG-17 jets, and that the few missiles in its arsenal for air defence are mostly of Tanzanian origin."

Notably more generous, considering its own limited resources, has been Cuba's aid. Fidel Castro visited Mozambique in March 1977 and Machel made a reciprocal trip to Cuba the following October, when he signed a twenty-year friendship treaty with Castro. "Since we are a small nation and an underdeveloped country—although we are in a better situation than Mozambique—we cannot do much," Castro said during Machel's visit, "but we try to contribute with something. We have doctors, nurses, sugar technicians, livestock technicians, agricultural technicians, fishing, construction and transport technicians. In total, there are about 300 Cubans in Mozambique working in these fields and the time will come when there will be slightly more than 400."

As a natural corollary of its nonaligned policy and its membership in the OAU, the Frelimo government has also tried to forge close links with neighboring African states, in particular with Tanzania and Zambia, two of its partners in the group of African front-line states closely involved with the crisis in Zimbabwe. President Julius Nyerere of Tanzania, Frelimo's constant supporter during its liberation struggle, was the first head of state to pay an official visit to Mozambique after independence, arriving on August 30, 1975, for a week-long tour of the country. At the end of his visit, on September 7, Mozambique and Tanzania signed a series of agreements providing for a special economic and diplomatic relationship between the two countries. Tanzania and Mozambique produce two-thirds of the world's cashew nuts, and it was decided that a permanent commission with eight ministers from each state should formulate plans for a joint marketing policy. The agreements also allowed each country to represent the other at a diplomatic level and to issue passports and visas for the other. Of particular interest was a clause instructing the commission to "take into account the possibility that other countries might wish to cooperate in mutually advantageous undertakings"—a hint that Mozambique and Tanzania might form a new regional African economic community, perhaps with Zambia and Swaziland.

Though there are some obstacles to Tanzanian–Mozambican cooperation, notably language barriers and a lack of direct road and telecommunications links, both countries' governments proceeded with the plans outlined in September 1975. On April 3, 1976, Marcelino dos Santos, the minister for development and economic planning, led a thirty-two-member delegation to Dar es Salaam to participate in the first session of the commission set up the previous September. Four subcommissions were set up, dealing with trade, industry, and finance; diplomatic and consular affairs; education and culture; and communications, transport, and public works. One key decision of the meeting was that a "Unity Bridge" would be built over the Rovuma River to provide a direct road link between the two countries. On January 12, 1978, the two countries decided to set up a joint "foreign relations centre" to train their diplomats.

Meanwhile, there have been increasing signs that this type of cooperation is being widened in scope to include Zambia. On April 11, 1976, for example, it was announced that, following a joint defense and security meeting in Maputo, the governments of Zambia, Mozambique, and Tanzania had agreed to set up a joint institute for the training of their defense and police forces. On April 20 Zambia's President Kenneth Kaunda flew to Mozambique for a five-day visit, at the end of which Kaunda and Machel signed the Maputo Agreement, which sets up a Joint Permanent Cooperation Committee and reaffirms solidarity between Frelimo and Zambia's ruling United National Independence Party (UNIP). The Maputo Agreement included a commitment to build a direct rail link between Mozambique and Zambia, linking Zambia's industries with the Moatize-Beira railway. In another move clearly designed to forge closer economic ties between the two countries, a paved road was built between Katete in Zambia's eastern province and Bene in Tete during 1976. In May 1977 the two countries signed a trade agreement; and in February 1977 Zambia, along with Tanzania, sent aid to Mozambique after serious flooding in Gaza province.

Mozambique and the Crisis in Southern Africa

The Mozambican people's victory and independence (like that of the Angolans somewhat later) had a profound impact on the remaining white-ruled countries of Southern Africa, above all because it provided an inspiring example to blacks in Zimbabwe, Namibia, and South Africa of what a determined struggle against white rule could achieve. In South Africa the Mozambican events gave added impetus to the growing black consciousness movement and to the South African Students' Movement (SASM). In fact, the Lusaka Accords prompted the Black People's Convention (BPC) and the South African Students' Organization (SASO) to call a pro-Frelimo rally in Durban on September 25, 1974. It was banned by the government, and over thirty black leaders, including Zethulele Cindi, the secretary-general of the BPC, were arrested under the Terrorism Act. "What stands out," the London

Times commented after this incident, "is that the South African government hopes to silence any response to the Frelimo triumph in Mozambique. This amounts to an admission of its realization that the advent of a black government in Mozambique after a successful military campaign against white rule is bound to stir deep feelings in its black population. Silenced or not, they are bound to ask 'is our turn coming?' "

The black victory in Mozambique posed still greater dangers to the white-settler regime in Rhodesia. Besides rousing the militancy of Zimbabweans, Mozambique's accession to independence raised the prospect that sooner or later the Ian Smith government would lose its trade routes through Beira and Maputo (on which Rhodesia had previous relied for the transit of over 80 percent of its exports and imports). In addition the likelihood now arose and was also realized later that Mozambique's new government would allow the Zimbabwean nationalists to set up bases on its territory and help infiltrate guerrilla units across Rhodesia's eastern border.

On a broader level the collapse of Portugal's African empire undermined a central tenet of the Pretoria government's strategy for the whole Southern African region: the reliance it had placed on a *cordon sanitaire* of white-ruled buffer states north of its border. In response, South Africa adjusted its strategy and decided to seek a rapprochement with the new Frelimo rulers in Mozambique.

Relations with South Africa

A spate of important speeches by leading members of the South African government in the last few months of 1974 sketched out the essentials of Pretoria's new policy toward Frelimo. While the Lusaka negotiations between Frelimo and Portugal were still in progress, the South African prime minister, John Vorster, on September 6 in a speech to the South African Parliament said his government had received "assurances" from Portugal that South African interests would not be harmed by the transition to Frelimo rule. "On the matters on which assurances were sought," he said, "positive answers were given." Nine days later Vorster wished Frelimo well. He declared that "a black government in Mozambique holds no fear for us whatever. We are surrounded by black governments as it is, and we ourselves are in the process of creating some more by leading our black homelands to independence."

At the same time, Vorster warned Frelimo that South Africa would hit back at Mozambique if the newly independent country allowed its territory to be used by guerrillas of the South African liberation movements as a "springboard" against the Pretoria regime. But it soon became clear that Vorster's optimism and talk of "assurances" were well-grounded. While Machel promised on September 20, 1975, that Mozambique would become a "revolutionary base against imperialism and colonialism in Africa," Chissano assured Pretoria that the new government was prepared to coexist with its powerful white-ruled neighbor. "We do not pretend to be the saviours of the world," he told a press conference in the capital on September 17. "We will not be saviours or the reformers of South Africa. That belongs to the people of South Africa." A month later, in an interview with the Mozambican weekly *Tempo,* Chissano explained that Mozambique would become a "revolutionary base" in ideas alone and would not interfere in the internal affairs of other countries.

The Pretoria regime has exploited Mozambique's chronic economic dependence on South Africa. Stressing Mozambique's stake in the maintenance of good relations with South Africa, Dr. Nicho Diederichs, then South Africa's finance minister and subsequently its president, made the point in November 1974:

> I need only mention the harbour at Lourenço Marques, the bulk of whose traffic derives from trade between South Africa and other countries, the tourist trade—mainly South African—of Lourenço Marques and other coastal resorts, the job opportunities provided in South African mines and industries for many thousands of Mozambique workers, and, finally, the Cabora Bassa hydroelectric scheme, which would not be remotely viable without the sale of power to the Republic [of South Africa].

A brief examination of the factors noted by Diederichs reveals the powerful leverage that Pretoria knew it could use to pressure Frelimo into cooperation on a political level.

South Africa's right to recruit labor in Mozambique derives from the Mozambique Convention, first signed with Lisbon in 1928. Under the Convention, 60 percent of the Mozambican mine workers' wages are deferred and paid to them on their return to Mozambique. Until independence, payment of deferred Mozambican mine workers' wages was made by the South African Reserve Bank to Portugal's *Banco Nacional Ultramarino* (BNU) in gold bars valued at the official gold price of $42.22 an ounce. The gold bars were traditionally transferred to vaults in Portugal, while the miners received their deferred pay at home in Mozambique escudos.

Before Mozambique won its independence Portugal was able to sell on the free market the bullion it received under the Mozambique Convention. In this way Portugal could have a handsome windfall profit, because the market price of gold soared in the early seventies far above the official rate to reach an all-time high of $195.50 per ounce on the London gold market at the end of 1974. In addition, Portugal's profits were boosted by a steep increase in the number of Mozambicans recruited by the South African mines at this time:

Migration of Mozambican Miners to South Africa

	1971	1972	1973	1974	1975
Departed	79,700	80,940	79,446	90,179	102,725
Returned	88,488	83,366	71,309	76,378	83,456

After independence, Mozambique was able for the first time to reap the advantages of this system for itself. The gold bullion was no longer transferred to Lisbon but was sold on Frelimo's behalf at the free-market price by the South African Reserve Bank. The relatively high market price of gold and the increase in the number of Mozambican migrant workers in South African mines stood to earn Mozambique some $175 million of foreign exchange in 1975, about a third of its entire foreign currency earnings. This situation, above all else, symbolized Maputo's overwhelming vested interest in preserving "normal" relations with South Africa.

During 1976 Frelimo's benefits under the system waned somewhat. First, the market price of gold began to drift downward, falling below $120 an ounce in the second half of the year, thus narrowing Mozambique's profits from its gold sales. Nevertheless, it rose sharply again in 1977 and stood at around $185 an ounce in March 1978. At the same time, however, the number of Mozambicans in South Africa's mines fell substantially. The recruitment rate dropped from 2,000 per week in 1975 to 400 a week in the second quarter of 1976. By August 1976 total Mozambican mine employment in South Africa was down to 75,000. By January 1978 this had fallen farther to only 38,000.

In consequence, Mozambique's earnings from the export of mine labor probably fell to around $100 million a year. But, with its total balance-of-payments deficit in 1977 estimated at $280 million, this still large source of foreign exchange earnings remained crucially important to the Maputo government.

Under new International Monetary Fund rules, the official gold price has been abolished as the norm for gold transactions between central banks (see Grundy chapter). When this happens Mozambique stands to lose the windfall profits it receives from reselling its bullion on the free market. But South African and Mozambican officials have been discussing a new arrangement to come into force when the official gold price ends. In the negotiations the South African government has doubtless again been using whatever concessions it has been offering to Frelimo as a carrot to ensure continuation of the state of peaceful coexistence between the two countries.

Mozambique's other major source of foreign exchange earnings on its current invisibles account is its shipment of South African exports and imports via the port of Maputo. Maputo's port, whose modern development began with the construction of the Transvaal railway in 1886, is one of the largest in Africa. In 1975 it handled 18 percent of South Africa's exports and imports and shipped about 25,000 tons of South African exports per day. Moreover, foreign exchange earnings from transport trade facilities (primarily, though not entirely, from the shipment of South African imports and exports) have averaged about 30 percent of the country's total foreign exchange earnings in recent years.

In the early months of 1976 the freight volume moving from South Africa to Maputo slumped when port productivity fell following an exodus of the port's Portuguese administrators and skilled workers. But the South African regime, as part of its campaign to keep on good terms with Frelimo, reaffirmed its long-term plans to route a large part of South African trade through Maputo (despite the construction in South Africa itself of a major new port at Richard's Bay), and by 1977 South African freight volume exported via Maputo had leveled out at around 17,000 tons a day. The state-owned South African Railways has put pressure on South African exporters to ship cargo through Maputo, has sent skilled technicians there to work in the port, and has invested some $70 million in modernizing the rail line from Witbank in the Transvaal to the Mozambique border, raising its capacity from 28,000 tons to 40,000 tons a day.

Another consideration for Mozambique's new rulers is South Africa's emergence as the country's main and most convenient source of imports. South Africa displaced Portugal as Mozambique's leading supplier for the first time in 1973. That year 20.3 percent of Mozambique's imports came from South Africa. Imports from South Africa totaled 2.3 billion escudos (compared to 2.2 billion escudos of imports from Portugal), almost double Mozambique's imports from South Africa in 1972 (1.3 billion escudos). South African exports to Mozambique include machinery, spare parts, iron and steel, fertilizer, and wheat. Like other black-ruled countries in southern and central Africa (Lesotho, Swaziland, Botswana, Zambia, Zaïre, and Malawi), Mozambique finds South Africa to be the closest and cheapest marketplace for the purchase of a wide range of manufactured goods.

The third main factor impelling Frelimo's leaders to maintain friendly relations with the Pretoria regime is the giant Cabora Bassa hydroelectric scheme, built in Mozambique's Tete province by a Portuguese-led consortium, ZAMBCO, to provide electricity to South Africa under the terms of a 1969 contract with the Electricity Supply Commission of South Africa (ESCOM). Vorster, telling South African members of Parliament on August 30, 1974, that Mozambique could not survive economically without cooperating with South Africa, noted that Cabora Bassa (the fourth largest hydroelectric scheme in the world) would become a "white elephant" if the electricity was not sold to South Africa (see Grundy chapter).

Work on the Cabora Bassa dam, sited on the Zambezi River near Songo, began in 1969 and was completed at the end of 1974. The first hydroelectric generators had been installed and tested by the beginning of 1975. Under the 1969 contract, ESCOM was pledged to buy electricity at 0.3 South African cents a kilowatt for twenty years. There is no alternative market to South Africa that could make the project viable, since Mozambique's own power needs are very small. So, on March 15, 1976, Mozambique and Portugal signed an agreement to set up a new consortium, the *Companhia Hidroeléctrica de Cabora Bassa* (HCB), which would sell electricity to South Africa. Led by the Portuguese government, HCB includes all those that have invested in the project, but Mozambique is not expected to take a controlling share until the huge debt incurred in Cabora Bassa's construction has been whittled away over the next fifteen to twenty years through the sale of electricity to South Africa.

Power was scheduled to start flowing along the twin 850-mile power lines to South Africa's Apollo station (and then into the South African grid) in September 1975, but although ESCOM was supplying electricity to Maputo the flow of power from Cabora Bassa was suddenly postponed early in the month. The reason was not political, but was the simple fact that at 0.3 cents a unit the electricity would have been so cheap that sales would have scarcely been sufficient to cover interest payments on HCB's debts, let alone repay the principal. So regular transmissions were held up while HCB pushed for a renegotiation of the 1969 contract. In March 1977 HCB finally started sending power to ESCOM after Pretoria had offered to raise the 1969 tariff to 0.5 South African cents a kilowatt.

Dependent, therefore, to such a degree on South Africa, the Frelimo government in Mozambique has charted a pragmatic, collaborative course toward the South African regime. As Vorster put it in Parliament on November 5, 1974:

> We have asked that certain agreements between Mozambique and our country be honoured because it was in South Africa's interest that the ports of Lourenço Marques and Beira remain open and the railways carry traffic. It is also in South Africa's interest that the Mozambique labour agreement be honoured and the Cabora Bassa power scheme be successfully completed. I am glad to be able to tell you that in spite of certain difficulties these agreements will be reasonably honoured.

Evidence of Mozambique's political and diplomatic stance toward Pretoria has been plentiful. In February 1975, for example, Oliver Tambo, the leader of the African National Congress of South Africa, said that there was "a gap between what Frelimo will do for us and what we would like them to do." Shortly before independence the South African consulate-general in Maputo was officially closed, but it soon reopened under the guise of a trade mission. South African technicians continued to work at Cabora Bassa, and SAR officials continued to work in their offices at Maputo port. In April 1976 one top Frelimo leader, Manuel Bandeira (the Mozambican minister of agriculture), entered a South African hospital for medical treatment, and on two occasions, in September 1976 and August 1977, South Africa sent specialized rescue teams to Mozambique after major mine disasters in the Moatize coal fields.

There were occasional incidents on the South African–Mozambican border in 1976, but they all involved Frelimo attempts to prevent Portuguese expatriates crossing illegally into South Africa. On each occasion both South Africa and Frelimo authorities have been eager to reaffirm their desire for friendly relations. Thus, in March 1976, after seventeen Frelimo soldiers had been detained at Nelspruit after being caught chasing a group of Portuguese across the border, the South African minister of police, J. T. Kruger, said that "I want to give assurance that I know what I am talking about. . . . There is no reason to think Frelimo will not respect our border once the fence has been repaired." On April 8 Kruger announced that the seventeen Mozambican soldiers had been released after Mozambique had given assurances that the border would not be violated again.

Mozambique's Impact on Rhodesia

By contrast, relations with the white Rhodesian regime had been far from pacific. Maputo and Salisbury had been virtually at war since 1976, with Rhodesian troops and planes repeatedly striking deep into Mozambican territory to attack economic targets as well as Zimbabwean guerrilla bases and refugee camps.

"Between March 1976 and March this year," Machel said on June 18, 1977, "143 acts of aggression against the People's Republic of Mozambique took place: 54 in Gaza, 33 in Manica and 56 in Tete province. Between May 1976 and mid-June this year, 1,432 civilians were murdered, including 875 Zimbabwean refugees at Nyazonia, and 527 were wounded. Today, at Massangena, Mapai, Navonde and Chioco, only ashes remain of what were once houses, schools, hospitals, people's shops, public services and factories. This destruction has cost more than 400 million escudos. Ian Smith's regime is in a state of open war against Mozambique."

In 1976–77, there were three especially serious Rhodesian cross-border invasions. The first was the attack on the Nyazonia refugee camp on August 8, 1976. The United Nations High Commissioner for Refugees put the death toll at over 600. By July 1977, according to the U.N., there were over 32,000 Zimbabwean refugees in Mozambique. Salisbury's second serious assault into Mozambique came on May 29, 1977, when Rhodesian troops moved fifty miles into the country to seize the city of Mapai, which they held until June 2. The bloodiest assault followed in November 1977, when, according to the Rhodesian government, its forces killed 1,200 blacks in raids on what it claimed were guerrilla bases.

Mozambique had sustained serious economic losses because of the continuing conflict. Railway lines, roads, bridges, telecommunication facilities, and other economic targets had been destroyed by Rhodesian planes and troops. The thousands of refugees in Mozambican camps had to be fed and assisted. And revenue had been lost since the closure of the Mozambican-Rhodesian border in March 1976. For all these reasons Frelimo had been anxiously awaiting a settlement of the Zimbabwean crisis.

This was the main reason why the Maputo regime, as well as the other front-line states, supported the détente diplomacy over Rhodesia's future in 1975. Mozambique supported the Dar es Salaam Declaration, adopted by the OAU Liberation Committee in April 1975 (and endorsed by the OAU's 12th Ordinary Summit in Uganda in July 1975), which in essence gave OAU approval to the bid launched by President Kenneth Kaunda at the end of 1974 in Lusaka to arrange, with South African assistance, a negotiated settlement between the Zimbabwean nationalists and the Salisbury regime. During this period, which coincided with the term of office of Mozambique's transitional government and the first few months of full independence, Frelimo did not allow its territory to be used by the Zimbabwean guerrillas, who had previously been entering northeast Zimbabwe from Frelimo's liberated zone in Tete.

But the Rhodesian regime's dogged refusal to make even minimal concessions to the Zimbabwean nationalists (symbolized by the fiasco of the August 1975 summit meeting between Ian Smith, Kaunda, Vorster, and the main Zimbabwean leaders at Victoria Falls on the Rhodesian-Zambian border) forced the Mozambican government, like the other front-line states, to endorse a new wave of guerrilla attacks against the Smith regime. Frelimo concluded from the failure of the détente initiative that only an intensification of military and economic pressures would force the settler regime to concede a transfer of power to the Zimbabwean nationalist leaders.

Mozambique coordinated its policy very closely with the other front-line states. It was at a summit meeting in Quelimane, in northern Mozambique, in February 1976 that Presidents Machel, Nyerere, Kaunda, and Seretse Khama finally gave the green light for a new guerrilla offensive. By this point there were some 10,000 Zimbabweans receiving—or waiting to receive—a rather rudimentary guerrilla training in camps in Mozambique; and in the early months of 1976 fighting spread throughout eastern Zimbabwe, far from the long-standing northeastern zone, suggesting that Mozambique was allowing guerrillas to cross into the country along the entire length of its border.

At the Quelimane meeting, the four front-line presidents also agreed that the Mozambican government should apply United Nations sanctions against

Rhodesia and close the Mozambique-Rhodesia border. Mozambique's first serious threat to apply sanctions had been given the previous October by Chissano in an address to the United Nations General Assembly. There, Chissano had appealed "to all members of the United Nations to apply a complete and total boycott against Rhodesia" and said that "Frelimo and the People's Republic of Mozambique are ready to assume all responsibility in conformity with their international duty."

The border closure came on March 3, 1976. Its immediate effect was to bar Rhodesian access to the ports of Beira and Maputo, the ports that had traditionally handled over 80 percent of Rhodesia's foreign trade, and to throw the Smith regime into precarious reliance on its two remaining rail links with the outside world, the railway through Botswana to Mafeking in South Africa and the railway from Rutenga to the South African border at Beitbridge. In addition, the expropriation of Rhodesian assets in Mozambique lost Rhodesia one-sixth of its rolling stock (2,300 railway wagons worth $46 million). In short, Smith became totally dependent on the good graces of the South African government for Rhodesia's economic survival. Moreover, along with the escalation of the guerrilla war, both the United States and South Africa redoubled their pressures on the Smith regime to agree to a negotiated settlement with the nationalists.

Though Mozambique took these economic and military initiatives against the Smith regime at the beginning of 1976, it too had not abandoned hopes of securing a negotiated settlement—as it later showed by its support for the British-sponsored Geneva Conference in October–December 1976 and its partial backing for the Anglo-American proposals unveiled by British foreign secretary David Owen and U.S. ambassador to the U.N. Andrew Young on September 1, 1977. In fact, Frelimo was keen to see an orderly transfer of power to a black government in Zimbabwe—very much on the model of its own transition to power after the September 1974 accords with Portugal. The relaunching of the guerrilla offensive in early 1976 was designed simply to force the Smith regime into serious negotiations on the transfer of power to a black government.

At the same time, Mozambique, like the other front-line states, had sought to keep the "armed struggle" under tight rein through its control over the guerrilla camps and the supply of arms and funds to the Zimbabwean nationalists. In line with a decision of the OAU summit conference in Mauritius in July 1976, all OAU funds for the Zimbabwean liberation struggle had been channeled through the OAU Liberation Committee and Mozambique's Bank for Solidarity. In addition, Frelimo and Tanzanian soldiers had effectively been running the guerrilla camps and had been responsible for the supply of arms and the training.

Meanwhile, the Maputo government, like the other front-line states, had intervened directly in the Zimbabwean nationalists' intense factional infighting to select out leaders for official approval and to deny organizing rights, funds, and guerrilla bases to their rivals. Thus, during the détente period Robert Mugabe, then secretary-general of the Zimbabwe African National Union (ZANU), was placed under house arrest for much of 1975 because he had publicly criticized détente.

After the split of the African National Council (ANC) in September 1975 into "external" and "internal" wings, the first led by Bishop Abel Muzorewa and the Reverend Ndabaningi Sithole, the second by Joshua Nkomo, Mozambique refused to allow the leaders of the "external" ANC's Zimbabwe Liberation Council (ZLC) to launch a new guerrilla campaign from its territory and even barred them from visiting Zimbabwean camps. In May 1976 Bishop Muzorewa felt impelled to write a letter of protest to Nyerere, the chairman of the group of front-line states, claiming that his supporters had been arrested and some killed in Mozambique.

Faced by the fiasco of the détente exercise and the split in the ANC, the Frelimo regime gave its support at the end of 1975 to a small ZANU faction led by Rex Nhongo, Elias Hondo, and Dzinashe Machingura, which, along with Nkomo's Zimbabwe African Peoples Union (ZAPU), formed an eighteen-member Joint Military Command (JMC) to organize a "Zimbabwe People's Army" (ZIPA). A year later, in coordination with the other front-line states, Maputo gave exclusive support to the Patriotic Front, a bloc formed by Nkomo and Mugabe in September 1976 as ZIPA's political leadership. The disfavored nationalists, notably Muzorewa and Sithole, were now completely ostracized by the Mozambican and other front-line governments; and, at the July 1977 OAU summit in Libreville, Gabon, the Mozambican and Zambian delegations led a successful diplomatic battle for exclusive OAU backing for the Patriotic Front.

At the same time, Frelimo showed little hesitation about jettisoning heretofore supported Zimbabwean factions that stepped out of line with Mozambican policies. Thus, in January 1977 Mozambican police arrested eighty-five ZANU members, including seven of the nine ZANU members of the Mozambican-backed JMC, among them Elias Hondo and Dzinashe Machingura. Their crime had been to oppose the Geneva Conference—to which, under pressure from Mugabe and the Mozambican government, they had arrived with great reluctance six weeks after it had started. Scores of other ZANU members were since detained and sent to "reeducation camps."

This type of repressive interference in the Zimbabwean nationalist movement tended to exacerbate the factional feuding that had always been one of that movement's most debilitating characteristics; in addition it gave Smith's regime more room for maneuvers by allowing it to employ "divide-and-rule" tactics to exploit the difficulties faced by ostracized nationalist leaders. The crowning example was Smith's success in wooing Sithole and Muzorewa into signing an "internal settlement" in Salisbury on March 3, 1978, which (considering the major concessions to white power and privileges it contains) they would almost certainly have rejected had they not been disowned—to their factional rivals' benefit—by the front-line states, and above all by the Mozambican government.

An Economy in Crisis

The conflict with the white minority regime in Salisbury, especially the loss of revenues from Rhodesia following Maputo's imposition of sanctions, added to the grave economic difficulties faced by Frelimo since it had come to power.

Portuguese colonialism left Mozambique's economy undeveloped and distorted. Very little industrialization took place under Portuguese rule, and five agricultural products (sugar, cashew nuts, tea, sisal, and cotton) traditionally accounted for more than 60 percent of exports. Even the country's rich mineral resources were not tapped, except for the coal at Moatize in Tete. With deposits there estimated at 400 million tons, even the country's coal output, which has averaged around 600,000 tons a year, was minor by comparison to what it could be. Year after year Mozambique ran a massive trade deficit, the value of its exports usually covering about half the country's import bill. The deficit was usually balanced by a surplus on invisibles. These funds came from tourist revenues, charges on the shipment of South African and Rhodesian goods through Lourenço Marques and Beira, and the export of labor to the farms and mines of South Africa and Rhodesia. In brief, Mozambique was "developed" as a source of cheap raw materials for Portugal, a protected market for Portuguese goods, and a service sector of the South African and Rhodesian economies.

Independence brought some immediate advantages to Mozambique. Freed for the first time from the economic restrictions imposed by Portuguese colonialism, Mozambique could sell the full range of its export crops at world-market prices instead of the artificially low prices previously fixed by Portugal. Thus, whereas in 1973 Mozambique had been forced to sell its sugar to Portugal at only £52 ($120) per ton, it sold its sugar in 1975 in a world market where prices fluctuated from £128 ($307) and £480 ($1150) per ton. Second, as we have seen, Mozambique was able to boost its foreign-exchange earnings substantially by its new-found opportunity to sell in the open market the gold received from South Africa at the official rate in part-payment for its migrant workers under the Mozambique Convention. The large surplus previously reaped by Portugal (due to the substantial rise in the free-market price of gold in the 1970s above the official gold price) now went to Mozambique for the first time.

On the debit side, however, Mozambique—like other underdeveloped countries—was hit hard at the time of its accession to independence by world inflation; the quadrupling of oil prices; and, with the onset of the world recession in 1974, a decline in commodity prices which hit export earnings.

Above all, because very few Africans were trained for skilled jobs in the colonial era, Mozambique was hit by the exodus of almost all the country's technicians, civil servants, skilled workers, experts, administrators, and farmers, a flight accompanied in many cases by deliberate acts of economic sabotage. At one abandoned firm, Monteiro and Company, which employs seven thousand workers and is now run by a government-appointed administrative committee, the company's Portuguese managers stopped paying wages before their departure, embezzled funds needed for regular operating expenses, smuggled out currency, failed to renew vital contracts, and plundered the firm's equipment. Once back in Portugal, they received 31 million escudos in Portuguese bank accounts between January 1975 and March 1976. Industrial production has continued to run well below capacity across the country because of not only the acute shortage of skilled technicians and managers but also the lack of spare parts and raw materials caused by strict import controls designed to conserve foreign exchange.

Agricultural production has also fallen by 50 to 80 percent in some areas since 1974 because of the departure of Portuguese farmers and plantation managers. Some Portuguese farmers succeeded in taking valuable agricultural equipment with them, driving their tractors across the border into Rhodesia or South Africa. On their own initiative the farm laborers struggled to keep these abandoned estates in operation.

As industrial and agricultural production slumped, government revenue also fell dramatically, forcing Frelimo to cut back on state spending. Even in monetary terms, the government budget expenditure slated for 1978 (12.6 billion escudos) was less than the 12.8 billion escudos spent in 1975. Considering the right rate of inflation, the fall in *real* terms in government spending was substantial. Even so, the government was projecting a 2.6 billion escudo budget deficit in 1978.

To reorganize the agricultural sector and revive production the government has nationalized the plantations and farms that were abandoned by departing settlers (just as it nationalized abandoned factories in the cities) and has encouraged peasants to set up cooperatives and *aldeias comunais* (communal villages) where economies of scale will accelerate improvements in both production and social facilities. But natural disasters have added new problems. Serious floods have ravaged agriculture every year since independence. In 1977 they washed away $10 million worth of crops.

The fall in agricultural production has caused serious food shortages in the cities—even though the government has been importing up to $75 million worth of food a year.

Speaking on June 25, 1977, the second anniversary of independence, Machel was quite frank about the extent of these shortages. "At the beginning of this year, we began to notice the scarcity of some essential items for consumption," he said. "There was a shortage of rice, sugar, meat. These scarcities led to the shortage of flour, pasta, condensed milk, preserves, chicken and fish. Long queues, often started the night before, became a common sight in our cities."

The fall in production was not the only cause of these shortages. The breakdown of the transport and distribution systems, which had been dominated by whites and Asians, also helped stimulate the government to set up a National Supplies Commission in 1977 to reorganize these sectors.

While the regime was forced to increase its food imports, export earnings fell sharply with the fall in output of the main cash crops. Production of cashew nuts, of which Mozambique has traditionally been the world's leader, fell from 236,000 tons in 1973 to only 95,000 tons in 1976, though the government hoped to bring production back to 180,000 tons in the picking season that began in October 1977. Up to 700,000 families pick cashew nuts, but exports have fallen because the marketing and collection system, which was traditionally centered in small Portuguese and Indian neighborhood stores, collapsed in the wake of the settler exodus.

Almost all the country's tea estates, which cover some 15,750 hectares in Zambézia province, were abandoned by their owners. Tea production fell from 19,000 tons in 1973–74 to 13,000 tons in 1975–76, and exports fell from 315 million escudos in 1974 to 226 million escudos in 1975. Since then an administrative commission has been appointed by the government, bringing 12,670 hectares of tea plantations and 17 of the 21 tea factories under direct state control. In 1976–77, tea production rose again for the first time, to more than 17,000 tons.

Sugar production fell from an average of 311,338 tons a year in 1972–74 to an estimated 253,600 tons in the 1975–76 harvest, though output was expected to be greatly restored in 1977–78, with an estimated 290,000 tons of cane in the ground. But raw sugar prices have been very low on the world market over the past two years, having fallen from almost £500 a ton on the London sugar market just before Mozambique's independence to only about £100 a ton in March 1978.

Finally, sisal production fell steadily after the settler exodus—from 21,000 tons in 1973 to 19,000 tons in 1974 and 15,000 tons in 1975—and cotton production declined by up to 40 percent from the 1974 output of 180,000 tons.

According to the U.N. Food and Agricultural Organization, the total value of agricultural exports fell by 44 percent between 1974 and 1976. Since Mozambique's five main cash crops have traditionally accounted for around 60 percent of total export earnings, this decline in agricultural exports has had a major impact on the country's overall trading position. Total exports fell from 7.6 billion escudos in 1974 to 5 billion escudos in 1975 and 4.5 billion escudos in 1976. So, though imports were kept in check (despite the rise in food imports) by a strict licensing system, the trade deficit has widened sharply.

As noted above, Mozambique's trade deficits have traditionally been offset by a surplus on invisibles. In 1974, for example, the current invisible surplus of 3.9 billion escudos almost exactly offset the trade deficit of 4.2 billion escudos. But since independence, not only has the trade deficit widened substantially, but earnings on the invisibles account have been trimmed because of the Rhodesian border closure, the end of the tourist trade, the sharp drop in the number of Mozambican miners in South Africa, and the slight fall in the volume of South African freight exports via Maputo. The total current account deficit is therefore believed to have risen from $7 million in 1973 to $30 million in 1975, $150 million in 1976, and $280 million in 1977.

Besides the fall in the number of Mozambican miners in South Africa (from 127,000 in November 1975 to 38,000 in January 1978), the single most important reason for reduced invisibles earnings was the closing of the Rhodesian border. Traditionally, Mozambique's railways and ports handled the bulk of Rhodesia's exports and imports, as well as shipments from several other countries that had to be carried via Rhodesia's railway system. The losses caused by the border closure were detailed by a U.N. mission that visited the country in 1976. According to the mission's report, which was published by the U.N. Economic and Social Council in April 1976, Mozambique's ports and railways normally expected to handle annually some 4 million tons of transit traffic passing through Rhodesia. Since 1972, however, the level had fallen to about 2.3 million tons in 1975, partly because Zambia closed its border with Rhodesia in 1973, thereby halting Zambian copper shipments via Rhodesia to Beira; and, after Portugal's decision to withdraw from Mozambique, because Rhodesia started diverting some of its traffic to South African routes in anticipation on an eventual border closure by Frelimo.

The United Nations mission estimated the reduction in foreign-exchange earnings by the railways and ports as a result of the application of sanctions at between $57 and $74 million per year. In addition, $5 to $10 million per year was lost by related services (clearing, bonding, forwarding, insurance). Nearly $1 million was lost in airport taxes and landing fees for Rhodesian aircraft; and annual tourism earnings of $4.5 to $5.5 million were lost. The United Nations mission also estimated that Mozambique lost $22 to $25 million in annual remittances from Mozambican migrant workers in Rhodesia (believed to number roughly 80,000). The total annual loss of foreign exchange earnings on Mozambique's current invisibles account was between

$89.5 and $115.5 million. In addition, the loss of export markets in Rhodesia, the U.N. mission calculated, would cost Mozambique about $16 million per year over the first eighteen months to two years of sanctions.

The mission further estimated that development projects made necessary by the border closure (the provision of alternatives to roads and facilities cut off by the closure of the frontier) would cost $31 million and the building-up of stocks (particularly of food), previously lower because of access to Rhodesian stocks, would cost $6 million. The mission calculated that 10,000 Mozambicans would lose their jobs, 5,000 in ports and railways and 1,000 in related transit agencies and organizations. All told, therefore, the U.N. put the full cost of the border closure at $139 to $165 million in the first year of sanctions, $108 to $134 million in the second, and $106 to $132 million per year thereafter.

Under Resolution 386 (1976), the U.N. Security Council voted to launch an international aid program to compensate Mozambique for those losses. But a year later, on June 28, 1977, in a speech to the Security Council, Marcelino dos Santos said that "the aid provided has been significantly less than what is necessary." By July 1977 only $102 million of aid had been pledged—and most of this was in the form of loans that will add to Mozambique's long-term external debt, raising the prospect of a heavy burden of future debt-service payments.

4.

South Africa: Growing Black-White Confrontation

Gwendolen M. Carter

When thousands of peacefully demonstrating African high-school students, exploded into violence in Soweto on June 16, 1976, in response to police brutality, they set off a chain reaction of black protests that have erupted intermittently ever since. From its side, the government has increased repression. In a massive crackdown on October 19, 1977, it banned virtually all black consciousness and related organizations, nineteen in all, including SASO (the black student organization), BPC (its adult counterpart), and UBJ (the Union of Black Journalists), imprisoned most of their leaders, and held them without trial. Moreover, on the same day it banned *The World* and *Weekend World*, the country's leading black newspaper, and *Pro Veritate*, the organ of the Christian Institute. It also placed under ban Beyers Naude, the Institute's internationally respected leader, and Donald Woods, editor of the East London *Daily Dispatch*. Despite the world-wide outcry following the brutal death while in police custody of the best known of the young African leaders, Steve Biko, arbitrary imprisonment continued, as did the death toll of those in prison. But so do the overt signs of black rage against their lack of effective power and the morass of discriminatory provisions in which they are embedded.

The heightening of black-white tensions within South Africa is paralleled by what is occurring around its frontiers. The once-secure bulwark of white-controlled territories that insulated the Republic from independent African states has either disappeared or is in the process of doing so. The outcome of the struggle for Zimbabwe, in which Mozambique was so deeply involved, and now for Namibia, with its significance both for Angola and for Botswana, is also vital for South Africa itself. The chief of its security police, Brigadier C. F. Zeitsman, declares that his men are building a "steel ring" around the country to prevent infiltration and to block the flight of exiles. He confirms gun battles with African National Congress guerrillas in rural areas of the northeast but admits that "the main battle is against urban terrorism."[1] The twofold pressures from outside and inside are creating a new situation for white-controlled South Africa and for the Western countries, including the United States, that have massive economic interests in that area.

South Africa's rich mineral resources, including three-quarters of the world's gold, and its commercial and industrial potential have long attracted foreign capital, notably from Great Britain and the United States. In the 1960s these two countries, that until then had enjoyed a virtual monopoly of South African imports and exports, were joined by West German, French, and Japanese interests in stimulating what has been called an "economic miracle"[2] by pouring in investments, loans, and the advanced technology that have created South Africa's present mature industrial economy. Among these five, France played a particular role in becoming the Republic's chief arms supplier during its ever-increasing arms buildup.

The French response to public needs was not as unique, however, as most American interests suggest. The South African government is buttressed by an all-pervasive state sector controlling transport and local energy sources. It also elicits and directs capital inflow through its Industrial Development Corporation to fill gaps in the country's primary and secondary industrial structure. This close relation between state and private interests meant that the presence in South Africa by 1976 of more than 350 major American companies with a $1.67 billion investment formed a significant reinforcement of that government's power. Even more so does the $2.2 billion lent by American banks during the past few years, much of it directly to the government or its parastatals. Such investments and loans also indirectly bolster the Afrikaner business community that forms the prosperous core of white Afrikaner nationalism. It is this white nationalism that has long been counterposed against the claims of African and now black nationalists for a major share of the country's political and economic power.

Unique to the South African situation are the presence of both white and black nationalism. The latter stems from the earliest self-generated African nationalism on the continent of Africa and is the only one, moreover, from which rights have systematically been taken away. Elsewhere, political rights were steadily conceded to Africans by the British and French colonial powers in the relatively short period before independence. The paradox thus exists that in the most developed and prosperous country in Africa, not one of the black majority, who are some 83 percent of the population of South Africa, has a voice in selecting the members of the legislature that determines the supreme law of the land.

The First Clashes Between White and Black

The long history of black-white relations in Southern Africa dates back to 1652, when the Dutch East India Company established a way station to the East at the tip of the African continent. The Dutch settlers, who landed near what is now Cape Town, were a purposeful and independent group whose elitist Calvinism filled them with a sense of mission to dominate the heathen and to build their own characteristic society in the new land.

Spreading out beyond the established confines of the settlement, they soon clashed with indigenous peoples for control of the land. The San, or Bushmen, were driven from their hunting grounds and in the long run virtually exterminated; the cattle-raising Khoikhoi, or Hottentots, fought the white encroachments but ultimately became little more than hangers-on and servants. In the meantime, slaves had been brought from the East Indies and Africa itself despite an imaginative proposal that the settlement should depend on white labor. Particularly in the early days, when there were few white women in the settlement, miscegenation was common. From the intermingling of slave, Bushman, Hottentot, and white blood come the varied peoples known as Coloured, an increasingly significant population group in South Africa. From the experience of slave-owning and of conquest came the expectation of domination over peoples of color that still marks much of Afrikanerdom, and indeed most of the white population of South Africa.

More effective adversaries than those in the Western Cape met the whites who spread east along the coast in their search of new land. Well-organized Nguni tribes that had been seeping south and west for centuries blocked the white advance along the line of the Great Fish River, which today forms the western borders of the Transkei and Ciskei. The first of a long series of frontier wars erupted in 1791. Ultimately, however, the African tribes were also crushed and scattered, their members turned into farm labor or squatters or driven into the limited areas once labeled "reserves" and now "homelands." Later, the same process of conquest by arms took place in Natal. But the spirit of African resistance was not quenched.

Dutch (Afrikaners) Versus British

The Dutch settlers also experienced the bitterness of conquest and the search for new homes. In 1795, when the Dutch were allies of France in the Napoleonic Wars, the English occupied the Cape; in 1815 they annexed it. The influence of British missionaries and the liberalizing trends in England itself led to a new status for Hottentots and Africans at the Cape: in 1834 slavery was abolished. British mores and commercialism reshaped the character of local society. The cumulative effect of what they viewed as interference with their chosen way of life resulted in a long slow movement of many Dutch (later called Boers, or farmers, and ultimately Afrikaners) away from the Western Cape in what became known as the Great Trek.

Some trekkers crossed the mountains with their ox-wagons and cattle and spread into the fertile lands of Natal. There they clashed with Zulus and suffered a massacre that they avenged at Blood River in 1838, a victory still commemorated by modern Afrikanerdom. But their efforts to create a separate state were foiled by British annexation of Natal in 1845. This largely English-speaking colony was subsequently to complicate the racial composition of South Africa by bringing indentured Hindu Indians to Natal to work in the sugar plantations. Though intended to return, most stayed and were joined by Moslem merchants and others over the years. Their descendants form the fifth strand of the country's complex racial structure.

Though frustrated in Natal, the Boer trekkers were successful to the north in establishing two republics, the Orange Free State, and the South African Republic (Transvaal). In both republics all-white male electorates affirmed the doctrine of "no equality of black and white in church or state."

The Boer republics might have been left alone had it not been for the discovery of great sources of wealth under their soil. Diamonds found at Kimberley in 1867 led to gerrymandering the border in 1871 to include that area within the English-controlled Cape. As British imperial interests in Southern Africa ebbed and expanded, the Transvaal was annexed in 1877 but returned to Boer control after a British army was defeated at Majuba Hill in 1881. But the discovery of gold in 1886 in the Witwatersrand reef in the center of the Transvaal spelled the end of isolation.

The Impact of Modern Capitalism

British and European entrepreneurs and capital flooded into the area to establish the elaborate underground equipment necessary to exploit the gold veins that lay deep in the earth, while thousands of Africans were recruited to provide the necessary hand labor. The nascent capitalism that had been an inevitable feature of Southern Africa since the earliest white settlement was transformed into a major, some would say *the* major, molding influence in what was to become South Africa. It thus became a part of worldwide industrial and commercial capitalism.

Before that time, despite the disruption of tribal organization, there were Africans who continued to produce not only for their own needs but also for sale. Some did well in adopting new crops and techniques. Although their relations with Afrikaners were often marked by roughness, there was little of the calculated racial discrimination that stamped many of their later interactions. As long as the struggle was primarily for land, it was possible to accommodate both black and white on what was fairly easily available.

Now the emphasis turned to labor. The ever-increasing demand for cheap manpower to service the mines and all the associated aspects of the economy led to the imposition of taxes and other measures that steadily squeezed out self-sufficient peasant economies to reduce their competition and to force Africans into the wage system. To the basic tensions between the black majority and the dominant white minority was added an ever-increasing gap between black labor (African and to a lesser degree Coloured and Asian) and white capitalists and workers.

The Afrikaner regime in the Transvaal resisted the impact of mining and finance capitalism by denying *uitlanders* (foreigners) the vote. In 1896 an abortive coup known as the Jameson Raid sought to overthrow the Transvaal's administration and provide the new economic interests with political power. Both Cecil Rhodes, Prime Minister of the Cape, and the British Government were implicated in the raid. The angry recriminations that followed led inexorably to the Anglo-Boer War, 1899–1902.

Despite the mobilizing of troops from all over the British Empire, including the Cape and Natal, the war was long drawn out because of the skill of Boer tactics and fighting. The herding of Afrikaner women and children from their farms into camps in which many of them died of disease added further bitterness to their final defeat.

South African Independence: A White-Controlled State

A generous peace coupled with the promise of self-government and independence under a South African drafted constitution helped to overbridge the hostility caused by the war. Moderate whites from all parts of the country joined in shaping what was to become the Union of South Africa in 1910, an independent Dominion like Canada and Australia within the British Commonwealth of Nations. But the political and economic price of such reconciliation was paid by the Africans.

In the Cape, Africans had possessed the vote since 1853 on the same qualified franchise (economic and educational qualifications) as whites and Coloured; in seven border constituencies in the Eastern Cape they exercised a strong political influence on the election of candidates. Cape liberals sought to expand these franchise provisions to the other provinces but without success. The most they could achieve was to entrench their own voting provisions in the new constitution by requiring a special procedure for their amendment (also extended to the equality of English and Dutch, subsequently Afrikaans). Moreover, the constitution provided that only whites could be elected to Parliament.

Africans had not been silent while whites designed the structure for an independent South Africa. Their nascent political organizations dating from 1882 had been reinforced by African political journalism, which began two years later with a widely read newspaper, *Imvo Zabantsunda* (Native Opinion), edited by an articulate and sophisticated African, John Tengo Jabavu. Opposition by educated Africans to discriminatory measures was paralleled by their claim to share the status and rights of "civilized British subjects." On the eve of South African independence, the National Native Convention protested the exclusion of Africans from Parliament. In 1912, three years later, the South African Native (subsequently African) National Congress was formed under the leadership of four extremely able British- and American-trained African lawyers. Until banned in 1960 following the Sharpeville massacre, the African National Congress remained the chief standard-bearer and articulate voice of African nationalism.

There was much against which to protest. Late nineteenth-century laws stimulated by pressure from mine owners were specifically designed to push Africans off the land to work in white-controlled mines, commerce, and agriculture. So were the Native Labour Regulation Act of 1911, the Natives Land Act of 1913 (which ejected squatters from white farmlands), the manipulation of the pass laws and influx control, and a succession of other governmental efforts to stimulate a flow of cheap labor for white use. There were also other factors forcing Africans and other blacks into the wage economy: growing population pressures, cheap food from abroad as ports and the growing railway network increasingly tied South Africa into the economy of the West, local crop diseases and periodic droughts, price fluctuations abroad, and the late nineteenth-century worldwide trade depression. Both blacks and whites suffered their dislocating impacts.

Afrikaners' Struggle for Power and the African Response

In the aftermath of World War I, Afrikanerdom confronted a new and in effect its greatest crisis. An increasing number of relatively unskilled Afrikaners were forced off their farms by persistent drought. As they flooded into the cities, they found that the English-speaking occupied the top positions in industry, commerce, and mining while Africans and Coloured held the unskilled jobs. In the 1920s Afrikanerdom faced the world's worst poor-white problem with some 60 percent of its people in or near disaster. Only radical measure by government seemed capable of meeting their needs.

Whites were clearly in control in the new Union of South Africa, but which whites? Originally and ever since, the Prime Minister has been an Afrikaner. But Afrikaners at large felt that the English-speaking were entrenched both politically and economically, and too greatly influenced by British imperial interests. In 1912 General Barry Hertzog broke away from the Cabinet dominated by General Louis Botha and General Jan Christiaan Smuts, which was dedicated to uniting the English-speaking and Afrikaners. Hertzog campaigned through his National Party for a separate Afrikaner nationalism capable of working on equal terms with the English-speaking, and ultimately of capitalizing on the Afrikaners' majority position within the white community. World War I saw an abortive rebellion by some Afrikaners against South Africa's participation in the struggle. In 1919 the Broederbond was formed to promote Afrikaner advance; three years later it became a secret society dedicated to the ultimate establishment of a *boere republiek*, that is, one controlled by Afrikaners. The Broederbond has remained one of the most potent influences on Afrikaner politics and education ever since.

In 1922 radical white miners on the Rand struck against an economy proposal by gold-mine owners to allow Africans to assume some semiskilled jobs. In bloody fighting the strike was put down by the government under General Smuts, who had succeeded Botha on the latter's death. Though temporarily defeated, white labor in the end was victorious. In 1924 Smuts was turned out of office by Hertzog at the head of a coalition of his National Party and the largely English-speaking Labour Party. The ultimate result was the enactment of what was known as "the civilized labour policy" that carved out areas of the economy reserved for whites.

As increasing numbers of Afrikaners became urbanized, the National Party, the political organ of Afrikaner nationalism, acquired its second major pillar of electoral support. Traditionally the Afrikaner farmers of the *platteland* (countryside) and the *dorps* (villages) had provided its base. Now they were joined by the growing mass of Afrikaner urban workers whose employment and living centers brought them directly into contact with Africans. White labor's real and imagined fears of African competition joined with the capitalists' objective of a controlled black labor force to stimulate the growing, intricate pattern of restrictions on all blacks, but particularly on the African majority.

Besides protecting white labor against African competition and providing it with an assured economic status, the Hertzog government was determined to eliminate the African vote from affecting electoral results in Cape Province, the one place within South Africa where Africans shared voting rolls with whites. Failing to achieve this result through his own political resources and confronting the crisis of the depression, Hertzog joined with Smuts in 1934 to form a new political party, named the United Party, to institute economic and political changes. Once again the Africans were sacrificed.

Africans were, and are as well aware as whites that the franchise is the key to political power. Rural and urban Africans protested the threat to the Cape African vote. Under a new umbrella organization, the All African Convention, more than four hundred delegates meeting in Bloemfontein in mid-December 1935 drafted a comprehensive charter of African grievances and urged that the African franchise be extended, not reduced. Their pro-

tests were in vain, and, by a constitutional amendment passed by the necessary two-thirds majority, Cape Africans were taken off the common roll.
After 1936 Cape Africans could qualify for a direct vote only on a separate
roll to elect three whites to the House of Assembly to represent their
interests, and indirectly with all other Africans through a cumbersome
procedure for four white senators. In 1959 even this small degree of representation was abolished.

Although the Africans were defeated on the issue of the Cape African
vote, their ferment in the late 1930s and 1940s resulted in a new spirit of
unity that transcended area and ethnicity and brought rural and urban
Africans closer together. Earlier there had been sporadic anti-pass demonstrations and strikes, but the African leadership had depended largely on
the conservative tactics of verbal and written protests and appeals. Now
new forms of pressure like mass action and boycotts were discussed. The
time would come when these means of pressure would be used by Africans,
and still later in conjunction with Asians and/or Coloured.

Afrikanerdom was no less in ferment. Dr. Daniel F. Malan broke from
Hertzog over the latter's decision to unite with Smuts and formed his own
"purified" National Party, which preached a more extreme Afrikaner nationalism. Moreover, the thirties saw a withdrawal of Afrikaners from
community organizations. Afrikaner students seceded from the country-
wide student organization to form a separate one of their own in a move
that was to be reflected at the end of the sixties by the black student
withdrawal into SASO (South African Student Organization) from the
largely English-speaking National Union of South African Students
(NUSAS). Afrikaner Boy Scouts seceded from the world body. In 1938 a
country-wide commemoration of the Great Trek was turned into an exclusively Afrikaner pageant. Out of it sprang the Ossewa Brandwag (ox-wagon
guard), whose militaristic organization competed with Malan's party during World War II for the allegiance of Afrikanerdom. Although decisively
defeated in the election of July 1943 by Smuts' United Party, Malan demonstrated effectively at that time that his party had the major political support
of Afrikanerdom. On May 26, 1948, the Nationalists, with the support of
the small Afrikaner Party, achieved a majority in the House of Assembly and
Dr. D. F. Malan became Prime Minister.

While rival groups were competing within Afrikanerdom for dominance,
new leaders and programs were arising within the African National Congress.
In 1943 the Youth League was officially inaugurated with members like
Anton Lembede, A. P. Mda, Nelson Mandela, Oliver Tambo, and Walter
Sisulu, whose names were to become household words. Nelson Mandela, im-
prisoned since 1961, is still the most widely acclaimed leader of black South
Africans. Also in 1943 the African National Congress issued its most im-
portant document since 1919, *Africans' Claims in South Africa,* which not

only emphasized African opposition to racial discrimination but also appeared to endorse universal franchise without qualifications. The Youth League set itself the task of generating a spirit of self-reliance and militant nationalism among the African masses to achieve these goals.

In its Programme of Action, adopted in December 1949, the African National Congress, spurred by the Youth League, specifically set forth tactics of direct action—boycotts, strikes, and civil disobedience—that could be used in the "struggle for national liberation." In 1946 some fifty thousand African gold mine workers on the Witwatersrand had staged a walkout protest against low wages and discriminatory conditions at the call of the African Mine Workers' Union led by John B. Marks, long a member of both the African National Congress and the Communist Party. In the same year the Natal Indian Congress had begun a passive resistance campaign in Durban against restrictions on Indian land ownership and occupation. In 1952, stimulated by these examples of protest and despite the harsh official response, the African National Congress was to call its own passive resistance campaign against "unjust laws." Most of the laws specified had been passed by the new Afrikaner Nationalist government, moving swiftly to systematize controls on the black population and enforce a more rigid racial separation.

Afrikanerdom Shapes Race Relations

In 1948, when Malan's Afrikaner Nationalists came into office, whites were startled to learn that the number of Africans who had moved perforce off the overcrowded and undeveloped lands in the reserves to white farms and into urban townships was greater than the numbers still remaining within the reserves. Moreover, white dependence on black labor for the country's growing industrialization and secondary industries had led, as the government's Fagan Commission disclosed in that year, to "a settled, permanent Native population" in the urban areas. To Afrikanerdom this was a new crisis.

Malan's National Party had campaigned on a platform of apartheid (racial apartness) without specifying how it was to be achieved. Once in power with its overwhelming Afrikaner support, the National Party has successfully increased its parliamentary majority at almost every election from then to the present. This majority has been used not only to push through progressively restrictive programs of racial segregation in white areas that have affected all black groups—African, Coloured, and Asians—but ultimately, and most significantly, their corollary of separate territorial development for Africans. The keynotes of the latter program were the denial of African rights in white areas, an emphasis on the ethnic diversity among Africans which African nationalism had long sought to overbridge, and the development of the scattered pockets of African reserves into Bantustans, or homelands, to which all Africans, regardless of domicile, experience, or desire, were said to belong.

The Nationalists began quickly to build up the intricate structure of legally enforced apartheid, the impact of which has been progressively extended. Their first real target was the Coloured, whom Hertzog had earlier called "an appendage to the whites" because of their long and close association. The Prohibition of Mixed Marriages Act, 1949, and the 1950 amendment to the Immorality Act, 1927, struck at Coloured-white marital and extramarital relations. The Representation of Voters Bill, introduced in 1951, sought and ultimately, after a long constitutional struggle, succeeded in 1956 in removing the Coloured from the common roll in Cape Province, as the Africans had been removed in 1936. All three measures have remained sources of intense bitterness for the Coloured, and the government's own Theron Commission recommended in mid-1976 that they be modified or rescinded. Nonetheless, despite other current efforts to conciliate the Coloured and considerable white sympathy for sharing the vote with them, the government immediately rejected these proposals.

Two other early and far-reaching pieces of legislation laid the cornerstones of the urban segregation policy: the Population Registration Act and the Group Areas Act, aimed at restricting each population group to defined places in or near urban areas as far as ownership, occupancy, and trading were concerned.

Traditionally, and still, Africans outside the homelands are closely controlled in their movements and living places by influx control, must at all times carry a pass (a document including information on ethnic origin, birthplace, age, employment, etc.) under penalty of summary arrest, and must secure official permission to accept or change jobs. Indians have been prohibited from living in the Orange Free State since 1891 and have long been subject to varying restrictions on property rights, occupancy, and trading in the Transvaal and Natal. The ultimate goal of the Group Areas Act was to extend restrictions in order to establish residential "racial purity" by shifting groups from one place to another. In the process Coloured and Asians have been moved out of long-established communities in Cape Town and Johannesburg to far less desirable sites, Africans have lost their limited urban freehold areas, a few whites have had to move, and all blacks are threatened with impermanence.

Insistent pressure, formalized in 1967 into far-reaching regulations, has forced Africans not born or long domiciled or employed in urban areas to return to the rural areas, notably the Bantustans, and be turned into migratory labor. Migratory workers, following the pattern long established by the mines, are forced to oscillate between rural areas and workplaces, sent to particular jobs by labor officials in the homelands, and forced to return to their rural bases at the end of specified periods of service, commonly a year.

Three other basic laws that were aimed particularly at Africans were the Bantu (the Nationalist term for "African") Authorities' Act of 1951, the Bantu Education Act, and the Native Labour (Settlement of Disputes) Act, the last two passed in 1953. The first of these laws was designed to reestablish the authority of government-appointed chiefs, and it made provision for the lowest tier of what was to become the structure of the ethnic homelands. The second, and at the time most bitterly opposed of the laws, moved African education from provincial to central government control, reduced the role of churches and other voluntary bodies in the educational process, and threatened to make education a handmaiden of apartheid by training Africans only for inferior roles in South African society. Subsequently, African higher education was also brought under central government control, and since then with some exceptions the small number of Africans, Coloured, and Asians who moved on to university training are forced to do so by correspondence or to attend segregated institutions with predominantly Afrikaner staffs and councils.

The legislation affecting African labor that was passed in 1953 did little to change the highly discriminatory conditions from which it suffered. Though far outnumbering all other industrial and commercial workers, Africans were long formally excluded from the definition of "employee" in the Industrial Conciliation Act, and thus from any direct participation in the industrial councils through which employers and registered trade unions worked out their differences. Nor could they participate directly in negotiations over wages. The closest they came to having an officially provided influence on their wages and conditions of work was through the mediation of a white official of the Bantu Labour Board, which rarely affected the outcome of such negotiations. Moreover, although African trade unions (contrary to the common view) were not illegal, have existed in the past, and do so at the present, they had not any assured rights. The government instead endorsed liaison, or works councils on a firm-to-firm basis, thereby giving management the predominant influence. In addition, until the spring of 1973, when there were persistent African walkouts in Natal, the ban on strikes by Africans imposed in 1942 continued to exist. When a modification of the strike ban was instituted in 1973, it was so hedged with restrictions as to be more significant in theory than practice.

African Pressures for Change—And Their Defeat

As the apartheid net tightened, Africans girded themselves for nationwide protest. In January 1952 leaders of the African National Congress demanded both the abolition of "differentiating laws" and direct representation in parliament and provincial and municipal councils as "an inherent right." If their grievances were not remedied, they declared, their intention was to launch a passive resistance campaign. In reply the prime minister's private secretary maintained that a claim of inherent right by Africans was "self-contradictory" since the differences between Africans and whites "were permanent and not man-made." To remove restrictions on "the possible gradual development of a completely mixed community," he declared, "is not a genuine offer of cooperation, but an attempt to embark on the first steps toward supplanting European rule in the course of time" that would lead to "disaster." The words have a contemporary ring.

On April 6, 1952, white South Africa celebrated the tercentenary of Jan Van Riebeeck's arrival at the Cape in 1652. Africans boycotted many of the celebrations and at one counter mass rally, Professor Z. K. Matthews of Fort Hare College, who was president of the Cape ANC, declared that "only the African people themselves will ever rid themselves" of "political subjugation, economic exploitation and social degradation." June 26, 1952, was selected as the date to begin the passive resistance campaign. Despite government bannings and subsequent arrest of some leading black leaders, the Defiance Campaign started on time. Batches of volunteers in one town after another courted arrest by open violations of apartheid regulations such as entering African locations without permits, or sitting on benches marked "for whites only," or using white entrances to post offices. Although the number of volunteers varied from month to month, more than eight thousand had been arrested by December 1952, most of them in the Eastern parts of Cape Province, and the second largest number in the Transvaal. The membership of the ANC swelled to one hundred thousand, the nucleus of a mass movement; defiers became future leaders; and the campaign began to enter the reserves.

But already there had been nationwide arrests of ANC and South African Indian Congress leaders, the latter lending moral and financial support. More serious for the continuation of the campaign were sporadic and unconnected outbreaks of violence in East London and Port Elizabeth in which a few whites and many more Africans were killed. White sentiment flared and as soon as Parliament reassembled in January 1953, the government introduced the Public Safety and Criminal Laws Amendment bills. The former made provision for proclaiming a state of emergency and was used in 1960 after the Sharpeville shootings. The latter instituted heavy penalties, including lashes, for supporting a campaign of passive resistance or soliciting or accepting help for such a campaign. It was a decisive step toward the ever-increasing coercive measures taken in response to open black protests.

Shifting from disobedience to demonstration and from an African to a multiracial popular front, the Congress Alliance (that is, the ANC and its allied Indian, Coloured, and white organizations) held a massive Congress of the People at Kliptown near Johannesburg in June 1955 at which the Freedom Charter was adopted by voice vote of the three thousand persons present.

Prepared through hundreds of small open discussions that formulated popular demands, the Freedom Charter opens with the words:

> We, the people of South Africa, declare for all our country and the world to know:
> that South Africa belongs to all who live in it, black and white, and that no Government can justly claim authority unless it is based on the will of all the people. . . .

It demanded that "every man and every woman" have the right to vote, that the people share the country's wealth under public ownership, that land be redivided among those who worked it, that education be "free, compulsory, universal and equal for all children," that there be houses, security, and comfort for all, and that South Africa be "a fully independent state which respects the rights and sovereignty of all nations." It ended with the words: "These freedoms we will fight for, side by side, throughout our lives, until we have won our liberty."

The government's answer was to arrest one hundred and fifty-six leaders of all groups of the Congress Alliance in December 1956 and put them on trial for high treason. In a case stretching over four years all the accused were progressively discharged or finally held to be not guilty of the government's charge of intending to overthrow it by force. While the trial was continuing, the ANC split between those who upheld the multiracial sentiments of the Freedom Charter and those who identified more with the Pan-Africanism sweeping the continent as country after country was moving to independence under African control. The latter group, under Robert Sobukwe, broke away in 1959 to form the Pan Africanist Congress (PAC). It was the PAC that organized the demonstrations against carrying passes on March 21, 1960. When police fired on an unarmed crowd at Sharpeville in the Transvaal, killing sixty-seven Africans and wounding some one hundred and eighty-six, including women and children, a new watershed was created in South African history.

The government panicked, declared a state of emergency, outlawed the ANC and PAC, arrested and detained some nineteen hundred people, including for the first time members of the predominantly white Liberal Party, which stood for a universal franchise under its leader, the internationally known author Alan Paton, and imprisoned thousands of so-called African "idlers." Urgent appeals from inside South Africa for consultation with Africans were disregarded by the government. International censure on the wanton killings was followed by an outflow of foreign capital. It was with the support of American bank loans that the economic situation began to return to normal, from which it subsequently burgeoned into the "economic miracle" of the 60s that was described earlier.

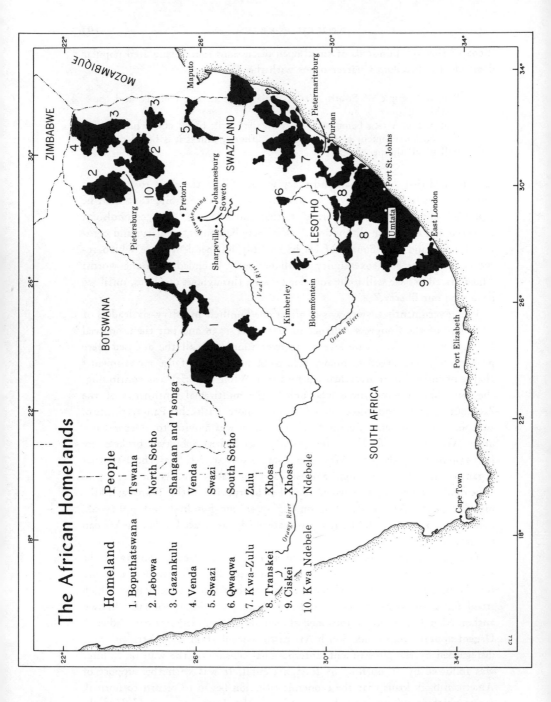

The African Homelands

Homeland	People
1. Boputhatswana	Tswana
2. Lebowa	North Sotho
3. Gazankulu	Shangaan and Tsonga
4. Venda	Venda
5. Swazi	Swazi
6. Qwaqwa	South Sotho
7. Kwa-Zulu	Zulu
8. Transkei	Xhosa
9. Ciskei	Xhosa
10. Kwa Ndebele	Ndebele

ZIMBABWE

MOZAMBIQUE

BOTSWANA

SOUTH AFRICA

SWAZILAND

LESOTHO

Maputo

Pietersburg

Pretoria

Witwatersrand
Johannesburg
Soweto
Sharpeville
Vaal River

Kimberley

Bloemfontein

Orange River

Orange River

Cape Town

Port Elizabeth

East London

Umtata

Port St. Johns

Durban

Pietermaritzburg

Despite the banning of their organizations, Africans made one last effort to construct a wide public front for public protest. Though its preparations were handicapped by internal dissensions, the All-In Conference, with more than a thousand Africans in attendance, met in Pietermaritzburg in Natal in March 1961. But raids and arrests frustrated its call for a three-day work boycott. It was the last effort by African nationalist leaders to organize a mass public demonstration. With all channels of peaceful protest barred to them, Africans turned to violence. Even then, sporadic targets for sabotage by the ANC's Umkhonto We Sizwe (Spear of the Nation) meticulously avoided taking human life.

The few terrorist acts in 1962 of the PAC-inspired Poqo spurred the government's counteractions, which systematically destroyed virtually all effective African leadership and organization in the country, except the ANC's underground headquarters at Rivonia, a suburb of Johannesburg. With its capture in June 1963, leaders still at liberty in the country and valuable files fell into police hands. Nelson Mandela (already in prison but tried again), Walter Sisulu, and other black and also white associates were sentenced in the 1964 Rivonia trial, the former leaders to life imprisonment on Robben Island off Cape Town. Sobukwe was already on Robben Island and, although subsequently released, remained under restrictions until his death in March 1978. The politically organized internal African struggle for rights was crushed. The ANC exile leadership under Oliver Tambo and Duma Nokwe and that of the PAC under Potlako Leballo and others sought what external support they could, but their contacts with persons within the country were tenuous, and their possibilities of organizing infiltration were frustrated by the distance between independent African-controlled countries and South Africa. Only after the independence of Mozambique, in June 1975, did a major African-controlled independent state share a boundary with South Africa.

The Bantustan (Homeland) Program: The Afrikaner Answer to the Racial Situation in South Africa

What had happened from 1960 to 1962 confirmed the government in its determination to push ahead with what it now termed "its answer to the racial problem in South Africa": territorial separate development. The subject of many Afrikaner *volks* conferences in the thirties, forties, and fifties, the Afrikaners' own history seemed to many of them to support the belief that a true nation evolves from ethnic exclusiveness. Neither Prime Minister Malan nor his successor, Prime Minister J. C. Strijdom, believed, however, that a far-reaching program of territorial separation of Africans could be implemented in practice when Africans already formed so substantial a proportion of the urban working force. The next prime minister, H. J. Verwoerd, and his secretary of native administration and development, Dr. W. M. Eiselen, were convinced, on the contrary, that such a program was feasible. They pointed to the High Commission territories, Swaziland, Basutoland (subsequently Lesotho), and Bechuanaland (subsequently Botswana), as prototypes of Bantu homelands. Even the possibility of ultimate independence for the ethnic units they envisaged did not disturb them since, as was said of Basutoland, which was embedded within South African territory: "It can become politically independent [as indeed it did in 1966] but it will always be economically dependent on South Africa."

The government had pushed through the so-called Promotion of Bantu Self-Government Act in 1959, which removed from Parliament the white representatives who were selected by Africans. Thereby it cut the last official link Africans had to the country's process of lawmaking. The same statute made provision for what the government called the Africans' appropriate form of representation. Territorial authorities were to be set up—and ultimately were—in nine (ultimately ten) "national units," or ethnic entities for different tribes, although by that time no substantial rural area was occupied exclusively by a single ethnic group (see Table 1). The national units were to be formed—and by government fiat have been—of scattered patches of land around the periphery of the country that had long been reserved for African occupancy (see map). The rationale for the program set forth in the preamble of the act was that "the Bantu peoples of the Union of South Africa do not constitute a homogeneous people, but form separate national units on the basis of language and culture."

This view and program were the antithesis of African nationalism. As such, they were bitterly opposed by nationally-minded Africans both then and now for denying African rights in a country built through the efforts of all its people, black and white. Moreover, they saw, and see, the Bantustan program as the capstone of apartheid since it promised to entrench inequality through balkanizing South Africa. The 87 percent of the land that was richly endowed with minerals and that included all the industrially developed areas was to be left, and it remains in the exclusive domain of the white minority, which comprises about 17 percent of the population. The Africans, who total more than 70 percent of all South Africa's people, were to be, and are restricted as far as rights are concerned, to a bare 13 percent of the land, nearly all of which lacks major exploitable resources, is largely undeveloped, and is seriously overpopulated in relation to carrying capacity.

The government's own Tomlinson Commission, which undertook an exhaustive examination of possibilities for the socioeconomic development of the reserves, reported in 1956 that no more than half the existing population of those areas could grow enough food on them to support themselves. It recommended that the other half of the population of the reserves be removed from agriculture and involved in a massive program to develop local commerce and

Table 1
Percentage Distributions of Ethnic Groups in the Homelands

People	Homeland	% of Each Group in Homeland of Own Ethnic Group	% of Each Group Outside Homeland of Own Ethnic Group — Other African Homeland	White Areas
Xhosa	Transkei Ciskei	54.97	1.16	43.86
Zulu	KwaZulu	51.10	1.92	46.97
Pedi	Lebowa	56.07 ⎫	6.35 ⎫	37.58 ⎫
N. Ndebele	Lebowa	25.77 ⎬ 53.00	12.75 ⎬ 7.01	61.48 ⎬ 40.01
Venda	Venda	66.87	3.32	29.81
Shangaan	Gazankulu	31.78	21.52	46.70
Tswana	Bophuthatswana	34.91	0.60	64.49
S. Sotho	Basotho Qwa Qwa	1.60	8.25	90.08
Swazi	Swazi	16.42	6.04	77.54
S. Ndebele		— —*	23.71	47.29
Other	— —	— —	5.94	94.06
Total African		42.13	4.34	53.53
Whites		99.46	0.54	
Coloureds		99.35	0.65	
Asians		99.45	0.55	
Total		59.20	3.22	37.58

Sources: Jeffrey Butler et al., *The Black Homelands of South Africa* (Berkeley: University of California Press, 1977), p. 5; Muriel Horrell, *The African Homelands of South Africa* (Johannesburg: South African Institute of Race Relations, 1973) pp. 37-39.

* No figure is available for the population of the future South Ndebele homelands, which is to be made up of territories from other homelands and from white areas.

manufacturing and create the necessary fifty thousand new jobs annually for the next twenty-five years. The magnitude of such a task was underlined by the commission's own statement that "as far as industries are concerned, the Bantu Areas are in fact a desert."

The government promptly rejected these major recommendations and the necessary financing of the equivalent of $70 million a year for the next five years and a total of $291 million for the coming decade. In their place it established a Bantu Areas Investment Corporation with limited funds to stimulate industrial development in the reserves. It also launched the border industries program in 1956, under which some white-owned industries were induced to relocate on the borders of reserve territories through a combination of lower minimum wage and other requirements, and restrictions on their further expansion in urban areas. These measures were quite inadequate to cope with the basic problem of developing peripheral areas confronted with the overwhelming attraction of highly developed industrial and commercial centers. The government's hope, however, was that the political inducements of the Bantustan program would outweigh economic considerations, would provide Africans with an acceptable alternative to the objectives of African nationalism, and would fend off growing foreign criticism of apartheid's legally enforced inequality and discrimination. Although none of these objectives has been realized, the program has had more success than might have been expected.

In October 1976 Chief Kaiser Matanzima accepted the government's offer of independence for his territory, Transkei, and in December 1977 Chief **Lucas Mangope accepted the same status for Bophuthatswana. Chief Patrick Mphephu of Venda accepted independence in September 1979.** In contrast, Chief Gatsha Buthelezi of Kwa-Zulu, who has long been a critic of territorial separate development, forcefully rejects the notion of independence, as do the leaders of Gazankulu and Lebowa. So does the international community that has unanimously refused to recognize homeland independence, which it sees as fragmenting South Africa in the interests of apartheid.

Matanzima maintains that only Transkei has the historical background and physical features to make independence tenable. To encourage him to accept independence, the Transkei was ceded Port St. Johns, a pleasant previously white watering place on the Indian Ocean. It is the only outlet to the sea possessed by any of the homelands and there are plans to build a floating harbor outside the silted-up port to make commerce possible. The three separate pieces into which Transkei is divided include more land and thus have more development potential than exists for any other homeland. Bophuthatswana, for example, although it possesses some rich minerals, is divided into seven (ultimately six) separate pieces of land, one of which near Lesotho is 250 kilometers from the nearest of the others. Government plans for Kwa-Zulu, with forty-four separate pieces of land, may only reduce them to ten (see Table 2). There is no African input to such arrangements.

Transkei is far from satisfied, however, with its present boundaries, despite having gained territory before independence at the expense of the Ciskei, which is similarly populated largely by Xhosas. In April 1978 Matanzima took the dramatic though not particularly effective step of breaking diplomatic relations with South Africa to publicize his anger that two sections of Transkeian territory are divided by East Griqualand, a rich white farming area, and that the government had transferred it from Cape Province to adjacent Natal to reinforce white interests. Since, like all Bantustans, Transkei depends heavily on central South African government funding (amounting to $130 million for 1978) for meeting its expenses and since these funds seem unlikely to be withheld, the chief purpose of Transkei's gesture seemed to be to attract external attention in the hope of ultimate foreign recognition. Nonetheless, when the training of Transkei soldiers was suspended by the South

Table 2
Black Homelands—Present Number of Land Units and Number
According to 1975 Consolidation Proposals[1]

Homeland	Present number of units (1975)[2]	Number of units after consolidation[3]
Bophuthatswana	8	6
Ciskei	19	1
Gazankulu	4	3
Kwa Zulu	44	10
Lebowa	13	6
Qwaqwa	1	1
South Ndebele	—	1
Swazi	2	1
Transkei	3	3
Venda	3	2

Sources: Department of Bantu Administration and Development; Muriel Horrell, The African Homelands of South Africa (Johannesburg: South African Institute of Race Relations, 1973).
From T. Malan and P. S. Hattingh, Black Homelands in South Africa (Pretoria: Africa Institute, 1976), p. 29.
1. Proposals tabled in Parliament on March 27, 1975.
2. Black spots excluded in figures.
3. The 1975 proposals do not distinguish between Lebowa, South Ndebele, Gazankulu, and Venda, but the 1973 proposals were used for determining the number of units.

African government, Matanzima temporarily barred South African military and naval passage rights over Transkeian airspace and territorial waters.

Matanzima argues that Transkei is different from all other homelands because historically it had as much right to be developed apart from what became South Africa in 1910 as the High Commission territories had. It is at least true that Transkei shared with the Ciskei the long political tradition of the Eastern Cape. Moreover, Transkeians had their own local representation through the quasi-political General Council of the Transkeian Territory from 1903 to 1955. The council, which had previously maintained an active interest in national as well as local affairs, was then persuaded to accept the Bantu Authorities system, the base of what became the Bantustan, or homeland, system. In 1963 Transkei became the first territory to accept this system.

The Transkei Constitution Act of May 29, 1963, made provision for an all-African Legislative Assembly consisting of sixty-four appointed chiefs and forty-five elected members. The election for these members was conducted on the basis of adult suffrage open to all Transkeians inside and outside the territory. It was the first time Africans had voted in South Africa without being restricted by property and educational qualifications. Only twelve of those elected supported the separate territorial development program; thirty-three envisaged Transkei's limited self-government as a step toward achieving rights for all Africans in a multi- or nonracial South Africa.

When Transkei's first government was chosen, however, on December 6, 1963, the votes of the chiefs determined that the post of chief minister should go to Chief Kaiser Matanzima, a forceful exponent of separate development who foresaw more opportunities for his own ambitions and for black nationalism within that territory than elsewhere in the country. The second and third Assembly elections confirmed his position and led to a formal request for independence. There remained considerable opposition inside the territory to this move, but on the eve of the fourth and last preindependence election in September 1976 the most vigorous opponents of independence, including members of the opposition whose election was not in doubt, were placed in detention on charges of associating with the ANC and conspiring to create violence at the time of the election. The final returns indicated that Matanzima's party would have secured a majority among the seventy-five elected members in any case, but with much of the opposition in custody it won an overwhelming majority among them as well as among the seventy-five chiefs who make up the rest of the current Transkeian Legislative Assembly.

Homeland Independence and the Citizenship Issue

Transkei independence, the first political structural change in South Africa since the Act of Union, 1910, marked a watershed in the country's history. To most nationalistic Afrikaners it signified the striking success of the program of territorial separate development that the government had promised would bring racial peace throughout the country. But even before the cession of independence a bitter dispute arose over a fundamental issue: what were the implications for African citizenship of Transkei independence?

The South African government claimed that regardless of their domicile all Xhosa and Sotho speakers who were not attached to another homeland automatically became Transkeian citizens and lost their South African citizenship. The Transkei government tried to maintain that apart from those born within the territory all others had to make formal application to receive citizenship. The fundamental difference between the two positions is clear: the Transkei government, supported by all other homeland leaders and by spokesmen for urban blacks, maintains that no African should be forced against his or her will to give up South African citizenship; but the South African government, which has the legal power in its hand, is divesting itself unilaterally of the citizenship of urban Africans it deems related to an independent homeland. Beyond this, the government's basic objective, as then minister of Plural Relations and Development (the new name for Bantu Administration and Development), Connie Mulder, told the 1978 Parliament and as the prime minister in the same body[3] confirmed in April, is that *all* Africans shall ultimately lose their South African citizenship. The result, of course, would be that by turning all South African Africans into foreigners, the whites would become the majority population within the country.

The issue is crucial on both sides. For the South African government to accept the African stand instead of its own policy on citizenship would be to abandon the basic tenet of separate development. For homeland leaders to endorse the South African government's policy of stripping Africans outside their territories of their existing South African citizenship would so alienate urban Africans that it might irrevocably divide the two groups (see Table 3). In June 1978 the Kwa-Zulu Legislative Assembly unanimously rejected the second Bantu Laws amendment bill, transferring the issuing of passes to homeland governments, on the ground that it required homelands to make "millions of blacks alien in our own country."[4] It determined not to implement the measure if it became law. Yet, in the end the homelands are as powerless as the urban Africans themselves if the government pursues its policy on African citizenship inexorably.

Table 3
Population of the Homelands, 1978

These population projections were provided by Benso (Bureau of Economic Research). They are based on midyear estimates of the Department of Statistics and take into account resettlement figures and border alterations as far as possible.

| | De Facto Population | | | De Jure |
	African	Other	Total	Population
Bophuthatswana	1,246,700	26,300	1,273,000	2,219,600
Ciskei	553,700	300	554,000	1,023,200
Gazankulu	353,200	600	353,800	858,900
KaNgwane	219,000	700	219,700	622,300
Kwa-Zulu	2,894,300	3,800	2,898,100	5,304,500
Lebowa	1,469,100	1,700	1,470,800	2,121,200
QuaQua	94,900	200	95,100	1,791,700
Transkei	1,783,700	700,000	2,483,700	4,142,800
Venda	357,400	200	357,600	473,200
Other*	—	—	—	1,072,600
TOTAL	8,972,000	733,800	9,705,800	19,630,000

* Includes North and South Ndebele, who are increasingly being resettled in the newly created KwaNdebele homeland north of Pretoria; foreign Africans; and Africans whose home language is English or Afrikaans.

Source: Survey of Race Relations in South Africa, 1979 (Johannesburg: South African Institute of Race Relations, 1979), p. 71.

The Lack of Viability of the Homelands

The homelands presently consist of ninety-seven separate pieces of land scattered around the periphery of South Africa (see map). Government plans for consolidation would eventually bring the number down to thirty-four, with most cut off from the others by white-owned property requiring special papers for transit. The final settlement is based on the 1936 Native Land and Trust Act, which promised in return for the loss of the Cape franchise on the common roll to increase African-held land from 7 percent to 13 percent of the country's land area. The density of population per kilometer in the nine homelands in 1972 ranged between twenty-three in Bophuthatswana and sixty-seven in Kwa-Zulu, with an average density of forty-six, compared to eighteen for the whole of South Africa and thirteen for "white" South Africa.[5] Not surprisingly, homeland leaders do not accept the limits on the land allocated to their territories.

Within these fragmented areas are domiciled some 50 percent of the African population, nearly nine million in 1978 and substantially more at the present time, both because of the high birthrate in these territories and because of the continuous resettlement of Africans either uprooted from so-called black spots in white areas or ejected from urban areas by redrawn boundaries or influx control. Since agriculture is mainly carried on in traditional fashion and exploitable resources are virtually lacking (partly at least due to redrawing of boundaries to include these resources within white areas), a high proportion ranging from between 35 percent and 55 percent of all males between the ages of fifteen and sixty-four must seek through migratory labor to earn what is needed to support themselves and their families (see Table 4). Transkei has

Table 4

Absence of Black Population from Homelands, 1970

Nation	Percentage of Inhabitants in Homeland			Number of men (15–64 years of age) temporarily absent
	Total	Persons 15–64 years of age		
		Men	Women	
Xhosa-Transkei	54.9	35.3	62.9	224,500
Xhosa-Ciskei	55.9	38.1	56.1	37,200
Tswana	35.5	24.4	32.8	37,600
North Sotho (Lebowa)	56.0	35.0	59.5	91,200
Shangaan (Gazankulu)	35.5	18.4	40.7	38,700
Venda	67.2	40.1	76.1	30,200
Swazi	17.2	12.5	16.4	5,000
Zulu	51.3	36.7	53.2	164,300
South Sotho	1.8	1.2	1.9	2,500

Source: Lombard, J. A., and Van der Merwe, P. J., *Central problems of the economic development of the Bantu Homelands* (*Finance and Trade Review*, June 1972), Table 3.

one of the country's highest proportions of males forced into migratory labor, nearly a quarter of a million in 1972, and more now.

Despite the government's stimulation of border industries and growth points within the homelands, at least a third of the 100,000 *new* work-seekers a year from the homelands are similarly forced to go as migratory labor to the industrial and commercial centers in "white" South Africa, from which the homeland policy is supposed to remove them, one of the fundamental contradictions riddling the system. Another third of these new work-seekers secure government jobs within the homelands, largely due to the substantial funding provided by the central government, amounting to between one-half and four-fifths of their annual budgets. Any reduction in this funding is quite likely to throw still more old and new work-seekers into the migratory labor pool, and to increase the pressures on scarce local sources of subsistence.

The compulsion on homeland Africans to engage in the oscillating migratory labor system results not only from the lack of work opportunities within those areas but also from the drastic restriction imposed under Section 10 (1) (d) of the Urban Areas Act, which provides that any African entering a prescribed (in effect, an urban or semiurban) area to work after April 1, 1968, is permitted to stay only one year at a time and must then return to his original domicile to await another call or job. While in the urban area, he must live in a unisex hostel where he shares a room with other migrants. Migrants must secure their first job through a labor bureau in their homeland, which allocates them in response to existing needs in the white areas and the migrant's preference. Thereafter, reemployment is generally at the same kind of job. Under the "call-in" system, the worker may be reemployed by the same mine or factory or firm after the compulsory return to the homeland. If not, he must await another opportunity for employment.

In general, the system limits opportunities for training and advancement, particularly since there are so many unemployed work-seekers always waiting in the homelands. The effect on the urban wage structure of so controlled a labor system is to keep it low. Despite the fact that well over five million Africans are already more or less permanently living in urban or peri-urban townships near white towns and cities, the government strongly favors the oscillating migratory labor system. It would prefer that most Africans be ultimately migrants, thereby undercutting the supply of skilled labor from which South African industry is so seriously suffering, another basic contradiction.

The social problems created by the oscillating migratory labor policy are vast. In the cities, where migrants live in close proximity to other males, there is rampant homosexuality, while not surprisingly migrants also cause a high percentage of illegitimate children in the African townships. In the homelands there is a dispiriting apathy among the women and children whose husbands and fathers are unemployed, awaiting jobs, or away for successive periods of service in the urban areas. When they return, there is a compulsion to procreate, which accounts for the abnormally high birth rate that resulted in almost half of all rural Africans being under fifteen years of age in 1970.

Moreover, health standards in the rural areas are poor, with comparatively few hospitals and clinics. Buthelezi once aptly characterized the homelands as "rural slums," far from the glowing picture presented by the government's propaganda.

The government's effort to decentralize industries and encourage economic development through larger economic units could be promising if implemented soon. More land and genuine consolidation of their territories, for which all homeland leaders call, could help to stimulate improved agriculture and cattle raising and labor-intensive enterprises like shoemaking, whereby these areas might support a higher proportion of their populations. What is obviously necessary, however, is to permit the African population greater mobility within the country by steadily reducing the rigid provisions of influx control. But this is only likely to happen as part of a comprehensive redirection of government policy.

The Problems of Urban Africans

Some nine to ten million Africans, twice the total white population, live in the so-called white areas, many of them far away from the homelands. About four million Africans work on white farms. The majority, however, comprising some six million, are in urban townships lying on the edges of towns and cities throughout the country. Except for Pretoria, where the number of white government workers swells the total white population, and Cape Town, where the Coloured are more numerous, Africans outnumber whites in virtually all urban areas. The white population of Johannesburg is less than half a million. In contrast, Soweto (the South Western Township), which covers about eighty-five square kilometers and lies about fifteen miles outside of Johannesburg, houses well over a million Africans, making it the fifth largest city in Africa south of the Sahara.

African townships, and in some areas also Coloured or Asian settlements, serve largely as dormitories for the workers who commute to their weekly jobs in white households, places of business, factories, and the like. A quarter of a million commute by train, bus, or other means from Soweto alone. The mines and complexes like ISCOR, the state-financed iron and steel corporation, and SASOL, which produces oil from coal, have their own compounds where migratory African labor is housed, often near the townships. The four largely urban centers of industrial concentration within the country—the Southern Transvaal, the Western Cape, Durban-Pinetown, and Port Elizabeth-Uitenhage—have a compulsive attraction for labor. Of these four areas, the Southern Transvaal, and particularly within it the PWV (Pretoria-Witwatersrand-Vereeniging) triangle with its spreading gold mine complex, heavy industry, and the commercial capital of Johannesburg, has accumulated the greatest concentration of black labor.

Only Africans who meet specific provisions can remain within a prescribed area like Soweto for more than seventy-two hours. These provisions are: (1) continuous residence since birth in that particular area; or (2) continuous employment with the same employer for at least ten years, or lawful residence for at least fifteen years; or (3) the wife or unmarried daughter or son under sixteen of anyone qualifying under (1) or (2); or (4) labor bureau permission to be in the area.

Those in category (1) qualify under Section 10 (1) (a) of the Urban Areas Act and are the best off. They have relative permanence of residence unless they are designated "idle" or "undesirable," in which case they too can be expelled. A university survey in 1969 found that 92.9 percent of those persons between eighteen and twenty-five and nearly 50 percent of all adults surveyed had been born in Soweto. The percentages are surely higher now. Category (2), qualifying under Section 10 (1) (b), provides approximately the same security except that the right of residence is lost if a fine of more than R100 ($140) is incurred or imprisonment for more than six months. Persons acquiring this status must have entered the prescribed area before April 1, 1968, and continue to work for the same employer.

Despite these restrictions the African urban population has grown steadily and continues to do so. What is distinctive is that such a high proportion of the teenagers and those in their twenties have known no other conditions. It is the completely urbanized youth that has demonstrated and rioted so persistently since June 1976. They have experienced discrimination and the humiliation of their parents all their lives. Moreover, they are better educated than earlier generations, and thus more sensitive to the deprivation they suffer compared with the conditions of the whites. Most Soweto dwellings are featureless four-room "matchboxes" without electricity or water, though there is also the middle-class suburb of Dube that has some fine houses. What is most galling to the youth are the lack of opportunities ahead; the tyranny of the police, black and white; and the pervading sense of government domination. They have absorbed black consciousness and nationalism out of the conditions under which they must live.

Fluctuating Government Policies for Soweto

Nationalist policy since 1948 has aimed not only to bring the African urban population around Johannesburg into one more or less consolidated area, Soweto, but also to extinguish all freehold rights to land. The Nationalist justification for this policy was that the urban African population, despite its long-settled character and significant role in the "white" economy, was only in the area so long as its members were needed by the whites. Although the government now acknowledges that there will always be settled Africans in the urban areas, there is still a rooted objection to permitting them to buy land in the townships, an objection that may be related to a long-held Afrikaner belief that ownership of land is related to citizenship. At the moment, it is only in recognized growth centers like Babelegi in Bophuthatswana that Africans may own land near "white" cities like Pretoria.

There is a serious lack of housing in Soweto, characteristic also of other African townships. Nearly 22,000 qualified families were on the Soweto waiting list for houses in mid-1977, some having waited more than a decade. About 2,000 additional houses are needed annually for newly married couples, yet only 422 houses were built in 1977.[6] The average number of people to a house in 1973 was 5.8. (Widows and divorcees cannot lease homes, but only sublease.)

The government's policies in regard to home ownership have gone through a bewildering cycle of changes that threatens to continue. After 1968 Africans were prohibited from building their own houses on thirty-year leasehold land, and, if those houses they had already erected were sold or if the owner died, they had to be turned over to the West Rand Administration Board, which is directly responsible to the central government. In the late spring of 1975 these provisions were modified to permit home ownership again on thirty-year leasehold land, but this concession was quickly nullified by restricting ownership to persons possessing homeland citizenship, which few Soweto residents were willing to adopt for fear it would further imperil their urban residence. Following the outbreak of disturbances in Soweto in June 1976, however, the government announced that this restriction was removed, though preference was to be accorded persons from Transkei or with homeland citizenship.

Early in the 1978 Assembly session, in an effort to conciliate Soweto-dwellers, the government gave notice of its intention to institute a ninety-nine-year lease system that would enable qualified Africans to buy, sell, improve, and inherit houses. Under questioning, then minister of plural relations, Connie Mulder, maintained in May that the descendants of citizens of homelands that had accepted independence would not be able to buy houses because they would not qualify for residential rights afforded other blacks, but this restriction has also now been dropped. Such contradictory moves have left uncertainty, however, about the possibilities of stable home ownership.

Most of Soweto is without electricity. The South African Urban Foundation proposed a plan in 1976 to bring electric power to Soweto, but it was turned down by the West Rand Bantu Affairs Board on the ground that Soweto residents would be unable to afford the cost of electricity plus the high interest payments on the loans the board would have to accept. A new plan described by the *Star* in its issue of April 29, 1978 (pp. 12–13), provides for the funds to be raised on a fifteen-year stock issue that the commercial banks, with the notable addition of the Volkskas Merchant Bank, would buy or be responsible for selling. The process has started but it is slow and costs rise continually because of the delays.

African traders in Soweto have long been allowed to deal only in "daily essentials," or "necessaries," although recently there have been modifications of these restrictions and there are now plans for a shopping center. In the meantime, goods such as clothing must be bought outside of Soweto, that is, from white or Indian shops. After 1968 African traders were not allowed to build their own premises, and they could operate only in premises leased from the local authority. In general each trader has been limited to one business in an urban area. This restriction may also be modified.

Although voluntary contributions to the Johannesburg *Star's* TEACH program had helped to ease the shortage of school buildings, there were far from enough classrooms for the primary level before the 1976 disorders and obviously still more serious shortages now. (Almost all TEACH-program schools were left untouched when government schools were burned.) Insistence on "home" language instruction in the lower grades has been particularly complicated for Soweto, where there is much ethnic intermarriage, and despite government efforts residence does not follow linguistic lines. Homeland leaders have asked the government to follow the language provisions for schools adopted in their own territories, in several cases English at a level earlier than that permitted in the urban areas, but this request has still not been granted. The government did withdraw its provision for teaching higher levels in Afrikaans as well as English after the June 1976 demonstrations.

The prevailing shortage in secondary school facilities continues, especially since Orlando High School was badly damaged by fire during the disorders, and rebuilding has been slow. (Nearly ten times as much was spent repairing liquor stores and beer halls as on damaged schools.) The government has changed its policy of restricting post-Standard Six schools to the homelands, and three were built in Soweto in 1978, but that township had no teacher-training institute until 1978 and still has no boarding school. Education for Africans is neither free nor compulsory, and lack of opportunities for those with educational qualifications contributes to the high drop-out rate. Improved educational facilities at all levels are high on the list of current demands, and have led to expanded programs for the 80s.

Soweto, like other black townships throughout the country, has long had no effective self-government. In 1968 the old advisory boards for the townships were replaced by Urban Bantu Councils (UBC). In Soweto the council was composed of forty-one elected members chosen by the eight ethnic groups. This council (called by the students the Useless Boys Club) had no legislative or executive power and was controlled after July 1, 1973, by the white West Rand Administration Board, whose members are appointed by the government. Such boards, which now exist throughout the country, are supposed to meet their expenses through the African rents and rates in the respective areas they control and they depend heavily on the revenue produced by the sale of liquor. This fact, plus the desire to curb adult drinking, explains why students have tried to destroy government beer halls.

During the disorders the Soweto council proved ineffectual and was disbanded. In the absence of any effective representative organ, a group of responsible Soweto citizens formed the Committee of Ten, headed by Nthato Motlana, which sought to negotiate new arrangements with the government. Instead, all of the members were summarily detained without trial. Dr. Motlana was ultimately released with four of his colleagues, but the rest remained in prison. In the meantime the government had adopted a new system designed to establish Soweto "autonomy." But in the general elections for a new community council held in February 1978, only 492 persons voted. Undiscouraged, the government endorsed David Thebehali, the former chairman of the Urban Bantu Council, as "mayor" and, after releasing Dr. Motlana, held another round of elections on April 15, at which, however, there was only a 6 percent poll.

The government now concedes that urban Africans will always be a permanent feature of "white" South Africa. It acknowledges the need to establish improved facilities in the black urban townships. Mulder spoke of theatres, cinemas (there is only one at present for all of Soweto), electricity, parks, chain stores, and means whereby residents can earn their own livelihood within the township itself instead of having to commute to Johannesburg. What it calls township autonomy, however, is a measure of self-government in local affairs, not a status paralleling that of the rural homelands, as was once requested, and certainly not comparable to the independence granted Transkei.

Many requirements must also be met before Sowetans will believe the government genuinely means to establish autonomy for their city. Not only must local staff be trained to assume the key positions at the top and middle levels of municipal service, but a freely elected community council must be able to appoint its own officials who will be directly responsible to itself. The Committee of Ten had suggested much the same arrangements for Soweto as white municipalities enjoy, but there are questions as to whether a strong mayor or a professional city manager or some other form of administration would be more suitable to Soweto's special needs and, by inference, to other African urban areas. It is also clear that the management of African municipalities is closely related to other basic questions such as labor relations, restrictions on the ownership of property, ability to finance services, planning for diversified needs like shopping centers, stimulation of business arrangements, and access to capital. Above all, even autonomous African municipalities would exist within a totally different environment from white municipalities because their members have no voice in decision-making bodies at the higher level to which inevitably they are subject. As in so many issues, the success of municipal autonomy for African areas turns on the basic question of ultimate sharing of power.

The Reemergence of African Protest

While worldwide attention has been focused on the demonstrations and disorders in urban townships throughout South Africa since June 1976, the way had already been prepared by black university students, black adults, and black workers during the years before. Indeed the characteristic features of black consciousness and protest were already widely accepted.

In the period following the Sharpeville shooting in 1960, the failure of the All-In Conference, the disruption of sporadic efforts to create change through planned violence, and the Rivonia trial and sentencing to life imprisonment on Robben Island of outstanding African nationalist leaders, most notably Nelson Mandela and Walter Sisulu, organized African protest had sunk to its lowest level. The combination of police surveillance, aided by African informants in the townships, legally permitted periods of continuous detention for suspected witnesses as well as those associated with banned organizations, and calculated brutality hidden from publicity except when cases came to trial shaped a period of black quiescence through fear and despair.

Throughout most of the sixties such vocal opposition to discrimination as there was in South Africa came through the liberal white spokesmen of interracial organizations like NUSAS (National Union of South African Students), the Liberal and Progressive parties, Defense and Aid with its efforts on behalf of the dependents of political prisoners, and from 1967 on, until banned, the University Christian Movement (UCM). The black members of these organizations kept in the background, under suspicion from the government by the mere fact of their membership and avoiding the kinds of actions that had resulted in sending so many of their fellows to prison and Robben Island. Inevitably the white leaders of these organizations came to be regarded as the spokesmen for all dissent; and all too often *pro forma* protest took the place of hard-headed planning.

The breakout from this syndrome of dependence came first from black university students on their segregated campuses. In a move comparable to the withdrawal of Afrikaner university students from NUSAS in the 1930s, the black students organized themselves in 1969 into what they called the South African Students Organisation (SASO). Shortly after, they broke away entirely from predominantly white NUSAS. In two ways SASO was distinctive: it sought to unite Africans, Asians, and Coloured within its organization, not simply to associate their separate movements in a common front as had the Congress Movement; and in addition its leaders made a calculated effort to instill a new black consciousness by deliberately and openly separating themselves from the liberal whites who had long supported African claims. In some ways they were echoing the Africanism of the Pan-Africanist Congress but with the larger aim of uniting blacks as a whole, all of whom shared a common experience of discrimination. Moreover, in their view, dependence or even formal relations with whites and the associated philosophy of multi-racialism diverted blacks from the essential awareness that fundamental change in South Africa could come only through their own purely black efforts; whites, no matter how sympathetic, inevitably form part of the discriminatory system that blacks must ultimately transform. Their opposition to and attacks on the Bantustans and their leaders were no less outspoken, for they saw the homeland concept as a Trojan horse to undermine the black resolve to secure rights in an undivided South Africa.

It was not without reason that this new organization arose on the black university campuses. The government itself had prepared the ground for this seed by isolating almost all black students on ethnic campuses, Xhosas and Zulus at Fore Hare and Ngoye respectively, other Africans at the University of the North at Turfloop, Coloured at Bellville in the Cape, and Asians at Durban-Westville; even the black medical school was effectively separated from the white medical students at Durban University (it is now being moved to Ga-Rankuwa in Bophuthatswana). The physical separation of the black campuses from each other was another incentive to the formation of SASO. So too was the earlier history of division between nationalist groups in South Africa and its reflection in the various student movements that surfaced surreptitiously in the sixties. The organizers of SASO saw themselves as unifiers by putting forward the objective of a black organization of blacks for blacks.

Tactics came first and ideology later. African leaders of independent Africa, African achievements in the sixties, and West Indian and African writers were strong influences: Fanon, Senghor, Sekou Toure, Nyerere. The American black power movement and the writings of black American leaders had their impact, but in the context of what SASO leaders looked on as the inevitability of a common society in the United States. They saw black consciousness as the universal. Their ultimate goal was to achieve not merely a better economic status or a modicum of political rights but a drastically different type of society to be shaped by blacks themselves in terms of their own inner motivation.

Following close on the formation of SASO came the Black Peoples Convention (BPC), sometimes spoken of as the adult reflection of SASO but with a wider, more specifically political thrust. The BPC, like SASO, opposed ethnically exclusive political organization and activism on principle as antithetical to the united black front. While older Coloured and Indian leaders, including those in the still functioning Natal Indian Congress, remained somewhat aloof, militant young Indians and Coloured identified themselves with black consciousness. Indian and Coloured students joined the 1973 African demonstrations against segregated educational institutions with predominantly white staffs, and they similarly had their colleges temporarily closed. The most striking sign of solidarity between African and Coloured youth came in September 1976, when they both erupted into white urban areas of Cape Town, thereby bringing the protest movement into the heart of the country's legislative capital.

The history of SASO, BPC, and the wide variety of black-consciousness movements (including one actually called Black Consciousness Movement, which claimed responsibility for the outbursts that marked Soweto Day on June 16, 1977), underscores the fact that government-enforced segregation provides a fertile seedbed within which such attitudes germinate. Moreover, the political changes that have already brought Mozambique and Zimbabwe to the borders of South Africa and are at work in Namibia inevitably intensify black nationalist sentiments within the Republic despite the government's efforts to crush its manifestations.

Not surprisingly, the African National Congress has been infiltrating guerrillas into the country and claims an increasingly important role in stimulating black activities. Most African activists charged in South African courts are accused of belonging to either the ANC or the PAC partly, however, because of their long-term illegal status. Inside the country it is claimed that ANC and PAC supporters often cooperate, for younger exiles as well as more recent ones are increasingly impatient with personal and ideological differences that stand in the way of unity. Nonetheless, the ANC is increasingly prominent because of its successful sabotage efforts.

Externally, the ANC has maintained its cohesion while the PAC went through a period of division over leadership from which it only emerged in 1981 with the selection of John Pokola, an experienced and widely accepted figure. The OAU Liberation Committee, which funnels African funds to its chosen movements and would prefer to support only one for each country, favors the ANC.

Inkatha: An Ethnic or National Movement?

An increasingly important African organization started in March of 1975 is Inkatha, whose 300,000 paid-up members are predominantly Zulu, but which claims to be a national cultural liberation movement. Its rapid growth led James Kruger, minister of justice, to warn its head, Chief Gatsha Buthelezi, in August 1977 not to broaden Inkatha's ethnic base beyond the Zulus. Nonetheless, Inkatha already has strong branches in Soweto, in other parts of the Transvaal, and in Bloemfontein; a number of prominent non-Zulus are among its leaders.[7] Urban African youth is bitterly opposed to

Buthelezi because of his homeland role, and deeply suspicious of Inkatha lest he use it as a power base in a reorganized South Africa. Steve Biko also repudiated him. There are other African nationalists, however, who accept the value of a movement with parallel values to their own[8] and one whose identification with Kwa-Zulu serves to protect it, at least so far, from government bans.

Buthelezi maintains that he revived Inkatha, originally a short-lived Zulu cultural movement founded in 1928, to oppose the fragmentation of South Africa and to work for black independence in an undivided country. Inkatha's members oppose independence for Kwa-Zulu, and they captured every seat in that territory's first general election in February 1978. The movement's black, green, and yellow flag duplicates the colors of the ANC, with whose external leaders Buthelezi has always kept in touch.

In January 1978 Inkatha leaders met those of the Coloured Labour Party and the Indian Reform Party and reached agreement on an alliance to work for a national convention. Buthelezi was elected chairman of the group. The Progressive Federal Party also calls for a national convention. White liberals like David Welsh, an internationally known author and professor at the University of Cape Town, endorse Inkatha's core values of nondiscrimination and equal citizenship. They are also attracted to Buthelezi, whose non-racialism extends to tactics as well as goals and who rejects the use of violence although he warns that it may come if change is long delayed. Confronted with the question of whether Inkatha insists on one man (or person)/one vote, Gibson Thula, Inkatha's strategy and publicity committee chairman who is based in Soweto, maintains that such "mechanics" will be worked out "through wheeling and dealing" in a national convention,[9] a more palatable approach to that basic issue for white South Africans but likely to be less popular with other liberation movements.

Inkatha is presently waging a campaign to persuade companies based in South Africa to establish black trade unions and negotiate with them. Buthelezi has been unwilling to urge that foreign companies leave South Africa, as many African nationalists do, but he does not appear committed to encouraging them to remain. His immediate objective for Inkatha is to encourage the growth of black trade unions as an economic force though not as a political one. The government, which fears the latter development, will be watchful as Inkatha's program continues.

Can Black Workers Create Change?

Potentially, the more than seven million black workers in South Africa's economy are the most potent force for change. Their latent power was demonstrated when three-day strikes called for by the students kept most

Soweto workers at home in September 1976. In an earlier demonstration of their potential, African workers seeking higher wages, and acting without any apparent organization, had struck approximately one hundred and fifty firms in Natal from January to March 1973. The absence of negotiating machinery had vastly complicated employer efforts to arrive at a resolution of the stoppages and led the government to require companies to establish either works or liaison committees to provide some link with their employees. Most companies had chosen the liaison committees, in which workers selected only half their own representatives, instead, as with works committees, all of them. But neither system proved effective in preventing strikes from continuing, particularly over wage demands.

Spurred by the protests of the black majority, by increasing criticism from abroad, and, above all, by the need to stimulate economic growth in the country's capitalist system, the government set up two Commissions in 1977: one, headed by Professor Nicholas Wiehahn, on labor legislation that affected Africans; and the other, by Dr. Piet Riekert, to investigate the system of influx controls and pass laws affecting the utilization of African labor. Their two reports, issued in 1979, had both liberating and restricting effects on the position of African labor within South Africa.

Until 1979, as we have seen, African unions, though not illegal, had been specifically excluded from registering under the Industrial Conciliation Act (1956). This law provided for a system of industrial councils through which employers bargained with registered and officially recognized trade unions of white, Coloured, and Asian workers. The Wiehahn Commission recommended that Africans be allowed to join registered trade unions and also that their own trade unions should be eligible for registration. These changes were made through amending the Act. The process of securing registration has been halting, however, and by early 1981 only nine all-African unions had been registered out of the twenty-two that had applied.

Even before the Wiehahn Report, there had been new developments in regard to African trade unions. In 1974, TUCSA (the Trade Union Council of South Africa), which was basically made up of twelve white unions and twenty-three with mixed white, Coloured, and Asian members, invited affiliation by certain African unions. Despite TUCSA's earlier history of three times alternately inviting and then excluding African unions from parallel association, affiliation was accepted by seven African trade unions, mostly organized in the craft tradition. The largest of these was Lucy Mbuvelo's National Union of Clothing Workers with over 20,000 members. By 1981 TUCSA, embracing the principle of multi-racialism, had 300,000 members (45,000 Africans in ten affiliated unions, 188,000 Coloured, and 74,000 whites). By then, virtually all job reservations had been repealed.

Other African trade unions, which sprang up after the mass strikes in

Natal in 1973, rejected "parallelism," charging that it was a device by TUCSA's white administration to protect their white workers from African competition. The "independent" unions formed two associations of their own. One developed into the Federation of South African Trade Unions (FOSATU) centered originally in Natal. Based on the principle of non-racialism, FOSATU had eleven affiliates by 1981 with some 60,000 members, almost all African or Coloured. The other association, the Consultative Committee of Black Trade Unions, based largely in the Transvaal, gave rise late in 1980 to a new federation of nine all-African unions called the Council of Unions (CUSA) with approximately 49,000 members. CUSA is closely associated with the Urban Training Project (UTP), a worker-service organization founded in Johannesburg in 1971. Both FOSATU and CUSA seek to follow the industrial trade union tradition of working through shop stewards but they still need technical assistance to develop their requisite skills and structure.

The Wiehahn recommendations did not differentiate between African urban dwellers and those in the homelands, but the Riekert proposals drew a sharp line between them. Not only did they endorse the maintenance of the pass laws and influx control, but also added the requirement that African urban workers must have housing for legal employment. It also proposed, and the government similarly accepted, that instead of the worker the employer must pay the penalty, a fine of over $700, for employing illegal African labor. Since there was an extreme shortage of housing in the townships and especially in Soweto, there was an immediate crisis in Johannesburg, particularly among housewives, few of whose servants could qualify. A temporary moratorium was granted but thereafter the enforced interrelation of "controlled employment and controlled accommodation" created what the *Guardian's* headline in its June 3, 1979, article on the Riekert Report called "Laagers around the towns."

The government caused bitterness and also confusion by originally refusing to approve the recommendation that "frontier commuters" from the homelands, who were linked by train to their jobs in the cities, and also migrants should be phased gradually into the trade union movement. By the time it had grudgingly extended such rights, first to commuters and then to migrants from inside the country's original boundaries, much of the goodwill generated by the extension to Africans of trade union rights had been dissipated. This was particularly the case in Natal where parts of Kwa-Zulu were adjacent to Durban. Another demand, only gradually conceded, was for mixed African-Coloured unions, and ultimately for "non-racial" unions. By 1981, TUCSA had two so designated, and FOSATU seven, with requests for two more pending. By then, trade union membership for migrants from outside the country was also under consideration.

The 1979 grant of trade union rights to Africans had set off a race for members between "parallel" African unions and "independent" ones. Employers tended to favor the parallel unions since they were used to negotiating with TUCSA officials and believed they could work more harmoniously with them than with the independent federations, some of whose members held black consciousness sentiments. A number of companies set up "paper unions" to avoid more effective union bargaining. African workers from their side began to group themselves into unaffiliated unions on a variety of bases including type of work, craft, or area.

The unaffiliated African membership unions, of which there were 21 by 1981, totalling over 87,000 members, have proved more militant than either the "parallel" or "independent" trade union associations. Several of these unaffiliated unions assumed a new, less structured and more aggressive style bordering on confrontation, and have sought new sources of support within local communities. The long-established African Food and Canning Workers Union in the Western Cape, for example, organized a widespread consumer boycott of "red meat" in 1980 to enforce its demands. Using another approach, the South African Allied Workers Union organized workers in a wide range of industries in the East London area ranging from motor assembly to food and furniture, and also concerned itself with the interests of local black communities and of migrant workers and commuters.

African trade unions have become influential interest groups in South Africa because of their growing numbers and assertiveness and some observers see them as potent sources of basic change. While only about 2% of the African work force is as yet unionized, the black proportion of the labor force is approximately the same as its proportion of the population, that is, 84%; since its numbers are growing by 2.5% whereas the white population is increasing by only 1.5%, there will be a still greater disproportion in numbers by the end of the century.

But black, and especially African, labor faces overwhelming handicaps. There are some two million Africans unemployed who are pressing to get into the labor market. Legal restrictions on African residence and movement are stringent and often arbitrarily enforced. Articulate African trade union leaders face possible arrest and/or banning. Most serious limitations are the inadequacies of the separate discriminatory African educational system on which the government spends an average of $97.50 a year per child as compared to $1,111 for a white child.

While a quarter of a million unskilled workers enter the labor market every year, the shortage of skilled workers grows by 5,000 annually. The South African National Productivity Institute estimates that the country will need an additional 700,000 trained professional and skilled workers by 1987. There were fifteen to twenty thousand artisan vacancies in 1981. But despite the obvious need for skilled workers, and the government's avowed goal of developing a stable black middle class, the National Manpower Commission reported in February 1981 that only 82 Africans had registered for apprenticeship training since mid-1979. Moreover, there are well-documented accounts, some related to American-owned companies, that Africans who have taken specialized training, as computer operators for example, are not accepted for known job openings.

The South African apartheid system cuts across what might otherwise be the solidarity of labor vis-à-vis employers and has long put white labor on the same side as white employers. Political authority, economic and financial policies, and labor relations have been tightly knit sources of power for the white minority. It was an unwelcome shock to the long favored white Mine Workers Union, therefore, when the government, as well as the Chamber of Mines, took a strong stand in March 1979 against its illegal strike which opposed the employment of a few Coloured workers in jobs previously held by whites. The veteran leader of the MWU attributed the poor showing of Botha's party in the subsequent Rustenburg, Transvaal, by-election to the white miners concern.

A still more forceful conservative protest against "reforms" being introduced by the Botha government came with the results of the April 29, 1981, general election. Not only the African labor advances but also the attempts to associate Coloured and Asians with the existing political system seem to have produced the backlash that provided the reactionary HNP with far more votes than ever before and thereby posed a threat to Afrikaner unity.

Manipulating the Constitution

Afrikanerdom has long been a tightly knit community whose interlocking organizations, reaching into every sphere of life, are unified and powered by the National Party's political control. The right-wing breakaway from that party by the HNP (Herstigte Nasionale Party) in 1969 to oppose Prime Minister John Vorster's "outward-looking policy" of cultivating relations with African-ruled states had almost created a crisis within Afrikanerdom. Its overwhelming desire for unity has continued to provide the HNP with more influence on national policy than its failure to secure seats in Parliament would seem to warrant. For Afrikaner political dominance is directed to protecting not only the white power position within South Africa but also the particular interests of Afrikaners.

It has been apparent for some time that the Nationalist government is convinced that change must occur, but its form and extent are still problematic. Attempts to maintain the basic Nationalist principles of ethnic and urban-homeland divisions in the labor movement have been gradually eroded, as much by the needs of the market place as by worker pressures, but whites are still dominant in the hierarchy of skills and managerial positions. In the light of international as well as internal pressures to reduce the blatant racialism in the political system, some tentative attempts have also been made in this realm to associate Coloureds and Asians by devices that might secure their support without undercutting white dominance in the all-important process of national law-making.

In place of restoring direct participation in the electoral process, which remains the basic objective of the Coloured, Prime Minister Vorster originally offered different opportunities that he maintained would provide them, and subsequently the Asians, with a meaningful voice at the seat of power, the Cabinet. This program involved a threefold program: upgrading the status of the Coloured Persons Representative Council (CRC); providing it with direct representation on bodies like the Wage Council, the Group Areas Board, the Road and Transportation Board, and the Race Classification Board that make decisions directly affecting Coloured and Asians; and establishing a Cabinet council in which white, Coloured, and Asian representatives could discuss matters of common concern like the budget. While the Asians tentatively accepted representation on the proposed Cabinet council, the CRC, which since March 1975 had been controlled by Sonny Leon's Labour Party, indignantly refused and called for a national convention to devise a new constitution for the country. When Leon and the Labour Party refused to endorse the 1975–76 government-proposed budget for the CRC, however, Leon was dismissed from his executive position in the Council and that budget and later ones were approved by a nonpolitical Coloured representative, A. Jansen, who was given her authority by the minister for coloured affairs. She and some other CRC members also agreed to participate in the Cabinet council.

The Coloured have a special importance in the eyes of most Afrikaners because of their mixed blood ancestry and the historically close relations between the two groups. Numbering some two and a half million, mainly in the Cape, the Coloured could form a powerful reinforcement of the Afrikaners, and indeed of the whites as a whole, should their allegiance be won. In addition to providing equal franchise rights, however, the government would have to renounce its recently reaffirmed insistence on maintaining the Mixed Marriages Act and the sections of the Immorality Act that refer to the Coloured. Both are bitterly resented by the Coloured and indeed no longer find unquestioning support among Afrikaners. Coloured have also suffered from their forcible ejection from their historic home sites in District Six of Cape Town.

It is also true, of course, that there are frequent tensions between the Coloured and Africans, and there is constant anxiety over the massive African majorities in most urban areas. At the same time, the urge for liberation and full political participation of both the Coloured and the Africans make an implicit underlying bond that will not easily be broken. Indeed, the failure to provide any role for Africans in this and subsequent proposals seeking the same purposes has led to their rejection by representative Coloureds and Asians.

Vorster's second offer, announced in the Assembly late in May 1978, was to associate the Coloured and Asians with whites in a three-parliament executive presidential system. The Coloured Persons Representative Council and the Indian Council were to be enlarged and made more fully elective so that in effect they could become ethnic parliaments with their own prime ministers and cabinets. They would then function side by side with the white parliament to deal with matters of exclusive concern for the particular group. Matters of common concern were to be considered in the Council of Cabinets, made up of ministers from all three bodies, and capable of initiating legislation if a consensus could be reached. Otherwise, the issue was to be referred to the Presidential Council, composed of nonpolitical experts, for advice to the President who, presumably, was to make the final decisions. The President was to be elected by an electoral college consisting of fifty white MPs, twenty-five Coloured MPs, and thirteen Asian MPs. Thus, it was apparent that the Nationalists would control all matters of common interest.

Dr. Gerrit Viljoen, formerly head of the Broederbond and subsequently Minister of National Education in the Botha cabinet, suggested that what he called "semi-independent homelands now on their way to independence" might form part of a cooperative association with South Africa and neighboring African states.[10] Thereby he added another concept to the thinking about changes in the constitutional system, which, as David Welsh pointed out in a thought-provoking article in *Optima*,[11] was in itself a revolutionary idea.

The Vorster government maintained that its constitutional plan received overwhelming support from the white electorate in the November 1977 general election, in which it won 135 of the 165 parliamentary seats. In fact, there was relatively little publicity about the plan during that campaign, which sought successfully to rally white voters against pressures from outside, notably from the Carter administration, to move South Africa toward providing full political participation for all its inhabitants. But since Coloured leaders in particular refused to participate in Vorster's elaborate constitutional structure, it also failed as had his earlier scheme. It was left to Vorster's successor, Prime Minister P.W. Botha, to seek yet another way to achieve the same purposes.

Alternative Constitutional Plans

In the meantime, the opposition had been attempting to devise their own constitutional plans. A 1976 attempt to define common principles and thus to lay the basis for a merger between the three opposition parties—the United Party (UP), the Progressive Reform Party (PRP), and the Democratic Party —had got so far as to secure agreement on three principles to underlie their policies: power-sharing between all groups at every level of the community; elimination of race discrimination; and consultation between all races on the drafting of a future constitution for the country. But while UP leaders agreed. the result was to split the party and thereby hasten its demise. In the 1977 election, two new parties, the New Republic Party and the South African Party, won 10 and 3 seats respectively. The PRP, now renamed the Progressive

Federal Party, which won 17 seats, thus inherited the UP's traditional role of official opposition.

In June 1978, Colin Eglin, then leader of the opposition, unveiled the Progressive Federal Party's long-awaited constitutional model.[12] It provided for an entrenched constitution incorporating a bill of individual and group rights, reinforced by a federal appeals court, and a federal system under which the central government would be restricted to national concerns and the states would possess maximum legislative, executive, and judicial powers. Thus it sought to decentralize the exercise of political power through federal arrangements and to entrench protection of individual and group rights against legislative or executive acts or those of the states. Additionally, in a radical change from its earlier position of restricting the franchise by a prescribed educational level, the final PFP constitutional plan accepted by its Federal Congress meeting in Natal on November 18–19, 1978, endorsed "a general adult franchise of citizens" to select the representatives of political parties elected "on proportional basis within each state."

The key principle pervading the PFP's constitutional plan is consensus. Constitutionally, this principle was to be reinforced by providing for a possible 10 to 15 percent minority veto on all decisions other than money bills, administrative details, and the election of the prime minister. But the party recognized that any constitutional arrangement drawn up without the participation of all racial groups in the country lacked the basic underpinning of trust essential for its acceptance and stability. Thus the PFP Federal Congress agreed that ultimately the constitution had to be the product of genuine negotiation among all groups, in other words in a national convention to reach agreed decisions reflecting the national consensus.

Among other constitutional proposals floated earlier was Chief Gatsha Buthelezi's plan, outlined in his 1974 Hoernlé lecture, for a federal system with substantial self-government for each of predominantly black and predominantly white areas, and free flow of labor between them. Yet another suggestion, said to have originated in 1976 with the powerful Bureau of State Security (BOSS), subsequently renamed the State Security Council, was for a Swiss-style cantonal system under a multiracial or confederal central authority.[13]

A model designed by Paul Malherbe for what he called a multistan,[14] that is, a region within which racial laws do not operate, seemed particularly appropriate for Natal, where parts of Kwa-Zulu are scattered throughout the province. The 1980 Lombard Report,[15] prepared by a team of academics from the University of Pretoria and financed by Natal's business sector, including its large sugar industry, proposed a multi-racial legislature for a largely autonomous Natal with an executive head (thought likely to be Chief Gatsha Buthelezi) elected on a one-man-one-vote basis. This plan was rejected by the government as based on black-white power sharing. Ongoing is the work of the Buthelezi Commission, established by Inkatha in May 1980, and endorsed by the Kwa-Zulu government, to investigate acceptable ways of overcoming this opposition.

Botha's Constitutional Plans

Prime Minister Vorster had resigned in September 1978 as the implications of the Muldergate scandal over the misuse of public funds through a secret account were becoming known. Pieter W. Botha, head of the Cape Nationalist Party, succeeded him, and lost little time in setting up the Schlebusch Commission on July 4, 1979, to advise on new constitutional arrangements.[16] Its report, presented in May 1980 and accepted by Parliament with the PFP dissenting, recommended the abolition of the second chamber, the Senate, and the appointment of a President's Council of 60 nominated members including "recognized" leaders of the Coloured, Asian, and Chinese communities as well as a preponderance of whites. The addition of a member from the small Chinese community reflected the new South African ties with Taiwan.

In the meantime, Botha himself had enunciated a twelve-point plan in August 1979 that dealt with both domestic and international relations. As far as the Coloured and Indians were concerned, Botha appeared to go farther than Vorster had done since he approved "a system of consultation and coresponsibility as far as common interests are concerned."

But the Botha plan reaffirmed separatism and like the proposals of the Schlebusch Commission excluded Africans from the process of national planning. The government offered a separate advisory Black Council but it was rejected by both urban and homeland leaders. The PFP voted against the Schlebusch proposals as constituting "in principle a continuation of white political baasskap [domination]." The Coloured Labour Party not only opposed participation in the President's Council but threatened that any member who accepted nomination would be expelled and subject to social ostracism. The Natal Indian Council was equally adamant. Those few Coloured and Asians who did accept places on the President's Council were labeled "sell-outs" though their role in constitutional planning may not be without value.

Among Botha's twelve points was a commitment to strive for "a peaceful constellation of Southern African states with respect for each other's cultures, traditions and ideals." Was this a new formulation for relations with the so-called independent homelands, Transkei, Bophuthatswana, Venda, and most recently Ciskei, a relation that could be extended through associate status to the other homelands? Was it to be related to still unfulfilled consolidation proposals? Subsequently in the House of Assembly, on June 2, 1980, Botha hinted that urban black communities that "for some practical reason or other" cannot be linked politically to a homeland might be related to a future council of state for the constellation. But any transitional plans must take into account the deep-seated opposition of nationally minded blacks to government-created structures like the homelands and township community councils and seek ways to involve all groups in their formulation and work.

When businessmen met with the cabinet at Carlton Centre in Johannesburg on November 22, 1979, their imaginations were fired by wider implications of a "constellation of states" involving "joint planning and action, as well as the pooling of resources" with African-controlled states in Southern Africa. But like blacks at home, those outside had other objectives. Thus in April 1980, nine Southern African states formed an association known as SADCC (Southern African Development Coordination Conference) committed to working together to reduce their economic dependence on South Africa.*

The 1981 Election and Its Aftermath

When Prime Minister Botha called a general election for April 29, 1981, a year before it was essential, he was responding to counter-pressures. On the one hand, industry and business, faced with a growing slowdown and the fall in the price of gold, were concerned to stimulate economic growth by capitalizing on the potentials of black purchasing power and abilities. Although several national universities, including Stellenbosch in the Western Cape and Witwatersrand in Johannesburg, were admitting limited numbers of black students, the growing need for more black skilled labor and administrative personnel was being frustrated by the inadequacies of basic black education, particularly for Africans, and their unstable living conditions. Industry's pressures, therefore, were for an acceleration of Botha's program of reforms which had been slowing down.

On the other hand, conservative elements in the Nationalist party, particularly in the Transvaal, resented Botha's Cape party base, opposed his constitutional maneuvers, and were concerned at the growing influence of African trade unions. Moreover, extremist right-wing groups had become increasingly active against what they interpreted as dangerous moves toward racial integration. Although leaders of the most prominent extremist group, the Wit Commando, were finally arrested in January and February 1981, the bombing of offices of liberal organizations and the homes of prominent individuals like Colin Eglin, former leader of the PFP, had been occurring intermittently. This was politically embarrassing to the government, and raised disturbing questions about the attitudes of the defense, security, and civil services.

Botha clearly hoped that the results of the election would confirm him as leader of Afrikanerdom, as well as of its standardbearer, the Nationalist Party, and thereby endorse the constitutional changes and race relations he had espoused. But although his party won what would elsewhere be considered an

* See chapter 11; see also chapters 7 and 8 in *International Politics in Southern Africa.*

overwhelming victory, 131 seats out of 165, the polls, with a seventy-percent turnout of voters, were widely interpreted as a defeat because of the unprecedented division in the Afrikaner vote. While neither the HNP nor Connie Mulder's new National Conservative Party won a seat, they received 210,000 votes, well over a quarter of the number secured by the Nationalists, and threatened some sixty previously "safe" seats. Almost a third of Afrikanerdom supported HNP policies, claimed its leader, Jaap Marais, who was quoted in *Rapport*, the Afrikaans Sunday newspaper, as saying "there can no longer be any talk of political unity in Afrikaner ranks." The PFP increased its numbers in the House from 17 to 26, unseating a Cabinet minister in the process for the first time in South Africa's history, and picking up 5 percent of the Afrikaner vote. The SAP, in contrast, lost its two members, and the NRP also lost two seats, ending with eight.

Following the election, discord in the Cabinet surfaced openly when Dr. Andries Treurnicht, well known for his outspoken conservative views, publicly questioned the government's labor policy reforms. However, Fanie Botha, Minister of Manpower Utilization and Treurnicht's own senior deputy chairman, supported them strongly and received the head committee's backing. Treurnicht in February 1982 then challenged Prime Minister Botha's leadership of the Nationalist Party. In an unprecedented action, Botha entered the specially convened meeting of the Transvaal head committee, called for and gained its vote of support, and gave Treurnicht an ultimatum to conform or leave the party. Treurnicht and sixteen of his supporters, including Minister of Education Ferdinand Hartzenberg, left the party.

Another Afrikaner, but this time liberal, challenge to Nationalist policies has come from the Afrikaanse Studente Bond (ASB), which has criticized squatter removals and arbitrary arrests. There was a still more forceful challenge from its July 1980 politically oriented break-away, Polstu (Politieke Studente). Numbering some 500 members, Polstu has called for equal citizenship and social and economic opportunities for all. This daring platform led to a death threat from the Wit Commando and a warning from the Minister of Police not to seek liaison with ANC-inspired black student bodies.

The annual congress of the more moderate ASB, held in July 1981, was treated to a speech by the Minister of National Education, Dr. Gerrit Viljoen, in which he made a formal rejection of racial integration, which he called cultural suicide. But he also asserted that in the future South Africa, whites, Coloured, and Indians "in one form or another" would have "joint responsibility for matters affecting the three groups," which apparently remains the goal of constitutional planning.

Internal Challenges and Their Cost

In June 1980, the African National Congress had scored its most spectacular success by bombing SASOL, the oil-from-coal facility that South Africa

depends on to help free itself from dependence on foreign oil. But the anticipated increase in urban terrorism did not materialize and the townships were
relatively quiet except for a brief flare-up in violence in Soweto in October,
and continued bus and school boycotts in the Free State and northern
Transvaal. The government continued population removals, sending the
families of farm labor that had long been domiciled in the latter area and
ejected urbanites to the newest homeland, KwaNdebele, whose more than
100,000 inhabitants now spread over relatively barren land north of Pretoria.
Political repression also continued with the harrassment of African activists,
the banning of black journalists, and, on the charge of promoting the aims of
the ANC by printing the Freedom Charter, the closing of the *Post* and Weekend *Post*, which had the country's largest black circulation.

Still harsher measures were taken after the election against Africans and
their supporters. Throughout June and July 1981, the security police undertook the most severe and widespread crackdown on labor and political activists
since October 1977. Sixty members of the unregistered South African Allied
Workers' Union (SAAWU) were detained, partly at least because of their
rejection of the homeland system, and their open opposition to the proposed
incorporation in the Ciskei of their home base near East London, Mdantsane,
which was said to be the second largest black living area in the country. The
government has indicated its intention to outlaw general membership unions
like SAAWU and restrict union activities to one industry or trade. But in
response, independent black unions representing more than 150,000 workers
vowed to support each other in defying anti-strike measures.

Behind the government's extended activities against militant trade unions
lies concern about the increasing influence of the ANC, whose non-racial class
consciousness is now more pervasive than black consciousness. Moreover, the
ANC continued to score spectacular successes after the election by sabotaging
key strategic projects, including rail lines and electricity plants in Durban as
well as two widely separated Transvaal power stations, thereby plunging
towns into darkness, and, most dramatic, launching a rocket attack on the
South African Defense Forces Voortrekkerhoogte military complex near
Pretoria. Immediately thereafter, the National Key Points Act barring reports
of attacks on strategic installations without specific state approval was rushed
through Parliament at the end of the session. It added yet another restriction
to the nearly one hundred laws affecting press reporting in South Africa.

Another target of the police has been student activists, many of whom
are associated with COSAS, the black Congress of South African Students and
the Black Student Society of the University of the Witwatersrand. While
many blacks, including Chief Gatsha Buthelezi and his Inkatha movement,
refused to join in the celebrations on May 30, 1981, of South Africa's 20th
anniversary as a republic, stressing their own exclusion from political decision-
making, the students openly declaimed against what they called a "racist
republic." The police acted most forcefully when the South African flag was

burned by unknown persons on the Witwatersrand campus, not, in fact, a unique event on that day. In addition to widespread African arrests, they also seized Azhar and Feroze Cachalia, whose parents were well-known Indian activists, and two white student leaders, Sammy Adelman, chairman of the Witwatersrand Student Representative Council, and Andrew Boraine, president of the National Union of South African Students (NUSAS), whose father is a PFP member of Parliament. All four students were banned for five years after emerging from detention.

The most spectacular arrests, however, were of members of the South African Youth Revolutionary Council, made up of young blacks who had fled South Africa after the 1976 Soweto upheavals and whose organization has been supported in Nigeria in preference to those of the ANC or PAC.* More dangerous in reputation than fact, they were soon picked up by the police after they infiltrated back into South Africa. What is apparent, however, is that despite severe repression, Africans, and those who embrace their cause, refuse to accept the inferior role within their country that is still assigned to them by law and force.

Harry F. Oppenheimer, chairman of the Anglo American Corporation, wrote in his 1981 annual report: "Economic growth and racial discrimination are in fundamental opposition to each other and economic growth is an essential element in building a peaceful and just society." He added "Nothing is more dangerous than half hearted reform." Bishop Desmond Tutu, general secretary of the South African Council of Churches, went deeper when he wrote late in 1981: "Real fundamental change . . . has to do with political power-sharing."

Population Pressures and the Economy

Whatever temporary measures may be adopted to neutralize the vast disparity in black-white population ratios in urban areas, South Africans must confront the inevitable fact that the current numerical dominance of Africans throughout the country is on a steady increase. Of the 27 million in the population in 1978, nearly nineteen and a half million (71.6 percent) were Africans, compared to under four and a half million whites (16 percent). Still more significant is that the African birthrate is 40 percent, compared to only 18 percent for the whites. Thus, while the number of whites will increase by about 40,000 a year, the number of Africans will increase by more than half a million (see Tables 6 and 7).

Speaking to the International Monetary Conference in Mexico City on May 22, 1978, Harry Oppenheimer estimated that by the year 2000, South Africa's urban population would total thirty million, with the black urban population forming a huge majority because the total white population would be only seven million by that time. If, as he anticipated, what he called

* See chapter 6, *International Politics in Southern Africa.*

Table 6

Population of the Republic of South Africa, 1978

	Numbers	% of total	Birth rate	Death rate	Growth rate	Annual increment Numbers	% of total
Asians	792,000	2.9	30	7	2.3	19,000	3
Coloureds	2,553,000	9.4	31	11	2.0	50,000	7
Whites	4,393,000	16.1	18	9	0.9	40,000	6
Blacks*	19,463,000	71.6	40–	11	2.9	570,000	84
	27,201,000	100.				679,000	100

* South African-born blacks only.

Source: Prepared by J. L. Sadie, director of the Bureau for Economic Research, University of Stellenbosch. Printed in his article, "Demographic and Socio-Economic Projections and Constitutional Alternatives," in *Constitutional Change in South Africa,* ed. John A. Benyon (Pietermaritzburg: University of Natal Press, 1978), p. 278.

Table 7

Population 18 Years and Older, 1978

	Numbers	Percent	Growth rate per annum
Asians	444,000	3	2.95%
Coloureds	1,298,000	9	3.45%
Whites	2,887,000	20	1.55%
Blacks	9,750,000	68	3.20%
	14,379,000	100	

Source: Sadie, p. 281.

"the advanced sector of the South African economy" continued to grow, a high proportion of the skilled workers would also be black. This situation, he suggested, would make separate development "less plausible." Others might well draw the conclusion that it would make it impossible, and also that what he envisages as a profitable capitalist system might well have become something much closer to the socially oriented model that black nationalist groups espouse.

South Africa's population figures make it clear why the Nationalist government is trying to neutralize the African majority through the homeland policy and by stripping Africans of their South African citizenship. It is also obvious why nationally minded Africans press for majority rule in an undivided country. The potential confrontation between irresistible forces and immovable objects seems to leave the choice between ultimate violence or negotiations among accepted leaders from all sides.

As the black-white confrontation grows ever more serious, the basic contradictions within the white-imposed system become still more apparent. Relieving the pressures from urban black unemployed or homeless creates still greater overcrowding on the scarce resources within the homelands that the government had hoped would develop into viable areas. Permitting white trade unions to maintain a virtual veto on African advance within the economy unless their own members are rewarded in wages and status limits the extent and kind of black training needed to spur production. Refusal to deal with the African urban leaders who possess community trust undercuts potential moves toward genuine accommodation, and enhances the role of those who preach boycotts, strikes, and confrontation. Arbitrary arrest and imprisonment and a growing use of the death penalty for sabotage only harden the resolve of those determined to secure genuine changes.

Afrikaner intellectuals, including Willem A. de Klerk, author of the distinguished study of Afrikanerdom *The Puritans in Africa*,[17] have been ready to criticize the paraphernalia with which the separate development policy has been overlaid but have maintained their faith in the conception as such. But contradictions within the system place severe strains on Afrikanerdom. The faith that separate development is not only *an* answer but *the* answer to the South African racial situation is difficult to maintain when Matanzima breaks diplomatic relations with Pretoria, and Inkatha calls for a national convention. Nor under such circumstances is it easy to convince taxpayers that the government should continue to contribute large subsidies to Transkei and Kwa-Zulu, although to reduce that support might well lead to still more serious ruptures. Buthelezi has successfully fostered urban links for Inkatha, especially in Soweto, and through the Black Alliance with some Coloured and Indian moderates. Urban Africans who reject Buthelezi because of his homeland base are nonetheless aware that rural misery and anger provide seedbeds for allies in potentially strategic areas. The geographical location of the homelands adjacent to South Africa's borders might in the long run prove stepping stones rather than barriers to penetration by liberation forces.

There seem two possible but very different ways in which the government may move. One feature of change that some observers suggest is that there is or will be a gradual reduction in the barriers between the homelands and the developed white areas in the interest of overall economic integration. Even the Minister of Finance, Owen Horwood, acknowledged in February 1981 that the homeland system had not proved economically viable. One evidence is that despite harsh rebuffs and expulsions, squatters from the homelands continue to seek a bearable life outside that does not exist within. The most poignant example of this fact was the persistent efforts of women and children from Transkei in the autumn of 1981 to establish themselves near Nyanga in the Western Cape despite a series of brutal efforts by the authorities to force them out.

Moreover, there are already twice as many Africans in the urban areas who meet the legal qualifications for residence than the total number there in 1948 when Afrikanerdom seized on the doctrine of separate development as a means of achieving ultimate racial harmony through separation. No less important is the bitter rejection by urban Africans of the notion of homeland citizenship in place of full South African citizenship which they see as their ultimate right. Pressure from public opinion, but even more the inherent defects and unworkability of separate development in its present form, convinces these observers that a gradual lessening of the more rigid features of apartheid is taking place as one feature of a progressive, if little publicized, process of change.

Those who support this view of likely developments point to the inclusion of a few Coloured and Asians in the President's Council and the growing expectation that those two groups will be provided in due course with some political rights, possibly leading to their elected members of the Assembly. They also note the planned extension of free primary and secondary education to all black children, and to the gradual easing of the industrial color bar even in the particularly sensitive area of mining where the right-wing Afrikaner-dominated union has long resisted any such moves. These developments suggest to those observers that while they do not involve any fundamental shift in power, they do at least alter the balance in the relations between whites and blacks, and that other forms of political manipulation may result in further stages in such a process of change.

But change to what? Is it a gradual removal of economic and educational discrimination that may lead ultimately to limiting political discrimination by gradually opening opportunities for African political participation in the making of national decisions? Or are these changes to be limited to the economic and educational spheres and even there through carefully controlled steps which do not challenge ultimate white control?

There is a second, less palatable, possibility inherent in South Africa's current moves. This possibility is much cloer to the desires of right-wing Nationalists who view with alarm any shift in the balance of either economic or political power within the country. They admit the need for more economic integration to keep South Africa rich and powerful but they are determined to prevent Africans from challenging Afrikaner dominance within the system. And Prime Minister Botha, whose support within the army remains a potentially powerful bulwark but whose position within the cabinet was seriously weakened by the HNP resurgence so visible in the election returns and thereafter, is determined that there shall be no split in Afrikanerdom.

How can be prevent such a split? To a degree by maintaining traditional apartheid; hence no moves are being made on such sensitive issues as the Immorality Act or Group Areas except by specific government exemptions. To believe that "apartheid is dead" or even dying is to ignore its obvious continuing manifestations, especially through intensified efforts at influx control. *The Economist* reported in September 1981 that almost half the prison population was the result of apartheid offenses. A significant trend is that commuting from the homelands is subsidized while subsidies to Soweto and other black townships are being reduced. Moreover, there is increased encouragement to homeland leaders to act as counter-magnets, both through the attraction of casinos as in Sun City (known locally as Sin City) in Bophuthatswana, where Frank Sinatra performed in September 1981, and through reinforcing their power structures.

A powerful argument being put forward by some Afrikaner as well as other observers is that survival rather than apartheid or separate development is and has always been the dominant ethic of Afrikanerdom. This may well be the ultimate touchstone for constitutional and other changes. It may also explain the massive if largely unpublicized increase in the number of Africans being resettled in the homelands, often in remote and seldom visited areas.

At this point, it is still difficult to choose between these two interpretations of the likely evolution of Afrikaner policies. The African and, indeed, black role in influencing the decisions on direction, whether through violence or, less likely, negotiations, is no less difficult to predict. What is obvious, however, is that the difference between the potential effect of the two different lines of development foreseen by different observers—manipulation to achieve changes that will reduce strains and move the country toward a gradual reduction of racial barriers, or increased rigidities of an authoritarian type—is of great importance to the West. It is not its responsibility to prescribe a new constitutional dispensation for South Africa. What it should do is to press the South African government to open channels of communication with the black majority that have long been kept closed, and to identify itself openly with the objective of a peaceful transition in South Africa to majority rule with minority rights.

In this situation it is the United States that should take the lead to urge a process of genuine negotiation between representative leaders of both blacks and whites. It seems safe to assume that Britain and other Western European countries would lend their support to any such initiatives with the South African government, as the United States had lent its support to the British in the Rhodesian negotiations for transfer of power in Zimbabwe to majority rule. The United States has a key importance for the South African regime, and should not be hesitant to make use of it for such a purpose. This may well be a long-term process; it is time that it began.

The Africans have tried for many decades to find ways to capitalize on their numbers within South Africa and throughout the continent. They are no longer prepared to depend on peaceful methods to urge fundamental change in the way South Africa is structured. Decisions on the future character of South Africa press ever more urgently upon the whites and particularly on the governing Afrikaners and are of great significance for Southern Africa as a whole. The answer they give may well mean the difference between war and peace in the state that has more to contribute to the African continent than has any other single country, but that still stands as its greatest affront.

5.

Namibia: Impending Independence?

Elizabeth S. Landis and
Michael I. Davis

The situation in Namibia presents itself to the unitiated as one of confusion. The World Court and the United Nations have characterized South Africa's occupation as illegal, but nonetheless, South Africa has maintained an ever-increasing military force and has also mounted attacks on neighboring Angola from Namibian bases. International negotiations and local meetings have been convened and broken off with bewildering frequency. The South West African Peoples' Organization (swAPO), which is recognized by the UN as a representative of the people of Namibia, has been waging a political and military struggle for independence while participating in negotiations as part of this struggle. In 1978, under pressure from the international community, both South Africa and swAPO agreed to a Western-formulated plan to bring Namibia to independence, but South Africa's withdrawal of its agreement in late September again plunged the situation into uncertainty.

The achievement of independence has been complicated by very deep and fundamental differences among all those immediately concerned about Namibia: the Namibians themselves; South Africa, which through its military might and police-state tactics has occupied the Territory in defiance of international law; the OAU, and particularly the African states south of Zaïre; the United Nations, which is the legal administrator of the Territory but which has been unable to eject South Africa; and the Great Powers, whose economic, strategic, and political interests extend to Southern Africa.

In order to understand what underlies the apparent confusion and the influences on the future of the Territory, it is important to visualize the area and to know a little of its relatively short recorded history. The name "Namibia" is said to derive from *Namib*, the Nama word for "shelter." In-

141

deed, for hundreds of years, while Europeans were exploring other parts of Africa, the waterless, uninhabitable Namib Desert, which runs along the entire coast of the Territory, discouraged explorers and settlers from penetrating to its interior.

The German Era

Such isolation could not last forever. At the beginning of the nineteenth century, German missionaries entered the Territory, which was called South West Africa for obvious geographical reasons. Beyond the Namib they found an arid, sparsely populated interior plateau, which was bounded on the east by another desert, the Kalahari.

The Germans must have been struck by the stark and austere beauty of the country, which still moves inhabitants and visitors alike. In the drier south central part of the plateau sheep and goats grazed. (Today the valuable karakul sheep is raised there.) Farther north there were vast herds of carefully tended cattle. All around were the wild animals of the savannah. After a rain, the dry, dusty plains came alive in a carpet of grass and flowers.

The pressure of population, small as it was, was already causing episodic intertribal warfare to control the vast acreage needed for each ruminant. But at a time of relatively plentiful rainfall and little or no disease—disease periodically thinned the herds—the country looked inviting even if it was too dry for grain crops.

The missionaries came with the benevolent intention of bringing the Christian message and European colonialism to the area. Were they to be judged simply by how well they achieved their religious objective—a test that their present-day successors admit is inadequate—they would be considered uniquely successful. The Lutheran missions, along with Roman Catholic, Anglican, and a few others, were so thorough in their self-appointed task that Namibia is today perhaps the country in Africa with the greatest percentage of Christian adherents.

Like missionaries elsewhere, however, they brought in their wake first traders, then settlers, and finally soldiers, administrators, and politicians, most of them Germans belatedly seeking a share of Africa. After the Berlin Conference of 1884–85 set the ground rules for colonial expansion in unclaimed or challenged territories, the German officials in South West Africa promptly induced or forced most of the tribes in the Territory to sign protection treaties. On that basis the Imperial German Reich proclaimed a protectorate over the entire area except "the Port and Settlement of Walfish [whale] Bay." (That enclave of 434 square miles had been claimed by Britain some ten years before.)

There followed a systematic looting of the local Africans. By the end of the century German traders and settlers had seized by legal trickery, guile, or force much of the best land and the cattle. In desperation, first the Hereros and then the Namas rose in rebellion against the government. But, fighting separately, they were defeated by superior weapons and organization and by Teutonic ruthlessness. The Hereros were literally decimated under an extermination order issued by the German command. The Namas were ruined because they had to forfeit all their cattle; landless and broken, they were reduced to acting as herdsmen for the very whites who had seized their traditional lands and their animals.

The Germans established their control over the entire Territory except the sector north of the "Red Line," which marked the limit of the area believed fit for white settlement. Within the "Police Zone" to the south of the Red Line they were unquestioned masters and treated the Africans as subhuman. They made only a partial exception for the Rehoboth Basters, a community of persons of part-white ancestry who had migrated from the Cape in mid-century; the German representatives signed a treaty with their leaders which gave that community substantial autonomy in their own area under the laws they had brought with them. However, Africans in the Territory were kept in economic and political subservience.

The Mandate Era

When the South Africans invaded the Territory in 1915 as their contribution to the Allied war effort, they were seen as presaging a better dispensation by the Africans. Their reputation was enhanced by the official Blue Book published in 1918, which documented German atrocities during the protectorate period.

The Union expected to take over Namibia at the war's end. But in the name of a peace without annexations, and under the mandatory concept devised by General Jan Christiaan Smuts of South Africa, President Wilson prevented South Africa from absorbing the Territory as a fifth province. Instead, the newly created League of Nations entrusted Namibia to South Africa as a mandate for the latter to "promote to the utmost the material and moral welfare and the social progress" of the Territory's inhabitants. The closest analogy is a court's entrusting the care of an orphan to a guardian. South Africa was allowed to administer and legislate for the former protectorate as if it were an integral part of its own territory.

It was clear almost from the start that South Africa had no intention of treating its mandated territory as "a sacred trust of civilization" (President Wilson's term), except as and when compelled to by the international community. It regarded the permission to treat Namibia as an integral part of its own territory as a license to establish its system of race discrimination— originally called "segregation," later "apartheid," and ultimately "separate development." Those Africans despoiled by German rapacity did not regain their lost lands or cattle. Instead, they were treated as vagrants and impressed into labor in the mines and on the farms of new South African settlers or of the many Germans who had remained. All other Africans were relegated to inadequate, poor-quality native reserves, and whenever the land-hungry whites desired land in a reserve, the borders were shifted, always to the detriment of the black inhabitants. The Blue Book on German atrocities was soon suppressed—before the South African air force put down a rebellion by a few hundred Bondelswarts Namas armed with knives and clubs by bombing their women and children. The Africans learned that they had exchanged an overseas tyrant for one from next door.

After the Second World War, South Africa was the only mandatory power that refused either to grant independence to its mandated territory or to place it under the somewhat more rigorous trusteeship system of the United Nations. At the first session of the U.N. General Assembly the South African representative sought permission for his country to annex South West Africa, but the General Assembly refused. The Union government thereupon refused to recognize the right of the Assembly, in substitution for the defunct League of Nations, to supervise its administration of Namibia.

The South African government also refused to accept the 1950 Advisory Opinion of the International Court of Justice concerning the legal status of South West Africa. That Opinion had held that the mandate continued to exist even after the dissolution of the League; that the General Assembly had the right to supervise South Africa's administration of its mandate; and that South Africa could not unilaterally change the mandate's status by annexing it without Assembly approval.[1]

The Union government was, however, unmoved and soon began to intensify the existing segregation system by applying the new and more rigorous doctrine of apartheid to the territory. It extended to Namibia many new laws mandating discrimination, either directly or through similar legislation enacted by the all-white territorial Legislative Assembly. The new South African laws were more extensive and ideological than those already existing and left little or nothing to more flexible local practice.

As one facet of extending apartheid to the Territory, South Africa had introduced the pass system, long functioning within the Union itself. The pass laws require Africans, but not whites, to carry on their persons and to produce on official demand numerous passes, i.e., permits, certificates, receipts, etc. Failure to produce them is punished by a fine or imprisonment. Pass laws function to prevent or restrict the movement of Africans, who may not leave their reserves or areas of employment without an appropriate pass. They have served at least three major purposes: to compel Africans to take particular jobs in particular areas only; to operate as "influx control" measures, to prevent unwanted Africans (wives, children, the elderly, and the incompetent) from entering or remaining in the white urban center; and to facilitate political control by limiting African movement and contact. The effect has been to keep Africans a source of cheap regimented labor.

Along with the pass laws, the government expanded the contract labor system. Under this system Africans from the north were recruited by white employers' organizations, which were later consolidated into the South West Africa Native Labourers Association (SWANLA), for work on the farms and in the mines of the Police Zone. Africans had no choice as to the kind of work or even as to their employers. They were involuntarily separated from their families, who were prevented by the pass laws from accompanying them for the duration of the contract (a year or more). They were subject to imprisonment if they left their jobs, regardless of the justification. Nevertheless, poverty drove them to the recruiters; and if it did not, their chiefs or headmen might deliver them anyway to fulfill their quotas. Namibians were also recruited to work in South Africa's own gold mining industry.

South Africa also undermined, if it did not alter, the international status of the Territory by having white representatives of the Territory in the South African Parliament and by making *all* Namibians involuntary South African citizens.

For over a decade the United Nations tried to reach some accommodation with the Union, alternately employing criticism, cajolery, and mediation, but in vain. Finally, in 1960 Ethiopia and Liberia brought a proceeding against South Africa in the World Court under an untried provision of the mandate agreement that provided for a binding judgment. After six years of arguments and one interim decision, the court eventually concluded that the two complainants had no status to bring the proceeding. It therefore refused to rule on the issue, leaving unanswered the basic legal question: whether South Africa was maladministering the Territory in violation of its obligations under the mandate agreement.

Post-Mandate Era

After years of being warned against taking any action that would prejudice judicial consideration of the *South-West Africa Cases,* the General Assembly was outraged by the court's ultimate nondecision. By 114 votes to 2 (South Africa and Portugal) and with the United States voting affirmatively, the Assembly on October 27, 1966, adopted resolution 2145 (XXI) (1966), which revoked South Africa's mandate on the political ground that by its maladministration of the Territory, the Republic had repudiated the mandate agreement. The Assembly also resolved to take over the administration of South West Africa until it should attain independence. A few months later it established an eleven-member Council for South West Africa to act on its behalf, and in 1968 it changed the name of the Territory from South West Africa to Namibia.

Resolution 2145 established the unique international legal status of Namibia. By removing the Territory from South African jurisdiction, the resolution automatically converted South Africa's presence in the Territory from a legal *administration* into an illegal *occupation*. It made the Territory the direct responsibility of the international community, which was legally obligated to bring the Territory to independence and self-determination. South Africa thus became a foreign state vis-à-vis Namibia.

South Africa has been occasionally referred to as the 'de facto administration (or government)" of Namibia. This designation is technically incorrect and misleading if used to indicate that South Africa exercised control there by reason of its superior force. A de facto government, in proper usage, is one that is recognized in international law as having *some* justified claim or right to govern. South Africa lacks *any* such claim or right vis-à-vis Namibia.

On June 21, 1971, the International Court of Justice confirmed this analysis in an Advisory Opinion presented to the Security Council on the "Legal Consequences for States of the Continued Presence of South Africa in Namibia." The court held that South Africa was obligated to withdraw its administration from the Territory immediately; that United Nations members should recognize the illegality of the South African presence in Namibia and the invalidity of its acts on behalf of or concerning Namibia; and that they should refrain from any acts implying recognition of the legality of the South African presence or giving support or assistance to that presence.

Not surprisingly, South Africa, which had defied the United Nations for the two decades before revocation of the mandate, refused to yield to the international community thereafter. On the contrary, it began to put into effect a plan, published in 1964 during the long Ethiopian-Liberian proceedings in the World Court, for a complete reorganization of the administration of the Territory.

Implementing the Odendaal Plan

The Odendaal Plan—named for F. H. Odendaal, the head of the commission that drafted it—consisted of two parts: the first part completely revised the legislative, administrative, and financial relations between the Territory and the Republic, greatly reducing local, white autonomy and binding Namibia far more closely than before to South Africa. The second part established a Bantustan system within the Territory very much like that evolving in the Republic (see South Africa chapter 4). The first part of the

Odendaal Plan was implemented primarily under the South West Africa
Affairs Act of 1969, which rewrote certain key provisions of the South West
Africa constitution.

The original contitution, granted by the South African Parliament in
1925, had created an all-white territorial Legislative Assembly elected by
universal adult all-white suffrage. The Assembly had broad legislative authority, effectively limited, however, to whites and the "white area" of the
Territory. In 1954 Africans in the reserves were placed under the jurisdiction
of the South African Ministry of Native Affairs (later Bantu Administration
and Development). Subject to veto by the governor-general (later the state
president), the Assembly could legislate on all matters of territorial concern,
with the exception of those in which the Republic insisted on identical laws,
such as "native affairs," courts, police, defense, immigration, and currency.

The 1969 Act amended the constitution by returning to the South African
government both legislative and administrative authority over virtually all
subjects previously under territorial control. It left only those of purely
limited, local concern. The Legislative Assembly and Territorial Administration were effectively reduced to the status of the four South African
provincial governments. As a consequence of this change, there was a great
increase in the next few years in the amount of South African legislation
extended to Namibia or applied in the Territory by executive proclamations
issued under a special provision of the 1969 Act.

In addition many sources of territorial revenue—in particular the corporate
income tax on foreign, including American, as well as South African firms
doing business in Namibia—were taken from the Territory and allocated
to Pretoria. This was done ostensibly to compensate the South African government for performing the many functions the territorial government had
performed before 1969; but the effect was to integrate Namibia with the
Republic economically, as well as legislatively and administratively.

The second part of the Odendaal Plan was implemented by the Native
Nations Act of 1968. This Act provided for the allocation of parts of the
territory as ethnic "homelands" to nine separate African groups and to the
Rehoboth Basters. These homelands were alleged to represent, with certain
modifications, the ancestral lands of those groups. Only the territorial Coloureds, who are of mixed racial descent, can claim no ancestral lands, in
the South African view; and for that reason they were allocated no homeland, but continue to be scattered in urban and rural ghettos.

All the land not assigned to the Africans or Basters was considered to
constitute the "white area." The 100,000 whites, who constitute some 10
percent of the total population, hold about 60 percent of the Territory's land
surface, while the remaining 40 percent of the land is divided among the
black 90 percent of the population. The white area contains most of the best
farming land, all of the urban centers, most of the known significant mineral

deposits, the entire seacoast (with all its alluvial diamonds), and most of the Territory's economic infrastructure, such as roads, railroads, airports, electric lines, and boreholes. Black homelands are overcrowded, overgrazed, underdeveloped, lacking in basic amenities, and, in some cases, waterless or with soils lacking in the chemicals needed to raise healthy animals.

The ostensible purpose of the Act was to allow each ethnic group ("people" or "nation") to develop separately, according to its own culture and genius. The decision as to which persons constituted a separate nation was made by South Africa, which also decided where each homeland was to be located. Thus, all whites, regardless of linguistic, cultural, and political differences, are considered to constitute one people; but, as designated in the Odendaal Plan, there are nine African peoples, including one referred to as "Tswana and other."

In theory, each homeland was to be uni-ethnic. In fact, the extensive population transfers that would be involved in some areas to limit the inhabitants to one group have prevented full application of the theory in some of the black homelands in the Police Zone. However, the government's stated intention was clear: that each people should advance according to the South African government's view of its desires and capabilities, from simple tribal structure through regional "authorities" to lesser, then greater "self-government," and possibly eventually to "independence." To facilitate this development only members of the ethnic group for which a particular homeland had been established could be citizens of the homeland and enjoy citizenship rights there.

The unstated but sinister intention of the government was to apply a more sophisticated version of the basic colonial strategy of "divide and rule." By isolating African groups from one another and by restricting common endeavors, the Republic was seeking to divert their common hostility from itself and refracting it among the blacks. In particular, the South Africans combined this strategy with a constant barrage of propaganda about the "Ovambo menace." The Ovambos, who represent some 40 to 50 percent of the total black population, have for years been accused by the whites of seeking to take over the Territory and dominate all the other blacks, a fate which they have endeavored to make sound far worse than the oppression by the white minority. Government propaganda has been aimed at linking the "Ovambo menace" with SWAPO, which had its start as an association with a primary Ovambo base before it became a national organization opposed to any ethnic orientation.

The effect of the law was, for all practical purposes, to strip the Africans of their common Namibian citizenship. It transformed them into rightless aliens in the white area, where, given the economic realities of the Territory, the jobs existed. While whites are theoretically aliens in all the homelands, the fact is that whites are never without rights anywhere in Namibia. In any case, virtually the only whites who had reason to go to the homelands were government officials or wealthy businessmen or tourists, who were protected by South African military and police power.

"Terrorism"

By the late sixties the full scope of Odendaal-style apartheid, by then called "separate development," and South Africa's ruthless enforcement of its repressive laws had become clearly apparent. At that point the fledgling black political movements faced a major political, practical, and philosophical decision: whether to resort to armed struggle or to limit themselves to exclusively nonviolent means. SWAPO opted for armed struggle; the others were against it.

The possibilities for successful armed struggle seemed very limited when SWAPO took that fateful decision; Portugal still controlled Angola, and the struggle for independence there seemed to be facing a long and bitter future. Nevertheless, it was possible for SWAPO to infiltrate across the Angola border into Ovamboland, since by reason of ethnic origin SWAPO had strong sympathy among the Ovambos, who straddled the border. Infiltration of the Eastern Caprivi Strip from Zambia was also possible despite the fact that Eastern Caprivi, which had been administered as part of South Africa's Transvaal province since 1939, was protected by a major air base near Katima Mulilo. The western portion of the Strip, a boggy, nearly impassable area with much close vegetation, was ideal for guerrilla movement but contained no significant targets.

The first guerrilla activities ended with the capture of a number of the inexperienced freedom fighters and the roundup of hundreds of Africans believed to support them. Although there was no law authorizing the action, many were detained incommunicado for periods of up to several years and tortured during their detention. Eventually several were brought to trial in South Africa, not Namibia, under the Terrorism Act. This law, enacted by the South African Parliament in 1967, was made retroactive to 1962 in order to convict many of the detainees against whom no existing statutory or common-law crime could be proved.

The Terrorism Act created a crime of "terrorism" so broad that virtually any political or social act falls within the definition. Such normally innocent behavior as cooperating with UNICEF to reduce infant mortality, undertaking an advertising campaign to secure an increased share of the detergent market, or revealing misconduct by a state official can be so construed. Under its provisions accused persons are presumed guilty and required to prove their innocence beyond a reasonable doubt. Section 6 of the Act permitted indefinite detention incommunicado of persons for interrogation, and it denied them the right to habeas corpus. Under the authority of that section government ministers have refused, on the grounds of state security, to give any information whatsoever about detainees—even their names—to inquiring families or even to members of the South African Parliament. One much-criticized provision permitted the retrial of persons already acquitted of an offense under the Act, while another permitted joint trials of persons accused of different crimes under the same Act. The same section authorized the trial in any place in the Republic or Territory of persons accused of terrorism, regardless of where the alleged crime was committed.

Although the Act defined the crime of terrorism broadly enough to cover virtually the entire range of social conduct, by and large only selected political dissidents have been *tried* under it, although thousands have been *detained* under section 6 and threatened with trial. The first prosecution, against Eliasar Tuhadeleni and thirty-six other Namibians was a "show" trial; it was designed to intimidate Namibian nationalists and to persuade whites that guerrilla activity on the border required further and more repressive action and legislation. While the failure of the first SWAPO guerrilla incursions did not—as South Africa confidently expected—put an end to such action, it did compel a period of consolidation and reevaluation of strategy.

The Advisory Opinion

At the same time the momentum that had been generated at the United Nations by the revocation of the mandate was also halted. Although most countries wanted some quick and effective follow-up on resolution 2145, the Western Powers insisted that, given the new situation, negotiations with South Africa should precede any other action. Ultimately numbers prevailed in the Assembly, and the Council for Namibia was created in a special session in the spring of 1967. But no Western country accepted membership during its first years, thereby denying the Council the political effectiveness and prestige that their participation could have assured.

The position of the United States, which had actively supported resolution 2145, was particularly resented by the Africans as hypocritical. Its delegate argued that the Council was a futile organization because it could not operate inside Namibia, and futile activities would only lower the prestige and credibility of the United Nations as a whole. This argument ignored the Third World position that the American failure to join the Council was a primary source of its impotence. In a related argument the United States justified repeated refusal to cooperate with the Council on the grounds that the related resolution 2248 directed that body to proceed to Namibia and to administer the Territory there, and that therefore actions taken by the Council from New York were technically not within its power.

As post-revocation doldrums set in, the General Assembly appealed to the Security Council for assistance. But Britain and France, two of the permanent members, still questioned the validity of resolution 2145, and the other members were unwilling to support any steps involving compulsion. So the Council, as a means of temporizing, decided to seek the advice of the International Court of Justice on the obligations of U.N. members in relation to Namibia.

It was at this point, in 1971, that the court specifically upheld the validity of the resolution, advised that South Africa should end its occupation of Namibia forthwith, and informed the Council that other states should refuse to assist the Republic to remain in Namibia or to recognize any action taken by the Republic on behalf of Namibia.

The Role of the Mission Churches

The court's opinion was quickly made known throughout the Territory and was greeted enthusiastically by the Africans. Shortly thereafter bishops Leonard Auala and Lukas de Vries of the Lutheran Mission Church addressed an open letter to Prime Minister Vorster. Taking a purely pastoral position, they asked for an end to discrimination, pass laws, and the contract-labor system as the sources of poverty, marital instability, and general social disorganization among the Territory's inhabitants.

The bishops' letter reflected the growing involvement of the mission churches—primarily Anglican (Episcopal) and Lutheran—in the Africans' political and social problems. White pastors, teachers, and doctors in Namibia were excluded from the territorial "establishment," for, unlike the local whites, the missionaries lived among the Africans. Lacking preconceptions as to color-based abilities or proprieties, they quickly and sympathetically responded to the moral and material problems of their parishioners, most of which seemed to originate in the political system imposed upon them.

The Africans, in turn, rallied to the sympathetic church, which provided assistance, education, doctoring, and a vision of a new and better way of life. In the church they were introduced to the concept of wider communities— African, Namibian, and Christian—and, more concretely, they met their contemporaries and coreligionists from other parts of the Territory and developed friendships and common interests across ethnic lines. It is not surprising, therefore, that the liberation movement has for years numbered among its most influential members black pastors and lay persons, as well as African mission teachers, nurses, and students. Nor is it surprising, given these facts, that three Anglican bishops and innumerable missionaries of both churches have been expelled from the Territory, and that dozens of other missionaries have been denied visas to enter Namibia. Afrikaner officials in the Territory have been particularly hostile to mission education in English, which they commonly believe to be the language of subversion.

The General Strike

At the end of the same year, 1971, the Africans began a general strike against low wages, the pass laws, the labor system, and the separation of workers from their families. The strike was a remarkable tribute to the organizing ability and cohesion of the black workers. Despite the lack of any formal labor movement and the prevailing restrictions of the pass laws and other prescriptions, it was effective throughout the territory. Offered their choice between returning to work or being sent home, they chose the latter. From all over the country—the mines, the farms, and the towns—Africans streamed back to their homes. Because the rains had been adequate, and newly harvested crops were relatively plentiful, there was no immediate pressure to return to work. Consequently, the stoppage, which had a devastating economic impact, lasted well into the spring of 1972.

In Ovamboland the restless strikers streamed across the frontier, tore down the border fences, and vented their wrath against some unpopular homeland officials. Without consulting Parliament, which was then in session, the South African government issued a proclamation (No. R 17 of 1972) which established quasi-martial law in Ovamboland. It prohibited entering or leaving the area except by special permit; banned all meetings except church ceremonies, sporting events, and local assemblies; permitted indefinite detention incommunicado; and made it a serious crime to make "subversive statements" or to treat a chief with "disrespect, contempt, or ridicule."

As soon as the proclamation was issued, journalists and other observers were banned from Ovamboland and were seldom allowed in thereafter, except on a limited or official-tour basis. South African police then freely rounded up hundreds of strikers, SWAPO members and others believed to sympathize with them. They were detained in special camps, most of them tortured, and many executed. It was a method of control to which South Africa would revert more frequently and more ruthlessly in succeeding years.

Meanwhile, every effort was being made to end the strike and, even more important, to convince the world that it had ended and that Namibia still remained a good place for foreign investment. When it was determined that the strike could not be broken by imported labor, a conference of employer representatives, South African representatives, and Ovambo and Kavango officials was held at Grootfontein. It excluded representatives of the workers and of SWAPO, which had obviously played a role in the strike. A settlement was announced at the end of the meeting; but it was another month or more before industry was operating normally again, and far longer before sporadic walkout and wildcat strikes ceased.

The "settlement" claimed to end the contract-labor system. In fact, however, it modified the system cosmetically but maintained its essentials:

SWANLA, the employers' association, was abolished, but labor recruitment in the homelands was not; it was carried out (for the first time among the Namas as well as in the north) through labor officers in the homelands —a change that substituted corruptible local individuals for the impersonal cruelty of a large organization. A worker could no longer be assigned to a particular employer against his will, but the operation of the pass laws and of the newly established labor bureaus achieved substantially the same results. The law that made it a prison offense for an African to breach his labor contract was repealed; but the requirements for official permission to leave before the end of the contract period were almost impossible to fulfill, and the administrative penalties for quitting without permission were only marginally less severe than the former criminal penalties. Although promises were made to allow at least some families to accompany their breadwinners to the mining centers, they were never carried out, ostensibly due to objections by homeland authorities.

Ovamboland Elections

With the restoration of an uneasy calm in 1973, Pretoria decided to impose slightly more "self-government" on the Ovambo (renamed "Owambo") and Kavango homelands by providing for election of some members of the homeland legislative councils. These councils were empowered by the Native Nations Act to enact ordinances on some matters of local concern and application. In a challenge to both South African and homeland authorities, SWAPO called for a boycott of the elections in Ovamboland. It also held rallies to support the boycott, in violation of the continuing ban on meetings.

Against these SWAPO actions the South African police also employed a new tactic. They arrested anyone believed connected with the movement and turned over such persons to the local Ovambo chiefs to be punished for that "offense." The chiefs, resurrecting a tribal "tradition" unknown to other Ovambos, sentenced the alleged "offenders," usually without even the pretense of a trial, to public floggings. Old and young, male and female, church deacons and student nurses were stripped and whipped in public, many until they lost consciousness.

The Lutheran and Anglican bishops, on behalf of their coreligionists and a victim of the floggings, joined in seeking an injunction against this practice. Their plea was refused by the local courts, thereby giving new life to the tradition, but it was finally granted on appeal by South Africa's highest court.

Despite this cruel use of local chiefs as South African surrogates, a tactic previously developed extensively in South Africa itself, the Ovambos were not intimidated, and the boycott was fully effective. Less than three percent of the eligible voters went to the polls—a number that hardly exceeded the roll of office-holders and their families and retainers. By way of contrast, in the neighboring Kavango homeland, where SWAPO did not mount a boycott campaign, a majority of the Africans voted.

In the period that followed, South Africa worked to undo the political damage done by the boycott. It set out to break SWAPO within the Territory, first by the floggings, then by mass arrests and political trials for offenses ranging from pass-law violations to sabotage. At one point the entire internal SWAPO leadership was either banned or detained in prison under the Terrorism Act. At the same time soldiers were sent to Ovamboland and began a new course of intimidation and violence that sent thousands of Namibians fleeing across the border.

When this program was well under way, the Ovambo authorities requested South Africa to promote their homeland to the highest level of "self-government." Pretoria promptly acceded to their wishes and, in connection with this change, scheduled new elections at the beginning of 1975 for members of the enlarged legislative council.

SWAPO was unable to mount another effective boycott campaign. According to South African figures, somewhat more than half the eligible population went to the polls. After the election new and released SWAPO leaders complained that the Ovambos had been dragooned into voting, some by sheer force and others by threats and intimidation, such as the denial of passes, refusal of hospital admissions, etc., to nonvoters. The International Commission of Jurists, which investigated the elections, graphically reported a classic pattern of force, fraud, and intimidation, nonetheless real because the purpose was to compel the unwilling to vote rather than, as in so many cases, to prevent potential voters from exercising the franchise.

Pro-Liberation Forces 1974–75

As of 1974–75 an altered balance of forces was becoming evident in Namibia, one that presaged either confrontation or some form of accommodation in the not too distant future. Starting soon after the 1971 Advisory Opinion of the World Court, the Africans had shown new militancy and organization within the Territory, as witnessed in the general strike and the boycott of the first Ovamboland election. Even the temporary disruption of SWAPO preceding the 1975 elections had not prevented an obvious increase in SWAPO's support throughout the Territory. A British observer who toured the Territory, including Ovamboland, while the flogging was in progress reported that everywhere the children chanted SWAPO's slogan, "One nation, one Namibia."[2]

At about that time a fragile coalition of virtually all the black political parties and groups in the Territory formed the National Convention (of Namibia). It ultimately broke up, leaving the abbreviated name NCN to the groups that gathered around Chief Clemens Kapuuo, and creating a new Namibian National Convention (NNC), in which SWAPO and SWANU (South West African National Union) were leading members. (Subsequently, a smaller group, originally brought together under the title of the "Okahandja summit," renamed itself the Namibian National Council [also NNC], to add to the alphabetical confusion.)

Outside Namibia SWAPO's quasi-diplomatic representatives at the U.N. and elsewhere were beginning to win increased humanitarian assistance in the West and more military assistance elsewhere. SWAPO was accepted[3] by the OAU and the U.N. as the sole authentic representative of the Namibian people pending independence and elections (although not without objections from other Namibian political groups). It was allowed to participate in U.N. debate (but not to vote) on Namibian issues, and it was brought more closely into the work of the Council for Namibia. The U.N. General Assembly upheld the right of the Namibian people to seek, by whatever means necessary—including force—the liberation of their country.

SWAPO's military arm, PLAN (People's Liberation Army of Namibia), was also becoming more effective. Raids across the border were more frequent and more successful, and the mining of roads used by South African troops also increased. Both civil and military members of the SWAPO command were able to hold an undisturbed week-long conference in the Caprivi Strip while a large part of the South African army and air force searched for them in vain.

At the United Nations also, the naming of a full-time commissioner, Sean MacBride, who had had practical experience in the liberation of his native Ireland, brought a burst of new activity to Namibian issues. Within twelve months the Council for Namibia had created a Namibia Institute in Lusaka. The Institute was designed to engage in fundamental research about the Territory and to prepare untrained Namibians in exile to participate in the administration of a future independent Namibia. The council also adopted a Decree for the Protection of the Natural Resources of Namibia.[4] That decree provided that no one might exploit or export Namibian natural resources without the consent of the council; that mining or exporting concessions or licenses issued to Namibia by South African authorities were invalid; that resources removed from Namibia without Council consent could be seized and forfeited on behalf of the Council for the benefit of the Namibian people; and that anyone contravening the decree might be held liable in damages by a future government of an independent Namibia. No proceeding has yet been brought under the decree; but it already appears to have had some influence on speculative investment in the Territory and on insurance and shipping of Namibian products.

Anti-Liberation Forces

On the other hand, as long as the Portuguese held on in Angola and Mozambique, South Africa appeared to have a sound, if not wholly comfortable, position politically, economically, and militarily both in Namibia and at home.

Changes proposed in the Odendaal Plan were being carried out relatively smoothly, despite considerable temporary embarrassment caused by the general strike and again by the boycott of the 1973 Ovambo election. The northern homelands (except the Kaokoveld, a poor and sparsely populated area) were being marched steadily along the "self-government" path. The chiefs and homeland officials, along with their dependents and retainers, were developing into a sizable group whose fortunes and futures were tied into the success of the divisive South African separate-development policy. South Africa appeared to envisage the possible outcome of a cluster of weak "independent" client states in Namibia. In the case of the Ovambos, who are also settled over a considerable area in southern Angola, a rash of irredentist statements led some observers to believe that a "greater Ovambo" encompassing the groups on both sides of the border was a feasible political possibility.

At home South Africa had begun to break out of the political isolation to which its apartheid policies and its unlawful occupation of Namibia had consigned it. Its policy of black-white détente in Africa was beginning to bring the more conservative African states into a sympathetic, potentially semi-client relationship. The generous economic assistance that bought quasi-clandestine support by some African states was, by South African standards, money well spent.

So was the increasing amount spent on propaganda and public relations in the United States and Europe. Perhaps as a consequence, the United States' position, announced in 1970—that American investment in Namibia should be discouraged—never advanced beyond the formal-letter-to-potential-investors stage. Certainly, it remained a secret from other government departments in Washington. And State Department representatives, although having no positive alternative suggestions to offer, continued to oppose United States participation in the U.N. Council for Namibia.

South Africa was also successfully implementing the Odendaal Plan in the economic sphere. It liberalized territorial policy in order to attract additional investment capital; hastened the development of the Cunene River project, which would supply electric power to the major mining and industrial centers of Namibia; and undertook to involve the power-hungry West and Japan in the development of uranium deposits found at Rossing, a short distance north of Walvis Bay. In addition, the price of gold was skyrocketing, and every increase strengthened South Africa's overall position.

Militarily, South Africa had begun in the late fifties or early sixties to fortify the Territory in defiance of the express prohibition in its mandate agreement. A major naval base was established at Walvis Bay, backed by an air force base a few miles away in the desert, and now tied by advanced electronic communications into South Africa's main naval base at Simonstown, in the Cape. An air-army base was built at Katima Mulilo in the Eastern Caprivi Strip, with another major airfield nearby. A major army base was also constructed at Grootfontein, close to the valuable copper mines at Tsumeb and not far from the border separating the Kavango and Ovambo homelands. All these facilities were greatly expanded over the years. In addition other lesser bases, connecting roads, military airfields, and airstrips were added until in 1976 it was calculated that there were at least ten major and fifteen secondary military bases in Namibia.

The Impact of the Portuguese Coup

The Portuguese coup affected the psychological and political balance of forces in Southern Africa long before the decolonization of Luso-Africa was in fact accomplished. It utterly undermined the basic American premise shaped by the option selected in the 1969 National Security Study Memorandum on Southern Africa that had argued that Africans could not change their condition in Southern Africa by their own efforts. Thus it assumed that, except as the outside world could convince the ruling white minorities in Southern Africa to change their ways, blacks would always have to be satisfied with handouts. Therefore, American policy should aim at increasing the handouts rather than pressing for basic change.

The basic South African premise that the Republic would be protected by the Portuguese from large-scale contact with black liberation forces was also shattered. Not only was the Portuguese buffer crumbling; white-ruled Rhodesia, which had constituted an additional barrier to black advances (thanks in part to South African undermining of sanctions and limited military assistance) was also, and immediately, endangered.

On the other hand, Africans were finally able to confirm, by their brothers' experience, that the whites of Southern Africa were not invincible. The planned African celebrations in honor of Frelimo and Mozambican independence and subsequent violent confrontations between white police and black demonstrators in South Africa reflected a new attitude on the part of Africans toward themselves, their white bosses, and their ability to determine their own future.

Even before the final form of the Portuguese African settlement was entirely clear, Pretoria had recognized the need for at least outward accommodation with the forces of change. Thus, in the fall of 1974 Prime Minister Vorster began to suggest that change was in the offing for Namibia; and he referred, somewhat vaguely, to a six-month interval for achieving it.

In December the U.N. Security Council took him at his word. In resolution 366 the Council gave South Africa until May 31 to make a solemn declaration that it would terminate its unlawful occupation. The resolution also required the Republic to take certain specific steps—releasing political prisoners, repealing apartheid legislation, etc.—toward that end. In particular it required the holding of territory-wide elections, under U.N. supervision and control, for delegates to a constituent assembly that would draft a constitution for a free Namibia.

During the spring of 1975 South Africa leaked word that the government had taken a first step toward change by repealing the pass laws and ending segregation of certain public facilities.

The vaunted changes turned out to be meaningless. Obsolete pass laws no longer used were repealed, but modern laws were retained. Optional desegregation of cafes, restaurants, and hotels was finally adopted with continued misgivings months after announcement. But general segregation was hardly affected: late in 1976 a theater where a Christmas concert was being given was still closed to blacks, and swimming pools were shut down rather than opened to all races.

As the end of May approached without the required declaration by South Africa, the African states decided to back an uncompromisingly tough line in the Security Council. They presented a draft resolution calling for an arms embargo against South Africa. When the draft gained the necessary nine votes for adoption, France, Britain, and the United States cast a triple veto. Since there was no backup draft resolution, the Council session closed without acting on South Africa's failure to comply with resolution 366. However, the speeches of the representatives of the three Western countries were read, signaling the Republic that they would not continue to protect it indefinitely from similar attacks if it did not move on Namibia.

The Turnhalle Conference

At the same time that Prime Minister Vorster asked for six months, he also made an obscure reference to some future time when South Africa would step aside to let Namibians govern themselves. Shortly thereafter the territorial leader of the National Party, apparently under pressure from Pretoria, announced a vague proposal to hold a constitutional conference to determine the future of "South West Africa."

The proposal, which progressed very slowly through party congresses and the otherwise defunct multiracial territorial Advisory Council, surfaced again in concrete form after the triple veto. By September 1, 1975, the conference was called into session in a converted gymnasium (*Turnhalle* in German, hence the popular name of the conference) in Windhoek.

According to the convenor, the conference was designed to represent all the "peoples" of Namibia. *Peoples* spelled with an "s" is a code word in Southern Africa indicating that the persons involved are considered only as members of ethnic ("tribal") groups and not as individuals. This restriction automatically excluded SWAPO and SWANU from representation unless they were willing—as of course they were not—to seek selection as delegates of a particular ethnic group.

Not only were the Namibians to be represented tribally whether or not they believed in the ethnic approach, but they were also to be represented at the conference whether or not they wanted to be represented at all. Thus, when the Damara Advisory Council and the Damara Tribal Executive at the behest of their people refused to participate, twenty-six hitherto unheard-of "Damara leaders" were recruited by the Damara United Front (itself a new organization allegedly created by the South African secret police) to represent the homeland at Turnhalle.

Most of the black delegates were chiefs or notables on the public payroll; some were teachers or civil servants also dependent on the government. Many were unable to adequately understand or speak Afrikaans, the working language of the conference, and required interpreters. None had had any sophisticated parliamentary experience, and few had dealt with whites in other than a subordinate-superior relationship.

The size of the delegations varied greatly but had no necessary relationship to tribal population; and the manner of the delegates' selection, when known, varied from one homeland to another. The largest delegation, numbering forty-four, represented the Hereros and the closely related Kaokovelders, who together constituted less than 8 percent of the Territory's total population; these delegates were chosen by the homeland authorities entirely from one of two groups competing for the chieftaincy of the Hereros. The Namas, who quarreled bitterly over alleged South African interference in the selection process, sent a delegation of twenty-six. Ovamboland, with some 40 percent of the Territory's population, sent a delegation composed of fifteen members of its legislative council; and the Rehoboth Basters and Coloureds sent slightly smaller delegations reflecting the results of recent communal elections. The Kavango and East Caprivi homelands were represented by a handful of members of their legislative councils, and the Tswana and Bushmen had the smallest delegations of all, chosen in an unknown manner. The whites, who started with only two delegates, both members of the territorial Legislative Assembly, ultimately included the whole assembly membership in their delegation.

Of the more than one hundred and fifty members, only a few became household names. Among the whites were Dirk Mudge, chairman of the conference constitutional committee; Eben van Zijl, a hardline *verkrampte;* and A. H. du Plessis, official head of the enlarged delegation. Among the blacks were the "autocratic" Dr. B. J. Africa of the Rehoboth Basters; A. J. F. Kloppers, a skilled politician from the Coloured community; Chief Clemens Kapuuo of the Hereros, head of NCN and of NUDO (the National Unity Democratic Organization, a once revolutionary party that had become largely a mouthpiece of the Herero Chief's council); and Pastor Cornelius Ndjoba, prime minister of Ovamboland.

Chief Kapuuo created a stir when he brought a white American lawyer, Stewart Schwartz, described as a constitutional expert, to the conference. But after some wrangling the lawyer was allowed to attend the sessions. After observing Chief Kapuuo, a number of the other black groups indicated that they too would like legal advice. Rather than face the risk that unknown and aggressive counsel might be chosen by any of them, conference officials arranged to supply counsel to any group that requested it. These lawyers, who were paid by the South African government indirectly through the homeland authorities, were all South Africans; most of them had previously represented their government against Namibia's interests before the World Court. Only the Chief's lawyers—the full complement of the team included a senior partner of the American lawyer, a Namibian junior counsel, and a London barrister—were not subsidized directly or indirectly by South Africa, according to their testimony before Congressman Fraser's Congressional subcommittee; they declared that the Chief or his party, NUDO, had available small "private contributions."

The first session of the conference adjourned less than two weeks after it opened. It produced a Declaration of Intent which urged that a constitution be drawn up within three years. But it was important primarily for its clear and unequivocal rejection of force to obtain independence or change.

It was not clear what the South Africans expected to emerge from the Turnhalle conference, probably some kind of loose, confederal system of semi-autonomous client states. Presumably such an arrangement would have protected the whites against any major change. In any case Pretoria must have been prepared to let the conference atrophy if external pressure eased.

South Africa itself, however, ensured that the external pressure would increase, rather than decrease, by intervening in the Angolan civil war. Crossing the border in August 1975, ostensibly to protect the Ruacana dam on the Cunene, it quickly converted that limited action into a major invasion with what it subsequently intimated was the implied, if not the express, blessing of the United States. In attempting to wipe out the MPLA and radical nationalism, it made common cause with UNITA, which had joined FNLA against MPLA in a two-front war for the control of Angola. The strike at MPLA in collaboration with UNITA enabled the South Africans at the same time to destroy many of the SWAPO guerrilla bases in southern Angola; SWAPO soldiers had previously shared certain UNITA bases, and UNITA was now willing to point out those bases in exchange for South African assistance against MPLA.

There were two major flaws in this military stroke: the MPLA was able, with outside help, to defeat both Angolan opponents; and the American Congress prohibited United States intervention in Angola. South Africa suffered a major military defeat when the troops it was using became bogged down in central Angola; in danger of being wiped out, they had to retire to Namibia, suffering considerable losses (see Angola chapter).

In January 1976, when information about South Africa's role in Angola was becoming clearer, the Security Council again took up the subject of Namibia. International outrage led to a new resolution, numbered 385, which was similar in content to resolution 366. The new resolution gave the Republic until the end of August 1976 to start its withdrawal from the Territory.

The South African military humiliation, combined with the unanimous adoption of resolution 385, put pressure on the Turnhalle conference to end its procrastination and produce positive results before the new deadline. A constitutional committee of thirty-six members representing all the population groups was established under the chairmanship of Dirk Mudge. It began to work on plans for a limited-power interim government, as well as on longer-range plans that alternatively or together might satisfy the Security Council.

With tight time-constraints, punctuated by sharp public criticisms and temporary walkouts, the committee finally produced a short statement of principles on August 18, 1976. It was described in the media as a "promise" of independence for the Territory by December 31, 1978, and a unitary state. The latter "promise" ostensibly complied with repeated General Assembly and Security Council demands that South Africa preserve the national unity and territorial integrity of Namibia. In fact, of course, the statement did not constitute a promise or agreement of any sort whatsoever. It was at best a statement of the wishes and hopes of one committee, which had not even been approved by the conference plenary. The South African government, which *officially* had no role in any of the discussions—whatever its role behind the scenes—was not bound by statements of the committee or even by decisions of a plenary session of the conference. It was noticeable that when the statement of August 18 was presented by the South African ambassador to the secretary-general of the United Nations, it did not carry any South African approval or endorsement of its conclusions.

A close reading of the committee statement, in fact, made it clear that independence would have to wait on an agreement on constitutional principles; the drafting of a constitution based on those principles; successful negotiations with South Africa on that constitution and a vast number of difficult issues (such as financial matters, the future of Walvis Bay, the division of property, the protection of South African property, etc.); and selection of the government of the future Namibian state.

Further analysis made it clear also that the statement did not promise a unitary state, but merely announced the "desire" of the committee that Namibia be "maintained" as a unitary state. Since Namibia was divided into Bantustans at the time the statement was issued, it was difficult to understand how it could be "maintained" as something which it then was not. Indeed, a new Rehoboth Bantustan was created by Parliament over serious conference objections, and the Namas were advanced toward full Bantustan status, both actions taking place while the Turnhalle conference was in session. Thus it was difficult to understand how Namibia could be "maintained" as a "unitary" state.

Contrary to media headlines, the statement, when read with the evidence— including news stories, conference documents, and the testimony of Chief Kapuuo's lawyers in Washington—suggested quite a different future for Namibia: the continuation of essential, if concealed, South African control of the Territory even after formal "independence"; the continuation of black domination by whites; the continuation of Bantustans; and the continuation of foreign exploitation of Namibia's vast mineral resources without benefit to the general black population. The major differences would be the existence of formal independence and the creation of a government in which a number of blacks would play visible roles.

Continuing white domination of blacks was assured in the first instance by persuading conference members to act by consensus. Since it was the blacks who wished to change the political, economic, and social situation in the Territory, the white delegates held an effective veto over conference proposals. They exercised that power in at least two matters of major importance: by barring integrated education, thus to assure the educational inferiority of succeeding generations of blacks, and by blocking a move to end the contract-labor system, which, over the protests of the blacks, government authorities decided was too efficient to give up. Even when the delegates decided on a territorial minimum wage, the white farmers' organization announced that its members had no intention of raising their black workers' pay to the set minimum.

Continuing white domination had also been assured in the draft constitution, which was proposed by Chief Kapuuo. (Chief Kapuuo was assassinated in early 1978, as mentioned below.) Under the proposed plan Dirk Mudge, the white chairman of the constitutional committee, would be prime minister and would control the government and the administration. In view of the inadequate education of most blacks, it was obvious that few would be able to qualify for positions of any importance. Those who might receive portfolios would undoubtedly operate with a white adviser at their side.

Continuation of the Bantustans was implicit in the August 18 statement; in Chief Kapuuo's draft constitution, which included an elaborate bicameral parliamentary structure representing Ovambos, Kavangos, and East Caprivians in one house and the rest of the Territory in the other; and in a subsequent three-paragraph-long committee proposal of September 16. That proposal envisaged a three-tiered government structure, the second level of which would consist of homeland governments.

Moreover, the continuation of foreign exploitation of Namibia's vast, still largely unexplored mineral resources was stated as a primary goal by the Kapuuo lawyers. It is evident that present or potential investors, rather than South African subsidy, were the source of the "private contributions" which the lawyers claimed had enabled Kapuuo to engage expensive legal counsel and public relations firms and to commute frequently to Europe and the United States with his retainers.

SWAPO: Opposing Turnhalle and South Africa

The conference had been harshly criticized because it failed to include SWAPO, which after all had been specifically recognized by the OAU and the U.N. as the authentic representative of the Namibian people. By the spring of 1976 some Turnhalle members were seeking SWAPO participation, although the basis on which it could have participated with ethnic delegations was far from clear. At one point it appeared that the South African government would withdraw its understood objections to such a development; but the failure to issue a formal invitation suggests that it finally held to its original position that it would never deal with SWAPO and particularly its president, Sam Nujoma. In any case it was clear that SWAPO would not have accepted an invitation to participate in the conference.

SWAPO objections to Turnhalle were well worked out. The ethnic basis of the conference was merely the first objection. Equally important was the fact that the conference was powerless to bring about independence or to effect fundamental change, particularly in view of its early decision to eschew the use of force. SWAPO felt, therefore, that the only relevant discussions would be those held with the South Africans, who had the power to grant independence, and not with other Namibians.

Furthermore, any detailed discussions held before independence concerning a post-independence government were bound to be subject to South Africa's constraining influence; conference members would constantly have to consider proposals not on their intrinsic merits but on the basis of whether they would improve or hinder the possibility of obtaining independence. An interim or final government set up under those circumstances was bound to serve South African rather than Namibian interests, and the persons who participated in setting up such a government were at best, in SWAPO's view, oblivious to Namibia's best interests.

Evidence to support SWAPO's objections was not hard to find. Thus, conference delegates meekly accepted data and analyses made by South African or territorial officials on economic and social questions affecting the future of Namibia instead of insisting on studies by their own experts. They also accepted without question the South African position that Walvis Bay, the Territory's only deep-water port and the key to its economic independence, if not survival, was part of South Africa, since it had been included in the Union in 1910 and never formally ceded to South West Africa. In fact, a strong argument can be made that under international law Walvis Bay has become part of Namibia, based on its administration, with South African consent, as part of the Territory since 1922, as well as on modern doctrines of self-determination, the international illegality of apartheid, and economic necessity.

U.N. members also criticized the conference for its advance refusal to hold elections under U.N. supervision and control. The element of "control" in this phrase implied more than mere observation of the conduct of elections. "Control" implied a process lasting a year or more that would ensure free territory-wide elections based on universal suffrage and full participation by all Namibians. It would involve establishing elections districts and voters' rolls; educating illiterate and inexperienced Namibians about the purpose and procedures of elections; supervising campaigning and actual voting and ballot-counting; and dealing effectively on the spot with such irregularities as intimidation or fraud.

Confident of its claim to majority support throughout the territory, SWAPO has been prepared to stand against all other parties in U.N.-supervised and -controlled elections, as called for by General Assembly resolution 2248 (S-V) (1967), to select members of a constituent assembly that would draft a constitution for Namibia.

After winning South African backing for his claim to the Herero chieftaincy, a claim which the government long opposed, Chief Kapuuo echoed Pretoria's line that SWAPO is a Communist (or Marxist) organization, as well as the agent of Ovambo hegemony. In fact, SWAPO has acted as a national movement and produced a draft constitution as a discussion document having strong human rights provisions, which would have precedence over other provisions in case of conflict; and allowed for an optional second house of the proposed legislature to represent chiefs and traditional elements.[5] Its position on foreign investments has not been extreme, considering that Namibia's minerals, which are exploited entirely by foreigners, are its most important source of wealth.

SWAPO has cooperated with the U.N. through years of delay and disappointment. It vainly sought aid from the West for its liberation struggle. It seemed likely, therefore, to become increasingly dependent on the Communist bloc and on radical nationalist states for military equipment if the U.N. could not bring about the peaceful withdrawal of South Africa.

South African propagandists have consistently played down SWAPO support in the Territory despite evidence of its growing strength, particularly among the young. During the second half of 1976 alone, thousands of Rehoboth Basters and Namas merged their own political parties into SWAPO, and a white territorial official admitted that he found more support for SWAPO than for Turnhalle in the Eastern Caprivi. During the same period SWAPO and SWANU inched toward a closer rapprochement than had previously existed.

It has long been recognized that with SWAPO divided among those inside Namibia who could operate legally and those outside (and the latter further divided among members of the guerrilla army), those in SWAPO headquarters in Lusaka, those in refugee camps, and others scattered around the world, some differences in perception were bound to occur. It was inevitable, therefore, that the South African secret police and their allies would try to exploit these differences to destabilize the movement. It is astounding that they had so little success.

The civil war in Angola offered extraordinary opportunities to exploit any serious differences in the organizations. SWAPO leaders in Lusaka were affected by Zambia's strong pro-UNITA stance as well as by the traditional ties of northern Namibians with their Angolan kinsmen in UNITA, whereas SWAPO soldiers at the fluid Namibian front were concerned with the more immediate problems caused by the then generally unrecognized UNITA-South African collaboration. It may be speculated that destabilization tactics operating to take advantage of the conflicting pressures generated in this situation led ultimately to the arrest, detention, and subsequent transfer to Tanzanian detention of about a dozen SWAPO leaders, including Andreas Shipanga (then minister of information), Solomon Mifima (secretary for labor), and Shangula Sheeli (secretary-general of the Youth Wing). Up to another thousand SWAPO members from the front were alleged to be interned in camps guarded by Zambian soldiers near the country's northern border as a result of their connections with the imprisoned leaders.

Nevertheless, unlike the liberation movement in Zimbabwe, SWAPO did not split as a result of this drastic action affecting so many of its leaders and followers. The need for unity proved stronger than any pressures for fission. Even some members who were adversely, if peripherally, affected continued to support the movement although they criticized its handling of Shipanga and others. More significant, perhaps, was the continuing support of internal SWAPO, which did not yield to the temptations held out to it to participate in the Turnhalle conference. In its convention at Walvis Bay in 1976 the party that operates legally within Namibia expressed its confidence in the part of the movement operating militarily and diplomatically outside the Territory by reelecting the present leadership under Sam Nujoma.

War in the North

While the Turnhalle conference was meeting sporadically in Windhoek, war was being waged in northern Namibia. It had begun years earlier with the infiltration of the first freedom fighters across the border and had continued in low-key, spasmodic fashion ever since. It accelerated greatly with the South African invasion of Angola. Although the alliance with UNITA enabled South African troops to wipe out SWAPO's Angolan bases, the push into central Angola made it impossible for the troops to exercise continuing control of the border area. Therefore, SWAPO fighters soon filtered back. When South Africa finally retreated out of Angola, SWAPO at last found itself with a friendly government to its rear.

When South Africa crossed back into Namibia in retreat, it promptly occupied the entire northern part of the Territory. "Operation Cobra" placed some fifty thousand troops in the area, except when some were hurriedly but temporarily recalled to Soweto in the early summer of 1976. Proclamation R 17, issued during the general strike, was extended to Kavango and the Caprivi and its application made more rigorous. A half-mile-wide free-fire zone was declared along the Angolan border. Africans living there (generally the best farming area) were forced to leave, within the area anything that moved was shot, and every male that was caught alive was hauled off to detention and torture.

South African troops raided into western Zambia and parts of Angola. Zambia brought a complaint before the Security Council, which condemned South Africa for its hostile act and for mounting it from Namibia, which it continued to occupy illegally. SWAPO has also charged that South Africa was training UNITA troops in Namibia to fight in southern Angola against both SWAPO and the new Angolan government. South Africa replied that the MPLA was persecuting UNITA partisans, causing them to flee to Namibia for refuge, where Pretoria was merely giving them humanitarian aid. On the Namibian side of the border, meanwhile, land-mine explosions, ambushes, and exchanges of fire between small groups had become everyday occurrences, with both SWAPO and the South African government issuing sporadic accounts of military action.

Reports in December 1976 spoke of increasing tension on the Namibia–Angola border, and the SWAPO representative at the U.N. accused South Africa of organizing UNITA elements to mount attacks on both the Angola government and the forces of SWAPO along the Angola border. Some observers saw in the South African moves a dual effort to strike at SWAPO and at the same time "destabilize" the Angola regime.

After a meeting of members of the Constitutional Committee of the Turnhalle conference and South African Prime Minister Vorster, the Constitutional Committee issued a draft constitution attached to a "petition for the establishment of an interim government." The petition was addressed to the South African government, and it requested that an interim government be established on the basis of the constitution drawn up by the Turnhalle conference and accepted by the conference on March 18, 1977.

This constitution, based on ethnic lines, involved a "three-tier" system of government. The tiers would be national, regional, and local and would function on the basis of ethnic selection.[6] Essentially the regional authorities would correspond to existing "homelands," with the whites retaining their present territory. The national executive, the Council of Ministers, was to act by consensus, so that any one minister could effectively block any move for change. This essentially would enable the white bloc to prevent any fundamental alteration in the constitutional scheme.

The overall balkanizing of the Territory among the eleven ethnic groups designated by the South African government conformed to the organization of the Turnhalle conference itself and was designed, as far as possible, to maintain a regime favorable to South Africa and to weaken the black population as a whole through divide-and-rule tactics. The overall result intended by the constitution was obviously a continuation of white domination over a territory fragmented into "homelands" and "population groups" among blacks and other nonwhite inhabitants of the country.

In the light of the current South African position that Walvis Bay does not and has not formed part of Namibia, it is worth noting that the reference to "metropolitan areas" under the chapter of the constitution dealing with local authorities includes the "areas of Windhoek and Walvis Bay." The petitioners evidently regarded Walvis Bay as part of the territory the constitution was to cover.

Shortly after the announcement of the constitution, the leader of the ruling white National Party was reported as saying that it would be enacted by South Africa as drafted and that an interim government under it would be set up in mid-1977.

The New American and Western Strategy on Namibia

At that stage, presumably, he was echoing the views of Prime Minister Vorster, but events in the U.S. as well as at the U.N. caused an abrupt change. The election of Carter as president of the United States brought Secretary of State Cyrus Vance into the administration in place of Henry Kissinger, and Andrew Young, the prominent black Congressman and 1960s civil rights activist, was appointed the new U.S. ambassador to the U.N. Discussions between the United States, Great Britain, Canada, West Germany, and France led to a decision to have representatives of these five countries confer with South Africa on new proposals for Namibia.[7] The Security Council took note of the efforts of the five and decided to defer further action on Resolution 352 and await the outcome of the negotiations that the five countries were to initiate.

The representatives of the five made it clear in their meetings with Prime Minister Vorster that the Turnhalle constitution would not be acceptable, and, with the U.S. taking the lead, South Africa was advised to come up with new proposals. It was evident that the Western five were concerned that intransigence by South Africa would result in a chain of events that would not only exclude South Africa from Namibia but would result in the installation of a regime hostile to those Western interests which had given visible though indirect support to South Africa. It was subsequently reported that Vorster had agreed to drop the Turnhalle constitutional proposals. However, Western diplomatic sources were also reported as stating that Vorster would not agree to elections under U.N. supervision or control.

Shortly after the initial meeting with the contact group, the Mondale–Vorster meeting took place in May 1977 in Vienna (see chapter on U.S. policies toward South Africa). Vice-President Walter Mondale was reported to say that South Africa had agreed to United Nations involvement and that its response was in some respect "most encouraging." However, it was evident that key questions of SWAPO participation, adherence to U.N. supervision and control, and withdrawal of South African forces were all points of fundamental dispute.[8]

At the end of May 1977 Vorster announced that a "Central Administrative Authority" would be established in Namibia by the South African state president to establish a provisional government that would precede final independence. The idea of an interim authority had apparently been discussed with Mondale in Vienna. After another round of talks in Cape Town between the Western "contact group" and the South African government, the abandonment of the Turnhalle formula was evident. Prime Minister Vorster declared that an administrator-general would be appointed to rule Namibia and that a Constituent Assembly would be elected. At the same time he announced that further legislation would be introduced to restore the administration of Walvis Bay to South Africa.

In the negotiations the issue of South African forces in Namibia continued to be a crucial point of difference. SWAPO had demanded a total withdrawal of South African forces, while South Africa insisted on maintaining its military and police forces in the Territory. The release of political prisoners was also a crucial point of dispute, as well as the fundamental issue of United Nations supervision and control.

Meetings between the ambassadors of the five Western countries and South African government representatives continued. There were also meetings in New York City in August 1977 between representatives of the five and a delegation from SWAPO, headed by its president, Sam Nujoma, at which according to a communique there was a "frank and useful" exchange of views.

In September there were further talks in South Africa with the ambassadors representing the Western five, and envoys subsequently traveled to various front-line states to discuss the negotiations. In November Dr. David Owen, the British foreign secretary, and Andrew Young met in London to review developments in Southern Africa, with particular reference to Namibia. Prior talks with the Western powers that were attended by President Nyerere had taken place in Dar es Salaam, after which the press reported Young as stating that the Anglo-American settlement initiative was continuing. In December another visit was paid to South Africa by representatives of the five, who had also met with SWAPO leaders previously in Lusaka, Zambia. Prominent among the Western envoys was Ambassador Donald McHenry, a high-ranking member of the U.S. United Nations staff.

After Vorster's announcement of the recessing of the Turnhalle conference, the South African Parliament quickly enacted a law giving its state president powers to rule by decree over Namibia, and under the law Justice Martinus T. Steyn was appointed administrator-general to exercise administrative and decree-making authority over the territory. Shortly after his appointment on September 1, 1977, a series of proclamations began to place legal and administrative control, previously exercised directly by South African officials, under the office of the administrator-general. This rather convoluted method of legislating obscured the reality that South African control remained largely unaffected. This was achieved by empowering the administrator-general to redelegate to existing South African officials the powers he had just assumed.

Some of the administrator's proclamations appeared to strike at apartheid doctrines—for example, those repealing the Mixed Marriages Act, forbidding interracial marriages, and the Immorality Act, forbidding interracial sex contact. However, the repeal of these largely symbolic laws had little practical effect. The modification of the pass laws effected by another proclamation also, on careful analysis, was revealed as more cosmetic than fundamental. Although the proclamation removed the main restrictions on the movement of blacks to and from various areas, residential segregation laws remained in force and the compulsory registration of black employees by white employers as a condition of employment was maintained. In addition, restrictions imposed by government-sanctioned tribal authorities continued.

Concurrently with the appointment of the administrator-general, another proclamation by the state president decreed that Namibia's only viable seaport, Walvis Bay, should be severed from the Territory and thenceforth administered as part of the (South African) Cape Province. Following this proclamation, numerous stringent apartheid laws were reapplied to the Walvis Bay enclave, in contrast to the ongoing purported "relaxation" in the remainder of Namibia. The response of SWAPO to the South African moves was again to insist on compliance with Security Resolution 385. SWAPO rejected the appointment of the administrator-general and his legislative and administrative actions. SWAPO also condemned South Africa's action on Walvis Bay as "annexation" and affirmed that Walvis Bay remains Namibian territory.

The shift in policy respecting Namibia by the Pretoria regime led to a split in the white ruling party within Namibia. Dirk Mudge, who had been a dominant personality in the Turnhalle moves, broke away from the ruling National Party, and with Herero Chief Clemens Kapuuo and other participants in the Turnhalle Conference he formed the Democratic Turnhalle Alliance (DTA). The white component of the DTA was the new Republican Party led by Mudge. The Democratic Turnhalle Alliance promptly began electioneering on the assumption that some form of elections would take place, even if not through agreement with the representatives of the five countries and the approval of the U.N.

Within Namibia the proliferation of small political parties and groups continued. However, it was clear that the contention was primarily between SWAPO, aiming at genuine independence for Namibia, and the DTA, aiming for a "South African" solution.

Meanwhile, the representatives of the five continued to hold meetings with the South African regime, the front-line states (Botswana, Zambia, Mozambique, Angola and Tanzania), and SWAPO. Ultimately, "proximity" meetings, which South Africa and SWAPO would attend separately, were announced for New York in January 1978, with the arrangement that neither would meet with the five in the presence of the other. This rather bizarre arrangement was due to South African intransigence against having any direct contact with SWAPO.

The proximity meetings actually took place in February 1978, and the five presented written proposals for settlement of the Namibian situation. Although the proposals were characterized as confidential, their full terms quickly became known. In essence, the five proposed that the secretary-general of the U.N. appoint a special representative who would be assigned by a "United Nations Transition Assistance Group" to monitor elections to a Namibian Constituent Assembly, which in turn was to draw up a constitution. It was suggested that governmental authority would be transferred during 1978 to the new government of Namibia upon the convening of the Constituent Assembly. The way in which this was to happen was left rather obscure.

The most controversial provisions in the proposals were those relating to the roles of the U.N. special representative and the U.N. Transition Assistance Group in the election process, and of the South African government, its armed forces, and administration. Under the proposals, the special representative was to "satisfy himself as to the fairness and appropriateness of all aspects of the political process at each stage." He was not provided, however, with any machinery for enforcing any decisions he might make or for acting effectively should he find out that the South Africans, or any group under their aegis, were proceeding contrary to the terms of Security Resolution 385 in relation to the election process or to any other aspect of the arrangements. The most striking feature of the proposals was thus the absence of any machinery for ensuring the "control and supervision" of the election (to quote the terms of Resolution 385) by the U.N. or its representative.

Furthermore, the proposals envisaged that the South African administration and its police forces would remain in place and in control even during the election process. Thus, they state that "primary responsibility for maintaining law and order in Namibia during the transition period shall rest with the existing Police Forces" that include armored paramilitary elements. Moreover, the proposals also stated that South Africa would be entitled to phase out its troop withdrawals during the initial stages of the election process and to retain a force of at least 1,500 troops throughout the entire transitional period, based at Grootfontein in northern Namibia, where the South Africans had built an enormous military complex, and at Oshivello in southern Ovamboland. This arrangement was to continue until after certification of the election. All SWAPO forces, in contrast, were required to cease hostilities and be confined to established bases.

The discussions on the settlement proposals were broken off abruptly when the South African foreign minister, Pik Botha, left New York, stating that he had to consult with the South African government. SWAPO then issued a statement emphasizing that Resolution 385 "should not be reinterpreted and watered down for the sake of expediency." It stressed that the transitional process to independence should be "effectively controlled and supervised by the United Nations," not by South Africa. SWAPO also pointed out that South Africa was maintaining more than a division of its armed forces in Walvis Bay under the pretext that the latter was a part of South African territory.

As a concession to the Western governments, SWAPO announced that it had agreed that a token force of 1,500 South African troops be retained in Namibia, but insisted that they be withdrawn from the northern sectors of the territory and placed in southern Namibia. Furthermore, SWAPO emphasized that the tribal forces in Namibia that the South Africans were engaged in training and arming on an ethnic basis would have to be dismantled.

Following the breakup of the New York talks, tension rose in Namibia, and in disturbances in the Katatura black ghetto of the capital, Windhoek, Chief Clemens Kapuuo was assassinated. The South Africans made no arrests but placed the blame on SWAPO. SWAPO leaders disclaimed any responsibility and suggested that the assassination might well have been a South African-inspired ploy.

In an effort to reactivate the Western proposals, the five sent representatives to South Africa and Namibia and held further meetings with the front-line states. In the meantime there was increasing impatience at the U.N. with what was perceived as South Africa's obstruction, and a special session of the

General Assembly was called to discuss the Namibian situation. Immediately following the opening of that session, Prime Minister Vorster announced in the South African Parliament in April that South Africa had accepted the Western proposals. This acceptance, he said, followed upon "clarifications" and "assurances" received from the Western five regarding the proposals. Vorster indicated that under these assurances South Africa retained the right to intervene militarily in Namibia "if peace is broken."

A dispute immediately followed on whether South Africa had in fact accepted the proposals submitted in New York, or whether there had been a substantial weakening of the safeguards against South African manipulation of the election process. SWAPO called for full disclosure, but although the Western five maintained that there had been no substantial change in the proposals, the nature of the clarifications and assurances was not revealed.

While the General Assembly session on Namibia was still in progress, the delegates were startled to hear that South Africa had mounted a paratroop invasion into Angola. Waves of aircraft attacked settlements as far as one hundred and fifty miles inside Angola, the site of what South Africa said was a SWAPO guerrilla base but which SWAPO and the Angolan government described as a refugee camp. Scandinavian reporters who visited the site after the South African attacks reported having seen over five hundred bodies, many of them women in unmistakable brightly colored print dresses.

On May 4, 1978, the General Assembly passed a comprehensive "Declaration on Namibia and Program of Action in Support of Self-Determination and National Independence for Namibia." Two days later the Security Council, at a meeting convened for the purpose, passed Resolution No. 428 (1978) condemning the South African attack on Angola. In the event of further violation of Angolan territory, it decided to meet again to consider the adoption of "more effective measures, in accordance with the appropriate provisions of the Charter of the United Nations, including Chapter VII thereof." Invoking Chapter VII would require a finding of a "threat to peace" and would justify military intervention in Namibia.

Following a meeting in Luanda on July 11 and 12, 1978, between SWAPO and the representatives of the five (with representatives of the front-line states also at hand), it was announced that certain points in the Western proposals had been clarified and that SWAPO agreed to proceed to the U.N. Security Council, thus "opening the way to an early internationally acceptable settlement on the question of Namibia." The Security Council met on July 27, 1978, and adopted two resolutions, 431 and 432. Resolution 431 requested the secretary general to appoint a special representative for Namibia "in order to ensure the early independence of Namibia through free elections under the supervision and control of the United Nations," and requested the secretary general to submit a report containing recommendations for the implementation of a settlement of the Namibian situation in accordance with

Security Resolution 385 of 1976. Resolution 432 stated that Walvis Bay should be "reintegrated" into Namibia, but it did not contain any directive or operative language on how this reintegration should be achieved.

The United Nations commissioner for Namibia, Martti Ahtisaari, was appointed by the secretary general as special representative for Namibia and was instructed to undertake a survey mission to that country. Accompanied by a team of United Nations officials and military advisers, the special representative spent just over two weeks in Namibia (from August 6 to August 22, 1978), traveling and holding meetings both with representatives of political parties and with South African officials, including the administrator-general. A key aspect of the visit was to make arrangements for UNTAG (the United Nations Transition Assistance Group envisaged by the Western proposals) to be set up and staffed.

While the special representative and his team were in Namibia, conflict broke out at Katima Mulilo. Both SWAPO and the South African forces suffered casualties, and the South Africans crossed the border into Zambia and carried out attacks on Zambian territory. On August 29, 1978, the secretary general reported to the Security Council that in order to carry out its tasks UNTAG would have to have a military component of 7,500 persons, as well as 360 police officers to assist the special representative in the election process. An additional 1,500 civilian personnel would be needed to act as a professional and field and general service staff, particularly in monitoring the election process.

South Africa attacked the report, stating its objection to the size of the military component and to the inclusion of any police forces as part of UNTAG. On September 20, 1978, Prime Minister Vorster issued a statement announcing his resignation and affirming South Africa's intention to proceed with its own election plans. At the time of writing, the immediate effect of this intransigence and disavowal of the U.N. was not clear.

The future course of events in Namibia remains uncertain. New alignments of political parties have emerged. The Democratic Turnhalle Alliance, under the leadership of Dirk Mudge, has been actively electioneering with reports of considerable financial backing, including the furnishing of a free luxury aircraft for campaigning purposes by a West German benefactor. Among the prominent personalities in the DTA were Pastor Njoba, the Owambo prime minister, and Kauimo Riruko, the Herero chief who succeeded Clemens Kapuuo.

Another group, which included right-wing National Party figures, was the "Akture" (the "Action Front For the Maintenance of Turnhalle Principles"). It also drew German support. Still another group was led by Dr. Benjamin Africa, with adherents in the Rehoboth community.

The Namibia National Front has emerged as an alliance of the Federal Party (formerly the United Party) led by a barrister, Bryan O'Linn, with elements from SWANU, including Gerson Veii (who had served a sentence on Robben Island), Andreas Shipanga, and other black former exiles. Shipanga, who subsequently formed what he called SWAPO-D (for democracy), was one of the SWAPO critics of Nujoma's leadership who had been detained in Tanzania but was released by Prime Minister Nyerere in May 1978. Before this release the South Africans had made play of the detention of SWAPO members in Tanzania when demands were made for the release of Namibian political prisoners held in South African prisons, notably on Robben Island.

South Africa's actions have strengthened the belief of SWAPO and the Third World generally that South Africa will continue to subvert or circumvent the U.N. on Namibia. This view was reinforced by the sweeping arrests of more than fifty SWAPO leaders in Namibia under a "Detention Without Trial" proclamation issued by the administrator-general. Although Proclamation No. AG 26 has provisions for the person detained to request that his or her next of kin be informed and to ask for the reasons for the detention, access to courts and counsel has been specifically prohibited, and the furnishing of reasons and the continued detention are entirely under the control of the administrator-general. It should be emphasized that other detention laws, including specifically the notorious Section 6 of South Africa's Terrorism Act of 1967, remain in force in Namibia and that Namibians can be seized without compliance with the next-of-kin notification of the proclamation.

Thus, it is evident that a peaceful solution for Namibia remains elusive, and U.N. military intervention may be a reality in the near future.

6.

Angola: Perilous Transition to Independence

John Marcum

In May 1981, just five and a half years after an alarmed Congress had closed down bungled, covert American intervention in Angola, Washington officials were once again proposing to intercede there on behalf of "anticommunist" insurgents. National security and intelligence officials argued that Angola had emerged from years of anticolonial warfare under a pro-Soviet, Marxist government that had been imposed by Cuban troops and that was bent on facilitating the expansion of Soviet/Cuban influence into Zaïre and Southern Africa. The author of the (Senator Dick) Clark amendment that prohibited American intervention unless approved by Congress, however, firmly opposed "getting involved, once again, in a local conflict in a distant country of no intrinsic strategic value to the United States."[1] After a period of confusion, President Jimmy Carter disavowed any such intent (an apparent defeat for his adviser on national security affairs, Zbigniew Brzezinski). Instead, his administration adopted a policy of talking with the government of Angola. Diplomatic rather than military initiatives proved promptly successful in gaining Angolan cooperation to reduce regional border tensions and conflict that had been diverting Angolans from the urgent tasks of economic reconstruction and political unification left in the wake of the civil war that had followed the collapse of Portuguese rule.

Portugal's last governor-general folded his flag and sailed out of Luanda the day before Angola's independence on November 11, 1975. During the preceding year and a half that followed the army coup of April 1974, Portuguese authority had dissipated. Having failed historically to associate Africans with the construction of a territory-wide administration or to allow Africans to organize and politicize within territory-wide associations, the Portuguese tried

175

to compensate for centuries of neglect by creating a broad-scoped transitional government, including all three of Angola's ethnically based liberation movements. But Lisbon's war-weary troops wanted to go home. They had no stomach for enforcing a rational "political solution." And they proved unwilling to oversee the dissolution and merger of three liberation armies into a common national army. As its authority evaporated, Lisbon was unable to conduct the Angolan elections that it had scheduled to set up a politically legitimate national government.

Moving into the power vacuum, Angola's nationalist movements, spurred on by their external backers, sought power via a "military solution." The result was escalating violence that thrust Portugal's oil-rich colony into civil war even before it had achieved statehood. And the world's great powers fanned the flames in a frenetic contest for privileged political and economic relations.

Lisbon had never devolved substantial political power on the resident European population, which numbered some 335,000 by 1974, many of them peasants sent from Portugal after World War II to relieve population pressures at home. Thus Angola's economically privileged but relatively unskilled and ill-organized whites were in no position to seize power. Instead, as intra-African violence mounted, the white population fled en masse to an uncertain fate in the political and economic chaos of postwar Portugal.

Although the goal of a unified Angolan state received widespread rhetorical support within the forums of the United Nations and the Organization of African Unity, neither of these collectivities was utilized to impose a peaceful resolution of incipient civil war and ethnic balkanization. Instead, outside powers, great and small, forsook multilateral peacekeeping action for the risks of self-seeking unilateral intervention: troops from Zaïre, military trainers from China, arms from the Soviet Union, covert funds from the United States, a commando column from South Africa, and, finally and decisively, an expeditionary force from Cuba. Angola emerged as a single state from the human tragedy of civil war that might have stalemated and left the country divided into three ethnic states (Bakongo, Mbundu, Ovimbundu) and the Cabinda enclave. But it had been unified by military conquest not by political consolidation.

Would continuing dependence on Cuban troops and technicians render Angola a long-term dependent of Havana? Did mutual defense provisions in the subsequent Angolan-Soviet accord of October 1976 signal that Moscow was intent upon acquiring naval facilities and a launch pad from which to expand its influence throughout the Southern African region? Or was Cuban intervention which provided a fortuitous opportunity to humble Yankee "imperialists" essentially a selfless action of solidarity on the part of a small, Third World country? Would the new rulers of Angola be able to reconcile the ethnic bailiwicks of those whom it had defeated in the struggle for power? Would the oil wealth of Cabinda, soon to pour some $700 million into the Angolan economy each year, enable the government to launch a successful program of economic reconstruction and development along socialist lines? Or would revolutionary "solidarity" draw Angola into a mounting confrontation with South Africa along the extensive southern boundary with Namibia (South West Africa)? Would the Carter administration establish constructive relations based on mutuality of interests with a regime that had come to power despite American efforts to block it?

Colonial Background to 1961

Portuguese penetration into Angola dates back almost five centuries to 1483. Early diplomatic relations with the Congo Kingdom of the north were followed by a slow, spasmodic conquest that finally extended Portuguese anthority over the interior in the nineteenth century. Depopulated and demoralized by a slave trade and related internal wars that ravaged it up until the middle of the past century, Angola became for Portugal a private preserve of raw materials and cheap labor.

The avowed goal of the *Estado Novo* of António Salazar (premier of Portugal, 1932–68) was to assimilate Angola into the Portuguese nation. For example, from 1951 Angola and other African possessions were considered "provinces," integral parts of Portugal. Yet as of 1950, only half of one percent of the African population had become *assimilados* (about 30,000), while over 99 percent remained *indigenas,* or unassimilated, "uncivilized" persons without political or civil rights. One reason for this situation was that it cost about $50 plus bribes to local administrators for those few who had the educational and other prerequisites for becoming *assimilados,* whereas a relatively well-paid African schoolteacher could earn only $17 per month. Therefore, the privileged status with its accompanying right to vote for Salazar government slates lacked appeal. Dr. Salazar himself recognized the snail's pace of assimilation when he said in 1961: "A law recognizing citizenship takes minutes to draft and can be made right away; a citizen that is a man fully and consciously integrated into a civilized political society takes centuries to achieve."[2]

Reforms following upon the outbreak of fighting in 1961 were timid. Absolute power remained vested in a governor-general appointed in Lisbon, reinforced by secret police (PIDE) and ultimately some sixty thousand troops. Severe literacy and financial qualifications continued to restrict the franchise for indigenous inhabitants, few of whom had the opportunity to learn to read and write Portuguese. No legal opposition was allowed.

After the Second World War, Angola emerged as an important economic asset for Portugal. In 1959 annual coffee exports rose to nearly fifty million dollars, diamonds to well over twenty, and newly discovered oil and iron reserves plus an influx of West German and other Western capital promised increasing revenue in foreign currency. Portugal's total exports paid for less than one half its imports; in 1959 Portugal's deficit in its balance of payments was about $150 million. This deficit was made up with a $45 million balance of payments surplus of exports over imports from "overseas provinces." The coffee, sisal, and cotton plantations, diamond mines, and other wealth of Angola, all owned by Europeans, were rendered profitable by African labor. For the latter there was still the economy of the *palmatorio*, a wooden mallet used to punish unsatisfactory workers. In a report on Angolan refugees in August 1961, two respected British observers wrote:

> The system of Contract Labour is one of the chief grievances of the African people in Angola. It is some indication of race relationships in Angola that about half a million Africans are held "in contract" and forced to work for the Portuguese government and Portuguese traders. African men are conscripted for periods of up to eighteen months of Contract Labour; women are forced to do work mending roads, and children from eight years of age upwards are known to have been employed in the copper mines and the coffee plantations. Labourers are frequently ill-treated. For years there has been a constant stream of Africans moving across to the Congo to escape Contract Labour. Some Contract Labourers have run away from their work but if they are caught they are severely beaten.[3]

Commenting on a relatively mild report on labor conditions in Angola made by a commission of the International Labor Organization, which conducted its survey under Portuguese surveillance and without any means of protecting African informants from reprisals, a former missionary in Angola, the Reverend Malcolm McVeigh, pointed out that "idleness" remained an offense. Moreover, obligations to work, either for the state or for private employers on the latters' terms, still defined the economic relationship of African to European. Referring to reforms in the labor code, the United Nations Committee on Portuguese Territories concluded: "Since vagabondage is punishable under the Portuguese Civil Code, the Committee considers that whether or not the new legislation brings an improvement in the daily lives of the indigenous inhabitants will depend to a great extent on how the laws are interpreted and applied." Meanwhile, Europeans continued to earn approximately three times the wages of Africans for doing the same work.

Perhaps it was in the educational field that the Portuguese colonial record compared most unfavorably with those of more advanced colonial powers. As of 1956 approximately one percent of the African school-age population was attending school; in neighboring Northern Rhodesia (subsequently Zambia) the figure for 1958 was 11 percent; and whereas the Northern Rhodesian government was spending approximately four dollars per capita for education in 1959, the Portuguese government was spending but one tenth of one cent per capita in 1956 ($476). Education was left to Christian missionaries. There were few secondary schools, populated mostly by Europeans and *mestiços*, a middle caste enjoying near-European privileges. There were no universities. Of the handful of Angolan students permitted to study in Portuguese universities, many fled Portugal after the outbreak of the Angolan war placed them under mounting pressures from the police.

This stagnant educational policy that prevented the emergence of a strong educated elite also facilitated political repression. Whereas in the unsettling wake of the Second World War, the comparatively permissive colonial administrations of Britain, France, and Belgium begrudgingly allowed socially aware Africans to organize, politicize, and gradually to acquire a measure of political power, the Portuguese remained constrastingly and implacably hostile to an organized expression of African cultural, let alone political, dissent. Coerced political docility, or silence, was the responsibility of local officials and police, supplemented by PIDE, which was introduced into Angola in 1957, by networks of police informers, and finally (1959–60) by progressively augmented European military forces. The Salazar government was thus able systematically to root out and destroy groups and individuals suspected of nationalist activity or sympathies.

As a consequence, surviving nationalist groups suffered common insecurity and shared common characteristics. Their leadership ranks were thin, coming from the politically aware portion of a tiny educated elite. Moreover, these group were handicapped by travel restrictions, police harassment, and general penury. Their range of action, life-spans, and political vision were limited. Localized, they remained parochial. Most were unable fully to surmount the bounds of primary ethnic (or regional) relationships (e.g., Bakongo) or of class ties (e.g., the multiracial intelligentsia of Luanda).

Clandestinity also left its mark. Decimated by infiltrators and corroded by the insecurities and tensions of underground politics, nationalists became exceedingly distrustful. Furthermore, when they sought refuge abroad, they immediately confronted a new situation that was no less suffused with insecurity and frustration. The debilitating condition of clandestinity gave way to the equally debilitating condition of exile.

Foreign refuge enabled some nationalists to avoid arrest and/or to regroup, seek international assistance, and then mount a new challenge to Portuguese rule from outside. Indeed, some left the country precisely in order to enter into political action. It was possible to organize among compatriots—émigrés and laborers—living and working within the more permissive political context of neighboring countries, for example the Bakongos residing in Zaïre.

Increasingly then, after 1957, displaced nationalist leaders and young militants congregated and reorganized abroad. Following the outbreak of the Angolan conflict in early 1961, they concentrated on building movements capable of effecting the politicization and military liberation of their homelands through action launched from exile. Their failure to attain this goal until 1974, and then only indirectly, was in part attributable to chronic frustration and fragmentation induced by long years of political repression, underground existence, and exile.

The Dynamics of Change

The liberation movements of Portuguese Africa served as powerful catalysts of social, economic, and eventually political change. At the outset of the northern Angolan uprising, it was generally anticipated by rebels and international observers alike that limited violence synchronized with diplomatic pressure at the United Nations would suffice to force Portugal to make a chain of concessions that would lead inexorably toward independence. But if such Bourguibist strategy had worked against the French in Tunisia and similarly if nationalist rhetoric, riot, and mutiny had stampeded the Belgians out of the Congo, armed uprising appeared only to steel Lisbon's resolve to hold on to its anachronistic empire. The Salazar government refused to step onto the slippery path of reform. It continued to deny Africans the right to political self-determination and clung instead to the principle of inalienable Portuguese sovereignty. Without its colonies, Portugal, it was felt, would shrink into a country of little political consequence and limited economic potential.

After an initial phase of fluidity (1961–63), the Angolan conflict stalemated at a rather low level of insurgency. Elsewhere, profiting from the Angolan experience which demonstrated the need for political mobilization of peasants and politico-military training of cadres *before* launching an insurrection, nationalists from Guinea-Bissau and Mozambique rather more methodically planned and phased into guerrilla operations by 1963 and 1964 respectively.

This chain of insurgency brought change to both Portugal and Africa. Portugal's armed forces more than doubled in size, consumed more and more of the government budget (by 1974, 45 to 50 percent), grew politically powerful, and, like the French army during the Indochinese and Algerian wars, developed an insatiable need for ever more material and psychological support. In official budgetary terms military expenditure rose from 35.6 percent in 1961 to 40.7 percent in 1969, whereas expenditure on socioeconomic development dropped from 22 percent in 1960 to 14 percent in 1968. Emigration from Portugal soared, reaching an annual rate of some 170,000 in 1971, including a large outflow of young men of draft age. In 1972, *The Economist* (London) calculated that 1.5 million Portuguese had found employment abroad, compared with a labor force of only 3.1 million in

Portugal itself. The results—manpower shortages, inflationary pressures, and stagnancy in the rural-agricultural sector—were only partially offset by industrial expansion (including light-arms manufacturing) and a growing tourist trade (West European and Americans).

In the African territories change was even more noticeable. Administrative and legal reforms such as liberalization of labor codes and abolition of the legal distinction between *assimilados* and *indigenas* constituted perhaps its least significant aspect. Africans were left as unenfranchised, voiceless, and politically impotent as ever. The real change came in education and economic development. Insurgency and international criticism jarred the Portuguese into a belated recognition that any possibility for converting the legal fiction of assimilation into a sociopolitical reality would require a massive program of general and civic education. Between 1960–61 and 1968–69, primary-school enrollment in Angola rose from 105,781 to 366,658 (including Europeans). Foreign Minister Rui Patricio claimed that in the decade 1962–72 school enrollment at all levels in Angola rose from 150,000 to 600,000. The nuclei of universities were created in Angola and Mozambique. Special programs were established to train rural elementary teachers (*monitores*), and army personnel began teaching in African bush schools. There was a decisive break with the lethargy of former years. Indeed, the elementary-school syllabus in Angola was sufficiently modernized to become superior to its antiquated equivalent in metropolitan Portugal.

Portugal's staying power was obviously dependent on increased economic capacity to finance both the overseas military effort and new educational programs. By 1964 financial pressures had reached the point where Lisbon felt compelled to reverse its long-standing policy of excluding or severely restricting the flow of foreign capital into its overseas territories. Traditional policy had been to screen the colonies from undue contact with foreigners, their ideas, press, and economic institutions. Except for what was viewed as the nefarious influence of Protestant missions assured of entry by the Congress of Berlin (1884), external influence was in fact kept minimal.

The right-wing Salazar government shared with Marxist-influenced African liberation movements a fear that because of economic weakness in capital and technology, an open door to foreign investors would result in replacing inefficient Portuguese monopoly enterprise with that of giant corporations based in the United States and Western Europe. Indeed, Portuguese and African nationalists shared a concern over the vulnerability of the African territories to the "neocolonial" effects of penetration by and dependency on powerful, self-interested American or multinational corporations. Premier Salazar went so far as to suggest that economic ambitions motivated the United States misguidedly to join the Soviet Union in attempts to undermine Portuguese authority in Africa.

By 1964, however, economic necessity and the counsel of Europe-oriented economists who argued for breaking out of economic isolation brought a major policy reversal. Investment laws were altered so as to become congenial to foreign capital, and *The New York Times'* annual economic review for 1965 correctly predicted a massive inflow into Angola of American, West European, and South African capital. The open-door policy brought investments in capital-intensive extractive enterprise: for example, Gulf Oil in Cabindan petroleum and Krupp in Angolan iron. And South African capital assumed a new and central importance not only in such massive projects as the hydroelectric dam on the Cunene River on the Namibian border, but in local industry as well.

By 1970 Portugal was no longer perched securely atop an economically hobbled colonial elephant. Disjunctive and irreversible changes were creating new and contradictory dynamics. On the one hand, African social and political awareness of relative deprivations developed along with educational and economic change. On the other hand, the 335,000 Portuguese in Angola, who were increasingly linked into South African security and finance, were intent upon maintaining their ever more prosperous ascendancy, both political and economic.

Nationalist Strategy and Portuguese Resilience

In general, the strategy of the African liberation movement was to rely on a combination of unconventional warfare and international diplomatic pressure to wear down Portuguese resolve. The goal was an Evian-type settlement such as was won by the Algerians after an eight-year war against France. At the outset, however, African nationalists (and many outside observers) misjudged Portuguese psychology and underestimated the willingness or ability of the Salazar government to commit scarce resources to a protracted defense of its colonial heritage. The intensity of this determination to stay (Lisbon openly disdained other colonial powers for capitulating to the demands of African nationalism) was evident in the size of the expeditionary forces sent to Africa—of Portugal's total armed forces of 218,000 in 1972, something in excess of 130,000 were in Africa.

In the face of this resolve, the liberation movements made some effort at developing a common, interterritorial strategy but relied mainly on developing separate guerrilla campaigns based on timetables and tactics suited to local conditions and capabilities. The Popular Movement for the Liberation of Angola (MPLA), the Mozambique Liberation Front (Frelimo) and the African Independence Party of Guinea and Cape Verde (PAIGC) cooperated within the loose framework of an association known as the Conference of Nationalist Organizations of the Portuguese Colonies (CONCP).

But their collaboration was limited to joint lobbying and propaganda work and exchanges of military information. The diffuse nature of guerrilla warfare and geographic separation militated against three-territory action so synchronized as to place maximum strains on the Portuguese.

With air- and sea-craft obtained from the North Atlantic Treaty Organization (NATO) powers, Portugal was able to shift its forces rapidly from one pressure point to another. In early 1971 the Nixon administration authorized the direct sale of Boeing 707's to the Portuguese government, known to want them for use as military transports, despite the American pledge to maintain an "embargo on all arms" for use in Portugal's colonial wars. And a report by a research unit of the U.N. Secretariat subsequently noted that "the increased use of aircraft for transport of troops is reported to have gone a long way towards solving one of Portugal's major military problems."[4]

Meanwhile, the African strategy of attritional warfare came up against a formidable economic obstacle to success. A Midwestern newspaper put the matter this way: "One optimistic supposition has been that, in time, the poorest of the West European countries would tire of the cost—in money and manpower—of supporting these rearguard colonial wars. But that thesis is tenable only if the price of holding on to the territories is greater than the return." The Kansas City *Star* (May 1, 1970) correctly judged that "major oil revenues"—which reached some $61 million in 1972—resulting from a Gulf Oil investment of $150 to $220 million in Cabinda would alter this cost-benefit equation "radically." As a result, African nationalists and those who supported their cause, suggested the *Star*, "will have to find another peg than economics to hang their hopes on."

Higher Portuguese casualty rates in Guinea-Bissau and Mozambique represented such a peg. In all three territories African insurgents came to use mines and booby-traps as part of a strategy of maximizing enemy casualties while minimizing physical contact and their own losses. Still officially considered at a "tolerable" level, Portuguese losses from 1967 to 1974 totaled some 11,000 dead and perhaps four times as many wounded (including many amputees). Its home population shrunk by emigration to as few as 8.4 million. Portugal's casualty rates compared proportionately to those suffered by the United States in Vietnam.

However, nationalist efforts from 1961 failed totally to prevail upon Western powers to refrain from selling arms, granting loans, or exporting capital to Portugal until African rights to self-determination were acknowledged. In return for a tracking station (Azores) and air base facilities (Beja), respectively, France and West Germany provided standard NATO weaponry on favorable terms. African nationalists were left to pursue attritional guerrilla war against Portuguese forces well equipped for counterinsurgency (e.g., Alouette II/III and Puma SA-330 helicopters) through the expenditure of funds dependent to some extent on economic relations with the United States and Western Europe.

After ten years of guerrilla warfare in Angola, the Portuguese government appeared resigned to continuing "military police action" for an indefinite period of time. It remained confident that it could confine guerrilla action to peripheral border regions, forest redoubts, and relatively empty areas of the arid south and east, well outside the territories' major population centers. While using some 65,000 troops (including a growing component of African conscripts) and local militia units to isolate and limit nationalist action, the colonial administration counted on long-term economic, social, and educational change to secure Portuguese sovereignty.

From 1961 through 1963 the Angolan insurgency was led principally by the National Front for the Liberation of Angola (FNLA) based in the Bakonga area of the north and led by a Bakongo politician, Holden Roberto. The apex of its ascendancy came in mid-1963 when its Government in Exile (GRAE) at Kinshasa was recognized by the newly founded Organization of African Unity and offered exclusive support from a Liberation Fund set up by the OAU. Concentrating on military action and giving only minimal attention to political education, organization, or strategic planning, the FNLA failed to maintain its revolutionary momentum in the face of stepped-up counterinsurgency, including effective Portuguese use of air power, land mines, and fortified villages. The fall of the Congolese government of Cyrille Adoula and the assumption of power by Katanga's pro-Portuguese Moise Tshombe (1964) severely handicapped FNLA operations, especially its ability to supply its forces inside Angola. Concurrently, internal quarrels brought forth primordial ethnic-regional rivalry, and in 1964 Ovimbundu soldiers mutinied and most central-southern leadership left the FNLA movement. During 1964–65 desertions and an abortive internal coup to overthrow Roberto reduced the FNLA to a defensive strategy based on the several hundred thousand Bakongo refugees and émigrés living in the Lower Congo. At the same time, it lost much of its *élan* and promising leadership as Roberto eliminated all potential rivals and asserted his own conservative direction.

The FNLA's constituency had largely transplanted itself from Angola to the Congo (now Zaïre). Angola's total Bakongo population has numbered around 600,000, and by 1966 up to 400,000 of them had reportedly moved across the border to join their ethnic kin in Bakongo regions of the Congolese Republic. This external political base along with renewed support from the Congolese central government after General (Joseph) Mobutu Sésé Séko came to power in late 1965 accounted for the staying power of Roberto's movement. It continued to carry out minor military action, ambushes, and raids from mountainous bases in the north and sorties across the

Kwango River and Katanga (now Shaba) border areas of Zaïre. But no coherent plan or cumulative political buildup seemed involved.

In return for exclusive use of Zaïrean territory and sole access to Zaïre's extensive borders with Angola, the FNLA cooperated closely with the Mobutu government. Perforce, it did not seek aid from foes of the Kinshasa government, in particular the Soviet Union. In the view of some observers, the FNLA constituted a rather safe, ineffectual organization that could be supported without provoking serious Portuguese reprisals. As Zaïre's economic relations with Angola and diplomatic contacts with Portugal improved in the early 1970s, the Kinshasa government seemingly increased constraints on FNLA actions. In March 1972 frustrated FNLA guerrillas mutinied and Zaïre forces occupied the FNLA's principal training base of Kinkuzu. In an apparent bid for Pan-African leadership at little risk, Mobutu then reversed field and undertook to retrain and equip the FNLA army. To this end, he also sought the collaboration of the OAU and China. By early 1974 the FNLA under Zaïre's tutelage had recruited a new army, brought in new administrative leadership, and planned to make a bid to become once again the preeminent insurgent movement.

Led by an urban intellectual elite from Luanda and its Mbundu hinterland, the rival MPLA found itself initially disadvantaged by geography and, to some extent, its class and racial origins. Its exiled *assimilado* and *mestiço* leadership moved from European exile to the Congo only after the outbreak of fighting. Once in the Congo, it managed to establish links with and gain the allegiance of some Mbundu guerrilla units in the forested Nambuangongo-Dembos areas northeast of Luanda. A Marxist orientation and sympathetic left-wing press won it considerable support within Western Europe and Scandinavia, and also among the more "radical" African states and from Communist countries. But this did not compensate for the lack of Congolese support essential for access to Angola's borders. Nor did it make up for the MPLA's slowness to build up military cadres. The result was a near debacle in 1963, when the OAU gave exclusive recognition to Roberto's militarily more active movement. The MPLA split into two, a loyalist wing led by Dr. Agostinho Neto and a smaller, Maoist-oriented faction led by the MPLA's original secretary general, Viriato da Cruz.

Regrouped in Congo-Brazzaville under Dr. Neto's leadership, MPLA loyalists mounted a significant guerrilla campaign in the Cabinda enclave by mid-1964. And then in 1966, following Zambian independence, Neto's movement opened up a new Eastern front. Emulating the program of political indoctrination carried out by the PAIGC in Guinea-Bissau, the MPLA trained political cadres from eastern communities (Luena, Luchasi, etc.), including émigrés in Zambia. It sent some of these cadres to Eastern Europe for military training, then equipped them with Soviet and Czech weapons and launched them (1966) upon a wide-ranging campaign in eastern Angola. This campaign carried MPLA patrols to the outskirts of Angola's population centers, notably the margins of the central Bie district. MPLA action extended from the Malange district in the north to Ovambo regions of the south. In addition, the movement continued minor guerrilla activity in Cabinda and the Nambuangongo-Dembos forests near Luanda.

In sum, the MPLA thus developed into the strongest Angolan movement. It was capable of hijacking an airplane and of disrupting the Benguela railroad (if Zambia had permitted), and it forced the Portuguese to resettle thousands of outlying peasants and pastoral peoples in fortified villages (*aldeamentos*). Moreover, the fact that it was the only Angolan movement that received OAU, Soviet, and Scandinavian aid significantly reinforced its advantage over its rivals. Beginning in 1968, the MPLA held regional party conferences inside the country. Its top leadership, however, like that of the FNLA, continued to spend most of its time in exile. And this absence, combined with military reverses in the face of Portuguese helicopter-borne search-and-destroy offensives in 1968–69 and 1972, produced internal schisms. In 1973 the MPLA eastern zone leader, Daniel Chipenda, openly broke with Agostinho Neto. The MPLA was thus in a state of political turmoil and military paralysis at the time of the Lisbon coup of April 1974.

Jonas Savimbi and most of the leaders of the Union for the Total Independence of Angola (UNITA), making a virtue of necessity, operated more or less permanently inside the country. UNITA's leadership enjoyed a strong ethnic base in the southern half of Angola. It was founded in 1966 by Savimbi, the former minister for foreign affairs in Roberto's exile government (GRAE), and by other Ovimbundu exiles and representatives from other southern and eastern communities (Chokwe, Luena, Ovambo). It lost its one contiguous exile base when the Zambian government closed its offices in 1967 after its forces had blown up the Benguela railroad and Savimbi had quarreled with Zambian officials. With a highly self-reliant, militant program, some press support, and a modicum of financial support from the Chinese, UNITA forces reportedly operated in areas west and south of Luso. Lacking any major external source of arms, and thus militarily the weakest of the three movements, UNITA concentrated on a relatively quiet strategy of building up a political underground. According to UNITA's own communiques, its guerrillas achieved an unprecedented series of "resounding victories" in early 1970. By 1972 it, like the MPLA, claimed to be operating militarily in both Bie and the Huila district (as far south as the Cunene-Namibia border regions) of the southwest. But its military action in reality was quite modest.

As of early 1974 then, guerrilla action still plagued large areas of northern and eastern Angola. Nationalists ambushed Portuguese convoys, blew up bridges, and raided military outposts. They were not, on the other hand, able to carry physical or psychological warfare to the more than 335,000

European town- and farm-dwellers, although in late 1969, and again in 1971, security police were obliged to move against persistent MPLA efforts to create and recreate a political underground in Luanda. Moreover, the nationalist movements were not able to thrust themselves deeply into the populous (over 2 million) Ovimbundu plateau areas west of the upper Cuanza River, a move that would have signaled real danger to the future of Portuguese rule.

Portugal's Africa Policy and the North Atlantic Alliance

Despite Portugal's heightened economic stakes and continued military superiority in Africa, its Eurafrican "mission" was steadily challenged and eroded. Although the post-Salazar government of Marcello Caetano disappointed those who anticipated a political liberalization of substance as well as style, domestic opposition to the colonial wars became a major problem. Lisbon was of course aware that war weariness and political disaffection, not military defeat, prompted the withdrawal of France from Algeria and the United States from Vietnam. And though antiwar elements in Portugal were denied the instruments of an open society—free press, mass demonstration, electioneering—with which to mobilize popular support, opposition became manifest in draft-dodging (*émigrés*), increasing army defections, and, most dramatic, military sabotage carried out by the country's first really effective and disciplined political underground, Armed Revolutionary Action (ARA). The core of the ARA, which destroyed seventeen military aircraft at Tancos Field in one operation and bombed ships, attacked trains, blew up ammunition dumps, damaged NATO facilities, and disrupted communications, all with skill and drama, managed, unlike more amateurish precursors, to elude the police. Other revolutionary groups emerged. The government felt obliged to declare a "state of subversion," and the minister of interior warned that the discovery and arrest of subversive elements within the armed forces, universities, and labor organizations would cause the political police (DGS) to use its power to detain without charges anyone suspected of activities against the security of the state. Premier Caetano and other officials spoke of the *real* enemy as "anti-Portuguese [read antiwar] collaborators" *at home*.

While Portuguese army deserters joined American counterparts in Sweden, the military leaders and hardcore Africa-first elements led by former Foreign Minister Alberto Franco Nogueira and Minister of Interior Gonçalves Rapazote continued to demand a military solution in Africa. But if Nogueira saw Portugal's claim to global status as residing in the hydroelectric power of Cabora Bassa and the oil of Cabinda, a growing number of young economists, businessmen, and politicians were concluding that Portugal's well-being would be best served by working for association with an economically integrated Western Europe. As *The Economist* noted in 1972, Western Europe provided some 58 percent of Portugal's imports and bought about 54 percent of its exports: "The comparable figures for Portugal's African provinces were 14 percent and 25 percent."[5] Consequently, an Africa-versus-Europe debate over national priorities emerged. It was reminiscent of that which had taken place two decades earlier in France during the waning days of the French Union. And it was sharpened by the economic and political fact that Portugal had enough difficulty preparing for its own gradual associations with the European Economic Community (EEC) without trying to fit its overseas "provinces" in too. Recognizing the benefits already accrued from membership in the loose European Free Trade Association (EFTA), Portugal's "European" advocates did not wish to be left sitting alone in the dust as Great Britain and other EFTA countries joined the EEC.

The dilemma underlying the Africa-versus-Europe debate, which increasingly polarized the ruling stratum of Portuguese society, was put thus by *Le Monde*'s Marcel Niedergang: "The Portuguese state cannot at one and the same time maintain its war effort and assure an indispensable economic development."[6] Seeking a way out of this dilemma, however, Lisbon turned to the United States and (1) found in "Vietnamization" a suggestive model for a new, less costly colonial policy and (2) obtained economic assistance that temporarily reduced the urgency for making tough guns-versus-butter choices.

As with its use of "strategic hamlets" *(aldeamentos)* and its threat of massive aerial retaliation against external support, Portugal borrowed from the United States' concept of Vietnamization and launched a program of "regionalization," or Africanization, that had three principal goals. First, in financial terms it meant that the "provincial" government of Angola, and Mozambique also, would bear an increasingly large share of the costs of counterinsurgency. Between 1967 and 1971 the percentage of defense costs borne by the overseas territories rose from 25.2 percent to 32.3 percent, and the secretary of state for the treasury, Costa André, predicted that it would be possible "to organize the defense of the overseas provinces more and more within the internal orbit of each province."[7] Because of "the rapidly increasing military budgets of the overseas territories," Lisbon was able to channel more metropolitan funds into socioeconomic development, and in 1972, for the first time since the early 1960s, estimated development expenditure was almost 80 percent of the amount spent on defense and security.

In military manpower terms Africanization, already well advanced, called for gradual replacement of metropolitan troops by local recruits. By offering literacy and technical training along with entry into special status commando and paratroop units, the government was developing the armed forces as *the* avenue of upward social mobility for thousands of young Africans. In constitutional terms Africanization means a modest devolution of administrative (as distinct from substantive) political autonomy to provincial authorities. Basically it represented a response to demands for a larger governmental role by local European settler interests—notably demands contained in a petition (1969) by predominantly white Angolan economic associations.

While its short-term expediency was patent, in the long term Africanization seemed likely to produce more problems than it solved. Could one recruit and train thousands of African soldiers for counterinsurgency and yet continue to exclude Africans from meaningful participation in the political, economic, and educational processes and institutions of their country? Could one promise more autonomy to settler interests and yet maintain a mercantilist economic relationship under which Angola's diamonds, petroleum, and iron were processed in metropolitan Portugal while Angola was compelled to sell its exports cheaply to Portugal in return for Portuguese goods at inflated prices? The overt, latent, and contradictory forces of African nationalism and white separatism suggested ample reason for doubt. And Africanization notwithstanding, did a Portugal that was able to settle only 277 families in Mozambique in 1971 at a cost of nearly $3 million, and was forced to import Cape Verdean and African workers (some 15,000 by July 1971) to meet domestic needs for unskilled labor at the risk of opening a door to racial conflict and political subversion, have the manpower and financial base to pursue a successful Eurafrican mission?

Attempts to answer that question had to reckon with external variables. In December 1971, as a quid pro quo for a two-year extension of United States base rights in the Azores, the United States extended some aid to Lisbon, up to $400 million in Export-Import Bank loan-drawing rights, $30 million in PL-480 agricultural commodities, and $5 million or more in excess "nonmilitary equipment" such as road-building machinery. Little of the available loan was in fact drawn. The aid was more important psychologically than materially, reinforcing Portuguese resistance to mounting pressures against the pursuit of endless colonial war. To be fully appreciated, of course, this aid had also to be placed in the context of unregulated American economic relations, which pumped an annual $300 million into the Portuguese economy through expenditures for tourism ($80 million), Azores base operations ($13 million), Cabinda oil (over $60 million), Angolan coffee (nearly $100 million), Mozambican cashews ($9 million), and so on. Moreover, it fell within the framework of a policy which, despite an embargo on arms for use by Portugal in Africa, provided specialized training for some one hundred Portuguese military officers annually (for a total of some three thousand by 1973–74), and access to U.S. jet transports, heavy-duty trucks, jeeps, and herbicides (defoliants) for use in Africa.

American assistance could be partially explained by a special desire to maintain antisubmarine, air-rescue, and refueling bases in the Azores, through which the United States routed supplies to Israel during the "Yom Kippur war" of 1973. But in a more general way, American policy simply reflected the thrust of strategic thinking and particular military and economic interests operating in the absence of any countervailing public pressures (notably the as-yet-unrealized potential for Afro-American political action). For fourteen years American policymakers paid scant attention to the small-scale wars for independence being waged by African guerrilla forces in Portugal's African colonies. With the advent of the Nixon administration in 1969, a major review of American policy toward Southern Africa (NSSM 39) concluded that African insurgent movements were ineffectual and not "realistic or supportable" alternatives to continued colonial rule. American policy became even more Eurocentric. The authors of the interdepartmental policy review, commissioned by then White House adviser Henry Kissinger, questioned "the depth and permanence of black resolve" and "rule[d] out a black victory at any stage."[8] They did not question the depth and permanence of Portuguese resolve. They miscalculated because of faulty intelligence, in both senses of that word.

By the early 1970s there were ample signs—economic disarray, political restiveness, military demoralization—that Portugal's days as a Eurafrican power were numbered. These indicators were visible to those with eyes to see. But when in April 1974 Portugal's armed forces overthrew the government of Salazar's successor, Marcello Caetano, the American government stood surprised and embarrassed by its close ties to the *ancien régime*. The debacle of America's subsequent involvement in Angola flowed from the same propensity to view what was happening there through the distorting lens of a larger strategic concern—this time a global shoving match with the Soviet Union.

Angolan Independence and Foreign Intervention

From the April coup until the end of 1974, the Portuguese moved steadily toward independence for Angola and attempted to lead Angola's nationalists into the unfamiliar arena of legal, electoral competition. In so doing they sought to achieve a degree of intermovement cooperation that a long series of conciliation initiatives by the OAU and its members had not. In early 1975 Lisbon's new military regime brought together the leadership of Angola's three liberation movements, first at Mombasa, Kenya, and then at Alvor, Portugal. The resultant tripartite accord created a transitional government to prepare the way for independence on November 11, 1975.

By July 1975, however, the transitional government collapsed, the victim of intermovement rivalry and external intervention. Enjoying an initial military advantage due to Chinese, Rumanian, and Zaïrean arms and training, Holden Roberto's forces occupied the coffee country of the Bakongo north, seeking FNLA ascendancy through military action. Finally able to organize freely in Luanda and its Mbundu hinterland, Agostinho Neto's MPLA (shorn of Daniel Chipenda's splinter group) implanted itself firmly within its own regional bailiwick and, as of late 1974, began receiving renewed arms and financial help from the Soviet Union.

In January 1975 the National Security Council's "40 Committee" had authorized a covert American grant of $300,000 to the FNLA, whose preference for a "military solution" and ostentatious spending spurred the Soviets, in turn, to increase their support for the MPLA. Partisan of a "political solution," UNITA, which had counted on an electoral victory based on its roots within the more than two-million-strong Ovimbundu population and a calculated appeal for support within the European community, found itself being squeezed out of contention by its better-armed, bitterly embattled rivals. With some belated assistance from Zambia and Zaïre, UNITA began building its own army. And in July 1975 the United States, eager to block the Soviet-backed MPLA from power, began funneling arms and money to both the FNLA and UNITA. In August South African troops occupied hydroelectric facilities near the Namibian border, and Cuban instructors began appearing among MPLA troops. At this point China stepped aside.

Finally, in mid-October a South African-led military column marched north from Namibia, turning the tide of battle temporarily in favor of loosely allied UNITA/FNLA forces. Before it was able to reach Luanda, however, thousands of Cuban soldiers equipped with heavy Soviet weaponry streamed in to reinforce the MPLA. By late 1975 MPLA/Cuban forces had smashed badly organized and badly led FNLA/Zaïre troops in the North. They then turned southward. Given Pretoria's white supremacist racial policies, no African state was prepared publicly to support its intervention (although at least two, Zaïre and Zambia, had seemingly encouraged it). Having underestimated Cuban/Soviet resolve and overestimated American nerve, South Africa found itself engaged in a lonely adventure. The U.S. Congress refused to fund further covert (but widely reported) CIA assistance to the FNLA and UNITA. South Africa, embittered by the desertion of an American government unable to pursue secret cooperation, pulled out. And UNITA's hastily assembled and outgunned army fled into the Angolan bush.

Following its military triumph, the MPLA controlled all major towns by February 1976. The OAU, previously split down the middle on the issue, recognized the MPLA government in Luanda. The United States alone among Western powers refused to recognize the People's Republic of Angola, to the extent of first vetoing, then abstaining on its application for United Nations membership. In the view of the American Secretary of State, Dr. Henry Kissinger, who had vainly pleaded with Congress to counter Cuban intervention with increased American assistance to FNLA/UNITA forces, the MPLA's victory represented a Soviet victory. He had inexplicably failed to contact the Soviets to seek an agreement to support the transitional coalition government—the obvious political solution—until the tide of battle had already assured an MPLA victory. Having been defeated in what he viewed as a global chess game with the Soviets, Kissinger then refused to "reward" the victors with American recognition. He clung to the hope that ongoing resistance by UNITA and FNLA guerrillas would bleed Cuban forces in a protracted Vietnam-like rural insurgency.

Angola Faces the Future

That independence came amid violence and chaos is directly traceable to colonial policies that were based upon divide-and-rule exploitation. Whoever ended up governing Angola was bound to face enormous problems, starting with the need to weld the country into a cohesive political entity. Convinced of the importance of political education, the MPLA, like its multiracial, Marxist allies in Guinea-Bissau (PAIGC) and Mozambique (Frelimo), plunged into the task of politicizing and molding a new, socialist society.

The constitution of the People's Republic of Angola (PRA) placed the MPLA, a "broad front" of "anti-imperialist" forces, "in charge of the political, economic and social leadership of the nation." After less than a year of independence, however, the powerful, long-time secretary of the movement, Lúcio Lára, announced plans to convert the MPLA into a "vanguard" socialist party. In November 1976 the MPLA Central Committee scheduled a congress for the second half of 1977 for the purpose of "transforming" the movement into a "Marxist-Leninist party." A new MPLA "action program" stated that, given the "intentions" of external forces to impose "neo-colonial domination" on it, Angola was obliged to embark upon the road to "scientific socialism." This meant adopting "the socialism of Marx, Engels and Lenin, scientific socialism that explicitly entails the ending of exploitation of man by man." The congress convened in December 1977 and launched the retitled MPLA–Party of Workers on a national program to revive agricultural production and promote political and ideological education. Inspired by an "internationalist" world view, the party rejected regionalist notions of "African socialism" or Pan-Africanism as diluted or constricted approaches to the goal of collective human liberation. For Angola's six million people, some 90 percent of whom remain illiterate despite an expansion of public education during the last years of the colonial regime, it prescribed an orthodox but flexible Marxism.

Did all this signify that Angola, as Henry Kissinger had feared, was becoming a Soviet-style, communist state? The October 1976 visit of the PRA's poet-physician president, Agostinho Neto, to Moscow, where he signed a Treaty of

Friendship and Cooperation with the Soviet Union, encouraged some to so conclude. The treaty included a military clause promising mutual support: "In the interest of strengthening the defense of the capability of the High Contracting Parties they will continue to develop cooperation in the military sphere on the lines of appropriate agreements concluded between them."[9]

But there was considerable evidence on which to base a contrary assessment. This view perceives Angola as setting out on a pragmatic, independent, and open-ended process of sociopolitical change. The MPLA Central Committee itself gave immediate priority to the task of "binding the wounds of war and getting the economy functioning again." Recognizing that Angola had only a very small urban working class, even the MPLA's principal ideologue, Lúcio Lára, warned against precipitous moves that would alienate such groups as the peasants, petit bourgeois, and intellectuals, whose participation was vital to national reconstruction. And it seemed reasonable to assume that the country's own particular historical, cultural, and experiential circumstances would play an important role in determining the final form that its socialist society would take.

Meanwhile, a visible measure of economic pragmatism was consistent with the PRA constitution, which "recognizes, protects and guarantees private property, including that of foreigners, provided these favor the economy of the country and the interests of the Angolan people." The fighting during 1975, or what the MPLA refers to as the "second war for national liberation," had left the economy in shambles. The departure of more than 250,000 whites crippled production and transport but also facilitated the nationalization of industrial and agricultural property. Repairing bridges, replacing transport vehicles (22,000 or 28,000 Angolan trucks left with the Portuguese or were wrecked), and obtaining technicians were the sort of problem that commanded immediate attention.

Just as Cuba's intervention was crucial to the MPLA's military victory, so its help was invaluable in coping with the postwar break in technical services. Cuban doctors, dentists, and medical technicians; education experts; and coffee, sugar, and forestry specialists arrived in force to join the battle of national reconstruction. They were joined by an influx of technical personnel from the Soviet Union and Eastern Europe.

Western business interests were also lured to Luanda by prospects of trade with one of Africa's potentially most wealthy countries. Scandinavian and Dutch firms had an advantage, given their countries' support for the Angolan cause prior to independence. But Luandan officials expressed a desire also to establish ties with the United States, which formerly imported much of the country's coffee, about one hundred million dollars worth annually. Indeed, the markets for many Angolan exports, including oil, diamonds, and iron ore, were perforce Western. And American fears that the Soviet Union would acquire a South Atlantic naval base at Lobito seemed overdrawn. Diplomatic sources have indicated that Soviet feelers pointing to that end were rebuffed. The PRA constitution, moreover, specifically prohibits "the installation of foreign military bases on its national territory." And Agostinho Neto has often stated that the PRA will "never be enslaved to any foreign country, be it the U.S.S.R. or any other power."

What should be expected, however, is a further expansion of the state sector of the economy, the creation of more state cooperatives in farming, manufacturing, and distributive enterprise. And through the medium of the National Union of Angolan Workers (UNTA), efforts are being made to infuse both technical training and greater discipline into the ranks of Angolan workers.

The long-term objective of the government is economic as well as political independence. Accordingly, firms such as the Gulf Oil Corporation face the prospect that their operations will ultimately be nationalized. But at present MPLA authorities are anxious not to disrupt the production of Cabindan oil, which translated into some $500 million in annual state revenue by early 1977. Indeed, in 1976 Cabindan oil accounted for some 80 percent of the country's export earnings (given the interruption of coffee and diamond production), or roughly 60 percent of the government's revenue. It was logical, therefore, for Luanda to follow a gradualist approach recommended by Algerian oil experts and to negotiate for a majority state in Gulf's Cabinda subsidiary for the duration of a new contract period. And a similar approach may be anticipated with respect to Angola's Cassinga iron and Lunda diamond resources as well as the Benguela railroad.

Over the long haul Western as well as other capital and technology will likely be welcomed, but on strict, toughly negotiated terms of mutual benefit. The PRA gives every indication that it will seek diverse sources of participation in the development of its unexploited but promising wealth in copper, manganese, titanium, and uranium, and in agriculture (less than 2 percent of its arable land is now under cultivation). Though they view the world through the prism of Marxist ideology, Angola's new rulers are manifesting a flexible rather than a doctrinaire approach to foreign economic relations.

The goal of reconstructing Angolan society within a new socialist order, however, will prove difficult. To begin with, the MPLA has been beset with internal dissidence. Organized in 1974, a *Revolta Activa* faction headed by Joaquim Pinto de Andrade, who had been named "honorary" president of the MPLA during his years as a political prisoner in Portugal, actively opposed Agostinho Neto's leadership. It was joined in opposition in Luanda by far left militants inspired by Portuguese ideologues, notably Maoists grouped within an Angolan Communist Organization (OCA). The government managed to snuff out these movements only to confront a more formidable challenge. A former black (Mbundu) guerrilla leader and critic of perceived white-*mestiço* dominance in the Neto administration, Nito Alves, emerged as a serious contender for political power. After his ambitions had provoked his dismissal as interior minister in November 1976, he drew high-ranking party leaders and army commanders into anti-Neto intrigue, which resulted in a bloody but abortive coup on May 27, 1977.

The previous February, Neto had alleged that French, South African, and other external "imperialists" were planning a multiphased "Operation Cobra" to destabilize his regime. Three months later internal *fraccionistas*, accusing Netoists of being responsible for acute food shortages, mismanagement by an excessively white and mestiço administration, and ideological weakness (even anti-Soviet sentiment), made their bid for power. According to an official inquiry into their attempted coup, which took the lives of such prominent leaders as minister of finance Saidy Mingas and set back plans for economic reconstruction, the fraccionistas had even managed to undermine confidence in the government among diplomats from "friendly countries."[10] This observation appeared to be an allusion to the Soviet Union. Unlike the Cubans, who gave prompt support to the Neto government, the Russians, whose personal day-to-day relations with Angolans have been less than ideal, were suspected of complicity in the unsuccessful power grab by reputedly pro-Soviet Nito Alves.

That the top levels of MPLA–PRA coup-riddled leadership are held by talented, well-educated, and dedicated men seems incontrovertible. That this leadership represents principally one elite, Portuguese-educated segment of Angolan society seems no less evident, if inevitable. The defeat of Nito Alves may bring temporary respite from the challenge of "black power" advocates. But it also serves to highlight a dominant characteristic of the MPLA government: the prominence of mestiço, white, and *assimilado* ministers and the corresponding paucity of African names among those in senior positions. This fact of course reflects an historical continuity within the MPLA. And the elimination of the FNLA and UNITA as political contenders in a contest of force sharpened and weighted an underlying social dichotomy that cleaved Angolan nationalism throughout the struggle for independence. The exclusion of leadership cadres of the vanquished FNLA and UNITA from government reinforced the preeminence of the MPLA's Portuguese-educated urbanites, who stress the centrality of class conflict as over against racial and ethnocultural considerations. It reinforces the political ascendancy of the *urban/acculturated-intellectual/multiracialists* over the *rural/ethno-populist/uniracialists*. But it has not blinded MPLA leadership to what Lúcio Lára, himself a mestiço, has described as an urgent need to improve economic conditions throughout the country and to overcome "tribal prejudices" within its largely rural populations.

Under the Portuguese the cultural values of Angola's diverse peoples were systematically denigrated. This practice has left a legacy of mutual ignorance and suspicion among ethnic groups. Consequently, any hope of building an integrated Angolan nation through a consensual as distinct from coercive process must rely on conscious, knowledgeable efforts to promote interethnic understanding and respect. To bind the wounds of war and construct a unified socialist society, the MPLA government will have to reach out, bring in new leadership, and transcend the limits of its Luanda/Mbundu/mestiço dimensions. But even if there is an awareness of the need and a commitment to do so, the task will not be an easy one.

Three years after independence the PRA still confronted a residual military challenge to its authority. Guerrilla forces—principally UNITA in the arid southeast, but also the FNLA in the forested northwest, and FLEC (the Cabinda Liberation Front) in the oil-rich Cabindan enclave—continued to harass the MPLA army. Persistent reports that Zaïre was supporting, or at least condoning, the use of its territory by FLNA and FLEC guerrillas were matched by similar reports of continuing South African and French help and new Arab-Iranian finance for UNITA.[11] Zaïre's hostility was evident as well in a refusal to allow its own and Zambia's copper exports access to the Benguela railroad—meaning a loss of some thirty million dollars in annual revenue for Angola. Whether externally supported guerrilla forces represented a serious short-term threat or a harbinger of long-term instability was unclear. Much would depend on the ability of the MPLA government to promote an inclusive, integrative participation by all sectors of Angolan society within the political process.

One obvious consequence of externally-backed insurgency against the government, however, was to prompt it to allow, if not encourage, Shaban (Katangan) exiles to mount armed incursions into Zaïre in 1977 and again in 1978. It also served to prolong, even increase, Angola's dependency on the continued presence of some nineteen thousand Cuban troops. The Cubans, engaged in training an Angolan army of some twenty thousand, were paving the way for their own eventual military withdrawal. But until the Neto government firmly established its authority throughout the country, the Cuban army would remain a vital guarantor of "law and order." Improbable as it might seem, a small island country of nine million people located six thousand miles away had become the arbiter of Angola's future, the decisive block to Ovimbundu, Bakongo, or Cabindan secession, the sole force preventing a return to (or what UNITA called perpetuating) foreign-fed civil war.

The punitive policy of nonrecognition pursued by Kissinger after the defeat of anti-MPLA forces in February 1976 did nothing but nourish anti-American sentiment and discredit American diplomacy in Africa as a whole. One of the first foreign-policy decisions to be faced by the Carter administration, therefore, was whether to continue that negative policy or to seek to establish relations based on the principle of "mutuality of interest." Among the arguments for entering into a more constructive relationship was the very role of Cuba that aroused so much hostility in Washington. If the United States could accept as a modus operandi the notion that it cannot and need not everywhere "shape events," to use one of Kissinger's favorite expressions, it might reduce or eliminate the phenomenon in which America's new "enemies" seek the support of its old "enemies" in violent reaction to its interventionist policies. Indeed, Angola suggested a good argument for "normalizing" relations with Cuba, for Cuba itself could only be rendered perpetually dependent on the Soviet Union by a punitive but futile American economic and diplomatic boycott. Why is it necessary or useful to perpetuate hostile relationships with either country?

The Carter administration did not, however, move expeditiously to recognize the Luanda government. Meanwhile, the MPLA's sense of "revolutionary solidarity" led it, without regard for what its relations with the United States might be, to play an active role in the regional struggle against South African apartheid. The MPLA provided sanctuary and operational bases to the South West Africa People's Organization (SWAPO), which was bent on replacing white minority rule in Namibia with its own. But more alarming to American policymakers, the Cuban army undertook to help train and the Soviets to equip SWAPO forces, as well as guerrilla units belonging to Joshua Nkomo's black Rhodesian (ZAPU) army. Cuba's effective 1978 entry into the Ethiopian-Somali war was facilitated by the presence of troops in Angola that could be quickly transported in Soviet ships to the Red Sea. And, American officials alleged, rebel forces that seized Kolwezi in Zaïre's copper-rich Shaba province in May 1978 were trained in Angola by Cubans (others alleged East Germans). As a consequence, just three years after an ill-fated covert Angolan intervention that was later chronicled in painful detail by the disaffected official who organized it,[12] the American government found itself considering renewed involvement in the form of (probably indirect) support for UNITA. Concern over expanding Soviet-Cuban influence in Africa, where the United States had too long propped up decaying colonial, racial, or imperial regimes, led some Carter officials to share Henry Kissinger's hopes of entrapping Cuban forces in their own Vietnam.

In the short run, however, Western support for anti-MPLA guerrillas could only increase Angolan dependence on the Soviets, Cubans, East Germans, and associates. Having denied itself a diplomatic presence in Luanda, the United States was in a poor position to work for diplomatic solutions. Then, in a surprising June 1978 reversal of the American posture, Ambassador Donald McHenry flew to Luanda. His mission set off a chain of diplomatic initiatives that led in short order to (1) active, perhaps decisive, Angolan pressure on SWAPO to accept Western plans for a United Nations supervised transfer of authority from South Africa to an independent Namibia, and (2) a new Angola-Zaïre agreement aimed at eliminating armed incursions from both sides of their shared borders. Angolan authorities moved quickly to implement the Zaïre accord by disarming Katangan (Shaban) soldiers and moving their refugee camps away from the Zaïre border; this was followed by a subsequent bi-lateral agreement to reopen the Benguela railway. In a separate move Agostinho Neto reached an agreement with President Eanes of Portugal by which thousands of skilled Portuguese cadres that had fled during the civil war might return to Angola to help rebuild its economy—and, incidentally, reduce its dependence on Cuba.

The Luanda government continues to see itself as having risen to power as part of a broader liberation struggle throughout Southern Africa, and it remains committed to the creation of a radical new order—egalitarian, mobilized, disciplined—within Angola and all of Southern Africa. The United States remains unwilling to embark on formal diplomatic relations with it. And UNITA forces still pose a serious challenge, leading to speculation that Agostinho Neto might eventually decide to seek an accommodation with Jonas Savimbi. Nonetheless, Angola seems to be entering a new, less tumultuous era.

In a lecture at the University of Dar es Salaam in 1974, Neto set forth his political ideas and hopes for his country. "What we want," he said, "is an independent life as a nation, a life in which economic relations are just both between countries and within the country, a revival of [African] cultural values which are still valid for our era."[13] These remain goals around which a country that is weary of war while rich in economic resources might be able to unite.

7.

Zambia: The Crisis of Liberation
Timothy M. Shaw and
Douglas G. Anglin

Zambia achieved independence after a comparatively nonviolent liberation struggle and with more promising economic prospects, based on its advanced and prosperous multinational copper industry, than most African states. Nevertheless, it inherited an appalling legacy of social deprivation, educational neglect, and racial inequality. In addition, it remained in 1964 an integral, if somewhat peripheral, dependency of the white-controlled south. Yet while economically the country was still an extension of the Southern African sub-system, politically it now stood in the front line of the struggle along the Zambezi—the river that divided it from Rhodesia and gave the country its name—for the liberation of the subcontinent. This contradiction has been central to all Zambia's difficulties and dilemmas since independence. History, geography, and economics thrust a destiny upon it that was not of its own choosing but one it could never shrink from fulfilling without betraying its deepest principles. Zambia held the keys—or at least one of them—to the gates of the white citadel, and it was determined to unlock them, almost regardless of the cost to itself.

Zambia since independence has been living in a state of almost constant crisis, domestic or international. These crowded years constitute an eloquent testimony not only to suffering and sacrifice but also to a remarkable capacity to accept and surmount national adversity. Nevertheless, by the late nineteen-seventies, the nation found itself confronted with the severest challenges in its brief history. This situation was largely the result of regional and global issues beyond its control, notably a calamitous combination of enforced austerity at home, precipitated by the catastrophic collapse in the world price of copper, and a sharp escalation of the racial conflict along its southern border. Coping

199

effectively with the cumulative consequences—economic, political, social, and strategic—of these simultaneous crises tested the wisdom and will of Zambia's leaders and the maturity and steadfastness of its people as never before. Even the independence of Zimbabwe in 1980 did not bring an end to its troubles.

Despite an ambiguous inheritance in 1964 and inadequate outside support, Zambia has responded with courage and style to the series of challenges that have dominated its independence years. As a result of its geopolitical position and its reliance on insecure transit routes, it has been exceedingly vulnerable to the vicissitudes of Southern African politics. Nevertheless, it has repeatedly resisted temptations to arrange a *modus vivendi* with the white-controlled south, and instead it has consistently supported and identified with the liberation movements. It has done so, in part, as an expression of it own independence and its advocacy of nonracialism and majority participation, recognizing that its own values are tenuous without regional liberation and stability. Moreover, given the slow and uneven pace of change in Southern Africa, Zambia seems fated to face many more crises and challenges before it celebrates the end of its second decade of independence in 1984.[1]

Introduction: The Challenges and Crises of Independence

The emergence of the Republic of Zambia on United Nations Day 1964, after nearly three-quarters of a century as a British protectorate known as Northern Rhodesia, symbolized not only one further step in the process of decolonialization in Africa but also the beginning of a series of setbacks for white power in Southern Africa. The new state of Zambia represented more than the successful conclusion of one more nationalist struggle; it also signified the assertion of the principle of racial equality. Zambia's independence constituted a move toward freedom not only from British colonial rule but also from the settler-dominated Central Africa Federation and the pervasive white racism of Southern Africa.

However, the impact of independence was limited by regional contsraints on the one hand, and by global interdependence and dependence on the other. Salient regional constraints included the pervasive racist culture of Southern Africa, trade, transit and investment linkages, and the presence of white minority regimes on several of Zambia's borders; global interdependence and dependence included participation in international organizations and communications, and reliance on the export of minerals and import of capital and manufactured goods, technology, skills, values, and assumptions.

The ambiguity of Zambia's colonial legacy was most apparent in its political economy, dominated by the production and exportation of copper. The rich Copperbelt meant revenue, but also racialism because of white economic controls, and an outward-oriented and highly dualistic economy; in short, growth without development. Zambia was, in many respects, the archetypal dependent state. At the same time, it was an underdeveloped Southern African state determined both to exemplify and to promote the positive aspects of majority rule. Furthermore, given the importance of copper in the world economy and Zambia in regional affairs, it has been able, on occasion, to take advantage of the politics of independence.

Zambia's agenda at independence was awesome enough. Since then, this agenda has lengthened even further as the processes of internal and regional change have become protracted and problematic. Yet the basic agenda items remain: national development, regional liberation, and international independence. These issues and levels are interconnected. Attempts to develop a nonracial society, to reduce dependence on copper, and to maximize control over the national political economy all impinge upon other regional and global interests and events. As a result, any assertion of Zambia's values tends to have widespread, if somewhat marginal, consequences, spreading outward like the ripples on a pond. In view of the weakness and vulnerability of Zambia's political economy, it is all the more remarkable that the government has dared to grapple so boldly with such a forbidding array of interrelated issues and entrenched interests, nationally, regionally, and internationally.[2] Zambia's leaders might have avoided certain difficulties and dilemmas by accepting with resignation their laissez-faire economic legacy, by treating with the white-controlled south rather than with the liberation movements, and by collaborating more closely with Western countries and corporations. Yet, such a stance of resigned detachment and ideological permissiveness was rejected from the outset on principle as selfish and shortsighted.

The determination of Zambia's first generation of political leaders to confront the issues of independence and dependence has served to multiply and intensify the crises they have had to face. Their tactics at times have been pragmatic, but their principles have remained intact despite pressures to modify or abandon them. On the contrary, Zambia's set of ideologies and priorities has challenged established interests at each level: humanism and nationalism at the national, liberation and nonracialism at the regional, and nonalignment and self-reliance at the global. Rather than compromise at any one level of interaction, Zambia has expressed and exerted its preferences at all levels simultaneously.

At the same time, Zambia's response to this series of challenges and crises has been more robust than radical; it prefers reasonable rather than revolutionary change at all levels. Its leadership eventually responded to the threats of national disunity and factionalism by institutionalizing a one-party state that incorporated significant elements of popular participation and choice and a comprehensive leadership code. It has also bargained effectively with mining and other multinational interests for better terms and relationships rather than imposing total and immediate state control over its economy. Nevertheless, Zambia saw nothing exceptional in the simultaneous encouragement of shuttle diplomacy in Southern Africa and the provision on its soil of facilities for freedom fighters operating against neighboring white-ruled territories, or in maintaining economic links with the West while accepting massive Chinese aid for rail and road projects. Similarly, President Kenneth Kaunda's pilgrimages to Western capitals pleading for capital, credit, and know-how to rescue his ailing copper-based economy have not deterred him from expressing his virulent denunciation of many of these same countries and corporations for their continuing collaboration with the racist minority regimes.

Zambia did not embark upon independence in a mood of resigned fatalism. Far from accepting the colonial legacy as immutable, its leadership has struggled to overcome the nation's inherent weaknesses and break the shackles of inherited dependence. Since 1964, considerable progress has been recorded in realizing a greater measure of independence. This has enabled Zambia to resist external threats and pressures more effectively. In the final analysis, however, its capacity to respond to regional and global challenges will depend crucially on its ability domestically to forge a united nation and to mobilize the energies of its people.

The Challenge of Nation Building

The national motto—"One Zambia, One Nation"—was, and to a considerable extent remains, more an aspiration than an actuality. This is probably inevitable in a country which, even more than most African states, is an artificial colonial creation—as its peculiar butterfly configuration so dramatically demonstrates. In addition to being a geographical curiosity, Zambia suffers from five mutually reinforcing cleavages. These have tended to inhibit the growth of a sense of national solidarity—particularly crucial in a state under siege for so long—and, at times, have generated politically dangerous subnational tensions. The five divisive tendencies are regionalism, ethnic and linguistic diversities, competing political allegiances, unequal economic development, and class differentiation.[3] Yet, the first serious threat to the fledgling nation's fragile unity was none of these; it was instead the outcome of a politico-religious confrontation.

On the eve of independence, violence erupted in the Northern Province when the fanatical followers of a remarkable prophetess, Alice Lenshina, who headed a puritanical Christian separatist sect known as the Lumpa Church,[4] went on a rampage. The origins of this armed uprising can be traced to a clash of absolutes: between the militant nationalism of Kenneth Kaunda's ruling United National Independence Party (UNIP) on the one hand, and the religious exclusivism of a possessed peasantry on the other. There was also evidence of efforts at external manipulation designed to embarrass Kaunda, whose home district of Chinsali was the center of the disturbances and whose own relatives were involved on both sides. In the struggle, the movement was quickly crushed with tragic loss of life as waves of crudely armed and near-suicidal Lumpas rushed police and army units dispatched to the area. Alice Lenshina was captured and held in detention until 1976. Nevertheless, the continuing consequences of the crises were minimal, though it did lead to the imposition of emergency regulations which have remained in force ever since.

Potentially more disruptive was the secessionist sentiment in the Western (Barotse) Province. Regional discontent surfaced periodically in various other parts of the country, notably in the Eastern, Luapula, North-Western, and Southern provinces, but only in Barotseland was a sustained independence campaign mounted.[5] The bases for this claim were ethnic particularism, the proud traditions of the Lozi kingdom, the distinct legal status Barotseland held as a British protectorate, and legitimate grievances against the established line-of-rail for its economic neglect of the peripheral provinces. President Kaunda's initial instinct was to try conciliation. In May 1964, shortly before independence, he signed an agreement with the *litunga* (paramount chief), Sir Mwanawina Lewanika III, who thereby acknowledged Barotseland's incorporation as "an integral part" of Northern Rhodesia in return for the retention of certain customary rights. However, following a resurgence of separatism, culminating in the repudiation of UNIP at the polls in 1968 and the almost simultaneous election of a former secessionist as the new *litunga*, the president moved swiftly to abrogate the Barotse Agreement by a constitutional amendment and to eliminate other symbols that implied (as in the case of Buganda within Uganda) that the province constituted "a nation within a nation."

What made the threat of Barotse secession particularly disturbing at the time was that province's strategic situation bordering Portuguese-ruled Angola and South African-controlled Namibia. Government fears were reinforced by mounting evidence of foreign intrigue. Portuguese agents had attempted at various times to exploit feelings of disaffection among the Lozi, and also among the Lunda in the North-Western Province. Subsequently, South Africa too sought to exert pressure on Lusaka by training, financing, and arming various dissident Zambian elements, who were then infiltrated into the Western Province from Namibia. The most blatant of these subversive interventions was the "Mushala gang" incursion in 1975.[6] While this initiative was politically ill-timed as it coincided with Pretoria's détente offensive, it has succeeded in creating considerable havoc in the countryside and embarrassment for the government, especially as Mushala himself has continued to elude capture.

Geographical, ethnic, and economic differences have also found expression in an almost continuous potential for political fission.[7] From the first, President Kaunda argued for a one-party state as an instrument of national unity. At the same time, he firmly rejected any suggestion of legislative action to outlaw opposition parties. Instead, he was content confidently to await the day when UNIP would sweep the country democratically at the polls, as TANU had done in Tanzania in 1958. UNIP popular strength had increased dramatically since the party (initially under the name Zambia African National Congress) had, on October 24, 1958, broken away from the African National Congress, the preeminent nationalist movement in Northern Rhodesia during the preceding decade. Moreover, as a result of its more militant though still essentially nonviolent strategy, it could legitimately claim most of the credit for the achievement of independence exactly six years later.

The party's expectation that the momentum of success would be maintained, if not accelerated, once it took over the reins of government proved excessively optimistic, as internal-external linkages effectively prevented both domestic tranquility and unity. To begin with, the ANC under its veteran, if ineffective leader, Harry Nkumbula, failed to wither away. Despite the implications for uneven local development of the slogan "It pays to belong to UNIP," the sturdy Tonga of the Southern Province remained unshaken in their political loyalties. Similarly, the Lozi of the Western Province transferred their allegiance to the United Party, which had broken away from UNIP in 1966 and, following its banning two years later, merged with the ANC. Thus, in the December 1968 general elections the ANC won twenty of twenty-five parliamentary seats in these two strategically-located provinces, providing considerable comfort to neighboring white regimes.

A major factor in this electoral upset, especially in Barotseland, was the voter perception that, as a result of the UNIP Central Committee elections in August 1967, the ruling party had become increasingly dominated by the Bemba of the Northern Province. (The Bemba language group constituted just over one third of the population at the time of the 1969 census.) So bitter in fact had tribal animosities within UNIP become that it took the shock of President Kaunda's brief "resignation" in February 1968 to save the party, and perhaps the nation, from disintegration. At the next party elections three years later, the political exploitation of political sectionalism,[8] was contained by negotiating an agreed slate of candidates in advance. Nevertheless, later in the year the party split, with Vice-President Simon Kapwepwe, a close friend of the President's since boyhood, forming his own essentially conservative United Progressive Party (UPP), mainly with support from his fellow Bemba. Subsequently, Kapwepwe and a number of his top officials were detained and the party banned. It was readily apparent that the country could ill afford another electoral free-for-all. If Zambia was to be made safe for democracy, let alone for development, a radical restructuring of the political institutions of the country seemed a prerequisite.

This was a major consideration in Kaunda's decision to institute a "one-party participatory democracy" by legislation rather than through the ballot box. In December 1972, Zambia's "Second Republic" was ushered into existence and a year later the first elections under the new constitution were held.[9] Although the party central committee wielded certain reserve powers (which resulted in twenty-six of three hundred fifty candidates being disqualified, presumably in most cases for suspected pro-UPP sympathies), both the primary elections (to select the three one-party candidates in each constituency) and the parliamentary elections (among the three official candidates) were remarkably free. One measure of this was the heavy turnover in the membership of the National Assembly. In particular, three cabinet ministers and eleven junior ministers went down to defeat. At the same time, five former ANC MPs and a dozen ANC supporters were elected. In many UNIP strongholds, where there had been selection by acclamation in the past, the 1973 election offered voters their first taste of competitive politics since independence. Moreover, the new House has proven more lively than its predecessors.

Nevertheless, Parliament remains a comparatively inconsequential, if colorful, centerpiece to the political stage. The center of gravity of power lies elsewhere—in State House (the Office of the President and his special advisors), the bureaucracy including the burgeoning parastatal sector, and potentially the military and the party, as well as in the business and professional community, Zambian and expatriate. These constitute the "modern sector" of society, the preserve of a competent, confident, and cosmopolitan coterie of managers and technocrats who largely guide the destiny of the nation. Whether this elite can yet be designated a distinct class and, if so, whether class has now superceded ethnicity, provincialism, and the urban-rural gap as the predominant cleavage in Zambian society are the subject of lively controversy inside the country and outside it, in both activist and academic circles. Much analysis of class formation in Zambia has to date tended to be rather nonempirical and polemical, and the perceived consequences of inter- or intra-class conflicts projected beyond what the available evidence would seem to justify.[10] Nevertheless, it is undeniable that class distinctions in some sense of the term are real, growing, and increasingly significant for decision making. At the same time, a convincing case has yet to be made that class interest offers a definitive explanation of all of Zambia's foreign policy behavior. This is particularly apparent in any analysis of Zambia's principled stance at the regional level on Southern African liberation, the cumulative adverse socioeconomic consequences of which for the country and its ruling elite have been substantial.

The Challenge of Liberation

The achievement of formal independence in 1964 created the potential for the realization of substantive political, economic, and social freedom in the future. However, because of the multifaceted impact of white power on Zambia, national independence was inseparable from regional liberation. Zambia's support for nationalist movements in Southern Africa is, then, an extension of its own continuing struggle. In particular, aside from other political and economic imperatives, it reflects Zambia's commitment to a nonracial society as expressed in its national philosophy of humanism. As formulated by President Kaunda, humanism advocates a person-centered development strategy in which human needs take precedence over politics or profit. It is a nonracial, participatory, ecumenical expression of idealism, with roots in traditional African society, Christianity, and Western social democracy. It was intended to mobilize the population for unity, development, and support. Its distinctiveness lies in its complete contrast to the racist exclusiveness of apartheid.

In the immediate aftermath of independence, Zambian energies were, understandably, concentrated on a crash program to overcome the grosser deficiencies in the country's domestic development. Disengagement from the south was also a strategic goal, but it was envisaged that this could be effected only gradually. Rhodesia's unilateral declaration of independence (UDI) abruptly reversed these priorities by directly challenging Zambia's support for a nonracial future for Southern Africa. Subsequent regional crises, notably the closure of the Rhodesian border in 1973, until then the major transit and trade route for landlocked Zambia, also threatened the development and direction of Zambia's own political economy.

Zambia's principal foreign policy preoccupation in its first fifteen years was, of course, Rhodesia, but it also continued to support moves toward independence in the other white-ruled territories with which it shares borders: Mozambique, Namibia, and Angola. The prospects for change improved only slowly throughout the 1960s. During this period, Zambia's advocacy of nonracialism was limited largely to diplomacy within the Organization of African Unity, the nonaligned movement, and the Commonwealth, as symbolized by the 1969 Lusaka Declaration on Southern Africa (which offered cooperation with South Africa but only if it began to dismantle its apartheid structure) and the 1971 Singapore Declaration of Commonwealth principles; these advocated nonviolence and nonracialism respectively but both added the imperative of rapid progress toward final decolonization and greater participation. The challenges continually posed by the UDI and by South Africa to Zambia's independence and the nationalist parties compelled President Kaunda gradually to accept the inevitability of violent pressure against intransigent regimes.[11]

Support for the liberation movement, however, served to multiply the threats to Zambia's own independence and territory, with frequent incursions and border violations by Portuguese, South African, and Rhodesian forces, culminating in major Rhodesian invasions of Joshua Nkomo's Zimbabwe African Peoples Union (ZAPU) camps in 1978. Earlier, in 1973, Rhodesian Prime Minister Ian Smith threatened to close his border if Zambia continued to provide assistance to the Zimbabwe African National Union (ZANU) and to ZAPU. Rather than accept Smith's conditions, President Kaunda called his bluff and forced him to proceed with the border closure. That Zambia could contemplate such a step was indicative of the growing strength and sophistication of its political economy as well as the new sense of confidence that characterized its leadership.

The real beginning of the end for the white regimes was the April 1974 antifascist coup in Portugal, which heralded the start of the rapid decolonization process in both Mozambique and Angola. The immensity of this change was recognized in Lusaka earlier than in most capitals. This enabled the Zambian president to play an important role as "midwife" in bringing the new post-Salazar and post-Caetano Portuguese leaders and the Front for the Liberation of Mozambique (Frelimo) together for talks that culminated in the Lusaka Agreement of September 1974, leading to the birth of the new Mozambique. Regrettably, the situation in Angola, like that in Zimbabwe, was more complex, with a long history of factionalism and feuding within the nationalist movement. Nevertheless, Zambia consistently supported the liberation struggles, whilst also pursuing every opportunity to unite the various parties. In the case of Angola, the 1975 Alvor and Nakuru accords on unity, negotiated under Portuguese and OAU auspices respectively, rapidly broke down, leading to a civil war situation which was quickly exacerbated by the major interventions of South Africa, the superpowers, and Cuba, as well as Zaïre. (See Angola chapter.) Zambia was alarmed by this development, not so much because of Soviet involvement and the prospect of another Marxist regime, but largely because the transition to independence in this instance reduced the autonomy and unity both of Angola and of the continent. Although Zambia had long hosted the forces of the Popular Movement for the Liberation of Angola (MPLA) and had expelled the National Union for the Total Liberation of Angola (UNITA) from its territory, in 1975–76 it urged unity and cooperation among the rival factions in Angola and the achievement of an African solution.

Consonant with its own experience of overcoming internal disunity, Zambia has consistently sought to encourage domestic reconciliation among rival liberation movements as well as between governments and dissidents in independent Africa, notably in the Sudan, Zaïre, and Ethiopia. At the special OAU summit of January 1976 on Angola, for instance, President Kaunda commented that:

> Since the birth of the OAU, this is the most serious and tragic crisis the continent has ever faced. Angola is serious and tragic to the people of that country; it is tragic in its implications for the unity and security of Africa. Angola is an emotional issue. . . .
> In the history of independent Africa, this is the first time that thousands of non-African regular troops and heavy sophisticated equipment have

been brought in to install one political party into power and in service of
their hegemonic interests. This is a most dangerous phenomenon which
constitutes a grave threat to the entire continent and unity of Africa. . . .
Time has come for us to reaffirm the basic principle(s) of Pan-Africanism:
no intervention by foreign powers in African affairs . . . Africa must understand that imperialism is imperialism. It knows neither race nor color
nor ideology. . . .

   In dealing with this grave issue, Zambia is in no way questioning the
sovereign right of each member state to make its own independent decisions. However, if we as member states fail to harmonize our views on
such issues as Angola, our organization will no longer be credible. We
run the risk of playing into the hands of the enemies of Africa. . . .

   Zambia wants a progressive and non-aligned Angola, completely free
from external pressures.[12]

   Similar questions of national and continental independence and unity, freedom, and nonalignment continued to arise in the case of Rhodesia/Zimbabwe
as well. But here, Zambia's policy was very much informed by its own experiences of Ian Smith's deception and ambiguity. Moreover, President Kaunda
had a long-standing and close association with one of the nationalist leaders
and parties—Joshua Nkomo of ZAPU—and developed certain reservations
(which appeared to be reciprocated) concerning the substance and style of
other factions such as Bishop Muzorewa's UANC and Robert Mugabe's ZANU
(see Zimbabwe chapter). State House in Lusaka was not only preoccupied
with Rhodesia/Zimbabwe; it also expended considerable resources over the
years in attempting to bring the leaders and parties together, both the liberation movements themselves and also, more recently, the nationalists and the
rebel regime. It was this effort that produced the ambivalent period of
"détente" between 1974 and 1976. This involved a tactical maneuver, undertaken in close concert with the other front-line states—at that time, Botswana,
Mozambique, and Tanzania—and even then with considerable reservations, to
enlist the support of South Africa in pressuring the Smith regime to accept
genuine majority rule in Rhodesia.[13] Its specific achievements were the abortive Declaration of Unity amongst the Zimbabwean parties in Lusaka in
December 1974, which established the short-lived unitary African National
Council, and the conciliatory 1975 Dar es Salaam Declaration on Southern
Africa, which recognized the need for diplomatic contact as well as armed
struggle to bring about change in the region.

   The demise of both these related initiatives over Rhodesia/Zimbabwe—
combined with difficulties in Angola and Zaïre as well as with the falling
price of copper—led to a further escalation in Zambia's rhetoric and action.
Its leadership remains fearful of more violence and radicalization in Southern Africa, but increasingly saw these as inevitable if minority rule was to
be finally overthrown. Hence Zambia's full support of the Patriotic Front,
particularly the Nkomo wing based in Zambia, and its initial skepticism about

the series of Anglo-American proposals, at least until it became clear that they were both distinct from and an advance on any "internal settlement" promoted by Smith. Zambia's regrets and anger at the failure of "détente" were expressed by President Kaunda after the breakdown of the earlier 1976 Smith-Nkomo talks, in which Zambia had a considerable investment and stake. He referred to the previous cavalier rejection of the conciliatory and reasonable 1969 Lusaka Manifesto on Southern Africa by the white regimes until they felt directly threatened following the collapse of Portuguese colonialism:

> Even at this late stage, we allowed peaceful change to have an opportunity in Zimbabwe. The total breakdown of constitutional negotiations in Rhodesia has now demonstrated to all and sundry that nothing can be gained by a peace strategy as an approach to ending racism and colonialism which have led to conflict in Southern Africa. We have left no stone unturned in our determination to achieve majority rule by peaceful means. We invested a lot in the peace program as an instrument for beneficial change; this has failed. But we place this failure squarely on the shoulders of rebel leader Mr. Ian Smith and his henchmen. . . . In the circumstances, Africa has no option left but to help intensify the armed struggle which is now in full swing. This is the gravest hour in the history of our subcontinent. . . . The armed struggle is a just war against injustice which must be waged until victory is won. . . . The whites in Rhodesia have made their choice, namely that they prefer change to come by violent means. . . . they should not blame anybody except themselves for opting for a course that is clearly not in their interests and has the gravest consequences for non-racialism in Southern Africa.[14]

So, despite Henry Kissinger's policy switch on Southern Africa announced in Lusaka in April 1976, and Kaunda's as well as Nkomo's own preference for nonviolent constitutional change, Zambia remained understandably highly skeptical of any agreement with the Smith regime. Dr. Kaunda was fiercely critical of the 1978 internal settlement for Rhodesia between Smith and three African leaders, and even at one stage uncharacteristically opposed the holding of preindependence elections because of the prospects of continued violence and their divisive impact on Zimbabwe:

> The Anglo-American initiative, like the Geneva Conference on Zimbabwe, is the product of the liberation war being waged by the forces of the Patriotic Front. Therefore, any effective ceasefire agreement would have to be between the two combatants, namely, the Patriotic Front and the Smith Regime. . . . [Muzorewa, Sithole, and Chirau] have already signed their informal Ceasefire Agreement with the rebels.[15]

Despite this rough talk, Kaunda greeted the diplomatic breakthrough in Lusaka and the successful conclusion to the Lancaster House negotiations in London with great relief. In the case of Namibia, Zambia remains dubious about the prospects for success of the Western initiative. Nevertheless, along with the other front-line states and Nigeria, it has actively encouraged dialogue between the South West African Peoples Organization (SWAPO) and the five-country Western Contact Group (United States, Britain, Canada, France, and West Germany) shuttling between Pretoria, New York, and Lusaka. While awaiting the outcome of these efforts, Zambia has continued to accord SWAPO strong public support. Fortunately, the Namibian situation is more analogous to that in Mozambique, where one liberation movement was dominant, and unlike the more fissiparous cases of Angola and Zimbabwe. Despite some dissension within SWAPO, Zambia has not had to expend many scarce resources in fostering its unity. (See Namibia chapter.)

Zambia's interests and role in Southern Africa are central, then, to the futures both of its own political economy and of the region as a whole. Kaunda, along with his closest colleague, President Nyerere of Tanzania, has played a crucial part in establishing the *entente* of front line states (which now includes Angola) and in orchestrating their sophisticated diplomacy of contact and confrontation for change in Southern Africa. It has recognized the need for multiple tactics and pressures and has accepted the validity of some kind of "domino theory" for the region. In particular, Zambia has been acutely conscious of the need to secure multilateral support for its initiatives, or at least prior collective approval for any "unilateral" moves. Almost all of its Southern African actions have been taken in concert with other front line states and increasingly with Nigeria too. Angola was the one major instance prior to Zambia's own opening of its southern border in October 1978, where serious differences in approaches emerged.

Zambia appreciates that its own liberation will not be guaranteed until the last citadel of white domination is transformed, namely South Africa itself. Yet, President Kaunda recognizes that the achievement of majority rule in Pretoria will be a much more demanding, dangerous, and divisive task because of that country's advanced industrial economy and the presence of a large, well-established white population. However, Zambia has prepared the way for this transition by attempting to reduce its links with South Africa despite the political and economic costs involved, and by developing a longer-term strategy to cope with the complexities of any transition to democracy in the white redoubt. (See Grundy chapter.)

The Challenge of Dependence

The character and intensity of Zambia's dependence have changed during the period of independence. Zambia has largely overcome reliance on the white south, and has reduced the closeness of its British connection, both governmental and corporate. Yet, despite those considerable achievements, the country remains highly dependent on the global economy both for copper sales and for inputs for its mining industry.

At independence, the national political economy, dominated by copper, relied heavily on regional transit and international exchange, particularly inputs from the south and exports to overseas markets. Zambia was dependent not only on foreign capital, technology, skills, and routes to produce and market its single export commodity, copper, but also on external values, assumptions, and approval. Any refashioning of this inheritance required a simultaneous assault at the national, regional, and global levels. Given the elusiveness of regional liberation, the task of effecting change at the other two levels was further complicated. Today, Zambian reliance on exporting copper remains and constitutes a pervasive factor influencing both domestic and foreign policy. However, the country has begun to reduce its degree of dependence on copper-related variables. In particular, the leadership increasingly recognizes the dangers to the whole political economy of its continuing vulnerability to vicissitudes in the production, price, and distribution of copper. Nevertheless, awareness and policy have evolved ahead of action, which requires both time and money.

Zambia has sought to disengage from reliance on the white south and the multinational mining conglomerates that dominated the Copperbelt by diversifying its import partners, energy sources, export markets, transit routes, corporate links, and technological transfer arrangements. Thus it was able to largely overcome its dependence on the Rhodesia-South Africa connection and, to some extent, on Britain, and to begin to widen its links with the European Economic Community (with which it is associated as one of the more than fifty African, Caribbean, and Pacific states) and North America, Japan, and China. But such drastic structural changes require more than determination to effect; time and external assistance are also needed, and neither of these has been available in adequate supply.

Given the strength of the earlier formal bonds of federation and the informal links with South Africa, cooperation within the structures of the Southern African subsystem would have been an understandable policy premise. But the imperatives of nationalism, nonracialism, and liberation undermined this easy assumption and option; and the unilateral declaration of independence excluded it altogether. Instead, with each new stage in Zambia's disengagement from the racially-defined subcontinent has come an increasingly outspoken commitment to the liberation movements and to the achievement of majority rule.

In pursuit of disengagement, Zambia has sought to optimize the number of alternative routes at its disposal. In operational terms, this has meant attempting to ensure that at least two of the three major outlets to the sea— the Rhodesia Railway south to Beira in Mozambique, the Benguela Railway west to Lobito in Angola, and the road/rail northeast to Dar es Salaam in Tanzania—were available at all times. Access to only one of these routes quickly precipitated a crisis. The primary result of the quest for alternative transit capacity has been the development of new links with Tanzania: the opening of the Dar es Salaam–Ndola oil pipeline in 1968, the upgrading of the Great East Road between Dar es Salaam and the Copperbelt in the early seventies, and the inauguration of the Tazara Railway from Dar es Salaam to Kapiri Mposhi in 1976. Following the closure of the border with Rhodesia in 1973, Zambia diverted the bulk of its traffic onto the Benguela route, until the Angolan civil war closed that outlet in August 1975. This proved a severe blow to the Zambian economy as the new railway to Dar es Salaam was not fully operational until the following year; and, when it was, it aggravated the chronic congestion that has plagued Dar es Salaam port. Accordingly, the search for alternative routes has continued.

Despite Mozambique's independence, the old route to Beira remained un-available, as both Zambian and Mozambican borders with Rhodesia were closed. However, a direct truck route to Beira through Mozambique's Tete province was prudently developed, and the road/rail route to Mozambique's northern port of Nacala through Malawi has been improved. Moreover, direct rail links with Malawi and/or Mozambique are under active consideration. More problematical is the possibility of a direct rail connection with the West Coast, terminating at Lobito or conceivably (with the independence of Namibia) at Walvis Bay. Moreover, the liberation of Zimbabwe and the re-opening of rail routes to Beira and Maputo have inevitably had a profound impact, particularly as they also opened up the possibility of a new regional grouping of independent states in East-Central Africa.[16]

Zambia has succeeded in lessening its dependence not only on the white south but also on Britain and the major global corporations. Regional dis-engagement has been matched by global diversification toward smaller states and smaller companies in the West and elsewhere. Zambia has ended Rhodesian and severely reduced South African involvement in its economy, although residual links remain with the Anglo-American Corporation (AAC), an Anglo-South African regional conglomerate. But the twin policies of regional dis-engagement and global diversification have not led either to the creation of its own welfare-oriented institutions or to the acceptance of new forms of dependence on socialist states.

Through a series of 51% takeovers of foreign firms and continual restruc-turing of the parastatal sector, Zambia has created a massive state capitalist system centered on the Zambian Industrial and Mining Corporation (ZIMCO) and the Industrial Development Corporation (INDECO). These are essentially state holding-companies which have a series of financial, technical, manage-ment, and other arrangements with a variety of foreign companies, among them the two mining corporations (AAC and American Metal Climax, now minority shareholders in Zambia Consolidated Mines), established British con-cerns (Dunlop, ICI, Lonrho), and new major (Fiat, Mercedes-Benz, Toyota) and minor (Atlas of India, Airam of Finland, Labatts of Canada) foreign investors. New copper-mining operations include the involvement of Canadian (Noranda) and Rumanian (Geomin) companies. And, in 1978, AAC established a new emerald-mining and -selling company jointly with the government. Emeralds, combined with new uranium and cobalt production, may improve receipts from mining but, until these ores and stones are processed further in Zambia and until they are related to some form of integrated industrial strategy, they will not lead to a significant redefinition of Zambia's political economy. Further, the enactment of an Industrial Development Act in 1977 provides a wide range of incentives for domestic and foreign manufacturers, particularly those investing in priority enterprises and rural areas.

Despite the rhetoric of "self-management" and "workers' participatory democracy" in industry, parastatals (government-owned corporations) in Zambia remain firmly integrated into the global capitalist system. Through minority ownership, management contracts, the provision of services, and control over technology, the multinationals are still in a position to influence the mode of production and the "national" industrial strategy. Many leading Zambians, reflecting their distinctive political economy, have been incorporated into a transnational society, and have largely eschewed the alternative of some variety of socialism and self-reliance. The dependence of Zambia in the world system, if no longer within the regional subsystem, may be explained in part through this interdependence of the Zambian elite in transnational activities.

The parastatal nexus manages, then, to reconcile national and external interests, and so to rationalize Zambia's involvement in the world economy. The series of negotiations to secure majority Zambian ownership in mining operations and branch plants constituted a significant shift in the balance of power between host state and multinational corporation within a transnational relationship; the negotiations did not of themselves involve a fundamental restructuring of Zambia's political economy, although they may be a prerequisite for such restructuring. The reorganization of formal control did, however, serve to appease certain nationalist and class interests, while widening the scope of state involvement and patronage. Potentially, the parastatals are capable of being transformed into more socialist or cooperative institutions along the lines of "industrial participatory democracy" and "Communocracy —a people's economy under Humanism" as advocated by President Kaunda,[17] but thus far they have operated essentially on normal Western lines, so constituting central pillars of a state capitalist system.[18]

The state capitalist political economy meanwhile has tended to exacerbate established domestic differences; regional and ethnic sectionalism has been supplemented by class-type divisions. The major beneficiaries of the system have been the middle classes and the labor aristocracy—the managers and workers in ZIMCO, INDECO, and the private sectors. The un- and underemployed and the peasantry have been the major losers and have seen their real incomes fall—in some instances quite dramatically—since independence. Some party members and intellectuals have supported the interests of the poor and relatively deprived by advocating moves toward a more socialist or cooperative society in which regional and class differences would be minimized. On the other hand, there is a growing group of entrepreneurs in both the parastatal and private sectors who are critical of excessive state involvement and favor more scope for private initiative and greater emphasis on criteria of economic efficiency. The former group—the radicals—seek a more social definition of humanism, whereas the latter—the technocrats—advocate a more capitalist definition. To date, the president and senior party leaders have successfully mediated between these and other forces, tending to accept the rhetoric of the radicals while practicing the policies of the technocrats. But given the prospects of class formation and structural problems with the economy, such fine balancing may become increasingly tenuous.

To date, Zambia remains a dependent society dominated by a consumerist ethic. Any transition to a more modest life-style for the rich and to a re-distribution of wealth from the more affluent regions and classes to the less advantaged remains rather problematic. Nevertheless, the president is aware of the need for greater self-reliance internationally and self-regulation internally if structural problems such as balance-of-payments deficits and domestic inequalities are to be tackled. Over the years, he has repeatedly denounced the middle classes for their antisocial values, criticizing "the rapid emergence of a powerful Zambian elite whose thoughts and actions are couched in terms of the very rapine system which Humanism in Zambia was meant to combat."[19] Class cleavages may yet prove a more intractable problem than racialism.

One attempt to ameliorate sectional and class tensions and to perpetuate Zambia's consumptionist high-cost political economy by enhancing the national income has involved the creation of a copper cartel: the Council of Copper Exporting Countries (CIPEC). Zambia was a founding member of CIPEC, and has supported its moves to stabilize supplies and improve prices. However, because several major exporters remain outside CIPEC, and because of the global recession and, above all, the nationalist policies of some members, notably Chile, CIPEC has not been able to stabilize, let alone increase, the price of copper.

A further attempt to avoid a choice between technocratic and radical definitions of humanist ideology and development strategy involves the bor-rowing of external funds. In 1973 and 1975, Zambia arranged for three Eurodollar loans totaling $250 million to help implement its self-management of the two major copper companies. And, in 1978 and 1981, Zambia secured $390 million and $950 million stand-by credits from the International Monetary Fund (IMF) to help it survive the consequences of the continuing low price of copper.[20] Zambia's ability quickly to amass such substantial debts is a tribute to its national creditworthiness and the dexterity of its negotiators. It is also indicative of the West's own involvement in the Zambian state—the 1981 loan being the largest yet to a black African government—and of the state's willingness to comply with stringent terms, which essentially define its development strategy until 1984. This strategy calls for accelerated rural development and a narrowing in the urban-rural gap, in part through a reduction in food subsidies for the urban population.

Eurodollar and IMF loans and links largely settle the question of Zambia's future development strategy without resolving the technocrat-radical feud. The president may continue to talk about a socialist definition of humanism, but Zambia's international bankers largely determine its definition in practice. IMF terms for special drawing rights in 1978 included a further 10% devaluation of the national currency (the *kwacha*) to protect jobs on the Copperbelt, following the earlier 20% drop in 1976, and austerity budgeting, particularly a rapid reduction in subsidies to agriculture, food, mining, and other sectors of the economy. These moves together constitute a remarkable return to laissez faire economics; along with the second declaration of a 15% cutback in copper production, principally because of congestion in Dar es Salaam (but also in keeping with CIPEC efforts to force up world prices), they indicate a considerable reevaluation and redirection of Zambia's economy.

The interrelatedness and intensification of the politico-economic crisis swirling around Zambia have been increasingly recognized in the West, particularly after the instability in neighboring Zaïre's own copperbelt province of Shaba. So, despite Zambia's growing indebtedness, it received a positive response for a further substantial injection of emergency aid over and above regular bilateral and multilateral forms: the May 1981 IMF loan was one of the largest ever made on a per capita basis. Accumulated foreign debts are slowly being paid off, national salaries and credit are being restricted, parastatals are to be retrenched and rendered profitable, and farming is to be the major growth sector. Western concern about Zambia has grown since a May 1978 editorial in the *Times* of London on "Zambia's Key Position":

> President Kaunda is visiting London and Washington at a critical moment for all Southern Africa. Zambia's near-bankruptcy is an integral part of the jigsaw of politics, economics, war and tribal and personal rivalries in the whole region. Dr. Kaunda must have help, but his influence on the course of events in Rhodesia is extremely important so he is not in a weak bargaining position. . . . Popular discontent is growing in an election year. Many Zambians ask more insistently why they must suffer for the sake of the black Rhodesians, whose leadership quarrels they see realistically; while other Zambians favour bringing in the Cubans to make a quick end of the torment. Dr. Kaunda . . . has therefore either to get Western credits to endure the siege a little longer, or he will be driven to accept Russo-Cuban intervention to finish the war fast.

Despite the recent purchase of Soviet MIGs, Zambia remains firmly within the Western world economically. However, Zimbabwe's independence has not led to the promised prosperity, so domestic dissatisfaction continues to mount. Per capital GDP has declined dramatically since 1977, and IMF-imposed constraints will further suppress urban living standards. Although the Kaunda regime received impressive support in the December 1978 elections, there is evidence of a considerable growth in popular discontent since then, and even some overt opposition: national plans and international loans cannot change the price of copper. Self-reliance remains as elusive as ever, with import restrictions effectively limiting local manufacturers. Moreover, international attention has shifted south to neighboring Zimbabwe. As a result, Zambia is more isolated regionally and more dependent globally than ever—a cruel irony after 16 years of advocating regional decolonization. Neither the technocrats' preferences nor the radicals' dreams have been realized. Instead, the regime seems more bewildered and embattled than ever. Given the structural roots of the present public mood, the widespread disillusionment cannot readily be overcome by either charisma or capital.

The Challenge of Interdependence

As a recently independent Third World state, Zambia is part of the new majority in world politics. Its entrance into the councils of the world strengthened demands for new global structures. Zambia has been identified most closely with its African neighbors, both contiguous and more distant in the continent, and then with other Third World countries. It inherited many linkages with First World actors, particularly with Britain, but it has attempted to balance these with relations with the Second, socialist World as well as with the Third World. Its own definition and practice of nonalignment has been important not only for the diversification of its socioeconomic associations but, perhaps even more forcefully, in the attraction of support against the white regimes. It has actively interpreted its policy of nonalignment both to enhance its prospects of economic development and to improve its chances of political survival in the hostile Southern African environment.

Given the range of geopolitical, economic, and social difficulties Zambia has faced since 1964, its ability to attract continued international sympathy and assistance has been crucial. Not only has it received political, psychological, and material support for itself, it has also offered its own support to particular ideas and movements. This mutual interaction has advanced furthest in the case of the six front-line states, but has also extended to other African states and structures. Aside from participation in conferences, institutions, and activities at both regional and global levels, Zambia has been actively involved in forums of the nonaligned states and in the Group of

77 less-developed countries. Such south-south, horizontal linkages help to balance inherited north-south vertical ties.

Zambia applied and negotiated for association with the now-defunct East African Community of Kenya, Tanzania, and Uganda in the mid-1960s, when it was still seen as a potential catalyst for wider forms of integration. But even before the collapse of the Community, Zambia had become more interested in a set of bilateral links with three neighbors, Tanzania, Botswana, and Mozambique, to reinforce its multilateral relations with these front-line states. Its bilateral relationship has become particularly close and comprehensive with Tanzania, reflecting the warm ties between presidents and state houses. The social, diplomatic, military, communication, and economic linkages based on this dyad are now maturing into a new regional grouping in east-central Africa, incorporating Zimbabwe as well as Angola and Mozambique, the BLS countries, and even Malawi.

Already some Zambians, particularly those in the technocrat group, appear concerned about the "radicalization" of the region, with the formal implementation of "people's democracies" in Angola and Mozambique, and would prefer associations with other mixed economies. Zambia's interest in becoming the core of a new region in Africa could probably be exercised only in association with Western interests, a claim that it continues to use effectively in attempts to secure Western financial support. Neither Zambia's present strategic concerns nor its economic interests would be particularly well served by association with Eastern-dominated states. It miscalculated over socialist involvement in Angola because of fears of a grand Soviet strategy; and some Zambians continue to fear politico-economic "contagion" in the Central African region. According to one of President Kaunda's advisors: "If Zambia goes down, the exponents of scientific socialism presently in Angola and Mozambique will have done what the Portuguese failed to do. They will have created a contiguous sphere of influence right across Africa."[21] In contrast to this global and ideological perspective, Zambia's advocacy of regionalism is intended to counteract South African designs and to reduce external, particularly extra-African, involvement in liberation and development.

President Kaunda has served as chairman of both the OAU and the non-aligned states. Nevertheless, given Zambia's preoccupation with regional, especially Rhodesian interactions, both cooperative and conflictual, the country has been somewhat less concerned with continental affairs and the nonaligned movement except as they have related to Southern Africa. Accordingly, it has sought support for its liberation goals at both levels. At the same time, as the front-line states have grown in number and maturity, so their reliance on the legitimization, as opposed to the support, of other African and nonaligned members has diminished. The conciliatory 1969 Lusaka Manifesto on Southern Africa, agreed upon by a subcontinental grouping of

Eastern and Central African states, symbolized this transition away from initiatives in the OAU or even its liberation committee and toward the front-line states themselves.

Zambia's reluctant acceptance of the necessity of armed struggle in regional liberation has not altered its commitment to reconciliation and participation in both continental and global affairs. Zambia has reacted to insurrection and secession in Africa by urging conciliation and negotiation, and even offered to mediate in the Somali-Kenyan and Nigeria-Biafran disputes. Similarly, President Kaunda has taken particularly strong exception to military coups, especially the overthrow of Kwame Nkrumah of Ghana and of Milton Obote of Uganda. Zambia has also supported moves toward more popular participation in both national and international affairs. Despite its declared aim of friendship with all governments and peoples, it has repeatedly denounced dictatorial regimes, whether they be white or black, socialist or capitalist, and encouraged moves toward changes in the global distribution of power and wealth. The 1970 Lusaka Declaration by the nonaligned states on peace, independence, development, cooperation, and democratization of international relations heralded the beginning of the debate about the New International Economic Order (NIEO), with its emphasis on economic issues and planetary participation.

Despite its preoccupation with regional crises, Zambia has supported longer-term moves toward a redistribution of influence and affluence at the global level from north to south. It sees the NIEO in terms of more than economic opportunity and security. Rather, it considers the north-south dialogue as a necessary precursor to any more egalitarian and nonracial world order. Zambia inherited not only an underdeveloped and dependent society at independence but also a racially divided one. For this reason, its concern with the NIEO reflects a desire not simply to complete the task of political liberation and commence the task of economic liberation but also to finish the task of racial liberation. This has meant principally the promotion of black majority rule in Southern Africa, but it has also been expressed in a concern for black minority rights in the First (and Second) World.

The Challenge of Development

Since independence, Zambia has sought to confront and overcome its inheritance of social deprivation, educational neglect, and racial inequality. Successive national development plans and interpretations of the ideology of humanism, combined with the efforts of some competent and creative planners and managers, have contributed to the construction of an adequate infrastructure, considerably improving the potential for development. But, while basic human needs are increasingly being met, particularly in the areas of education and employment, housing and health, popular demands and expectations continue to grow. Moreover, the "honeymoon" period of independence has long since passed, as have the earlier and easier stages of growth, such as import substitution and Africanization. The political economy now faces the need for structural change if it is to cope with rising unemployment and inflation, and declining productivity. Moreover, the prevailing ethos of a consumer society has tended to corrupt values and behavior, contributing at times to a lack of initiative, attention, and direction. These, combined with a relentless population explosion, declining national income, continuing urbanization, and mounting food imports, merely exacerbate the economic difficulties associated with both the low price of copper and the high price of principles.

At independence, Zambia constituted a classic case of underdevelopment as well as of dependence. Although not a "least developed country," national income and government revenue fluctuated with the price of copper and both were maldistributed along racial lines. Since independence, Zambians have come to occupy most positions within the bureaucratic elite and have begun to invest in land and companies. But rural, regional, and class inequalities persist. Despite the considerable effort and substantial sums devoted to the development of agriculture, education, welfare, and communications, and the progress made, many basic human needs remain unfilled.

The national ideology of humanism is concerned not merely with non-racialism but also with the quality of life; its man-centeredness is compatible with a basic human needs approach to development. However, the obstacles to the achievement of equality of opportunity are considerable and, with the emergence of class-type distinctions, may even be growing. Although many Zambians remain apathetic or apolitical, a lively debate continues between those technocrats who would resist any further moves toward an egalitarian distribution of resources and a radical core who argue that any nonsocialist definition of humanism is largely irrelevant. The perpetuation and even intensification of inequalities, combined with the growth of state capitalism and a tendency toward solidarity within the ruling class, could lead to increased opposition to the regime either in the form of political apathy and resistance, or conceivably in the form of violent challenges to the state apparatus.

Rumors of coup attempts have multiplied since the second election under "one-party participatory democracy" in 1978 and the transformation of Rhodesia into Zimbabwe in 1980. Such reports—some of which have had official sanction—may represent only the more conspicuous expressions of discontent that set in when it became apparent that the end to the Rhodesian war would not herald the anticipated golden age of prosperity in Zambia. At the national level, the economy is stagnating even if not decaying; at the regional level, South African economic dominance is more evident than ever; and at the global level, international recession and high oil prices continue to depress the value, and increase the production costs, of copper. In the circumstances, the prospects of successfully breaking loose from such inter-related constraints become highly problematic, especially as the regime has so many political obligations at each level. Moreover, the liberation of Namibia and South Africa will continue to drain energies and resources. In short, any transition toward more self-reliance will likely have to wait upon either major changes in the regime at home or a dramatic turn of events in the region.

The first two five-year development plans were preoccupied with the crea-tion of an infrastructural and industrial base. With the logic of the import-substitution phase largely over and the persistence of agricultural and rural stagnation, the third national development plan focuses on rural agrarian transformation as well as agricultural and mineral processing. Agriculture in Zambia has suffered from the departure of expatriate farmers, ineffective development strategies, and a social environment which has a largely negative orientation toward the countryside. In addition, growth in the importation of foodstuffs, especially from South Africa and now Zimbabwe, has hit the balance of payments and restricted economic development.

Despite the now widely perceived need for some kind of agrarian revo-lution, Zambia has yet to discover an appropriate mode of rural development. Considerable sums have been written off following the failure of successive attempts to encourage cooperatives, promote state farms, and implement intensive development zones, a series of concentrated rural development nodes. Thus far, the only form of food production that has borne fruit is that of agribusiness: large-scale, capital-intensive corporate undertakings. Zambia has an immense potential for the production of grain and beef—crucial ingre-dients in a hungry world—and has already become self-sufficient in sugar. But while agribusiness may resolve certain aspects of the food importation problem, it may further intensify dependence on external capital, technology, skills, and imported inputs. Two of its major promoters in Zambia—AAC and Lonrho—are already heavily involved in other sectors of the economy, and the large-scale farms owned by Zambians are often run by expatriate man-agers along agribusiness lines. Despite the growing official awareness of and attention to rural, agricultural issues, the green revolution in Zambia remains elusive.

Conclusion: The High Price of Principles and the Low Price of Copper

Given Zambia's dependence on copper, communications, and capital, and associated problems of economic structure and social inequality, it may appear somewhat surprising that its commitment to the liberation of Southern Africa has been so unqualified. It is a tribute to the country's leadership, as well as to the strength of its nationalism and nonracialism, that Zambia was prepared to pay such a high price for its principles during the years of UDI.

However, the set of policies which have enabled Zambia to weather the storm —humanism, participatory democracy, and state capitalism—may yet create the conditions for future political change. In particular, structural constraints, especially the continuing low price of copper and high costs of production, may severely limit the capacity of the state to cope adequately with popular expectations, without resort to repression. If inflation, recession, unemployment, and debt continue to increase, a point may ultimately be reached when the reasonable balance of forces sought by the present regime may become untenable. In this extremity, the alternatives facing the nation may be either further drastic financial retrenchment—the remedy many technocrats would prescribe—or social revolution—the prayer of the radicals.

As the Smith-Muzorewa regime experienced its final dying convulsions in 1978–79, it lashed out savagely against Zambia as well as Mozambique, in a desperate attempt to break the power of the encircling guerrilla armies. While the targets selected included Zimbabwean military bases and Zambian defense installations, they were more commonly civilian refugee camps and vital communication facilities. Their purpose was as much psychological as military —to demoralize the Zambian population and compel the government to withdraw from the war. In material terms, the successive attacks on economic targets proved the most damaging. Rhodesian commando units and aerial strikes knocked out the vital Chambeshi river bridge cutting the road and rail links with Tanzania, periodically disrupted traffic along the Great East Road to Malawi and Mozambique, and sank the Kazungula ferry to Botswana. As the Benguela Railway westward to Lobito had still not been reopened following the Angolan civil war, only the southern rail route through Rhodesia remained. After having been closed in January 1973, it had to be reopened in October 1978.

The end to UDI and the independence of Zimbabwe refocused the attention of Zambians on domestic shortcomings. Preoccupation with the external threat—as earlier with the independence struggle—had fueled unrealistic expectations that the country's ills would quickly dissipate once the immediate crisis had passed. It soon became apparent, however, that these high hopes would not be readily realized. Despite the resolution of the Rhodesian conflict, many of the problems which had plagued the country persisted, thus revealing them to be essentially structural rather than simply contingent, global as well as regional.

Not that peace made no difference. Trade with Zimbabwe was resumed (to the extent that foreign exchange permitted), secure access to the sea by the southern route was restored, the war damage was repaired, and the guerrillas and refugees were repatriated. Nevertheless, as a landlocked state, Zambia remained vulnerable, with the Benguela Railway out of commission and Tazara operating at far below full capacity. The continuing drought accentuated dependence on imported—especially South African—maize, the national oil bill spiralled even higher, and the world copper price once again dipped below cost of production—ironically, partly in response to the improved security situation. By early 1981, copper was fetching barely half the price prevailing a year earlier. Even cobalt prices, which had provided a temporary cushion to the economy, have collapsed. For the mass of workers and peasants, the cost of living continues to soar, and essential goods remain in short supply. Moreover, Zambians have suffered an added blow to their pride; after all their sacrifices on behalf of Zimbabwe, they find Salisbury has suddenly over-shadowed Lusaka in terms of diplomacy, aid, and international sympathy.

Disillusionment with the false dawn has inevitably bred some disenchant-ment with the government and party among a broad spectrum of Zambian society despite the president's convincing majority in the December 1978 elections. Certainly, there has been evidence of considerable nervousness on the part of the nation's leaders, especially at the prospect that the Liberian mili-tary coup might prove contagious. Their fears appeared confirmed when, in October 1980, a plot was uncovered. Visibly shaken by this revelation and by the subsequent damaging wave of unofficial strikes by copper miners early in 1981, the government redoubled its efforts to tackle the country's seemingly intractable economic difficulties. Foremost among these has been the failure to achieve agricultural self-sufficiency. Yet, despite the launching of an am-bitious Operation Food Production in May 1980 and the end to three years of drought, there are few solid grounds for optimism.

In the longer term, government strategy seeks to take advantage of recent political changes in the region to lessen further the trade and communications links with South Africa. Approaches for closer association with East Africa have been revived and, more significantly, in accordance with the "Lusaka Declaration" of April 1980, a Southern Africa Development Coordination Conference (SADCC) has been established to promote the "economic liberation and integrated development" of Pretoria's nine black neighbors—without South Africa. At the same time, the chronic balance of payments crises have again forced the government to turn to the West for record loans. In March 1981, $150 million was raised on the Euromarket and, in May, a $1 billion IMF standby credit was secured. The road to economic independence promises to be long, hazardous, and uncertain.

Botswana, Lesotho, and Swaziland: The Common Background and Links

Bordering on South Africa are three independent African states—Botswana, Lesotho, and Swaziland. Despite differing degrees of economic dependence on their much larger neighbor, these sovereign countries sharply oppose apartheid. Although long expected to form part of South Africa, their people rejected this alternative in favor of separate independence. Botswana and Lesotho raised their own flags in 1966, Swaziland in 1968. From the late nineteenth century until that time, however, the British administered all three as the High Commission Territories. The top British official in the area was the high commissioner to South Africa. This was a somewhat unique arrangement because the section of the British home administration responsible for these territories was the Commonwealth Relations Office, not the Colonial Office as was the case with most protectorates and colonies.

The first of the three to come under British control was Lesotho (then Basutoland) when King Moshoeshoe, a man of great diplomatic skill, requested British protection in 1868. His kingdom was faced with encroachment from the Afrikaner Republic of Orange Free State.

Botswana (or Bechuanaland, as it was called until 1966) came under British "protection" in 1885. It was the missionaries' "road" to central Africa. It was also an avenue of Afrikaner expansion for settler-farmers from the Transvaal and for Cecil Rhodes' pursuit of his dream of a central Africa as rich as the Rand. An index of the strategic location of Bechuanaland was the abortive attempt in 1895 by Rhodes' British South Africa Company to thwart collusion between the Afrikaners in today's Transvaal and the Germans in Southwest Africa (today's Namibia) to close off British access to the north.

Both Afrikaner encroachments and the intentions of the Company led the Batswana chiefs to appeal to London for assistance in protecting their lands and traditional autonomy. In response, the British declared the land of the Batswana, or Bechuanaland, a protectorate of the Crown in 1885. Bechuanaland was not thought to be valuable for either industry or agriculture, but it provided a corridor between the Cape and the northern territories.

Swaziland was the smallest of the three territories. For years there was an active dispute over who should control it: the Afrikaner republic of the Transvaal or Great Britain. In 1894 Great Britain recognized the right of the Transvaal to protect Swaziland. But at the conclusion of the Anglo-Boer War, the country came under the administration of the British governor of the Transvaal. In 1906 Swaziland became a British protectorate.

These territories shared features that distinguished them from the neighboring "native reserves" in South Africa. They had a common British civil administration. There were no passes or other racial restrictions, as in South Africa. Nonetheless, the three had close ties with South Africa and to a great extent were dependent. Their posts and telegraphs, currency and banking, and customs and tariffs were operated by the South African government.

Moreover, opportunities for industrial wage labor and higher education for their people were available only in South Africa. South African newspapers and radio programs were their principal sources of information. White farmers in these territories belonged to the South African Farmers' Union and received the subsidies that South Africa gave its farmers. Such transterritorial interdependency made it logical and convenient for white South Africans to perceive the three British territories as the equivalent of their own African "reserves."

Contributing to this view was the very tentativeness of the British commitment to these territories. The South Africa Act of Union of 1909 carried an addendum explicitly noting that the three High Commission Territories were expected to become part of the Union in due course. The British seemed to share the white South African view that the logic of geography, economics, and ethnic ties between and among the peoples of the High Commission Territories and the Union of South Africa pointed to incorporation as the sensible path for the future.

It was precisely their fear of incorporation, however, that led the people of the High Commission Territories to resist the move. Through the first half of the century, the chiefs of the three territories continued to remind the British that they had an obligation to protect the autonomy and basic human rights that would be denied their people if they were formally incorporated in South Africa.

After 1948, when the Afrikaner Nationalists came to power in South Africa, the incorporation issue took on different and more menacing dimensions because apartheid was installed as official policy and restrictions were steadily increased. From the South African side incorporation became more attractive as the white Nationalists developed the Bantustan, or homeland, program. This was made explicit in the Tomlinson Commission report of 1956 (see South Africa chapter), in which maps of the three territories were included in its view of an overall separate development strategy.

By then, however, external events had strengthened the resistance to incorporation. African nationalists in British colonies to the north (Ghana, Nigeria) were nearing their goals of political independence. Their example helped spark a spirit of nationalism in the High Commission Territories that made it more difficult for the British to yield to South African plans. Also, apartheid had become an international issue, and pressure on the British government to spare the people of these territories the oppression of white supremacist hegemony came from world capitals and the United Nations, as well as from their own citizens.

In 1962, Prime Minister Verwoerd signaled that he was reconciled to the High Commission Territories becoming separate self-governing states. A year later, however, he asked Britain to allow South Africa to appeal directly to the African people in the territories and explain how they would benefit from the Tomlinson formula for incorporation in his country. The formula involved both economic threats and incentives, but the tactic was transparent and came at a time when Britain was already moving toward constitutional changes and political independence for each of the three territories.

Despite the territories' attainment of statehood in the mid-1960s, important institutional linkages between them and South Africa remained and, although modified, still exist today. The most important regional institution is the South Africa Customs Union Agreement established in 1910 that provided for the free interchange of goods between South Africa and the three territories and a sharing of the area's total import and excise revenues accruing from the common external tariff. (The territories originally collected their own duties only on alcoholic beverages.) Although the percentage share of the three smaller territories varied slightly under the original allocations, in each of the three cases it was less than 1 percent, leaving about 98 percent for South Africa.

In 1969 the Customs Union Agreement was renegotiated at the collective insistence of Botswana, Lesotho, and Swaziland. The objective was to improve the revenue position of the three smaller states relative to South Africa or, more accurately, to reduce the inequities so apparent in the 1910 formula. The new agreement is complex. In brief, instead of the former straight percentage basis, customs revenues are now divided according to a formula based on the value of actual imports to each country in relation to that of the common customs area as a whole.

Although this new customs union formula still allows South Africa to benefit disproportionately due to its large industrial economy, income from the duties since 1970 has represented a significant portion of the public revenues of the three new countries (Table 1). It has enabled the two eco-

Table 1

Representative Proportions of Ordinary Government Revenues
from Customs and Excise:
Botswana, Lesotho, and Swaziland (in percentage of total)

Country	1959–60	1965–66	1973–74	1974–75	1975–76
Botswana	25	21	50.1	48.5	31.0
Lesotho	50	35	68.7	63.3	48.0 (1976–77)
Swaziland	11	32	46.5	N.A.	N.A.

Sources: 1959–60 and 1965–66 are drawn from Kenneth Grundy, *Confrontation and Accommodation*, p. 37; 1973–74 and 1975–76 from *The Europa Year Book, 1977: A World Survey. Vol. II* (London: Europa Publications, 1977), pp. 180, 976, and 1553.

nomically stronger members—Botswana and Swaziland—to terminate their dependence on British subsidies. The agreement also provides that the three smaller members can impose protectionist measures against South Africa for selected infant industries.

Botswana, Lesotho, and Swaziland ultimately buy most of their consumer goods from South Africa, where prices are lower for the three smaller states than those on the world market but *only* because of the high external tariff of the customs union. Any economic arrangement which includes one large industrial country and several nonindustrial ones tends to perpetuate inequalities whereby the poor to some extent subsidize the rich. The dilemma for the three smaller states is the high cost of surviving alone.

They are, however, moving inexorably, if at different paces, toward their own currency and central banking systems. Swaziland issued its own currency in 1975, Botswana in 1976. Although the former still accepts the South African Rand as legal tender, the latter does not. By the end of 1977 Botswana had revalued its currency 5 percent from par with the Rand. (For a more detailed account, see Grundy chapter.)

The most substantial institutional link within the three states was the University of Botswana, Lesotho and Swaziland (UBLS). Its core campus at Roma, Lesotho, evolved in the mid-1960s from long-established Pius XII College. Satellite campuses were established in Botswana and Swaziland in the early 1970s. This arrangement greatly expanded the opportunities for higher education in the three countries. It also represented a more economical alternative to establishing separate national universities in countries with small populations.

However, by 1975 the centrifugal forces of nationalism within Lesotho had begun to affect the cohesion of the institution. Disagreements over proposals for devolution that were designed to provide more equitable sharing of facilities and programs led to Lesotho's precipitous withdrawal in October 1975 and the establishment of the National University of Lesotho, independent of UBLS. The University of Botswana and Swaziland was subsequently chartered. It is presently developing two separate university colleges, but professional schools such as the College of Agriculture and the Faculty of Law will not be duplicated. A surviving regional legacy of UBLS is the Institute of Development Management, a tri-country institution specializing in high-level administrative and management training for both the public and the private sectors.

Thus, apart from some additional plans to establish scheduled air links among the three national airlines, the common characteristics and functional linkages of Botswana, Lesotho, and Swaziland are fading. Emerging national identities, differential resource endowments and development, different politico-geographic locations, and, perhaps most important, different political systems now more aptly characterize these three distinct entities.

8.

Botswana: Development, Democracy, and Vulnerability

E. Philip Morgan

As in the early days of the protectorate, landlocked Botswana occupies a strategic position. It is almost surrounded by the two white-dominated territories in which there is dramatic pressure for change: Namibia to the north and west, and South Africa to the east and south. Botswana thus has hundreds of miles of exposed borders. These were violated so frequently during the war in Rhodesia that the government reluctantly formed a small army in 1977.

Botswana is a large country, roughly the size of France, with a population of only 936,000. As the vast Kalahari Desert occupies the southwestern quarter of the country, the bulk of the population is distributed north-south along the eastern corridor's "green strip." Communication is difficult, though improving rapidly. Radio helps to bridge the physical barriers since most Batswana speak a version of the same indigenous language: Setswana.

Within Southern Africa, Botswana occupies an increasingly prominent position. Per capita, it has become one of Africa's richest countries. The late president, Sir Seretse Khama, as the leader of one of the front-line states, was intimately involved in the negotiations over the transfer of power to majority rule in Zimbabwe. Botswana has also been a refuge for people fleeing from the tyrannies of Rhodesia and South Africa. In 1978 President Khama received the Nansen Medal from the United Nations High Commission for Refugees for the country's open and courageous refugee policy. He was also awarded an honorary doctorate by Harvard University in the same year. These distinctions are a tribute both to the stature of Sir Seretse Khama and to the respect accorded his country's efforts to overcome great economic and political obstacles while maintaining a nonracial, open society. When

Khama died in July 1980 the vice-president, Q.K.J. Masire, became president in accordance with the constitution.

The location of Botswana, the effects of British "protection," the specter of incorporation within South Africa, and the salience of color have combined to shape Botswana's position and to a certain extent its prospects.

Political Vulnerabilities

Transport Links

The railway connection to Zimbabwe remains a lifeline for Botswana. It is the principal carrier of goods between Botswana and the seaports of South Africa. Within the country Zimbabwe Railways, as it is called, consists of tracks running the length of the eastern part of the country, a number of stations, and some housing for Batswana maintenance workers. All the major repair facilities are located in Zimbabwe, and until 1978 the company owned all the rolling stock.

Because of this real as well as symbolic constraint on the independence of Botswana the government went on record during the election campaign of 1974 as planning a takeover, six years before there was to be a friendly regime in Zimbabwe. The slow pace of implementing this large step can be attributed in part to the war in Rhodesia, but also to the formidable requirements of money and manpower. Official statements after an extended study by Canadian National Railways consultants put the cost at P60 million and 350 trained technicians.[1]

In late 1977, however, major moves toward takeover were announced. Some new rolling stock bearing the insignia of Botswana Railways was purchased, thus enabling Botswana to move coal on its own branch lines. Batswana are being trained in such nontechnical areas as shunting, checking, plate laying, and clerking. Over fifty percent of the commercial clerks are now Batswana. Training in technical categories has begun with eighteen locomotive driver trainees sent to Malawi. Zambia, Kenya, and Swaziland have also offered help in technical training. The West German government has given P14 million to assist. Five British Rail management experts make up the team spearheading the takeover. After the country owns its own equipment and has its own personnel, the final transaction projected in 1986 will involve the outright purchase of track and rights-of-way that belong to Zimbabwe.

As part of an official strategy of outreach to its African-governed neighbors to the north, Botswana has given high priority to a road project financed by the United States and several other western countries connecting Francistown with Kazungula, which is linked by ferry to Zambia. The importance of this all-weather road running the north-south length of the country is more strategic than economic. Although the routes are costly, Botswana now has access to the sea via Zimbabwe and the ports of Mozambique, or through Zambia and the Tazara railway to Dar es Salaam, Tanzania (see Grundy chapter), in the event that political forces should interfere with its usual routes through South Africa. The Botswana government has announced its intention to build a rail link westward to the sea when a political settlement is reached in Namibia.

Refugees

Another aspect of the country's vulnerability is the prospect that it might become a staging area or, as in the Rhodesian war, a victim of assaults by the contending sides in the liberation of Namibia or South Africa. The government provides political asylum for what it calls "genuine" political refugees: those in danger of harassment or imprisonment in their own country. But it has not condoned the use of Botswana territory as sanctuaries or training bases for active guerrilla partisans.

Most persons seeking political refuge in Botswana since 1975 have come from pre-independent Zimbabwe or South Africa. An increasing number now come from Namibia. Despite the departure of Zimbabwe refugees in 1980 an estimated 10,000 refugees still remain[2] for whom Botswana has not nearly enough housing, school places, or employment possibilities.

The government's open refugee policy has been based on "a moral obligation," but with resources and opportunities already scarce for the indigenous population, there is danger of domestic resentment. South African refugees, mainly urban in background, are thought to have a potentially disruptive influence on local politics. Accordingly the Botswana government attempted in 1980 to resettle them, and other refugees, in a fully serviced camp at Dukwe in the northeast but with little success. The refugees used South African claims that refugee camps were "terrorist bases" against the Botswana government and refused to go fearing South African raids like the earlier ones by Rhodesian security forces.[3]

Reaction to Separate Development

Apart from location, the legacy of South African efforts to incorporate Botswana into the Republic still affects present relations between the two countries. Botswana has only arms-length relations with South Africa, and there has been no exchange of diplomatic representatives.

Moreover, Botswana is unalterably opposed to apartheid and refuses to recognize any of the so-called homelands, including that of the Batswana people in South Africa, Bophuthatswana. Although the chief minister of Bophuthatswana, Lucas Mangope, once indicated a willingness to become federated with Botswana, the latter country did not respond. Such a move would legitimize the balkanization of South Africa and more than double Botswana's population all at once. President Khama once said that Botswana will not recognize a "child of apartheid and separate development."[4] Although part of Bophuthatswana is contiguous with Botswana and movement between the two has historically been frequent and informal, the Botswana government will not accept any travel document from that country. Since that stand could create many personal and family hardships, the external affairs ministry of Botswana issues its own special entry permit to such persons, as to others from the so-called independent homelands, a device it does not regard as tantamount to recognition of their governments. Since the railway between Botswana and the South African ports runs through Bophuthatswana it is conceivable that the latter could hold rail transit hostage to official recognition by Botswana. But Bophuthatswana would only do this if it had clear backing from South Africa—a card the latter has so far withheld.

Economic and Social Vulnerabilities

Although politically aloof, the interdependence of Botswana's economy with that of South Africa forces continuous contact. In addition to being Botswana's principal import supplier, South Africa is responsible for a greater percentage of foreign investment in Botswana than any other country. This investment is primarily in the emerging industrial sector of mineral exploitation, where profits are highest, and secondarily in light manufacturing and service industries. The majority of the engineering and building contractors who bid on development projects (that are not tied to donor agency contractors) are also South African.

Almost 20,000 Batswana work annually in the mines of South Africa (gold, coal, diamonds, etc.). The Rand mine organizations still hire foreign labor, and the Botswana government does not feel it can restrict the movement of its citizens to the South African mines so long as it cannot provide jobs for them at home. Despite the hazardous living and working conditions in South Africa for the Botswana worker, he can make more money there than at home. Taken in conjunction with the common customs union described earlier and the reliance on South Africa both for goods and as a market, there remains a close, reciprocal relationship as regards commerce, industry, and employment (see Table 1). This inhibits Botswana's efforts to establish genuine independence but at the same time provides the incentive for an aggressive outward policy.

Cattle: Backbone of the Agricultural Economy

Botswana's traditional exports of beef and beef products increased enormously between the droughts of 1965–67 and 1979–80. The national herd recovered from numbering under one million head of cattle in 1966 to an estimated 3 million in 1979. Botswana Meat Commission (BMC) sales in 1979 amounted to almost P70 million ($73.5 million), up 53 percent over 1976, 83 percent over 1973.[5]

Table 1

Botswana: Direction of Trade by Source and Destination, 1976–79
(in millions of pula)

	1976	1977	1978	1979
Exports				
Customs area*	23.2	18.1	26.2	25.6
Other Africa	11.5	13.1	14.3	31.0
Europe	66.0	82.8	98.0	245.2
of which: United Kingdom	(63.3)	(61.5)	(9.1)	(47.8)
North & South America	52.1	42.0	53.1	63.6
Other	0.3	0.6	1.1	1.8
Total	153.2	156.7	192.7	367.3
Imports, c.i.f.†				
Customs area*	147.6	205.5	260.0	384.2
Other Africa	22.1	23.8	30.5	30.3
Europe	6.1	5.3	8.1	14.0
of which: United Kingdom	(3.0)	(3.9)	(5.1)	(9.9)
North & South America	3.7	4.1	6.2	5.9
Other	1.9	1.0	2.2	3.9
Total	181.4	239.6	307.1	438.3

Source: Statistical Bulletin, December 1980, Central Statistics Office.
* Comprising Lesotho, South Africa, and Swaziland.
† Inclusive of customs, excise, sales, and additional duties.

In fact, Botswana's beef industry has become so attractive to a traditional cattle-holding people that expanded grazing has created problems of potentially irreparable damage to the country's limited range. The need for systematic range management and water resource development has caused the government to embark on a far-reaching Tribal Grazing Land Policy. Under this new land tenure arrangement, what was always regarded as communal grazing land for respective ethnic groups is now subject to surveying, fencing, and allocation by commercial lease. A number of cooperative mechanisms are supposed to protect the small herders so that several can take out a lease collectively and graze their cattle according to a modern management regime. Some communal land will also be set aside for those who have only a few cattle and do not join any group. Finally, there is "reserved" land that will be held for future use. This fundamental change has been compared to the eighteenth-century enclosure movement in Britain.

Marketing Botswana's beef has become a problem, however, for two reasons. First, beef products have been exported in the past to essentially two markets, South Africa and Great Britain, with over 60 percent going to the latter. When Britain entered the European Economic Community its imports of agricultural products became subject to the Common Agricultural Policy of the EEC. That policy subjects those foreign imports of beef which are admitted to the market to a 46-to-51-percent levy on sales receipts. During the mid-1970s the Botswana government negotiated a reduction of the levy based on the Lomé Agreement of 1975 between the EEC and the African, Caribbean, and Pacific countries dealing with trade preferences. The 90-percent reduction of the levy for Botswana's beef is extended for only short periods of time, however, requiring recurrent, time-consuming renegotiation. This uncertainty makes it very difficult to plan for the future.

The second problem confounding predictability for beef marketing has been the recurring outbreaks of foot and mouth disease since 1977. Because Botswana has always had high marks for animal health, persistence of the disease is logically attributed to fugitive cattle wandering across the border from the disrupted areas of pre-independent Zimbabwe. Whatever the cause, the outbreaks resulted in the closure of the European market to Botswana beef. In turn the BMC experienced a reduction in 1980 export earnings to about half those of 1979.[6] Through vigorous efforts involving containment and vaccination the country was declared free of the disease in early 1981.

Since the European community will not accept meat from the infected areas for twelve months, the government instituted a number of measures to compensate cattle holders: protection against speculators, interest-free loans against cattle as security, and the waiving of school fees. The foot and mouth problem has also disrupted implementation of the already delayed Grazing Land Policy.

In order to cope with uncertainties in the primary beef market the BMC has moved toward more value added in Botswana. A cannery and a tannery are now operating in Lobatse and construction is soon to begin on a second small abattoir and cannery for corned beef in Maun. The long-awaited major abattoir for the north is scheduled for construction in the Francistown/Tonota area beginning in 1982, a move which reflects official optimism that marketing uncertainties can be overcome.[7]

The 1979–85 development plan also includes major attention to the long-neglected arable side of the agricultural equation. The new policy is to raise crop production and provide for the country's needs for basic grains. It is anticipated that this will have the additional effect of narrowing the presently widening gap between urban and rural incomes and stem the tide of urban migration.[8] The Arable Lands Development Program (ALDEP) is moving very slowly, however. Small farmers in the demonstration areas are finding the substitution of donkeys (for oxen) as draft animals difficult. Moreover, crop farmers without livestock to offer as security are unable to get loans from the National Development Bank.

Mineral Resources and Exploitation

The remarkable improvement in Botswana's economic position since independence results principally from a number of mineral discoveries. Diamonds, copper-nickel, and coal are now being commercially exploited under complex agreements with a number of multinational corporations. So far the most lucrative development is in diamonds.

Botswana is now the fourth largest producer of diamonds in the world. DeBeers Botswana Mining Company (Debswana) invested heavily between 1977 and 1979 to increase the output at Orapa and Letlhakane from 2.3 million to 4.5 million carats per annum. Total output increased 85 percent to P245 million in 1979.[9] A lucrative third new pipe located at Jwaneng will yield 4 to 6 million carats per annum beginning 1982. Diamonds accounted for 70 percent of Botswana's exports in 1980.[10]

A number of technical constraints are delaying realization of the full benefits from the copper-nickel mine. Despite good world prices in 1979, the copper-nickel company, Bamangwato Concessions Ltd. (BCL), lost P16.5 million and has not yet shown a positive cash flow.[11] Poor world prices for copper and nickel in 1980/81 will likely require the financial restructuring of BCL once again.

Coal production was over 350,000 tons in 1980. Because of newly discovered reserves of at least 17 billion tons, plans are under way to build a coal-fired power station at Morupule.[12] The goal is to produce for export as well as supply the power station making coal an important part of the economy in the near future.

The concerted efforts in both mineral development and livestock production must be seen in the context of Botswana's need for export earnings. Without these earnings Botswana cannot diversify its economy and increase its total economic capacity. At the moment export earnings are perceived by the country's policymakers as the principal sources of revenue for productive investments in rural development, administrative efficiency, and manpower development.

The Need for Skilled Manpower

Another major economic constraint is skilled manpower. Although this is a common problem in new states, it is particularly acute in Botswana for peculiar historical reasons. Relative to the financial commitment Britain made to most of its other African colonies, Bechuanaland was sorely neglected. Whereas, in West Africa, British-inspired and sponsored secondary education goes back to the early years of this century, there was no government secondary school in Botswana until after independence in 1966. There were a few poverty-stricken ethnic and missionary secondary schools, but the protectorate government spent very little on the development of human resources. Nor were there any significant development expenditures related to the creation of local wage employment. In fact, the colonial government cooperated with the South African mine labor recruiting organizations in the mobilization of Batswana for mine work. External employment provided a source of cash income to pay the head tax.

The lack of British commitment to the development of Bechuanaland goes back to the incorporation issue. The land and climate of Bechuanaland were inhospitable to large-scale white settlement, and the territory never attracted a large European community which would have made developmental demands of its own on the British. The migratory settlement that occurred was composed of South Africans who established large cattle ranches and looked south for protection of their interests rather than to Great Britain.

At the very time an independent Botswana is attempting to pursue a rapid development policy—certain aspects of which are highly capital intensive and technologically complex—it must invest heavily in the basic social overhead capital to develop human resources, that is, schools, clinics, roads, and communications facilities. This state of affairs has resulted in a heavy reliance on expatriate manpower in the short run, and it has serious implications for the country's future demand for qualified manpower and for labor relations.

The educational infrastructure has expanded greatly since independence; however, for a variety of reasons only about 10 percent of those who enroll in the now fully subsidized primary schools will go on to secondary school, or 20 percent of those who actually complete primary school. The number completing secondary school has averaged about 1,200 per year for the past several years. Although current completion and pass rates stand in marked contrast to those of the early 1970s, there is continuing concern for improving the number of passes at higher levels. A pattern of poor performance in science and math—fields crucial to a developing mineral economy—has resulted in priority teacher education in these subjects. The University of Botswana and Swaziland has made great strides through pre-entry programs in science and math to make up this deficit. However, the university itself is far behind in its enrollments and output targets. The 1980–81 year was to have 1,100 students on the Botswana campus, whereas the actual number was 760. Batswana earned only about half of the 116 degrees and 168 diplomas and certificates awarded by the university in 1980.[13]

While the civil service has made great progress in localizing general administrative positions, the technical posts in government and in the parastatal corporations still tend to be occupied by foreigners, and vacancies continue to be filled with expatriates. Localization in the private sector is lagging far behind the public sector. This is partly because most industry is foreign owned and companies want to bring in their own management personnel. Government complains about the pace of training locals for managing Botswana-based units of foreign enterprises. The investors complain that locals with adequate schooling are either unavailable or, when hired, are unduly impatient about promotions.

Essentially, government and the private sector are rivals for the same small pool of potential managers. An incomes policy keeps salaries close to par in the public and private sectors. It is designed to give government an equal chance at keeping able people in senior posts who would otherwise be attracted to private firms by larger salaries. This works to a point, but a pattern of retirements from the civil service by supergrade officers who subsequently take up management positions in the private sector would suggest that firms have ways of getting around salary ceilings with other perquisites.

The growth in demand for personnel by government over the next decade is going to be mainly in local government. Expanded responsibilities are in store for local authorities under the present Plan, both with respect to development projects and land matters. Presently the Unified Local Government Service employs 2,700 people; by 1990 the figure is projected to be 5,000. Meeting this goal will add even greater stress to existing institutions and procedures for manpower development.

Given this human resource dilemma, the salience of race politics in the region at large still emerges from time to time in Botswana. There is an open and still healthy debate about the wisdom of importing large numbers of foreign technical assistance people, most of whom are white. The foreigners who appear most credibly to be impeding the upward mobility of local people are those on contracts who do semi-skilled or technical work at middle and elementary levels of sophistication in posts and telecommunications, works, mining, construction, banking, and similar job categories. Too often counterparts are not trained and the difficulty of identifying them is used as an excuse not to look for them. Racial problems are sometimes created when a group of expatriates with a particular skill is coterminous with a particular nationality and is concentrated in one place, such as South Africans at the mining sites.

The Botswana government tends to tolerate the idiosyncrasies of foreigners only so long as their behavior does not include racism. The use of racially pejorative terms is subject to prosecution. Black employees use the law in defense of their own dignity in the event of racial slurs by employers or supervisors.

To the extent that there have been vocal protests about white *citizens* in positions of public power, the government has held to a firm line. The late president always defended the few white citizens in pivotal positions on the basis of their competence and their loyalty to the country in the early days of independence. Because he married a white woman in 1949 and was persecuted by the British through denial of his chieftainship and banishment from his own country (1950–56), Sir Seretse Khama was particularly sensitive to the development of "anti-whiteism" in Botswana. He defended his country's official policy of nonracism out of conviction and cited Botswana as an example of moral commitment.

Given the national and international environment, racial attitudes in Botswana are still encouraging. Whether this continues, however, will depend on whether the technical requirements of an industrial economy outstrip the ability of a country with such a small population and educational infrastructure to maintain a rapid pace of localization; and on whether the resolution of the struggle for democracy in the neighboring states is relatively more benign or bitter. Certainly the untimely death of Sir Seretse Khama removed the most positive single influence.

Political Characteristics and Opportunities

Botswana is a regional symbol of liberal democracy: an African state with a multi-party system that has held regular open elections for successive popularly elected governments. The openness of the Botswana political process stands in sharp contrast to those of both Swaziland and Lesotho as well as to that of Zambia, much less South Africa. It provides a refutation of the paternalistic assumptions underlying the ideology of white supremacy.

The Botswana Democratic Party (BDP), headed by Sir Seretse Khama, formed the government after the preindependence election of 1965 and has been returned three times since. There was little doubt in 1969, 1974, or 1979 that the BDP would emerge with a majority. However, the three opposition parties—the Botswana People's Party (BPP), the Botswana National Front (BNF), and the Botswana Independence Party (BIP)—along with independent candidates collectively contested enough seats for the National Assembly in 1974 and 1979 to offer, arithmetically at least, the possibility of an alternative government (see Table 2). In a political system where the governing party is constantly returned, opposition votes are nonetheless interesting as indicators of issues and of the extent to which the governing party is meeting the perceived interests of the public.

The third national election in Botswana took place on October 20, 1979. The campaign itself was conducted against a backdrop of several national crises: drought, foot and mouth disease, and the domestic effects of the war in what was then Rhodesia, e.g., border incursions, security threats, and many thousands of refugees. Accordingly the majority party cast much of its election rhetoric in terms of these threats to Botswana's fragile democracy and the need to reelect the BDP to protect the gains of the recent past.

The tone of the 1979 election was more strident than in 1974. The presi-

Table 2

National Assembly Elections

1969

	BDP	BNF	BPP	BIP	IND
Total vote	52,518	10,410	9,329	4,601	—
% of total vote	68.3	13.5	12.1	6.0	—
No. seats contested	31*	21	15	9	—
Returned unopposed	3	0	0	0	—
Seats won	24	3	3	1	—

1974

	BDP	BNF	BPP	BIP	IND
Total vote	49,047	7,358	4,199	3,086	321
% of total vote	77.7	11.5	6.6	4.8	.5
No. seats contested	32	14	8	6	3
Returned unopposed	4	0	0	0	0
Seats won	27	2	2	1	0

1979

	BDP	BNF	BPP	BIP	IND
Total vote	101,098	17,324	9,983	5,813	278
% of total vote	75.2	12.9	7.4	4.3	.2
No. seats contested	32	16	14	5	2
Returned unopposed	2	0	0	0	0
Seats won	29	2	1	0	0

* One new constituency added in 1974.

Source: Data compiled from three reports on the general elections of 1969, 1974, and 1979, prepared by the supervisor of elections, published in March 1970, December 1974, and December 1979 respectively by the Government Printer, Gaborone.

dent and his party colleagues pictured the opposition, especially the more left wing National Front, as an insidious threat to democracy by intimating they were plotting revolution. To reverse the embarrassingly low turnout in 1974 the population was re-registered between 1977 and 1979. Twice the number of actual votes were cast in 1979 (134,496) as in 1974 (63,011) and the turnout in contested constituencies was 58.4 percent of voters compared to 31.2 percent in 1974. Since only 25,000 more citizens had been registered for 1979 than in 1974, the almost double turnout must be attributed to vigorous mobilization of voter participation.

The governing BDP won 29 of the 32 elected seats in the National Assembly, in contrast to 27 in 1974 and only 24 in 1969. The opposition parties were crushed. The BNF won two seats, standing firm with its performance in 1974. The BIP lost the single representative (Motsamai Mpho) that it had had since 1969. The opposition parties got almost 33,000 votes in 1979, a total which contrasts positively with 1974 in which the collective opposition secured only about 13,700. This higher opposition vote notwithstanding, the result was a net loss of two seats for the collective opposition because it was scattered among various constituencies rather than focused on a few.

Botswana has a pragmatic and pluralistic party system. The preoccupation with ideology is very limited indeed. The Botswana Democratic Party "national philosophy" is presented in terms of four concepts—democracy, development, self-reliance, and unity—and these themes were constantly reiterated in the president's speeches. Apart from preambles to public documents, party conferences, and manifestos near election time, there is little attention to developing or propagating these themes. The media are clearly government instruments, but they are seldom used for ideological cant. BNF and BPP documents and pronouncements by their respective leaders are more ideological than those of the BDP. At the same time, opposition statements are often fragmented, their issues diffuse, and the tone of debate more contentious than ideological or suggestive of an alternative program. Fifteen years of independence seems to have attenuated the previous affinities between the BPP and African nationalist sentiments in South Africa, although these could be rekindled by events.

Notwithstanding the turnout in the last election, the degree of political mobilization in the country is low; popular response to public policy is partial, if not passive. There is more participation and organizing among the elite (civil servants' and teachers' organizations) but such pluralist activity is inchoate. The mass public is still unmobilized except for pockets of traditional loyalty and emerging localized interests such as self-help groups and rural development associations.

All Botswana parties can be characterized as hierarchical and centralized in principle but loose and undisciplined in practice. Local BDP branches are not well organized between elections; the party is simply not an identifiable instrument of government/developmental policy at the village level. However, the lack of vital local party organizations between elections does not seem to affect the ability of the BDP to pull itself together when it counts most. Tsholetsa House, one of the three high-rise buildings in Gaborone, is owned by the Botswana Democratic Party, testimony to an ability to mobilize resources that sets it apart from the other parties.

Both the BDP and the BNF established youth wings in 1977, suggesting that youth would be the target for future mobilization. After the 1979 election the government set in motion a national service corps for secondary school graduates, a move with implications as much perhaps for containment as for mobilization.

The electoral success of the BDP indicates that Botswana has a one-party-dominant system; that is, it includes only one party truly capable of governing but cannot afford to ignore other parties, as interests are articulated *both* within the major party and through the smaller parties. Is it, in fact, changing into a one-party system in which other parties exist, but the major party can ignore them?

In Botswana the BDP is clearly the major party and the only one capable of forming a government. The experience of four elections confirms this fact. But the question of whether the BDP can ignore the smaller parties is less clear. Without its only former M.P., the BIP is nonexistent. The BPP has a lingering regional base in the northeast, but it lost its most important seat to the BDP in 1979 and is now without a nationally known leader (following Philip Matante's death in 1979).

The BNF on the other hand still represents a loose coalition of traditional and modern urban interests. The former chairman, Bathoen Gaseitsiwe, was one of the best known traditional chiefs, representing a conservative opposition to many of the structural changes the central government has undertaken, especially the modern local government arrangements in which traditional authority has been highly circumscribed. The much younger present chairman, Kenneth Koma, a powerful speaker, has an appeal for the urban unemployed, junior and mid-level civil servants, and the shop assistant and bank clerk stratum. The BNF is able to maintain the salience of such issues as the condition of the rural poor, which some attribute to the corrosion of traditional authority and others to the acquisitiveness of governing elites and the accumulating inequalities in the country. In recent years BNF rhetoric has had its impact on the younger majority party backbenchers who sometimes surprise their BDP colleagues with the sharpness of their criticism in Assembly debates.

There is also a constitutional provision which, over time, could add to the attitude of cynicism. Four seats in the National Assembly are filled by presidential appointment, not by election. This allows the President to bring into parliament and the cabinet able people who are not otherwise politically inclined. It also gives him the opportunity to save a member who has been defeated at the polls, e.g., Q.K.J. Masire (now president) in 1969, or to co-opt former opposition candidates by giving them seats and even junior ministerial posts. The power of appointment has also been used in local government elections, where the power of nomination lies officially with the minister of local government and lands. The use by the BDP of the power of nomination to convert electoral defeats in district or town councils into majorities has caused some bitterness.

Possible Cleavage Factors: Ethnicity and Class

There are at least two cleavage patterns that might offer clues to the direction of party system change in Botswana: ethnicity and socioeconomic class. Despite the fact that most Batswana speak the same language, they themselves distinguish nine separate "tribes" with a considerable degree of ethnic consciousness. There is a keen awareness that the Bamangwato, the late president's group, is the single largest ethnic group in the country. At the same time, the governing party has not used an ethnic spoils system in political appointments; rather, the BDP has attempted to capture loyalties all over the country, as is reflected by its performance in non-Ngwato constituencies. Although the opposition BNF was originally a Bangwanketse party, the BDP has always selected some cabinet ministers from that ethnic group, the new president, Masire, among them.

Ethnic arithmetic is nonetheless relevant as a potential basis for bifurcation. Although ethnic polarities are pretty well confined to the northeast, which is the location of 120,000 Kalangas, some majority party M.P.s claim from time to time in the Assembly that Kalangas are overrepresented in both the public and private sectors. Government sensitivity to this complaint is illustrated in the recent appointment of a new rector for the University College. The logical indigenous candidate to fill the vacancy left by the former rector, himself a black citizen, was passed over in favor of a British expatriate recruited from outside. University students demonstrated in front of the president's office, submitting a statement protesting the appointment as "delocalization." Since the logical indigenous figure the students had in mind is perfectly credentialed and experienced for the position, it can be surmised that the government felt it could better withstand student pique than appoint a Kalanga to yet another highly visible position.

The second potential cleavage is socioeconomic. The salaried group, principally civil servants and politicians, enjoys an urban life style and is investing in cattle. (Of the 119 ranches leased under the new Grazing Land Policy, 60 have been allocated to individuals, as opposed to groups.) Despite a wages-and-incomes policy designed to avoid a lopsided distribution of wealth, the cost of living in urban areas is so high that the government has yielded four times since 1973 to demands by civil servants for increased salaries. The latest Salaries Review Commission recommened an increase in salaries of between 21 and 46 percent.[14]

As career civil servants put their savings into cattle over the next decade, a modernized landed gentry might emerge. If rural incomes do not increase more than they have in the past fifteen years—from about $39 per capita per annum in 1966 to about $63 per capita in 1980—there will indeed be cumulative cleavage. So the potential bifurcation which could become self-reinforcing is less likely to be ethnic than socioeconomic; the haves pitted against the have-nots.

In such a bifurcation the interests of the salaried—especially the bureaucrats—remain close to those of the ruling party. The civil servant who chafes under an awareness of the maldistribution of income might vote for the opposition if he knows his vote will not really affect his own earning situation, but he will rarely quit his job on principle in a situation where the alternatives to government employment are so meager. The choice is presently one of co-optation or returning to the land. As long as the major party can provide the monetary inducements, the bureaucracy will ally itself tacitly with the governing party. The official acceptance of the inflationary salary recommendations must be interpreted in this context. It remains true, for now at least, that maintaining a one-party-dominant status in a multi-party setting, rather than ignoring the opposition, is seen by the regime to be necessary to legitimate the political system.

Economic Prospects, Constraints, and Options

Until recently Botswana was on the United Nations list of the world's twenty-five poorest countries. Per capita income was about P60 per annum in 1966–67, the first year of political independence. Botswana suffered large balance-of-trade deficits because it had to look abroad for supplies of capital. In 1966–67 the national budget included P17.8 million ($24.9 million) in expenditures and only P11.6 million ($16.2 million) in revenues There were no development funds at that time.

However, in fourteen years what was an extremely bleak picture has become much more encouraging. Annual per capita income in 1980 exceeded P450 ($585). National budget estimates for 1980–81 show P271.6 million ($353 million) for recurrent expenditures plus P120 million ($156 million) for development expenditures.[15] Revenues exceeded expenditures in both accounts until 1980. Also, the Gross Domestic Product almost quadrupled between 1971 and 1979, from P102.6 million ($133 million) to over P500 million ($650 million).[16] Real economic growth was about 16.1 percent per year between 1970 and 1978, the best in Africa according to the World Bank. However, because of soaring import costs and a sagging private (nonmineral) sector, real annual GDP growth in the near future will be much lower.

It is generally agreed that the high growth rates are not sustainable. Overall agricultural performance is poor except in the Barolong area. Agricultural output as a percent of Gross Domestic Product has decreased from 45 in 1968/69 to 17.5 in 1978/79. Although mineral output is up to 25 percent of GDP, full substitution of mineral output for agriculture will distort the national economy, increasing unemployment and the food import bill. Greater diversification of the economy is recognized to be imperative.

Botswana has one of the most lenient of tax structures for new investment. The former minister of commerce and industry said publicly that the country's company tax was among the "lowest in the world and that land in Botswana is at present plentiful and cheap."[17] Moreover, government cut personal income taxes in 1980; 15 percent in the upper brackets and 25 percent in the middle and lower brackets. These are attempts to cope with the recession in the private sector which has obtained since 1978; a government in search of investors. Cutting taxes at the same time that a salary increase for public servants averaging upwards of 30 percent has been approved seems dangerous. In addition it is questionable whether the tax policies are constructed in such a way as to turn the types of private investment that are attracted into long-term national gain.

Another future set of constraints relates to the effects of technology transfer on employment. Much of the technology required for modern mineral exploitation is capital-intensive. What are its effects? Is the employment of, say, two thousand local people in the service of a several hundred million dollar investment a fair capital-to-labor ratio in a country with severe employment problems? Is the technology being transferred increasing employment and per capita real income as well as decreasing the unemployment rate in the country? Is it conducive to a wide sharing of the benefits, or will they accrue largely to a small class of people who understand and can arrange to benefit from its use? Finally, what are the effects of the technology on the environment, on rural-urban migration, and on food production as more lucrative industrial employment is sought?

Local mining companies do not pay Batswana miners as much as they are getting in South Africa, so the latter often prefer to work outside the country. If the mining companies really wanted to pay locals a competitive wage, the government would no doubt accede even though it tries to avoid too wide a gap between mining and other wages. The paradox derives once again from the country's location: the effort to maintain equity in incomes is having negative effects on the development and use of local labor because of the proximity of South Africa and alternative employment.

Another option is encouraging foreign investors to use more "appropriate technology." This requires taking a hard look at the inputs into mineral exploitation, house construction, road and dam building, and other economic activities and attempting to identify local resources that can substitute for imported ones in the design of technology. For example, the Botswana Housing Corporation, after much public criticism for using expensive imported materials in the homes it builds, has begun experiments substituting indigenous materials—such as sulphur, mud, and stone for concrete blocks. Soaring power costs and the desire to be free of dependence on electricity for heating water have finally turned some people and several public buildings to solar units. But force of habit results in even these "appropriate" techniques being imported from South Africa even though they can be, and in some cases actually are being, manufactured in Botswana.[18]

On the financial side, the Botswana government has made a number of moves in the direction of taking greater control of its financial affairs. In 1975 it established the Bank of Botswana, an institution which has gradually taken on all the functions of a central bank: governance of exchange reserves, regulation of financial institutions operating in Botswana, and repository of government funds. As a first step the bank began issuing its own currency in 1976: the monetary unit is called the Pula, meaning "rain." The value of the Pula was originally on a par with the South African Rand. However, as the result of inflation in South Africa and higher import costs, the Pula was later pegged to a combination of the Rand and the unit of account of the International Monetary Fund (the SDR). Control over monetary policy not only gives Botswana control over its own money supply, it permits actions to protect and enhance capital formation, e.g., controls on the repatriation of profits and wages.

Finally, one option looms large and begs analysis: whether Botswana should remain a member of the Southern African Customs Union Agreement. Does Botswana really benefit over the long run from the renegotiated agreement of 1969? The answer to this question depends on (a) an assessment of the revenue generated by the formula as compensation for Botswana's loss of fiscal sovereignty and for having to import some commodities from South Africa at prices greater than those on the world market, and (b) an analysis of the extent to which the customs union has inhibited or will inhibit the growth of industry in Botswana. Point (b) suggests the need to examine the effects of withdrawal in terms of the potentially enlarged domestic market along with reduced exports to South Africa, changes in revenue resulting from the country's setting up its own import-duty structure and administration, and changes in the cost of living in the country. An exploratory analysis suggests that the results are most encouraging in the area of "shiftable" industries: those for which, though they are presently located in South Africa, the magnitude of Botswana imports would justify shifting production to Botswana. Examples include dairy products, milling industry products, beverages, pharmaceuticals, soap and candles, and rubber articles including tires. The preliminary analysis is not so encouraging in the areas of export markets, revenue and cost-of-living projections.[19] A recent analysis by the governor of the Bank of Botswana is skeptical of the above analysis. He argued that withdrawal from the Customs Union for purposes of import substitution would mean greater costs per unit of production in Botswana. This, in turn, would mean higher prices for the goods produced and consequently less consumption of the product. The prevailing official view in Botswana is that South Africa is still the lowest cost country in Sub-Saharan Africa in terms of industrial goods production.

Of course, the best economic analysis does not yield a forecast of the likelihood of outright retaliation by South Africa in the event of a Botswana withdrawal. Such a move could cripple the landlocked country. Nonetheless, more economic analysis of the kind suggested might allow the Botswana government to move more aggressively toward a strategy of calculated risk in its economic planning.

The longer Botswana remains a part of the customs union the higher the potential costs of withdrawal. Membership in customs unions always involves a certain amount of interdependence that derives from specialization. But the extreme differences in the economic structures of the members could, even with the liberalized aspects of the 1969 agreement, stunt the development of the three smaller members and make their relationship to South Africa one of acute and increasing dependence.

Zimbabwe, a potentially rich country, is now independent. That, combined with a resolution of who is to govern in Namibia, will give Botswana a clearer picture of its immediate and potential economic environment. What likely economic relationships will emerge between Botswana, Zimbabwe, and Namibia? As the changing political situation is consolidated over the next few years, prospects for new economic alliances will be greatly enhanced, affecting markets and access to the sea. A study for building a railway from Botswana due west through Namibia to the coast has already been completed. Whether the risks of withdrawal from the customs union are worthwhile depends on these imponderables.

Botswana's Political Options

What are the political options open to Botswana for enhancing its circumscribed position? Since independence, the country's leaders have attempted to compensate for the country's vulnerability by using the tools of statecraft on the international stage to alert the world to their own plight and that of the African majorities in the region. The late President, his ministers, and the small but very able external affairs staff constantly put a global construction on the crisis in Southern Africa. Sir Seretse Khama's speeches in the late 1970s became less oblique and more categorical regarding the universal issues of race, human rights, and democracy that are at stake.[20]

Botswana attempts to adhere to the general Pan-African principles of nonalignment, noninterference, and self-reliance. The government has always been an active member of the Organization of African Unity, the United Nations and the specialized agencies, and its representatives have attended most of the international conferences of the nonaligned nations. It was Sir Seretse Khama who took the lead in establishing the Southern African Development Coordinating Committee (SADCC) in 1979. He chaired the meeting in Lusaka in April 1980 which formalized its arrangements, allocated sector responsibilities among the nine countries, and provided for a (now permanent) secretariat in Gaborone.

The goal of SADCC is to enhance cooperation and the coordination of resource development along a range of sectors among the nine countries of the region excepting South Africa. It represents an important political as well as economic opportunity for Botswana in the 1980s. The selection of Gaborone as the site for the secretariat is not only a legacy of the early efforts of Sir Seretse Khama, but also a reflection of the way in which Botswana is perceived and the political role the country plays in the region. Botswana's is the small but steady hand. Its pragmatic leadership is trusted by the governments of the other eight countries. The economic viability of the country contributes to a robust and stable image. Botswana has developed and maintained easy relations with countries with very different political ideologies, both in the region and abroad. All of this contributes to the logical role of Botswana as the principal broker among the SADCC countries.

The role of Botswana as a bridge across several dimensions of the international relations among the majority-ruled independent countries of the region is illustrated by President Masire's remarks at the opening of the SADCC conference in Gaborone as reported in the *Botswana Daily News* on October 27, 1981: "Our experience in the struggle for political liberation has now found expression in the SADCC initiative which is a vehicle for promoting our struggle for economic liberation and cooperation. . . ." The use of the rhetoric of "struggle" and "liberation" by Botswana's leaders is not perceived by her SADCC neighbors as inconsistent with the country's pragmatic conduct. Mixing the symbolic political language of the SADCC region is natural, given its heterogeneity: "Commonwealth countries and former Portuguese colonies, evolutionary and revolutionary regimes, capitalist and Marxist ideologies, fragmented and unified societies, democratic and autocratic governments and vibrant as well as stagnating economies."*

Perhaps this is because, Botswana's economic prospects notwithstanding,

* See Richard F. Weisfelder, "The Southern African Development Coordination Conference (SADCC): A New Factor in the Liberation Process," in Thomas M. Callaghy, et al., *South Africa in Southern Africa* (New York: Praeger Publisners, forthcoming).

the country is dependent on its SADCC neighbors to the north and east. In fact, its very economic viability depends upon efficient means for getting its mineral exports to the sea. This gives SADCC members like Zimbabwe and Mozambique a sense that Botswana also needs them, that they have some leverage on the broker in exchange for not having the ecretariat in Salisbury or Maputo. Botswana also needs the patience and understanding of her SADCC neighbors in that its economy is perhaps more tightly linked to that of South Africa than some of the other members, so that disengagement from South Africa will be longer and more difficult for Botswana.

Significantly, representatives of the African National Congress, the Pan African Congress, and the Southwest Africa People's Organization (the political arm of the nationalist struggle for independence in Namibia) were present at the October 1981 conference as "observers." This confers a neutral or evenhanded status on the Botswana government in regional affairs which no other country can claim. Advantage of this unique position was taken by Botswana Democratic Party Chairman D. Kwelagobe at the end of the conference when he soberly admonished the SADCC conferees that success would depend upon "self-criticism" as well as the need for change in others. He warned those assembled that a number of efforts at African cooperation had foundered on the selfish and petty political rivalries of individual members which defeated the larger goal.

Botswana's foreign policy is not ideological and is quite independent. Almost all its external assistance comes from the western industrial countries. This did not deter the country from establishing diplomatic relations with the Soviet Union (in 1970) and the People's Republic of China (in 1974). The government was not intimidated by South African reactions to its refugee and outreach policies. Botswana refused to attend the OAU meeting in Uganda in 1975, publicly accusing Idi Amin of being inhumane. Very late in the struggle in Rhodesia the patience and suffering of the Batswana were tried to the point that they warned the Patriotic Front leadership to get together on a position for settlement or the Botswana position would soon be "a plague on both your houses." Through it all, Botswana's independent posture is greatly respected. The best evidence for this is the close cooperation with the new government in Zimbabwe and the successful state visit of President Machel of Mozambique in July 1981.

During the 1970s Botswana moved consistently from a posture of risk avoidance to one of more calculated risk-taking, the result both of external circumstances and improved domestic prospects. Botswana has exerted its symbolic and moral force both effectively and with dignity. The legacy of Sir Seretse Khama is a vindication of tireless diplomatic efforts and vision. President Masire inherits a viable polity and economy, enhanced in no small measure by the settlement in Zimbabwe.

Ironically, however, Botswana is still in the center of great political uncertainty. So long as the struggles in Namibia and South Africa remain
unresolved, the government's ability to maintain an open domestic democracy
that can balance vigilance against threats to its own security will constantly
be tested.

9.

Lesotho: Changing Patterns of Dependence

Richard Weisfelder

The Legacy of Domestic Conflict

Lesotho has several political attributes which are distinctive from patterns in many other African and Third World states.[1] In contrast to disruptive ethnic diversity, the Basotho are a single people sharing a common language, culture, and history of struggle to sustain their national identity against great odds. Data on income distribution, land holding, and cattle ownership portray a society in which an egalitarian heritage is only beginning to be offset by sharp differentials in income and in living standards. In addition, the Basotho have very strong traditions protecting basic human rights, including indigenous concepts of free speech, equal justice, due process of law, tolerance for diversity, and accountability of public officials.[2] A highly competitive multiparty system and a firm commitment to parliamentary democracy characterized Lesotho's constitutional development and its initial years of independence. Finally, the Basotho have long been proud of an unusually high level of literacy and political awareness that belies their rural setting and their level of economic development.

Given this unusual background, why has Lesotho not been spared from intense factionalism, outbursts of fratricidal violence, and endemic political instability? The concept of "marginality" seems particularly appropriate for interpreting the Basotho experience. Marginality occurs between groups of substantially different wealth, status, or power that exist in close proximity, and in which the less privileged are incapable of achieving the higher standards they envy. For over a century geographic encapsulation, labor migra-

249

tion, and growing literacy have accentuated the Basotho experience of economic, political, and social marginality vis-à-vis white-controlled South Africa. The result of their protracted and inescapable dependence has been debilitating competitiveness and suspicion. A natural human reluctance to concede that their nation is less than master of its own destiny has led the Basotho to hold their fellow nationals largely accountable for the failure to achieve their desired objectives. The result has been politicization of virtually every conceivable line of demarcation within the society. Internecine conflicts have involved dynastic rivalries, hereditary prerogatives vs. elected authority, traditional administration vs. modern bureaucracy, senior chiefs vs. lesser chiefs, chiefs vs. commoners, rural agriculturalists vs. urban wage earners, Protestants vs. Catholics, and conservatives vs. radicals. Since many of these cleavages have been mutually reinforcing, the tendency toward unrelenting recrimination and obstructionism has been maximized. It has usually been possible to organize a body of the discontented against any political incumbent.

Lesotho's political evolution from 1965 to 1970 fully reflected this turbulent pattern.[3] Chief Leabua Jonathan's National Party (BNP) assumed power in 1965 after gaining a scant two-seat parliamentary majority and a bare 40 percent plurality of the votes cast in the preindependence election. Few observers had predicted that Chief Jonathan's poorly organized, conservative amalgam of rural peasants, junior chiefs, and Roman Catholics could prevail against the militant, Pan-Africanist thrust of Ntsu Mokhehle's Congress Party (BCP) and the royalist imagery of the Marematlou Freedom Party (MFP). Once in power, Chief Jonathan's inexperienced cabinet confronted even greater obstacles. The BCP, which had its base among commoners, townspeople, Protestants, and the more highly educated, commanded the sympathies of much of the civil service and dominated politics in Maseru, the capital. Moreover, King Moshoeshoe II's persistent efforts to win substantial executive powers put the prestige of the monarchy solidly in the opposition ranks. Because of the new prime minister's precarious grasp on power, his opponents joined in a constant barrage of parliamentary, legal and agitational maneuvers to force the government from office. The BCP boycott of the independence celebrations on October 4, 1966 symbolized the reality that Chief Jonathan's government was to have no respite from political confrontation between its assumption of power in 1965 and the general election of 1970.[4]

Until 1971, the BNP leadership seemed preoccupied with the notion that maintaining friendly relationships with South Africa was essential for national survival and economic development. The prime minister and his colleagues clearly believed that their basic electoral support had derived from "realistic" BNP policies of sustaining and augmenting "bread-and-butter" relationships with the Republic. Moreover, these leaders vociferously argued that the peaceful dialogue exemplified by Chief Jonathan's face-to-face meetings with Prime Ministers Verwoerd and Vorster should serve as a model for other African states seeking to end white supremacy. Exponents of economic sanctions, guerrilla warfare, or other hostile actions were denounced as infantile extremists and terrorists whose futile efforts would only heighten white intransigence. Similarly strident critiques were aimed at BCP and MFP opponents, who constantly characterized the ruling party as "stooges" or "sellouts" to South Africa. In his effort to hammer home the validity of his approach, Chief Jonathan tended to go beyond symbolically or economically necessary links with South Africa. For example, the employment of loaned South African civil servants in key departments such as justice, information, and planning seemed as much intended to prove that the BNP had South Africans doing their bidding as to enhance efficiency or technical expertise in the civil service. Undoubtedly such graphic evidence of a South African presence in Lesotho was instrumental in the BCP's stunning electoral victory in 1970.[5]

In the midst of this bitter political infighting, Chief Jonathan decided to abrogate the independence constitution and remain in power despite his party's defeat at the polls. His action was understandable but dealt a serious blow to Lesotho's fragile sense of constitutionalism. The initial transfer of power to an opposition is a critical test for any new state since it requires an act of good faith by the incumbents. In Lesotho, the shared dimensions of common identity and experience between the winners and losers were outweighed by the effects of marginality and by the all too familiar excuses that the opposition victory resulted from fraud and irresponsibility rather than genuine support. But the disregard of constitutional norms meant that Basotho leaders vying for power in the future would be tempted either to mobilize the requisite force or to strike a bargain with incumbents instead of trusting the ballot box.

Images of Self-Assertion

Unfortunately, most images of Lesotho and of Chief Jonathan's administration seem to have become fixed during this early period of independence, without adequate regard for some remarkable transformations taking place in the meanwhile. Most commentators had treated the BNP position regarding South Africa as an immutable ideological necessity rather than an expedient in a struggle for domestic power and national security. But a shrewd and pragmatic politician, Chief Jonathan proved more than willing to adopt his opponents' more strident line toward South Africa when his own approach became demonstrably unpopular. Even if the BNP had triumphed at the polls in 1970, subsequent developments in Southern Africa would have compelled some tactical adjustments. In particular, no prime minister of the politically

conscious Basotho could long afford to be upstaged by increasing outspokenness from Bantustan leaders like Chief Gatsha Buthelezi or urban spokesmen
like Bishop Desmond Tutu and Dr. Nthato Motlana.

Lesotho's position as a resource-poor ministate wholly surrounded by the
Republic, and the latter's pervasive impact, have led to skepticism regarding
any significant Basotho role in the regional struggles to attain majority rule.
But while geopolitical realities continue to impose major constraints, the recent performance of the Lesotho government compels serious reevaluation of
these commonly held presumptions.

Since 1971, Chief Jonathan and his government have mounted a crescendo
of public criticism of South African racial policies. Incidents such as the killing of eleven Basotho miners at Carletonville in 1973 fueled strident warnings
that escalating violence would be the inevitable consequence of continued
South African failure to redress the fundamental grievances of the black majority. Revolutionary action by liberation movements was accepted as legitimate, if not desirable. Relations were swiftly established with the Frelimo
government in Mozambique, and regular direct flights to Maputo were instituted. South African expatriates gave way to technical assistance personnel
from international organizations and other bilateral aid donors. Lesotho's increased willingness to risk confrontation with South Africa gained international visibility in December 1976 when Foreign Minister C. D. Molapo
brought an urgent complaint before the United Nations Security Council.
Molapo argued that South Africa had illegally closed much of Lesotho's eastern
frontier by unilaterally transferring control of border posts to the Transkei
government despite prior treaty obligations to Lesotho regarding their operation. Unanimous Security Council endorsement of Lesotho's position and rapid
provision of emergency assistance for affected areas gave strong evidence that
challenging South Africa could even be financially profitable.

Some additional signs of increased national assertiveness are worth noting.
Visits to Lesotho of African leaders such as Presidents Khama of Botswana and
Tolbert of Liberia provided excellent opportunities for speeches and communi-
ques affirming mutual solidarity and joint commitment to the liberation of
Southern Africa. Likewise, Lesotho has hosted a number of major international
meetings that must have caused considerable discomfiture in Pretoria. The
African-American Institute conference held in November 1976 brought to-
gether delegates from thirty-five countries. These included outspoken critics
of South Africa like U.N. Ambassador Andrew Young, Congressman Charles
Diggs, Senator Dick Clark, Percy Qoboza, editor of *The World,* Manas
Buthelezi, head of the Soweto Black Parents Association, Alfred Nzo of the
ANC, and David Sibeko of the PAC. One year later, representatives of sixty-two
African, Caribbean, Pacific, and EEC states also met in Maseru. Both occasions
permitted Chief Jonathan to provide an array of influential foreign statesmen
with firsthand knowledge of Lesotho's precarious situation, to seek their

assistance against South Africa, and to enhance his own militant credentials by vigorously denouncing the white minority regimes. As the Basotho prime minister had told the nonaligned meeting in Sri Lanka, he wanted his country to be thought of as "more than a frontline state," because Lesotho operated "right behind the enemy line, shoulder to shoulder with our oppressed brothers in the thick of battle."

Possibly the most telling evidence of shifting emphases within the Lesotho government was the decision to establish diplomatic relations with Rumania and Yugoslavia and to consider links with other communist states, including East Germany and the Soviet Union. "Familiarization" visits to Lesotho by Cuban delegations and discussions of a Russian embassy in Maseru triggered anxious speculation in the South African media. Yet, no principle had seemed more central to the ideology of the ruling Basotho National Party and its founder, Chief Jonathan, than adamant anticommunism and uncompromising opposition to direct dealings with the socialist world.

All of these improvisations point to the unusual durability and flexibility of one man, Leabua Jonathan, whose lengthy tenure in office has encompassed these diverse strategies. But far from having undergone some complete metamorphosis, the Basotho prime minister still leads an array of conservative forces only partially different from those which brought him to power in 1965. Lesotho remains active in conservative groups such as the World Anti-Communist League and is virtually alone among African states in continuing full diplomatic and commercial relationships with Israel, Taiwan, and South Korea. These anomalies and gyrations in Lesotho's foreign policy may explain why some observers have contented themselves with simple stereotypes of Chief Jonathan's regime to the exclusion of less easily explained realities.

Lesotho's political behavior can only be understood as the cumulative product of forced choices among unpalatable and unsavory alternatives. From precolonial times to the present, the Basotho have sought strategies for maximizing national autonomy while dealing with hostile neighbors which possessed far greater economic, military, and organizational resources. A century of British rule prevented a physically truncated Lesotho from being incorporated into South Africa, but at the price of becoming a stagnant rural backwater whose primary productive activity was to supply cheap labor for the burgeoning economy of the Republic. But while gradual development within existing patterns promised continued economic subordination and racial oppression, Basotho leaders were aware that a frontal challenge to the established South African order risked immediate strangulation. The political violence of 1970 and 1974, that destroyed Lesotho's multiparty constitutional processes, had its origin in acrimonious debate over which of these unacceptable alternatives to embrace. Interpretation of Lesotho's role in contemporary Southern African conflicts requires further insight into this complex economic and political underpinning.

International Influences and Policy Choices

Based on the assumption that any obstacle can be surmounted, a thorough and cogent World Bank Report on the Basotho economy is euphemistically entitled *Lesotho: A Development Challenge*. Like virtually all such analyses, this document demonstrates the pitifully slim resources with which Chief Jonathan had to make his record before submitting his administration to the harsh scrutiny of Basotho voters in 1970. When juxtaposed to prior economic malaise, there appeared to have been a remarkable amount of new, if somewhat disjointed, activity during the first four years of independence.[6] Visible accomplishments included construction of a major tarred road, opening of a Holiday Inn and casino, establishment of a national development corporation with several affiliated small-scale industries, and initiation of a substantial agricultural improvement scheme in one locality. Changes with long-term payoffs, such as the creation of a central planning office and the favorable renegotiation in 1969 of the Southern African Customs Union Agreement (see Interchapter), occurred too late and were too remote from ordinary voters to have much impact on the electorate. The inexperienced new government might also have deserved some plaudits for facilitating open access to needed South African goods, services, and employment opportunities or for simply maintaining existing domestic services despite woefully inadequate financing. However, the failure of Chief Jonathan's policies to produce tangible improvements in living standards for most Basotho was more often attributed to gross malfeasance or outright betrayal to South Africa than to his having undertaken a nearly impossible task.

In the late 1960s Southern Africa was hardly a central focus of great power concern. Leosotho could expect a modicum of development assistance from various bilateral and multilateral donors in addition to emergency famine relief from governments and charitable organizations. Plagued by its own financial crisis, Britain's major interest was reduction of its annual grant-in-aid, which had initially funded 50 percent of Lesotho's recurrent expenditure. Prior support from socialist states to Jonathan's political rivals, together with the militant anticommunism of the National Party, effectively ruled out a tilt to the East. No individual state or collection of overseas donors appeared likely to make major commitments to a country where positive results seemed improbable and genuine independence so questionable.

Under these circumstances, the Lesotho government could reasonably conclude that only South Africa might have the motivation and capacity to deliver the level of assistance required to make a meaningful impact upon Lesotho's economy. The financial and technical assistance which the BNP had received from South African sources during its rise to power provided a precedent. If further South African aid could help to perpetuate cordial relationships with a more stable Lesotho located in the heart of the Republic, the Pretoria regime would be the prime beneficiary. In addition, drought-prone South Africa appeared to have much to gain from developing Lesotho's major water resources and hydroelectric potential while simultaneously permitting Lesotho to fund further growth from the revenues earned by these commodities. What Jonathan did not anticipate was that the actual South African contribution would be far too niggardly to offset the huge domestic political costs of that association imposed upon his party. By prematurely flaunting their commitment to cooperation with South Africa, Lesotho's leaders heightened domestic opposition while also weakening Pretoria's incentive to provide economic inducements. Nevertheless, the South African government had evidently concluded that few propaganda points could be scored by providing extensive aid to Lesotho since enhanced relationships would only be interpreted abroad as more definitive evidence of a Bantustan-type arrangement. Moreover, the Vorster regime could hardly justify major assistance to Lesotho without also making substantially greater commitments than intended to its own black homelands.

Following the 1970 coup, many observers presumed that Lesotho would become even more closely bound to the Republic than before. Whatever the truth of alleged South African complicity in that event, at least tacit collaboration with Pretoria seemed required to maintain Chief Jonathan's manifestly unpopular regime in power. However, the Lesotho government proceeded on just the opposite track once it had reestablished full control and reevaluated its situation.

Distancing itself from South Africa may initially have been a short-term BNP expedient for political survival. The Pretoria regime had no acceptable alternative to continuing business as usual with Chief Jonathan. Adopting portions of the opposition message regarding South Africa in order to rebuild popular support was an inexpensive means of relieving pressure on the Lesotho government's severely strained security capacities. This strategy also served to make Jonathan's efforts at national reconciliation under his leadership a bit more palatable to erstwhile opponents. In any event, the BNP leadership had regularly denounced apartheid and demanded the return of conquered territories when speaking before local audiences. Only the insertion of more strident language and delivery of such attacks on national occasions in the presence of the international media were now required. This emphasis on Lesotho's victimization by its neighbor's apartheid policies also tended to dissuade aid donors from retrenching their programs in reaction to episodes of violent repression which had followed Jonathan's coup. High profile criticism of South Africa could also lessen the effectiveness of opposition efforts to mobilize African states and organizations in support of their claim to be the legitimate government of Lesotho. Finally, movement to a harsher line had some potential for persuading South Africa to provide increased assistance in order to restore earlier harmonious relationships.

Significant alterations in the international environment have enabled Chief Jonathan to sustain and expand this more assertive approach. Growing emphasis in the United Nations on the plight of the twenty-five least developed countries has stimulated enhanced flows of multilateral aid to Lesotho. More importantly, as conflict in the Portuguese colonies and Rhodesia widened during the early 1970s, Western governments came under intensified pressure to buttress their rhetorical support for racial justice and majority rule with more tangible actions. Expanded aid to sustain the independence and development of black governments in Botswana, Lesotho, and Swaziland provided a convenient means of achieving this objective short of lending support to radical liberation movements. This trend was strongly reinforced when Southern Africa became a prominent and chronic international issue in the wake of the collapse of Portuguese colonialism, the Angolan civil war, the Soweto insurrection, the Biko affair, and the continuing war of attrition in Rhodesia. For example, American aid to Lesotho, which averaged $1.9 million per year from 1966 to 1970, and $2.7 million per year from 1971 to 1975, reached approximately $8.6 million in fiscal 1978 and $17–19 million per annum in the early 1980s. Under the South African Special Requirements Fund, an additional $25 million of funds from the United States were committed toward building a major road, which will obviate Lesotho's dependence on the Transkei by linking Lesotho's southeastern mountain areas with the densely populated western lowlands. Although Lesotho's authoritarian political format may cause it to be somewhat less favored than democratic Botswana, the overriding determinants of American aid decisions have become the general international salience of the region and the "moderate" credentials of the prospective recipient.

The Costs and Benefits of Dependence

Even though the bulk of its technical assistance, project aid, and foreign investment comes from non–South African sources, Lesotho was more economically dependent upon the Republic in 1978 than it was in 1966. Despite potentially negative long-term consequences, two of the more visible components of these linkages have spurred rapid economic advances. Lesotho's share of Southern African Customs Union receipts, which have provided roughly two-thirds of current government revenues, has increased at a rate consistently exceeding expectations. As a result, Lesotho attained a surplus in its current account by 1973/74, thereby terminating dependence upon British subsidies. Moreover, the growth of customs revenue, combined with rising external assistance, has permitted expansion of the budget from $15.7 million in 1970/71 to $92.5 million in 1977/78, with a 53 percent spurt to $141 million in 1979 and 30 to 40 percent increments recently. Although its membership in the Customs Union and use of the rand currency permit Lesotho to devote scarce administrative resources to other matters, most discretion in selecting appropriate trade and monetary policies has been lost because of these arrangements. Lesotho has no voice regarding the valuation of the rand, a decision of crucial importance to its economic well-being since the rand and new maloti currency are fully interchangeable. Furthermore, an alarming potential for harassment was revealed in January 1977 when the South African government delayed payment of Lesotho's quarterly share of customs revenue for a month. Inflation, austerity, and unemployment there are equally devastating potentials.

To remedy these deficiencies, Lesotho's monetary authority might follow Botswana's example and break the rand-maloti linkage. Autonomous, if costly, customs arrangements could also be developed. By contrast, Lesotho could not possibly create alternative jobs for a significant portion of the 200,000 Basotho migrants employed in South Africa, nor begin to replace the 40 percent of the gross national product generated by their labors. The most optimistic estimates indicate that only 27,500 persons, or 5 percent of the adult Basotho work force, were employed in Lesotho's modern sector in 1975. At best, 6,000 new positions were created between 1971 and 1975, while the work force expanded by ten times that number. The second five-year development plan failed to fulfill its objectives, as only 12,500 additional employees entered the wage-earning sector or just a sixth of the actual *increase* in the work force by 1980. In short, Lesotho continues to rely on the ability and willingness of South Africa to absorb the bulk of its new workers as well as growing numbers of existing laborers from its stagnant subsistence agricultural sector.

On the positive side, a fivefold increase in the minimum cash wage in mining and the generally rapid upward trend of black earnings in South Africa from 1971 until 1976 permitted some Basotho households to make modest improvements in their standard of living. Citizens of Lesotho employed in the Republic during 1975 earned an estimated $250 million, a figure more than double the gross domestic product of their country. The repatriation of goods and cash by migrant workers plays a major role in offsetting Lesotho's trade deficit, where imports are nine times greater than exports. Under a deferred payments scheme for migrant workers begun in 1975, 60 percent of cash wages, previously held without interest by the Chamber of Mines until the end of the contractual work period, must now be deposited in interest-bearing accounts at the Lesotho National Bank. The revolving fund thus created enhances the pool of domestic capital available to provide credit for development programs, but has not yet fulfilled initial expectations.

There is ample documentation that this constant exodus of the most motivated and capable Basotho has had starkly negative consequences for agricultural productivity and rural family life.[7] Rising wages in South Africa have made even less inviting the meagre rewards from the backbreaking toil required to increase subsistence agricultural productivity. The resignation of over a hundred members of the Lesotho Mounted Police in 1977 to seek better paying employment in the mines highlights the general problem that Basotho at all skill levels can invariably find more remunerative positions in the Republic. Hence, Lesotho's economic strategists must choose between using sparse revenues to finance spiraling domestic labor costs or permitting South Africa to continue to be the prime beneficiary of Lesotho's substantial educational and vocational training expenditures.

The most alarming potential inherent in the migratory labor pattern is that South Africa can create economic and political havoc in Lesotho by repatriating even a small portion of the total work force or simply cutting back on recruitment. When unexplained outbreaks of violence between Xhosa and Basotho mine workers resulted in the sudden but brief return of more than 10,000 migrants during 1974, Basotho politicians were quick to characterize the problem as a South African reprisal for Lesotho's more strident critique of apartheid. Likewise, a decline in recruitment during early 1977 was thought to be a reaction against Lesotho for bringing the Transkei border issue before the United Nations. Even in the absence of Pretoria's arm-twisting, similar effects may result from the Republic's efforts to automate, "stabilize" the work force, and reduce dependence on foreign nationals by employing more South African black workers. Despite the creation of a national employment service and labor-intensive construction unit, Lesotho lacks the emergency capabilities to withstand more than partial or short-term dislocations.

Several other manifestations of acute dependence bear comment. Rapid population growth and declining agricultural yields, resulting from erosion and poor husbandry, have forced Lesotho to import 50 percent of the grain consumed. The bulk of this food, like other imports, is purchased in the Republic. The remainder, together with wool and mohair exports, must transit through South African port facilities and railways. All of Lesotho's electricity is purchased from the Republic's ESCOM power grid. Infant industries assembling television sets, producing handicrafts or electric fixtures, and retreading tires are all dependent upon the South African market. The thriving tourist trade relies on a predominantly South African clientele to create profits and recover its huge initial investments. Each of these sectors is incredibly vulnerable to outright sabotage or, more probably, petty harassments, including power failures, shipping delays, price increases, or, in the case of tourism, a bad press regarding political violence.

A Development Balance Sheet

Preparation of a balance sheet evaluating Chief Jonathan's economic stewardship since 1970 is highly problematic. Because of the sudden surge of outside interest in the region many significant projects have been launched too recently or operated too briefly to be judged on their merits. At best, these endeavors can merely provide more breathing room, not fundamental alterations of Lesotho's precarious existence. At worst, they are institutionalizing a new layer of dependency relationships where domestic self-help efforts are drowned in a sea of imported techniques and expatriate advisors.

Chief Jonathan's greatest triumph to date was persuading De Beers Consolidated Mines to invest $46 million in mechanized diamond mining at a site rejected by two other multinationals. Less spectacular successes in road construction, electrification, provision of local water supplies, and creation of over fifty small enterprises through the Lesotho National Development Corporation seem more directly applicable to the needs of ordinary Basotho. In particular, newly established marketing boards seeking to maximize the return from exports and small factories producing commodities like flour and clothing for domestic consumption are appropriate means of lessening dependency. Implementation of the Rand Monetary Agreement of 1974, establishment of its own currency, regulation of the operations of local financial institutions, and creation of parastatal credit organizations may eventually augment the mobilization of Lesotho's financial assets for development objectives.[8] Similarly, several externally funded agricultural projects were designed to reverse the declining productivity of the vast portion of the Basotho work force engaged in subsistence agriculture. However, their results provide little hint of marginal improvements or future transformations.

In Lesotho, as elsewhere, the desire to create national symbols has occasionally distorted priorities. Although the life-styles of both UNDP and AID personnel provide some precedent, it is certainly questionable whether construction of a $2.6 million palace for King Moshoeshoe II was the most appropriate way for Lesotho to celebrate its tenth anniversary of independence. There also must have been more pressing needs than the $9.1 million stadium in Maseru. The replacement of Lesotho's outmoded airport with a new international facility costing up to $70 million will provide reassuring access to the outside world in times of crisis. However, the high emotional commitment to this project, which will in fact benefit relatively few Basotho, contrasts with a surprising sluggishness in harnessing the nation's ample hydro-electric potential. The government has seemed fixated on its 1965 campaign promise to construct the massive Malibamatso hydroelectric scheme which would earn substantial revenue through the sale of water and power to the Republic. But despite South African slowness in concluding a mutually beneficial agreement on that project, Lesotho has quite belatedly begun to consider small projects at producing water for irrigated farming and power for domestic consumption. With Lesotho's dry and unpredictable climate, only irrigated horticulture is likely to generate sufficient increases in productivity to retain the more ambitious workers on the land. Since hydroelectric projects could terminate dependence on South African power and benefit large numbers of

Basotho, it is difficult to imagine why even high cost factors could have kept such ventures from the top of the development priorities list.

Most observers agree that Lesotho's weak project implementation capacity is the greatest obstacle to effective development in almost all sectors of the economy. Expenditure of available funds is frequently delayed. The rapid expansion of external assistance will mean further proliferation of expatriates, projects designed and executed with marginal Basotho input, and greater difficulty in obtaining the informed cooperation of ordinary citizens. While Maseru is strangled by urban sprawl, the countryside remains unchanged.

Much of the problem can be attributed to colonial-type deference to decentralized mission-school systems almost totally devoid of vocational, technical, or managerial curriculum content. Beyond the scarcity of qualified and experienced managers in the various government departments, implementation is complicated by continued reliance upon chiefs and headmen to fulfill local administrative functions. Thus a diffuse, poorly disciplined, neo-traditional framework bears major responsibilities for assuring local compliance with the requirements of highly specialized, technologically complex projects. Even if the funds and alternative manpower were available, fundamental changes in these patterns would be unlikely. In lieu of a popular mandate, the prime minister relies heavily on his long-established power bases in the lower echelons of the chieftainship and the Catholic Church. He and his party have argued forcefully that economic modernization can and should occur under the aegis of established religious, social, and administrative patterns, reoriented and retooled to accomplish their new tasks.

Project implementation may also have been hindered by failure to utilize effectively the skills of professionally qualified individuals known to have supported the opposition parties. Indeed, the most crucial aspect of Chief Jonathan's policy of national reconciliation may be the active recruitment and reemployment of experienced Basotho civil servants who were ousted from their positions or sought refuge abroad during the political turmoil of 1974 (see below). Nonetheless, demonstrably low-level governmental legitimacy remains a potentially devastating barrier to improved implementation capabilities. If decisions or regulations which would normally be carried out voluntarily require constant administrative oversight and coercion, shortages of indigenous personnel and rising costs will be greatly exacerbated. Therefore, the revitalization of Lesotho's dismal agricultural sector and of the economy at large is contingent upon the minimal acceptability, if not broad popularity, of its basic political institutions.

The Format of Authoritarian Rule

Following Chief Jonathan's coup in 1970, some writers (myself included) predicted continued conflict and endemic violence in Lesotho. This conclusion rested on the assumption that the BNP government lacked a sufficient security capacity and popular base to overwhelm its opponents conclusively. After all, Mokhehle's Congress Party had demonstrated the organizational strength to garner 50 percent of the national vote despite the numerous structural advantages favoring the ruling BNP. It did not seem farfetched to think that the BCP leaders could bring at least enough pressure upon Chief Jonathan's overextended administration to compel him to make significant concessions. John D. Holm correctly forecast "the emergence of an autocratic regime willing to quash public resentment . . . and, as a consequence, to mitigate substantially the present internal conflict." He contrasted Chief Jonathan's decisive use of force against any form of resistance to his rule with the BCP's hesitance at adopting violent or conspiratorial techniques. Lacking the capacity to sustain an armed struggle, the opposition seemed "largely limited to negotiating with [Jonathan] for the conditions under which they will offer their support to the new political structure."[9]

Since 1970 Chief Jonathan has remained firmly in control of Lesotho's authoritarian political format. Even the continued absence of a constitution has been turned into an asset. The resultant institutional flexibility has permitted the prime minister to skillfully co-opt segments of the opposition without permanently rebuffing the remainder. The royal Marematlou Freedom Party and the minuscule United Democratic Party (UDP) were quickly persuaded to support Chief Jonathan's efforts at national reconciliation because they were assured considerably greater visibility than their electoral base could justify. However, Ntsu Mokhehle, whose release from detention had been contingent upon his accepting the abrogation of the election, continued to demand parity for his party in a coalition arrangement with the BNP. In 1973, Chief Jonathan successfully cracked the BCP phalanx. He persuaded Mokhehle's longtime deputy, Gerard Ramoreboli, to lead a Congress Party contingent into the new interim National Assembly under arrangements far less favorable than Mokhehle had sought.

Frustrated by the defection of Ramoreboli's group and by harassment of party activities under tight new security legislation, the Mokhehle wing of the BCP attempted to seize power by force. Although the abortive "clumsy coup" of January 1974 superficially substantiated images of endemic violence, it actually vindicated John Holm's premises. This diffuse, poorly organized operation was swiftly crushed by the paramilitary Police Mobile Unit. Irregular formations of BNP youth launched a reign of vigilante-style reprisals against suspected BCP supporters. The top leadership of Mokhehle's faction either was jailed in Lesotho or sought refuge in Botswana and Zambia. All party assets, including buildings, vehicles, loudspeakers, and printing facilities, were transferred to the more pliant Ramoreboli faction. The Vorster regime allowed the BCP fugitives to transit the Republic, after first trying to exchange them for refugees in Lesotho. During the past three years, however,

BCP supporters trained in Libya and Uganda have begun an insurgency under the name Lesotho Liberation Army. Further schisms among the exiled Congress leadership have undermined opposition pressure on Chief Jonathan. But continuing acts of sabotage within Lesotho demonstrate the precariousness of the government's grip. Indeed, the recent murders of several prominent opposition figures may presage a decline of political civility and remergence of acute conflict.

What seems most surprising about the present authoritarian pattern of rule in Lesotho is how little the basic governmental structures and operational routines differ from their constitutional predecessors. Under the Westminster-style institutions embodied in the independence constitution, the prime minister and his Cabinet already possessed enormous latitude for independent initiative and discretionary action. Chief Jonathan, like several ministerial colleagues, had always exhibited a somewhat bombastic and assertive style based on the belief that leaders gain respect from visibly displaying their power and leaving no doubt who is in charge. Confronted with a vigorous opposition, the narrow BNP majority in the popularly elected National Assembly had showed little inclination to risk undermining the government by breaking ranks with the Cabinet. Hence parliamentary democracy had meant the imposition of the majority will upon an opposed legislative minority with little room for mutual give and take.

Nullifying the election, terminating executive accountability to parliament, suspending the power of courts to guarantee basic rights, and tightening security legislation already enacted removed all potential for popular resistance to arbitrary power within the system. However, the implementation and enforcement of ministerial decisions rested on the three bureaucratic structures that had always exercised these roles, the police, the civil service, and the chieftainship. Because of glaring abuses of power and violations of human rights during the temporary breakdowns of civil order in 1970 and 1974, the greater salience of force within the new system is well recognized. Nevertheless, the retention of the incumbent government in office provided an element of continuity quite unusual for an illegal regime. Habitual compliance with Chief Jonathan's directives was certainly no more problematic to many Basotho than acceptance of an unfamiliar new authority of Mokhehle.

The rhetoric of government spokesmen and the all-encompassing language of the security laws may conceal how much autonomous political activity and criticism has persisted in Lesotho. To be sure, the detention of political opponents and the banning of newspapers at the height of the crises have had a chilling effect on the freewheeling dissent of the 1960s. Nevertheless, the "holiday from politics" which Jonathan announced in 1970 did not mean the abrupt demise of political parties, but that they function in a more constricted context. Various church newspapers continued to criticize gov-

ernmental policies and readily denounced police brutality. Public trials of
BCP insurgents also provided a vehicle for assailing government behavior.
While announcing minimal punishments, the late Chief Justice Mapetla mani-
fested thorough outspokenness in condemning "brutal and humiliating assaults" by the police and in blaming the insurrection upon "relentless
repression." The establishment in 1973 of an entirely nominated interim
National Assembly containing opposition spokesmen restored the outward
form and a fair amount of the substance of parliamentary criticism. Inclusion
of Gerard Ramoreboli of the BCP and Patrick Lehloenya of the MFP in the
current Cabinet marks partial attainment of the goal of national reconciliation. From the evidence presented, there has clearly been constitutional re-
gression. However, Lesotho's present political system has demonstrated far
more in common with the benign colonial authoritarianism of the 1920s than
with the modern dictatorships of Mobutu and Amin.

Since Lesotho's political institutions are especially inchoate and fragile, the
future course of authoritarian rule depends heavily on the interaction of
the civil service and police with the established elements of the BNP political
base, the lesser chiefs, and conservative Catholics. Chief Jonathan's support
within the chieftainship appears to have been strengthened by the addition of
senior chiefs previously aligned with the royalist MPF. However, the price of
this allegiance has been minimal governmental interference with local chiefly
administration and land tenure practices. This configuration may help to explain Chief Jonathan's caution in embracing irrigated farming methods,
which would necessitate substantial adjustment of traditional roles. The
colonial dualisms remain largely unaltered.

Former Catholic teachers are quite evident in the Cabinet, and the entire
government retains a dominant Catholic flavor. However, the church hierarchy seems less wedded to Chief Jonathan than previously. Reforms affecting
Catholic schools, relations with communist states, reconciliation with opponents, confrontation with South Africa, and violence against fellow
Basotho are issues which create uneasiness among many Catholics. While no
massive defection seems likely, critical appraisals from conservative Catholics
have intensified. Within the BNP, this element has joined several chiefs
who have held Cabinet posts in opposing any rapprochement with Ntsu
Mokhehle or rival claimants to the BCP leadership like Koenyama Chakela.

For the past five years, top civil servants who had long been associated
with policy making have been recruited directly into the Cabinet to enhance
its technical competence. On the other hand, the BNP has consistently facilitated rapid entry of its supporters into the civil service, which in the 1960s
had been a stronghold of Congress Party sentiment. This complex inter-
penetration has opened the bureaucracy to frequent charges of nepotism,
favoritism, and incompetence, but has also permitted talented professionals
and aspiring militants to gain acess to ruling circles. Chief Jonathan's more

assertive policies toward South Africa were undoubtedly influenced by two outspoken ministers, J. Kotsokoane and J. Moitse, who rose from the civil service. In addition, the central bureaucracy provides a mechanism for the articulation of the interests of wage earners and townspeople who had previously been represented through the BCP. Hence civil servants are likely to provide the government with a net impetus toward modernization which runs at cross purposes to traditional interests.

To date, no Lesotho Mounted Police official has been elevated to a Cabinet post, and the supremacy of civilian authority has been maintained. Nevertheless, experience elsewhere in Africa suggests that any number of highly unpredictable variables, ranging from low pay to the degeneration of civil order, could precipitate military intervention. Despite its small size, the paramilitary unit of the police has amply demonstrated its coercive preeminence in Lesotho. Although police recruits have been carefully screened and top officers retired before becoming too well entrenched, only Chief Jonathan's political skill precludes intervention. So long as there is no agreed-upon standard of political legitimacy, the police are as likely to assert their claim as anyone else.

King Moshoeshoe II's unprecedented willingness to steer clear of controversy and maintain the posture of a constitutional head of state has been a major factor in Chief Jonathan's ability to consolidate his authoritarian rule. Following a period of exile in 1970, the King formally assented to ceremonial status rather than risk forced abdication and the denial of the throne to his sons. Nevertheless, many observers have sensed the King's lack of enthusiasm for his role and barely concealed distaste for the pretentious uniform and ostentatious royal palace provided by his government. His publicly expressed concerns about human rights questions reinforce this judgment.

This contrast with the power of the Swazi monarch is often attributed to Lesotho's greater penetration by facets of modernity and to Moshoeshoe II's alleged lack of leadership qualities. What is not sufficiently emphasized is that modern politicians in Lesotho gained the initiative during the long female regency preceding Moshoeshoe II's installation in 1960. Due to the vicissitudes of the timing of succession, there was no ruler like Sobhuza II, whose reign conveniently spanned the entire period of Swazi constitutional evolution (see Swaziland chapter). Hence the Basotho kingship had been compelled to surrender control of key organizational elements of traditional power well before Moshoeshoe II assumed his title. Unlike Sir Seretse Khama of Botswana, who could make his bid for secular authority in a relative political vacuum, Moshoeshoe II would have confronted experienced politicians if he had risked his throne to enter the electoral arena. Despite setbacks, the Basotho monarch bears the historically rich and respected mantle of kingship, which could permit him to assume authority at some future date. Should the present political fabric begin to unravel, there is little doubt that Moshoeshoe II's traditional authority and legal training make him a potential law giver to whom the nation could turn.[10]

Regional Interactions and Prospects

Before majority rule was achieved in Zimbabwe, Lesotho's role in Southern African conflicts seemed likely to remain sporadic, peripheral, and primarily symbolic. But now that international initiatives are being focused on the liberation of Namibia and the Republic itself, mechanisms chosen to achieve that objective automatically place Lesotho closer to the forefront of the struggle. Lesotho government spokesmen no longer unequivocally oppose international sanctions against South Africa, because of their certain detrimental impact upon Lesotho. Instead, Basotho leaders use that prospect in soliciting additional aid to promote greater economic independence and in seeking commitments to help their nation survive the crises ahead. Ironically, any muting of conflict and decline of international involvement in Southern Africa would now seem more of a threat to Lesotho's development strategies than the risks of strangulation by the Republic.

From all appearances, South Africa has not hesitated to take punitive steps when annoyed by the escalating anti-apartheid rhetoric or the United Nations initiatives of its tiny neighbor. The sudden withdrawal in 1977 of a long-standing subsidy on Lesotho's grain products is symptomatic. But this petulant act did not have the desired deterrent effect. Instead, Lesotho's difficulties were made good through increased international assistance and greater understanding of its predicament. Basotho leaders seemed convinced that the Pretoria government had enough international problems on its agenda without risking the adverse reactions to efforts to throttle Lesotho's economy. Indeed, utilization of South African economic levers to secure political objectives in Lesotho would undercut the usual arguments advanced by Western nations opposed to sanctions against the Republic. Nevertheless, the South African authorities appear to have responded to Maseru's conversations with Moscow and Havana by turning a blind eye toward BCP insurgents infiltrating through the Republic into Lesotho. Jonathan's unexpected summit meeting with P. W. Botha at Peka Bridge in August 1980 has been attributed to this not so subtle pressure. The resultant economic agreements and softening of acrimonious exchanges may testify to its effectiveness.

Another line of thought suggests that South Africa has more to lose from poor relationships with Lesotho than in the past. With cutbacks in the flow of labor from Malawi and Mozambique, experienced Basotho shaft-sinkers and other migrant laborers are no longer expendable. Similarly, the insatiable needs of the Witwatersrand and the dubious reliability of power supplied from Cabora Bassa have made Lesotho's hydroelectric potential far more inviting. The Peka Bridge meeting and the good offices of aid donors appear to have broken the long-standing bottleneck on appropriate terms for the water. Negotiations with South Africa and feasibility studies for a massive highland water and power project are again underway. It should be noted parenthetically that talks with South Africa remain sensitive to events within the Republic. In June 1976 Lesotho broke off similar discussions when the Soweto uprisings and resultant mistreatment of Lesotho nationals made dealings with Pretoria inopportune. Finally, the South African economy continues to experience severe strains from inflation, recession, military expenditure, and decreased capital inflows. Even though interactions with Lesotho constitute a tiny portion of the whole, this is hardly the moment for the Republic to disrupt relations with a country whose overseas aid provides needed foreign exchange for the rand area.

Basotho leaders meeting with the South African Prime Minister and Foreign Minister have been careful to portray the deliberations as hard-nosed interchanges necessitated by geographical realities. Despite the Peka Bridge talks, Lesotho has begun to live down its earlier reputation throughout Africa as a pliant satellite of Pretoria, little different from a Bantustan. Nonetheless, Lesotho was never made privy to front-line deliberations about Zimbabwe or regularly consulted in advance of key political decisions. There is little evidence that Lesotho has opted out voluntarily because of concern about possible South African reactions. Indeed Chief Jonathan's assertions of his country's crucial "behind-the-lines" role reflect a bit of pique at being left on the periphery. Part of the problem was that Lesotho had not been on the best of terms with Botswana and Zambia, the moderate front-line states, which might otherwise have pressed its claim to a larger role.

Lesotho's occasional grievance with Zambia stemmed primarily from President Kaunda's sympathetic attitude toward Ntsu Mokhehle and other BCP refugees resident in Lusaka. However, the more comprehensive squabbles with Botswana have deeper historical and psychological roots. BCP refugees were again an immediate cause of the problem. Botswana's refusal to hand back the fugitives and allowing them normal access to local media were interpreted as support for their cause. At one point, Chief Jonathan ordered Lesotho local passports invalidated for travel to Botswana. It was alleged that the Khama government was knowingly permitting Basotho youth recruited by the BCP to transit Botswana for guerrilla training farther north. Although this dispute was later ironed out by high-level emissaries, it reflected an alarming tendency for both sides, but especially for the Lesotho government, to put the worst possible construction on the other's behavior and to act accordingly.

Competition for scarce resources among former British High Commission Territories has been an underlying source of these tensions. Basotho can rationalize Swazi economic gains as the product of having surrendered much Swazi land to the whites. However, the Basotho had always perceived themselves as more advanced and modernized than the Batswana, so that Botswana's economic surge ahead became suspect. Rather than looking to differential resource endowments, suspicious Basotho observers have been inclined to think that the Botswana government has somehow taken unfair advantage of Lesotho's political turmoil to make itself the favorite of aid donors. Competitiveness was accentuated because some embassies, aid missions, international agencie, and voluntary organizations maintain a single center serving all three countries. Until recently the U.S. embassy was located in Gaborone, the AID mission in Mbabane, and the Information Service in Maseru, so that the Basotho perceived themselves perpetually at a disadvantage. To be sure, Lesotho got fewer than its share of key regional headquarters because of the obvious geographical constraints posed by locating there. In short, there was a strong sense of a fixed pie available for the "BLS" states, and a larger slice could be provided to one only at the expense of the others. The acrimonious unilateral withdrawal of Lesotho from the joint University of Botswana, Lesotho, and Swaziland was a nationalistic response to seeing the Roma campus mark time while new centers in Botswana and Swaziland were given a chance to catch up. The whole concept of a "BLS" group had become an affront to the national self-image. Fortunately, the far greater abundance of development funding presently available for all three countries has mitigated these short-term antipathies. There is no inherent reason that precludes the Basotho and Batswana, who share a mutually intelligible language and culture, from broadly based cooperation to achieve common objectives in Southern Africa.

In the wake of Zimbabwean independence, the front-line states are resolved to draw the more conservative states, including Lesotho, into a new regional venture in economic liberation, the Southern African Development Coordination Conference. As the only noncontiguous participant in the SADCC bloc, Lesotho appears ambivalent about the nature of its contribution and the probability of attaining tangible benefits. Some Basotho policy-makers fear that newly independent Zimbabwe and SADCC will simply diminish the donor support available for Lesotho's own development priorities. However, possible political returns may be more immediate. Front-line leaders, eager to solicit Lesotho's greater involvement, have been increasingly reluctant to accommodate Basotho refugees or to have any connection with Ntsu Mokhehle and his insurgent LLA. Beyond this implicit support for his government, Chief Jonathan has gained leverage in negotiations with Pretoria as well as a safety net when the inevitable recurrent crises place Lesotho under South African pressure. Nevertheless, festering domestic strife could easily negate this political and economic opportunity.

Even if Lesotho becomes an active participant in SADCC and front-line efforts to promote majority rule and economic independence in Southern Africa, its well-known vulnerabilities set limits upon its possible contributions. Providing sanctuary for a few freedom fighters has already caused difficult interchanges with Pretoria. However, direct air links to Gaborone, Mbabane, and Maputo have enhanced contact with Maseru and provided an outlet for political refugees. Hence, Lesotho's position as a conduit for information could prove its most valuable asset. Not only do its migrant workers have access to key industrial centers within the Republic, but there are more than 1.6 million ethnic Basotho who live in the Republic and are nominally affiliated with the QwaQwa "homeland," but are otherwise indistinguishable from citizens from Lesotho. In fact, part of the recurring controversy with Botswana stemmed from the difficulty of identifying Lesotho nationals who posed as refugees from the Republic. Geographic proximity to portions of five Bantustans, the Ciskei, Transkei, Kwa-Zulu, QuaQua, and Bophuthatswana, also contributes to Lesotho's informational capacities. Lesotho, like all OAU members, refuses recognition to these offspring of apartheid, but bows to local realities by allowing their citizens to enter the country. Political figures from the five have already developed informal contacts through unofficial visits and attendance at international conferences in Maseru. The Lesotho government could play an instrumental role in stiffening Bantustan resolve to prevent physical fragmentation and to make maximal demands upon the Republic. Lesotho's mountains would also provide an excellent location for radio transmitters providing an alternative to the SABC message.

Whatever role Lesotho assumes will remain viable only if overseas aid donors continue to provide the level of support presently forthcoming and a diplomatic shield against South African pressures. Some may argue that such aid is counterproductive, inducing only further dependency. There is some solace in the fact that the new surge of assistance comes from a wide variety of multilateral, bilateral, and philanthropic donors. Furthermore, the bulk of past and present funding has taken the form of outright grants, leaving no huge backlog of debt service and repayment. Throughout their history, the Basotho have been compelled to make pragmatic choices among less than optimal alternatives. Although the present situation is fraught with new pitfalls, Lesotho seems to have achieved a slightly greater margin of survival than before and has some minimal prospect of attacking its fundamental problems.

10.

Swaziland: From Tradition to Modernity

Absolom Vilakazi

Wedged between Marxist Mozambique and apartheid South Africa, Swaziland seeks a middle way that will not alienate either of its neighbors, with which its stability and prosperity are intimately involved. Maputo has been the country's natural outlet, particularly since a rail link to the east was built in the sixties to ship iron ore to Japan. Recently, with the iron ore virtually exhausted, and with the growing possibility that Mozambique's current good relations with South Africa (see Mozambique chapter) might disintegrate under guerrilla pressures, Swaziland has secured another rail link, this time to Gollel in Natal, where it joins with the main South African line on the north coast that goes via Empangeni and Richards Bay to Durban. The move is typical of shrewd Swazi efforts to maximize opportunities for its flourishing export-oriented economy. The Swazi are no less characteristic in seeking to balance external influences in their own interests. Basic to current Swazi policies is the effort to maintain within the changing Southern African scene its own characteristic way of life, which contrasts so sharply with those of its two closest neighbors.

The Swazi Social Order

The social order of Swaziland has always been overwhelmingly traditional, and the social, political, and economic actions of its people are generally carried out as a result of ingrained habit. Undergirding all their actions is the "value-orientation" of traditionalism, which ensures that the social actions of persons will be determined by what seems to them to be required by duty, honor, personal loyalty, and proper standards of right and wrong. Value-orientation acts as a binding social imperative. This social order derives from the sacredness of tradition, whose validity is reinforced socially and psychologically by fears of the anger of ancestral spirits which could cause magical evils if tradition were transgressed. The living symbol of Swazi traditions and of the unity of the nation is the King (*Ngwenyama*), who is, as it were, draped in "the mystical credentials of authority," which give legitimacy to what he does or says. When the Swazi speak of "our way of life" and of "our traditions," they refer to the social relationships and social actions that take as their point of departure age-old customs validated by the ideology of traditionalism and legitimized by the King. Tradition and kingly authority, then, stand as the pillars of their social, political, religious, intellectual, and moral order.

The social hierarchies that derive from this structure are the King, the Queen Mother, and the royal household. While it is customary in the literature to put the King and the Queen Mother on an equal footing, the position and power of the Queen Mother are in fact derivative. As the wife of the King's father, who was also the King, she acquires the awesome dignity and ritual sacredness of the King's person. She is a very important political and religious figure without whom certain religious rituals cannot be performed.

Next in the social hierarchy are members of the aristocracy. These are the Dlaminis, or members of the King's extended family, that is, his brothers and cousins and other princes of the realm who have been elevated for meritorious service. Such, for example, are war heroes, army generals, powerful medicine men, and commoners who marry royal women.

The traditional political structure rests on the social structure described above. The King is the supreme ruler and all the people owe fealty to him. He is the symbol of the unity of the nation and he is its religious leader; he is "hedged around with divinity," which gives him his mystical powers of authority.

Preindependence Developments

The traditional order was interrupted by colonial rule and control from 1900 to 1968, when Great Britain was the administering authority. The King was reduced to the status of Paramount Chief, who was subordinate to the British Resident Commissioner, who had ultimate responsibility for policy. The British administrators in Swaziland did not practice the traditional British system of indirect rule but developed a type of dual administration. Because a large number of white settlers were allowed to buy land in Swaziland, and because the protectorate was expected ultimately to become part of South Africa, the British administration issued proclamations and enforced them directly, set up a national police force in 1907, and controlled the system of criminal justice. Although British administrators often consulted

with the Paramount Chief, the responsibilities of the traditional Swazi authorities were limited in practice to the collection of taxes and to matters
that were strictly within the traditional sector, always providing that tradition
was not "repugnant to natural justice."

The colonial period introduced a new form of legitimacy in Swaziland, a
legal authority based on the validity of certain concepts. According to these
concepts, a given legal norm may be established outside traditional authority,
and claim obedience from the population. Moreover, whoever is in authority,
whether the King or the British administrator, is himself subject to an impersonal order of law. In other words, the King's powers are limited by law.
It is assumed further that the persons who obey the authority do so in their
capacity as members of the state, and therefore their obedience is to the law,
not to the individual who represents it. Thus, there is no personal loyalty to
the man in authority; rather, there is loyalty to a country, a flag, or a set
of laws.

These concepts introduced a dualism between the traditional and the
modern in the social, cultural, political, religious, intellectual, and economic
sectors of the social order. This dualism continues to this day but with the
difference that the King presently is at the top of both structures.

Initially, the new legal concepts were such a radical departure from Swazi
norms that they almost (but not quite) dealt a death blow to the influence
of traditional authorities. It is significant that political unrest and political
agitation in Swaziland had their beginnings during this period. It is also important to note that Swazi political "agitators" were not merely critical of
the colonial presence in Swaziland. They raised the much more serious question of the basis of legitimacy in Swazi society. The idea that legal norms
can and should be established by agreement became popular, and people began
to question the right of the King and the aristocracy to exercise absolute
power. The political agitators who sought a new kind of social and political
order were admittedly a small minority, but they represented a growing
number of the educated and urbanized members of the community.

By 1963, five political organizations had emerged: the Swaziland Progressive Party (SPP), led by K. T. Samketi; the Ngwane National Liberatory
Congress (NNLC), under the leadership of Dr. Ambrose Zwane; another
Swaziland Progressive Party (SPP), led by John Nquku; the Swaziland Democratic Party (DSP), led by Simon Nxumalo; and the Mbandzeni National
Convention, led by Dr. George Msibi. All five programs were variations on a
common Pan-African theme. Notwithstanding differences among them, they
agreed at constitutional talks in London to form an alliance, with Simon
Nxumalo as chairman. The alliance made three basic demands: that Britain
give independence immediately to Swaziland; that the King become the
constitutional monarch under a new constitution; and that all forms of discrimination on the basis of race and color be abolished forthwith.

Despite the activities of the political organizations, the dominant figure in the Swaziland struggle for power and independence was the King. He accepted the challenge of the Pan Africanists for an elected legislature, organized his own Mbokodvo Party, and in the elections of 1964, conducted under a constitution which gave 30 percent of the seats in the legislature to the white community, 30 percent to the Swazi tribal hierarchy, and 30 percent to the national roll, he decisively defeated the other parties. All of their candidates lost their deposits, and the King's party became the sole ruling party. Thereafter, the Mbokodvo Party, which had been dismissed everywhere as subservient to South Africa, pulled off what was almost tantamount to a coup. They disenfranchised all white South Africans resident in Swaziland and challenged the provisions of the 1964 constitution on the ground that they were racist. They then declared for "independence now," and demanded that the King be designated the head of state. The British later acceded to these demands, which became the basis of the Swazi constitution accepted by Britain on February 22, 1967.

It is important to note that the Swazi rejected radicalism and Pan Africanism as the basis of national policy. They voted for moderate policies that would ensure coexistence with their white neighbor. The defeat of the Pan-Africanist leaders did not mean that the Swazis endorsed racism and the apartheid policies of their white neighbors, however, but simply that they rejected both apartheid and radicalism; otherwise their rejection of incorporation into South Africa is meaningless. The policy of coexistence was dictated to them by their political and economic circumstances.

After the striking Mbokodvo victory many young and dynamic Swazi left their old parties and joined the King's movement. The King, characteristically, welcomed his people "back home," saying, "It is their land, their party, their government. Even if they are communists, as some people tell us, they are our sons and therefore our communists."

The injection of this new blood had an important influence on the Mbokodvo. The men with Pan-Africanist leanings broadened the general political and ideological outlook of the party and moved it from its original rightist and traditionalist position toward the center. Thus, young radicals could find a home in the Mbokodvo. They became a very important influence in orienting the party toward the black states of Africa and toward positive positions on questions of Pan-Africanist ideology. They were also instrumental in developing strategies of disengagement from South Africa, especially in the economic sphere. Moreover, by rejecting in the constitution any racist reservation of seats in the parliament, they upheld the premise that to be a Swazi was not simply a matter of color or race but an act of commitment to the aims and purposes of the Swazi State. The party therefore followed a nonracial policy.

These policies had external effects. The liberalization of the Mbokodvo made the South African government rethink and even modify its self-assumed position of protector of African peoples everywhere against "communism" or any form of radicalism. There was a time when South Africa assumed the right to decide, based on its own definition of communism, who could or could not be admitted into Swaziland. When the Swazi King and the Mbokodvo movement showed that they were not afraid of Swazi radicals and that they could, in fact, find a home within the ruling party for them, South Africa had to relax its arrogant assumption of guardianship of the peoples and policies of Swaziland. Finally, the new blood injected into the Mbokodvo Party made it possible for the government of Swaziland to accept South African refugees so long as they did not use Swaziland as a base to launch attacks on South Africa.

Independence and the New Constitution

Swaziland achieved independence on September 6, 1968, under a constitution drawn on the Westminster model. The constitution recognized the King as a constitutional head of state. Even the new elite still proclaimed their loyalty to the King and insisted that the monarchy be retained. The constitution created two houses of Parliament, the members of which were to be elected by the general population on the principle of one man, one vote. It institutionalized a two-party system, with the majority party forming the government. A significant effect was to legalize the opposition (a fundamental departure from Swazi tradition) and to establish the right of commoners to share in power and the making of policy. A civil service was introduced, appointed by a civil service commission according to well-established bureaucratic rules and standards.

This latter feature inevitably created a class of government workers who were outside traditional control, and so created a dualism with Swazi National Council (SNC) employees, who were directly under the control of traditional authorities. SNC employees thus became the poor cousins of the elitist civil servants. The creation of the civil service helped somewhat to eliminate nepotism in government and introduced moral norms alien to Swazi traditional culture and society.

These changes had far-reaching effects on the government of Swaziland and on the country's social structure. The immediate result of having a popularly elected government was that many people who previously were only commoners now assumed positions of power, influence, and wealth which, under the old precolonial order, had been the prerogatives of the King and the aristocracy. Members of the royal house and most of the aristocracy did not have the necessary education for exercising power. The King, chiefs, and the aristocracy in general had disdained education, mainly because it was in the hands of the missionaries and the King and the aristocracy were not attracted to Christianity. The aristocracy also disdained hard work because they were accustomed to ascriptively acquired wealth and privileges. Furthermore, the discipline of schooling and being under teachers who were commoners caused problems for royal children, who often did poorly in the schools and failed their examinations.

The feature of the constitution that the King most resented was the legalization of the opposition, since traditionally opposition was seen as *umbango,* an illegitimate contest for power that rightfully belonged to the King and the aristocracy. Legalization of the opposition was an extension of the principle of legal authority which had first been introduced by the British as a new form of legitimacy in Swazi life. It soon led to trouble, for in order to contain the opposition, the King's party deported dissident people, who nevertheless regarded themselves as Swazi citizens. This led to court cases where the King's party lost. Thus, the King and the aristocracy felt that their powers had been subverted by the constitution and by the judges who ruled against them in court.

The Overthrow of the Constitution

It was this conflict which led directly to the suspension of the constitution and the takeover of the government by the King on April 16, 1973. In the preamble to the proclamation of the takeover, it is stated, among other things, that "the Constitution has permitted the importation into our country of highly undesireable practices alien to and incompatible with the way of life of our society and designed to disrupt and destroy our own peaceful and constructive and essentially democratic methods of political activity; increasingly this element engenders hostility, bitterness and unrest in our peaceful society."

The overthrow of the constitution and the takeover by the King of decision-making in the day-to-day operations of government was an attempt by the traditionalists to contain change and especially to deal with the harsh intrusion of new forms of legitimacy that industrialization, urbanization, modernization, and Western-style education are forcing onto the Swazi sociopolitical landscape. It had the effect of subordinating the modern arm of government to the traditional structure, which is dominated by the Swazi National Council. Operationally this means that any development in Swaziland which has to do with land use is thwarted unless it has the explicit approval of the King and the concurrence of the Swazi National Council because land is the Council's particular concern and involves serious sensitivities.

The Traditional Structure of Government

The Swazi National Council is the supreme sociopolitical body of the Swazi nation. It meets once a year, between July and August, at Lobamba, the

King's ritual and ceremonial capital. The Council is analogous to a national parliament but it is also the Swazi highest court of appeal. It is the citadel of Swazi traditionalism and conservatism.

In theory, every adult male Swazi can attend and participate in the deliberations of the SNC; but in fact, due largely to geographic factors, attendance tends to be limited to those with special functions, the aristocracy, and those who live near Lobamba.

The effective body which conducts day-to-day SNC business is a small executive committee composed mostly of members of the aristocracy and headed by an executive secretary who keeps the minutes and records and manages the SNC offices at Lobamba.

The Swazi National Council maintains its communication links with the rest of the country through the *tinkundla,* which are meeting places in the different rural areas throughout the country where matters of regional or national importance are discussed. Such meetings are attended by local adult males and their chiefs and are presided over by a special King's appointee (none of the local chiefs is given that honor).

A new trend in the country is to make the *tinkundla* focal points not only of socioeconomic organization but also for the dispensing of rural social services. It is also planned that in the future they will be used increasingly as employment centers where rural youth will go to find out about job opportunities in the country.

By tradition, the King rules the land through the chiefs, whom he vests with authority. The chiefs are district administrative officers and all are subject to the King. He has effectively "castrated" them politically and economically by refusing to pay them regular salaries; most chiefs have thereby been reduced to penury. The chief's most important function is that of allocating land to the people through what is known as the *khonta* system. It is customary for a man who wishes to acquire land to give the chief a *khonta* beast or an equivalent R10 (U.S. $11.50).

The *khonta* custom establishes a feudal relationship between the chief and his subject. He can *memeta,* or call on the men in his area to give free labor on his fields; and he expects occasional gifts of food, beer, and meat, especially when one of his subjects has a feast. At harvest time the people on the chief's lands are expected to *ethula,* or give to the chief a portion of their produce, normally one bag of whatever has been reaped from the field. In Swaziland, it is often a two-hundred-pound bag of maize or sorghum. Failure to perform these feudal services strains relationships between subject and chief and, if persistent, may result in the eviction of the man from the chief's land. Everybody has, theoretically, a right of appeal to the King. The right is rarely exercised, however, since, as a matter of practical politics, appeals follow certain procedures and a man can only go to the King through the very chief against whom he has a complaint. Cases are quoted of men who have gone directly to the King, but the simple peasant generally despairs of ever getting near the King through the complicated protocol.

A commoner has the political right to attend and participate in the *Libandla* (chief's council) and to express his views. Again, theory differs from practice in that although most adult men attend the *libandla,* the real discussions are carried out by a few outstanding men, and the multitudes register their agreement by vociferous choruses of *elethu* (hear! hear!) or, if they disagree, by a discreet silence.

Economically this social order, like all traditional orders where rational agricultural techniques are unknown and much of agricultural activity is accompanied by magical ritual, is based on subsistence farming and is characterized by low productivity. Swazi agriculture still reflects conservatism, self-sufficiency, and traditionalism, although important changes are taking place in Swaziland at the present time. Many traditional Swazi have sought changes because they have seen the resulting advantages. Many others, however, have had change imposed upon them by industrialization and by other agents of change, such as Christianity and education. At the present time, most Swazi remain outside the factory system and even outside the rapidly growing urban centers of Manzini, Mbabane, and other, smaller towns. But new socioeconomic groups have been created by the mining industry in neighboring South Africa, by the large sugar estates in Swaziland, and by growing industrial development in the country. These groups depend primarily on earned incomes for their livelihood, although they still practice some agriculture, particularly cattle-keeping and subsistence farming.

In some rural areas a growing system of market agriculture has replaced the traditional system of local subsistence production. In the south, for example, tobacco and cotton have become important cash crops. This growing trend toward market agriculture, especially in tobacco and cotton, is due largely to new market opportunities. Similarly, there is growing interest in cash-crop production of green maize, potatoes, and beans for the expanding urban markets.

Market agriculture, in particular, raises problems for the social structure and even more acutely for the traditional land-tenure system. For example, the concentration in the south on cash crops which were not for consumption enraged the traditional rulers and brought forth an angry outcry against nonfood crops from the highest political authorities in the land. Their indignation fortunately was short-lived, and the farmers were allowed to continue raising their cotton and tobacco. The point is that the traditional rulers were powerless to stop this development. Increased production of high-value crops like cotton, tobacco, and sugar also requires more land and improved methods of production that are alien to traditional Swazi agricultural technology.

Another direct challenge to the traditional social hierarchy results from the fact that enterprising farmers are almost exclusively commoners and they become conspicuously wealthier than either their immediate chiefs or the neighboring aristocrats. These new men clearly find it impossible to support the present feudal-aristocratic structure. This creates in the community a new source of power, the rich farmer who becomes more prestigeous than the traditional leaders and on whom the chiefs become dependent for handouts in the form of bribes camouflaged as traditional *ethula* gifts.

Successful people are resented in traditional societies and become the targets of all forms of social attacks ranging from accusations of witchcraft and sorcery (for that is the only logical explanation to a peasant for the sudden riches of a neighbor whose grandfather and father were known to be as poor as the rest of the community) to charges of disloyalty to the King. As an example of this disloyalty, people cite the owners of Vuvulane irrigation farms in the Lebombo district who voted for the opposition at the last election to be held in Swaziland. Even though the man whom they elected to parliament had been certified as a citizen before the election and had been allocated a plot in Vuvulane on the basis of his Swazi citizenship, he was subsequently declared a prohibited immigrant by the government. This ruling was overturned by the courts.

Characteristically, the reaction of the government to the opposition was in the traditional rhetoric of *umbango* (an illicit disputation for power), and indicated a complete failure to grasp the meaning of constitutional restraints on the King's power and the meaning of "opposition" in a democratic political setup which assumes sociocultural pluralism. It was this traditional-aristocratic attitude that led to the overthrow of the independence constitution.

But traditional attitudes and solidarities have been very much shaken by new developments in Swaziland. The migration of the young to towns and to South African mines and cities gives rise to social alienation, for they tend to develop contemptuous attitudes toward traditional culture and traditional attitudes. They desert rural areas and prefer urban residence which frees them from the impositions of rural authorities and from the empty and largely unmonetized existence of the rural areas. Material acquisition remains a less important goal for rural peasants, and this is seen particularly in their reluctance to sell their cattle in spite of the high prices the cattle can fetch in the market. Most rural peasants seem content with a lower standard of living. Not so their children and the urbanized section of the population.

The Modern Economy

A recent study by the World Bank shows that up to mid-1975 Swaziland was less affected by the downturn in worldwide economic activity than many other developing countries. This was largely because prices received for its major exports remained high and also because South Africa, with which Swaziland's economy is closely linked, continued a moderate growth rate.

While several indications suggest that such external influences may not be as favorable in the immediate future as in the past, the economy is now in a stronger position to withstand an export-induced downturn than it was only a few years ago. During the recent period of high real growth the base of the economy has broadened and manufacturing activity has diversified.

The main sectoral development has been the expansion of the share in the GDP held by manufacturing, from 15 percent in 1971/72 to 22 percent in 1974/75. Although much of the increase stems directly from higher prices for sugar and wood pulp, real output in manufacturing is estimated to have increased by around 10 percent a year. Agriculture and forestry, as well as community and social services, have grown at roughly the same rates as GDP, and they have continued to provide about 32 percent and 17 percent, respectively, of total production, while the share of mining and quarrying fell from 10 to 5 percent, reflecting mainly a leveling off of production, stagnation in prices, and an increase in intermediate consumption.

The pattern of resource utilization shows that the ratio of investment to GDP has remained roughly stable at an average of about 23 percent over the period, with private fixed investment accounting for nearly three quarters of the total. The share of consumption declined slightly from 67.2 percent in 1971/72 to 65.2 percent in 1974/75, whereas the share of net exports of goods and services increased from 8.8 percent to 11.4 percent.

Agricultural and pastoral production still form the major economic activity in Swaziland, accounting directly for an estimated 29 percent of GDP, while the processing of agricultural products forms the basis for much of the manufacturing sector. Agricultural products, both raw and processed, comprised more than half of total exports in 1974. Approximately twenty-three thousand persons are employed by the modern agricultural subsector, while about half the total population of half a million depends directly on traditional agriculture.

Swaziland's land and water resources are only partially exploited. About 20 percent of the total land area of 1.7 million hectares (6,560 square miles) is considered suitable for intensive agriculture, but only half this area, or about 170,000 hectares, is currently under cultivation. About 25,000 hectares of this land is irrigated, and there is potential for irrigation of an additional 15,000 hectares. A further 65 percent of the total area is utilized for grazing cattle.

The Dual Economy

The agricultural sector consists both of larger-scale, cash-crop oriented farms, which are mainly expatriate-owned, and of traditional (mainly subsistence) farming on Swazi nation land. This dualism results in part from nineteenth-century land concessions made to Europeans. In 1970 less than 40 percent of the total land area was under Swazi control. This land is still held by the King in trust for the Swazi nation, and its use is determined according to traditional arrangements. Various programs have been formulated over the years to transfer additional land to the Swazi nation, including an E 2.6 million ($3.9 million) grant from Great Britain in 1970 to finance the purchase of non-Swazi-owned land for incorporation into Swazi nation holdings. These programs have resulted in a rise in such holdings to about 55 percent of Swaziland's land area today. The government also enacted legislation in 1974 to tax underutilized land in an attempt to force expatriate landowners either to cultivate idle land or to sell it. The original legislation has not been implemented and is at present in the process of being redrafted.

There are about 790 individually owned farms in Swaziland, covering 45 percent of the total land area. The average size of these "individual tenure farms" is about 800 hectares. Approximately half of these farms are considered to be fully utilized, with an average of only about 140 hectares per farm being cultivated. Nevertheless, they account for some 60 percent of total production in the agricultural sector. The remaining approximately 40 percent is produced by some 39,000 Swazi farmers working communal land. On average these farmers cultivate less than 3 hectares each.

Animal husbandry is the largest source of cash income in the traditional sector. An estimated 80 percent of the nation's 600,000 head of cattle belong to Swazis. These cattle have traditionally been more highly valued for social than for economic reasons, leading in some cases to overgrazing and soil erosion. It has also resulted in a low annual offtake (slaughtering and exports) of around 10 percent. Recently, however, the government programs for introducing new grazing systems, new breeds, cattle fattening farms, and sales yards appear to have led to an increasingly commercial attitude among Swazi farmers. Commercial-managed estate ranches account for the remaining 20 percent of cattle. Management standards on the estates are high, and the annual offtake is almost 15 percent. Swaziland's disease control programs are extensive; nevertheless, periodic epidemics and droughts result in stock losses, and the ratio of deaths to offtakes has declined little in recent years.

Government agricultural policy is focused on developing the traditional sector from subsistence to semicommercial and commercial farming. Agricultural development expenditures have been about E4 million in recent years, with about three-fourths financed from abroad, mainly by Britain and the United States. In addition, substantial technical assistance has been provided through the United Nations Development Program.

Development efforts are concentrated in a few large rural development areas (RDAs) located on Swazi nation land. In these areas an integrated approach is being followed that includes road improvements, water resource development, the construction of terraces, and the provision of extension services for both animal husbandry and crops. In the northern RDA, where most of the effort has been concentrated thus far, output and yields of a number of crops have improved significantly, as have farmers' incomes. The number of farmers outside the RDAs seeking information and advice has increased to such a degree that the requests now exceed the capacity of the extension service staff of the ministry of agriculture to respond. The government plans to divide the RDAs into "high input rural development areas" and "minimum input rural development areas," the difference reflecting population density, resource bases, and physical development potential. The government also plans national projects in dairy farming, beef production, and marketing arrangements.

Swaziland has one of the world's largest planted forests, mainly coniferous, originally started by the Commonwealth Development Corporation in the late 1940s and now constituting a major forest-products industry. In the north at Piggs Peak, the output is mostly in the form of logs, but in the south at Utusu, a large pulp mill is located in which a major British fiber corporation (Courtaulds) has a 50 percent shareholding. The Usutu forest, with its attendant processing facilities, represents one of the largest foreign investments in Swaziland. Forestry exports consist mostly of wood pulp and amounted to E36.2 million in 1974, or 30 percent of total exports. In spite of the depressed wood-pulp market in 1975, the long-term prospects are good, and a Japanese company is tentatively considering plans for a second pulp mill at Piggs Peak.

Manufacturing is the second most important activity in Swaziland and has been increasing rapidly in importance in recent years. The two largest industries are sugar refining and wood-pulp processing; other processing industries are meat packing, cotton ginning, and fruit canning. New industries recently established include a TV factory, financed by Finnish capital, for production of color sets mainly for the South African market, where Swaziland, after hard bargaining, has been granted a share of twenty thousand sets a year. Also producing mainly for export to South Africa is a new fertilizer plant. Investors from Hong Kong have established an E6 million cotton-spinning plant, which will eventually employ about two thousand persons. Swaziland has itself developed a small tractor, the Tinkabi, which is particularly suited to the needs of developing countries. Since the domestic market is so small, new industries on any significant scale must be export-oriented.

Swaziland, as a member of the Customs Union with South Africa, Botswana, and Lesotho, enjoys access to the large Southern African market, and this has contributed to its success in attracting foreign investments. Swaziland has also signed the Lomé Convention with the EEC, which provides preferential treatment in that market. Investors are attracted by the fact that goods manufactured in Swaziland are generally accepted by other African countries where imports from South Africa are banned.

Swaziland also offers investors a number of generous tax incentives. Over and above the normal depreciation allowances, investors are allowed to deduct 30 percent of the cost of new industrial buildings, plants and machinery during the first year.

With Swaziland's wide range of scenic beauty, tourism has been one of the most dynamic sectors in its economy in recent years. Although tourism in the past has consisted of weekend visitors from South Africa, the recently established Tourism Development Authority is now promoting longer-duration package holidays. The TDA is also encouraging greater diversity in tourism by building another hotel-casino complex in the south near Big Bend, away from the well-developed Mbabane-Manzini area. A second game park may also be opened.

There has been a steady increase in paid employment in Swaziland, from a reported forty-seven thousand in 1971 to sixty-two thousand in 1974, when it equaled about one-third of the active labor force. About 20 percent of domestic employment is provided by the public sector, which employed 13,000 in 1974, and 80 percent is provided by the private sector. In addition to this domestic employment, some eight thousand Swazi workers find paid employment in the mines in South Africa.

In the immediate future, it appears that commercial production of small-scale tractors, expansion of plant capacity for processing agricultural produce, and continued growth of the Small Enterprise Development Corporation (SEDCO)-sponsored small-scale industries will all contribute to a more rapid growth of employment opportunities in manufacturing than in most other sectors of the economy. This growth in employment opportunities has allowed and is expected to continue facilitating a gradual shift in employment from the subsistence sector of agriculture, where labor is often underemployed, into paid employment, both in primary production and in manufacturing.

The Modern Swazi Scene

Swaziland, like most of the new states, nurtures what Pareto referred to as accepted truths and laws which turn out to be rationalizations of either the hopes and aspirations, or the interests of those who hold these concepts and who originated them; what are thus held to be objective truths really constitute the ideology of the society. Although Swazis do not recognize that their beliefs and rationalizations form an ideology, any student of the Swazi scene is struck by the fact that there is a very strong, if implicit, body of beliefs which are accepted without question throughout the various levels of Swazi social structure. If one asks how the ruling aristocracy maintains its position of power without the exercise of coercive force, the answer is given that the general mass of Swazi acknowledges the legitimacy of the ruling aristocracy. The question then becomes: How is this achieved?

The Swazi aristocracy, particularly the King, has been most successful in invoking the ideology (clothed as he is in his "mystical credentials of authority"). He states his aims and dreams for Swaziland in ways which show that his interests are not for the perpetuation of his personal power or that of his family, but for the general good (moral, material, and social) of the Swazi nation. He talks not as a representative of the traditionalists, or of the aristocracy, or of any other sectional group, but as a representative of all Swazi: literate or illiterate; Christian or non-Christian; black, white, or Coloured. This strikes a responsive chord in the hearts of the Swazi. The message appeals to the generally accepted moral and political principles and values of the society and to the worthwhileness of basic Swazi norms of conduct and custom. It extols stability in Swazi society and decries any new forms of public expression and protest like the 1976 teachers' strike, or the school children's supportive demonstrations, or the agitation of the opposition party, which is cast in negative terms of illicit disputation for power (*umbango*).

This ideology, which is generally accepted and to which the King gives expression in his messages, supports the status quo: the continuation of the aristocratic structure of the society. This structure has very strong "feudalistic" features; a high correspondence exists between the status of individuals and the various dimensions by which people may be classified: kinship, economic position, and political power. Those who occupy high positions in the kinship structure also occupy high positions in the political structure, and are economically privileged as well. This parallelism holds also for those in low positions; a low status family goes with low economic and low political power and status. This characteristic is one of the greatest obstacles to the politics of development.

As we have seen, however, this correlation in status alignments is breaking down rapidly, and men and women from low, commoner families are beginning to occupy high positions in educational, economic, and political fields. This, of course, gives rise to further questioning of the social structure by those who are no longer willing to accept the ideological rationalizations of Swazi society and who are resentful of and reject the Swazi aristocratic view that commoners are not entitled to participate in government.

It would be wrong to suggest that what Lensky and Landecker (1950 and 1963) call "status crystallization," by which "diverse positions of individuals or of groups along diverse status dimensions align themselves," does not take place any more. It does, but to a lesser degree. More and more, nonconformity to the Swazi traditional aristocratic social structure is taking place.

The high degree of "status crystallization" in the past was a product of the educational system of Swazi traditional society. In this connection, Ralph H. Turner's (1960) two ideal types of educational systems are useful. He differentiates between what he calls (1) the sponsored mobility system and (2) the contest mobility system. Each system represents the operative norms of the society in which it operates and may be said to articulate the ideological assumptions of that society. The sponsored mobility system as it existed and still operates today exercises a powerful influence in Swaziland in that it buttresses traditionalism and helps to prepetuate the values which support the traditional elites and the ruling aristocracy. Obviously, this system was not, and could not have been, meant to produce a new rival elite in the country. It was meant, rather, to emphasize the values and attitudes which support the traditional structure. It finds expression today in traditional rituals and celebrations which forcefully affirm the old social structure and support the authority of the King. They are, in a sense, rituals of authority, confirming and validating the King and all he stands for.

These "rituals of authority" are for the Swazi the expressions of what they believe to be the eternal verities embodied in Swazi Kingship. Interestingly enough, the King, Sobhuza II, is keenly aware of this, as is shown by an address to the nation which he made during an independence celebration in which he tried to explain the workings of the new government to his subjects. He pointed out that the colonial governments ruled for the British and therefore were "Her Majesty's Governments." The new government is the "Ngwenyama's Government"; but he hastily asked rhetorically: "Who is the Ngwenyama?" He proceeded to answer the question: "You are the Ngwenyama; you give validity to all that supports the Ngwenyama. The person of the Ngwenyama is not important; but the values embodied in the institution of the Ngwenyama are."

Modern Swazi education is, however, different from the sponsored mobility system. It belongs to the contest mobility system, in which the elite status is open to any person who is successful in a contest in which all may enter and in which the circumstances of one's birth are irrelevant. Modern education creates the new "marginal men" who form the "aristocracy of the diploma'd." They are the questioners of the established system and, in many cases, they are the ones who hold positions of importance in Swaziland today.

The system approximates somewhat what might be called a "meritocracy," although it is not one; a meritocracy could not develop under present conditions because there are still too many loopholes in the administration that allow for serious distortions to any merit criteria which might be applied. For example, royal children are awarded scholarships on command rather than on merit. Similarly, the bureaucrats who control scholarships can easily be pressured into giving scholarships to children of important people in the society and denying them to children of the poor, however deserving the latter may be on academic criteria. Indeed, it is a common complaint among Swazi students abroad that scholarships to universities, especially to overseas universities, have gone to the most undeserving and delinquent children of those in high places who, it is asserted, squander national funds and resources and return to Swaziland with nothing to show for the years they have been abroad.

But all the above does not explain the workings of the Swazi socio-political system until we grasp one central fact of Swazi life: that it is a confusing mixture of traditionalism and modernity in unequal parts, and not in a syncretistic fashion where the old and the new are welded together to form a new institution that derives form and value from the two antecedent structures. The situation in Swaziland is a coexistence of the old and the new and their constant interaction.

Amitai Etzioni's development model of "epigenesis" or "accumulation," as expounded in his essay "Epigenesis of Political Unification" (1964: 481–97), attempts to explain this kind of development. Etzioni suggests that while the differentiation model of development is popular in studies of social change and development, there is an alternative model which he calls "epigenesis," or the "accumulation model." The differentiation model assumes that "on the societal level, the evolution of a primitive society, from a traditional to a modern one, is . . . seen as a differentiation process. All societal functions are fulfilled by the primitive tribe; they merely become structurally differentiated: i.e., they gain personnel, social units, and organizational structures of their own. Religious institutions gain churches; educational institutions gain schools; economic institutions gain corporations, and so forth" (p. 483). The accumulation model differs from this. It postulates that "adult" units emerge through a process in which the parts that carry out new functions are added to existing ones until the entire unit is assembled. Earlier parts do not include "representations" of later ones. In other words, traditional institutions remain intact and perform the old functions; and the need for new functions is met by bringing in new institutions not as substitutes for old ones but as additions to them. This was first expressed in an anthropological theory of change by Bascom and Herskovits (1959) when they suggested that "change is not necessarily substitutive; it may be additive." As Etzioni explains his accumulation model, the processes (differentiation and accumulation) are mutually exclusive in the sense that new units are either the "institutional embodiments" of old functions or serve new ones. They may occur at different times in the same social unit: for example, a unit may first follow a differentiation model of development, then shift to an accumulation model (or the other way around); or it may simultaneously develop some subunits following one model and some following another (p. 483).

How does the theoretical framework outlined above fit the Swazi socio-political scene? Very neatly. In the first place, the traditional social institutions are still very much in place. When the Swazi nation was challenged to meet the need for modernization, a dual sociopolitical system developed, analogous to the one which had developed earlier when the economy faced the challenge of industrialization and modernization. Traditional institutions, with their cultural and ideological supports of the social structure, persisted. The family system, for example, remained essentially traditional. There are still the extended family units; the old polygynous family and practices are still honored; and the same validation of marriage, *ukugcoba libovu*, without which a Swazi traditional marriage is incomplete, still persists. Yet the Swazi realize that they have to meet new sociocultural needs and they therefore have accepted new institutions and practices to accommodate new social groups such as the Christians and the urbanized Swazi. It is instructive, in this respect, to note that for a modern Swazi there may be two marriage ceremonies: a church wedding in which Christian requirements and values are met, and a traditional one at home in which the traditional practices and validations are performed. Thus a modern Swazi bride might wear a ring to indicate marriage by Christian rites and still go through the *ukugcoba libovu* ceremony for traditional validation.

Education is another institution which lends itself to this analysis. The old "sponsored mobility system" of education, which meets the needs of the old order, and the "contest mobility system" of education coexist, albeit somewhat uneasily, to meet the differing needs of the different sections of the Swazi nation. One of the practices of traditional Swazi education which causes much apprehension among modern Christian parents is that of *ukuklekla*, in which children's earlobes are "slit." The theory behind it is that the *klekla* is to symbolically open a child's ears so he or she can hear and learn quickly.

The dualism in the economy has, of course, been documented for a long time; it, too, illustrates the applicability of the accumulation model in explaining development. The old, subsistence economy meets the special needs of peasant, rural, and mostly illiterate communities, while the modern, monetized economic sector meets the needs of the rapidly growing class of educated, urbanized Swazi.

The most important and, I think, impressive example of the accumulation model in Swaziland is the political system. The old, traditional system is not only in place, but very active and aggressive, and in many cases it is the one system which can either initiate or block any kind of political activity in the country. Its dynamism and power come from the fact that it represents by far the most powerful section of the population, the traditionalists, of whom the King is the head. It meets regularly at Lobamba, the traditional Swazi capital, from where it transacts the business of the nation. It is very powerful and is very jealous of its powers and prerogatives. It does not pass laws but reaffirms and enforces traditional Swazi custom, practices, and privileges.

With the need for modernization, especially when independence loomed ahead, the Swazi people, through the Swazi National Council, decided that new forms of political institutions and new political activities should be instituted. Thus the King, as head of the Swazi National Council, formed the Mbokodvo Party and had the Council nominate men to stand for election for a new governmental body: the Parliament. Although there were opposition parties which arose at the time and contested the elections, they lost to the

Mbokodvo, which emerged then as the single most powerful party. The Mbokodvo Party was the nearest thing to what Ruth Schachter-Morgenthau (1966) calls the "Patron Parties." It had the personal leadership of the King, it was weakly articulated in the sense of having no clearly stated ideology, and it was comparatively undisciplined and had little, if any, direct membership participation. In fact, this writer has not encountered a single person who held a membership card. The Mbokodvo was also based on traditional authority. It differed, however, from Morgenthau's characterization in that it was a very strong integrative force because it was the King's movement, and support for the Mbokodvo was seen as support for the King.

It was precisely at this point that the opposition quarrelled with the Mbokodvo. They insisted that by involving the King in politics, the Mbokodvo reduced his effectiveness as a national leader and as a symbol of unity in Swazi life. They argued that this exposes the King to contumely, because any criticism or derogatory remarks aimed at the party or movement could be interpreted as directed against the King. The opposition parties also accused the Mbokodvo of appropriating unto itself national rituals and celebrations like *umcwasho* and *Incwala* where the King as the leader of the nation plays the leading role.

Since the Mbokodvo was the government in Swaziland, it is inevitable that questions about its democratic character should be raised. It is difficult, however, to assess the democratic nature of the movement unless one falls back on Zolberg's (1966) elaboration of Apter's concept of "one-party democracy" in which he states that "one-party democracy is not merely a debator's trick. It implies a distinction between one-party systems striving for total control of society and regimes in which one party is dominant but exercises a substantial degree of self-restraint in the form of respect for the rule of law, for certain forms of opposition and for free associational life." There is no doubt that the Mbokodvo belonged to the latter category.

There was, however, a serious problem about the determination of human rights in Swaziland under the Mbokodvo government. In the first place, discussion of human rights always took place in a vacuum because no contextual definition of human rights was ever offered. In traditional societies (and this is true for most African societies today) human rights were, and continue to be, defined as rights to land; and to use of pasture and forests; rights to protection by the family; the right to participate in public and private activities and rituals of the society. Seventeenth- and eighteenth-century American and French revolutionaries defined human rights in political terms. These were rights to freedom of speech, to freedom of assembly, of a free press, of conscience, and, of course, the right to vote. It remained for nineteenth-century socialists to hark back almost to traditional views of human rights when they raised the issue of "the Social Question" and emphasized the rights to jobs, to proper social services, to participation in government, to proper housing, etc. It is important to note that when Western political scientists discuss human rights, they think much more in terms of the political rights and show their ethnocentric biases toward freedom of the press, freedom of speech, and freedom to vote.

To assess Swaziland's record on civil rights in the sociocultural context of Swaziland, one would have to ask if people have been denied access to land, to pasture, and to participation in the traditional social, political, and religious institutions of their society. From this point of view, it would be difficult to make any case for the violation of human rights. In a society that did not have a press until very recently, the question of a free press would be academic. But in terms of modern political freedoms, it is easy to conclude that Swaziland is culpable, especially since the suspension of the Westminister Constitution and the dissolution of Parliament in 1973. The King has ruled by decree since then, and the peoples' participation in decision making and in their own government has been nonexistent.

The Swazis are troubled by the negative image that the country has had because of the King's autocratic rule by decree since the suspension of the constitution in 1973 and the absence of a representative parliament. The King announced in February 1978 that there will be elections soon under a new constitution. The new constitution will be put first to the people and will then be the basis for new elections. Opponents of the King's autocratic rule have already criticized the new constitution of falling far short of meeting the aspirations of a people who are trying to shrug off traditionalism and move into the twentieth century. This criticism is led by a former opposition party, the banned NNLC (Ngwane National Liberatory Congress), whose leader, Dr. Ambrose Zwane, has been in and out of detention several times.

A major objection to the new constitution is its use of traditional institutions. The polling areas will be *tinkundla* (community councils), which are under the control of the King and also have no relevance in urban areas. The candidates are to be nominated by the people at these meeting places; the names so selected are to be sent to the King for approval. There will be no secret ballot. (*Africa Research Notes*, February 1–28, 1978). Such provisions can hardly satisfy current demands for functioning representative institutions.

There have been signs of internal discontent in Swaziland for some time. Much of this discontent has focused on nepotism by high-ranking officials and on the privileged position of members of the Dlamini clan in regard to government jobs, housing, and scholarships. In 1975, the Wamalwa Commission was set up to investigate civil service salary scales, but its report, and subsequent ones, were not published. Although primary school teachers were granted the recommended pay increases, many who changed schools did not in fact receive their checks for months because of bureaucratic inefficiency. When the army received an unexpected pay raise and the commission reports remained secret, the primary school teachers struck in July 1977, and secondary school teachers soon followed them in a sympathetic strike. The administration responded angrily by banning the three-thousand-member Swaziland National Association of Teachers, and by threatening to take away housing and other teacher benefits if they did not go back to work. Students, with final examinations looming, struck in October in support of their teachers, and three thousand students from Matsapa and Manzini marched on the offices of the minister of education, Pym Dlamini. Received with scorn as "pups" and ordered back to school, the students demonstrated in the streets, and Swaziland's first anti-government rioting broke out. Before the two-day outburst was brought under control, not only students but also three prominent government officials had been injured, though not seriously, and were briefly hospitalized.

The immediate reaction of the government was to accuse the several hundred Soweto and other South African refugees with having fomented the discontent. Though this accusation could not be proved, the sophistication of the Swazi students' actions suggested they had learned some useful tricks from the South Africans. That the antigovernment sentiment went deep, however, and extended to the King himself was demonstrated forcefully when he called the nation to the Royal Cattle Byre at Lobamba and scores of his audience, composed mainly of teachers and politically minded parents, walked out in an unprecedented fashion while his hour long speech was still continuing. Although the teachers and students returned to their classes shortly afterwards, open criticism of Sobhuza as being "too old and out of touch" continued, and has not abated. Subsequently, evidence has appeared of an underground movement named Swanlu which opposes the ruling regime.

In the troubled Southern African context, Swaziland seeks to maintain social and political stability at home and to insulate itself as far as possible from the impact of events in neighboring countries. So far the King's hold on power is unshaken, partly perhaps because of the buoyant economy. Confronted with the potential strains resulting from its buffer position between Mozambique and South Africa, Swaziland has tilted its links toward the latter, with which its economic ties are so strong, by building the connecting railway line to Gollel in Natal, where it joins the main line to Durban. Thus instead of being dependent for a route to the sea upon the line to Maputo, Swaziland will have a second outlet to service its growing sugar industry, its wood-pulp producers, and its fruit—especially pineapple—producers.

The King has also decided to forge marriage alliances with neighboring black peoples. One of his daughters has married the Zulu king and another has married the son of a prominent Soweto businessman, in both instances with great ceremony and publicity. It is suggested that looking ahead, the Swazi King has come to the conclusion that current South African political arrangements will not last forever and that it will be valuable to cement relations with the largest Nguni groups, the Zulu and Xhosa, across Swaziland's borders, which may well emerge as forces to be reckoned with in the future.

It may be noted that there are approximately as many Swazis in South Africa as in Swaziland, but the two groups have sharply differing traditional loyalties which effectively separate them.

Swaziland's greatest cause for concern is the interaction within its boundaries between the South African security forces, which operate almost as freely as within their own country, and the South African ANC and PAC members who infiltrated across the Mozambique border (see South Africa chapter). Anxious to maintain stable relations with the latter country, the Swazis are reluctant to protest what has become fairly constant movement of South African refugees escaping to Mozambique and nationalist adherents entering their country.

Early in 1974, a small ANC group in Manzini, including the son of Govan Mbeki, one of the best known of the ANC leaders, was forced to leave the country. The young Mbeki is now a prominent ANC leader in Zambia. The Swazis subsequently charged that some ANC members were kidnapped by security forces and forced into South Africa. One of the most publicized cases was that of Mludli, who died at the end of his first day of captivity, as a result, it was charged, of police brutality.

Early in 1978, rivalry between the ANC and PAC erupted inside Swaziland. Previously, the OAU Liberation Committee meeting in Tripoli had been quietly considering the withdrawal of OAU recognition from the PAC, a move urged by Angola, where the chief ANC center is in Luanda, and Algeria, but tacitly opposed by Liberia, Lesotho, and Tanzania, which extend hospitality to the PAC. The move was dropped and a committee set up to attempt the nearly impossible task of uniting the two movements. Shortly after, some fifty PAC members in Swaziland were rounded up and deported. One charge against them was that they had been involved in military training of the followers of Chief Ntunja Ngomezulu in the Lubuli area, a clan head from northern Natal who had fled to Swaziland several years ago after South African authorities installed his half-brother as head of the clan. It was also suggested that the PAC had a "training camp" near Sidnokodvo south of Manzini where arms were kept (*Africa Confidential*). At least for the time being, the PAC seems likely to be kept out of Swaziland.

The ANC, on the other hand, appears to continue its infiltration of Swaziland with considerably less hindrance. Technically, of course, what it is doing, particularly in training South African refugees, many of whom are black consciousness adherents, is treasonable, but the Swazis do not have the power to stop them. Like Botswana and Lesotho, Swaziland has a very considerable number of so-called Soweto refugees needing further education, and susceptible to nationalist activities. With its common border with Mozambique, Swaziland is in a particularly difficult position to limit either infiltration or ANC training. Its best policy, and the one it appears to be following, is to turn a blind eye to what is happening.

So the Swazi scene is by no means calm. It will continue to be subject to outside influences. Moreover, the greater the impact of modern developments, the more precarious will be traditional rule. There is very little doubt that when the present King dies, and he is nearly eighty, there will be such changes in the country that people will often think of Ethiopia after the Emperor to illustrate their magnitude.

11.

Economic Patterns in the New Southern African Balance

Kenneth W. Grundy

Until the Portuguese military coup of April 1974 the white-ruled states of the region, and the Republic of South Africa (RSA) in particular, dominated regional economic life. Even when ostracized by other states, the white regimes had an intimidating effect on their neighbors. They sat astride a good part of the region's transport and communications infrastructure, were major suppliers and purchasers of the imports and exports of their less-developed neighbors, provided much of the latter's financial and functional support, and attracted to their modern mines, farms, and industries the workers that the local resources of the less economically vibrant states could not support.

Economic linkages are like neurological paths that, once traced and repeated, cannot easily be erased or replaced. Southern Africa was not an economic tabula rasa. Life had been conditioned by a routinized set of economic givens. Geopolitically, Zambia and Rhodesia, for examples, were still landlocked and still bounded by the same neighbors. A country does not abandon a railway route or a port on signal, nor can it build a new transport network overnight. Familiar economic relationships, fashioned originally by and for the benefit of colonial interests, governments, or minority settler regimes, were in one sense the raw materials from which changes had to emerge. "Free" market considerations and environmental constraints were not alone allowed to prevail. The reason was simple. They had never been "free" in the first place. Patterns of interaction had been pieced together for a variety of political and economic reasons. Why should not new ways of doing things emerge for compelling political as well as economic reasons?

Slowly, painfully for some, old patterns were eventually modified as governments began to alter their thinking and policies. Rhodesia's UDI (see Rhodesia chapter) provided the first test of the long-established bonds. Try as they might, well-intentioned black governments could not easily sever old ties. But they did try, and in the process searched for and tried to move in new directions. The Portuguese fall and the attendant independence of black Marxist governments in Mozambique and Angola provided added impetus to change.

The history of political-economic relations in the region since 1974 has been one of continual effort on the part of governments either to revise prearranged detrimental power factors or in the cases of Rhodesia and South Africa to reinforce and defend the givens that have favored their continued white rule and economic well-being. The changes have not been insignificant, especially when considered against the backdrop of relative powerlessness and poverty. The railway from Dar es Salaam to Zambia (Tazara) opened new transport facilities and probably was the single most important factor enabling some governments to consider closing borders and revamping trading patterns. New hydroelectric projects, expanded port facilities, reduced migration of workers, and new sources of technical assistance and investment did not come without other political and economic trade-offs. But the theme of this chapter is that they were instituted as governments in the region tested and widened the parameters of their economic independence and political leverage.

South Africa's Shrinking Hinterland

Before the coup in Portugal the centrality of the white-ruled states was undeniable. No better could this be illustrated than by the structural economic domination of the Republic of South Africa and by the geographical significance of the Portuguese-held territories. These facts, more than any others, determined the economic, military, and diplomatic realities. This domination or asymmetry is evident if we compare gross domestic-product data (see Table 1).

Superficially, little has changed from the 1966–69 to the 1976–78 periods. Many of the economies have fallen on difficult times, but most have generally retained their relative positions and their relative shares of the total regional product. The most discernible trend has been the shrinkage of the share in the hands of white-governed states—this is not because white regimes are now less productive or because black regimes have not become economically dynamic, but rather because black governments have come to power in the Portuguese-ruled territories and in Zimbabwe.

South Africa, and increasingly Zimbabwe, are the only industrialized countries in the region. The Zimbabwean change of fortune has resulted from decisions forced by sanctions. Rhodesian industrialization as a substitute for foreign imports nonetheless compounded other economic difficulties. Other states in the region, however, have remained largely structurally unchanged.

Table 1

Gross Domestic Products of Southern African States

	GDP in millions of U.S. $	date 1965–69	%	GDP in millions of U.S. $	date 1976–78	%
Republic of South Africa*	12,645	1967	62.5	44,500	1978	70.7
Transkei	—			582	1976	
Bophuthatswana	—			552	1976	
Rhodesia	1,270	1968	6.3	3,609	1978	5.7
Zambia	1,369	1968	6.8	2,750	1978	4.4
Zaïre	1,441	1968	7.1	1,918	1977	3.1
Mozambique	1,028	1965	5.1	1,479	1978	2.3
Angola	834	1965	4.1	2,174	1978	3.5
Tanzania	822	1968	4.1	3,029	1977	4.8
Namibia	300	1966	1.5	1,120	1978	1.8
Malawi	300	1968	1.5	1,098	1978	1.7
Botswana	64	1968/9	0.3	500	1978	0.8
Swaziland	78	1968/9	0.4	338	1978	0.5
Lesotho	65	1967/8	0.3	391	1978	0.6
Total	20,216		100.0	62,906		99.9

* Includes all homelands.

Sources: Diverse yearbooks, U.N. publications, Africa Research Bulletin (Economics series), and *1979 World Bank Atlas* (provisional figures).

They continue to produce primary products for export, often a single important commodity in each territory. For example, mining activities predominate in Zambia (where copper accounted for 91 percent of all export earnings in 1977), Namibia (around 60 percent of GDP in 1973), and Zaïre (77 percent of all foreign-exchange receipts from mining in 1978). Agriculture is dominant in Malawi, Mozambique, Swaziland, and Tanzania, although in the first two countries the supply of labor and other services to neighboring white-ruled countries accounts for significant foreign-exchange earnings. The export of labor ranks foremost in Lesotho.

Except for Botswana, which is combining cattle-raising with mining activity, and Angola, which has moved from agriculture to oil, the past decade has seen little fundamental alteration in patterns of production. Only in Rhodesia did the political factors growing out of United Nations sanctions make a difference. These sanctions have had considerable impact on the whole region, however, through altered transport routes, increased costs associated with transport, production, and supply, and distorted labor flows. It has been estimated that the implementation of sanctions against Rhodesia cost Zambia $932.3 million in the 1976–77 period alone. After the artificially induced initial boom in Rhodesia (construction, secondary industry, and the service sector), the long-range effects of sanctions proved to be quite debilitating (reduced immigration, minimal new investment capital, and imported technology).

Regional Trade Patterns

With its substantial industrial and agricultural output, South Africa has long looked northward for markets.[1] For years South Africa's business and governmental leaders have seen the country's economic strength as a major lever in conducting foreign policy, particularly in regional terms. Economic strength and a vigorous foreign policy, whether called an "outward policy" or "détente," complement each other. There is an economic component of foreign policy that Pretoria has not ignored. Commercial dependence, government officials reasoned, can serve to neutralize radical, anti-apartheid policies by the country's black neighbors. The rhetoric, they have contended, will be diluted in actual policy. Their reasoning has not been flawless.

For years South Africa's leaders have been dreaming about displacing Great Britain as a dominant economic and political force in its hinterland.[2] Despite repeated commercial disappointments, the optimism survives. Witness the Johannesburg *Star* on February 10, 1975:

> South Africa is on the brink of a multimillion rand explosion of trade with Black Africa. The government is using South African exports as a powerful instrument in the service of detente and the trade offensive extends up to equatorial and sub-Saharan Black States.[3]

The report went on to indicate that trade missions from throughout black Africa were arriving in South Africa with large orders. A year later, as the policy of détente looked increasingly moribund, South African businessmen continued to wax positive about prospects for trade in black Africa.[4]

In fact, South African trade with black Africa has not provided its industries with the hoped-for outlets. Through the 1950s, 17 to 19 percent of its total exports went to Africa. They declined steadily as a percentage of trade (although exports to Africa grew steadily in absolute terms from 1957 until 1974), from a high in 1956 of 19.33 percent to a low of 11.70 percent in 1963. At that point the percentage of the total sent to black Africa grew again until it reached a post-independence high of 18.9 percent in 1971. The decline since then has been precipitous, plummeting to 10.1 percent in 1976, and it is likely to stay low until the policy of apartheid and its successor policies ("separate development" and "plural democracy") are abandoned. There appears to be a clear correlation between shifts in South Africa's regional political standing and its trading fortunes. Because the trade with its African neighbors has provided a favorable balance for South Africa, offsetting unfavorable balances elsewhere, South Africa is concerned as its export hinterland in Africa narrows. Only with respect to white-ruled neighbors, limited of late to Rhodesia, has trade been strengthened.[5]

Nevertheless, those black states most obviously in the geographical orbit of South Africa have found their trade with it important and even vital. In some instances they still do: 18 percent of Mozambique's imports, 29 percent of Malawi's, around 66 percent of Botswana's, and over 90 percent of Swaziland's and Lesotho's originate in South Africa. Even Zambia (8 percent) and Zaïre (4 percent) still buy from South Africa, and Namibia and Rhodesia are completely locked into South African trading patterns.

The overall impact on many regional states of this trade with South Africa is, however, diminishing. According to U.N. estimates, South Africa's share of Rhodesian imports and exports reached a peak in 1969, with 55.8 percent and 28.6 percent respectively. It is apparent that South Africa is still Rhodesia's major trading partner, but the trade is declining in proportionate though not absolute terms. Zambia has virtually broken its trade linkages southward.[6] Zaïre's have lessened. Angola and Mozambique have shifted directions. To be sure, the level of South Africa's exports is a function of the state of its domestic economy. If domestic productivity lags, so will exports. But increasingly, regional trade volume is a function of the political-military environment. Post-1974 tensions, increased militancy by nationalist movements, and economic sluggishness all contribute to the commercial problems of South Africa. This, in turn, adds to the conviction by most regional black governments that anything more than the minimum necessary association with South Africa is unwise and immoral. By reducing their trade dependence on South Africa, some governments have also helped deny South Africa profitable markets. In short, South Africa has failed to parlay its active trade policy into political acceptance or foreign-policy clientage. South Africa is a regional economic giant, one whose neighbors would like to keep at arm's length.

This is not possible, of course, for Botswana, Lesotho, and Swaziland (BLS states), with which trading patterns are formalized through the Customs Union Agreement (see Interchapter), or with Namibia and most recently Transkei and Bophuthatswana, which are also in the free-trade area.

The 1969 customs agreement permits the unilateral imposition of additional duties to protect infant industries in Botswana, Lesotho, and Swaziland. In practice, however, the three territories have accused South Africa of trying to prevent the establishment of industries that might compete with established South African industries—among them a fertilizer factory, a Japanese television assembly plant, and a Japanese motor assembly firm in Swaziland. Although the 1969 agreement provided for the establishment of a Customs Union Commission with minimal powers for intergovernmental consultation on a variety of common problems, the commission has provided little help in countering South African economic muscle.

The association of the BLS states with the European Economic Community in February 1975 may help expand mercantile alternatives. The Lomé Convention provides for free access to the EEC for all industrial goods and for 96 percent of agricultural output. The EEC insisted on firm guarantees that South African firms or the government of South Africa would not use the BLS states as a covert means of entry into the EEC market. But South African companies need only invest directly in these states to obtain access to the EEC. Despite the Lomé Convention, the Republic will be the principal source of imports for some time.

Among the constraints of being in the common rand currency area was the fact that South Africa, virtually alone, determined exchange control and other fiscal policies to protect the rand, decided on the issue of government bonds and treasury bills, and collected the interest on securities held in the South African Reserve Bank. In addition, Pretoria unilaterally has altered sales taxes and imposed import surcharges to the detriment of the BLS states. The BLS governments have thus sought to find alternative monetary relationships. In December 1974, Swaziland, Lesotho, and South Africa signed an agreement governing their currency controls and monetary affairs. The South African rand remains legal tender in these three countries, but Lesotho and Swaziland are permitted to issue their own currencies, provided they are fully backed by rand deposits. Swaziland thus issues its own currency, the *lilangeni* (plural, *emalengeni*).

Botswana refused to sign this agreement. Instead it established its own central bank and issued its own currency, the pula, in August 1976. Except for a change of name, Swaziland is still a prisoner of the South African monetary system, as is Lesotho (see Lesotho chapter). Botswana, on the other hand, has sought to demonstrate its monetary independence of the rand. The pula was revalued against the dollar and is now worth more than the rand. Nonetheless, Botswana is hardly independent of South Africa's currency. Nor is Mozambique, which is committed to dismantling the apartheid system and, by no means a formal partner in the Customs Union or the rand currency area, compelled to devalue the escudo in line with the devaluation of the rand in September 1975.

From time to time governments sign trade agreements. Angola-Zambia (November 1977) and Mozambique-Swaziland (October 1977) are two recent examples. By and large, with the possible exception of the Malawi-South Africa trade agreement signed in March 1967, few have had a noticeable impact on trading patterns. This agreement, while it did not lead to a radical growth in Malawian exports to South Africa, helped lay the foundations for the establishment of diplomatic relations, and led to various aid and loan agreements tied to purchases of South African goods.

Ten or even eight years ago there was talk of forming a larger regional common market, or "co-prosperity sphere," as it has sometimes been called. Although the South African government preferred expanded bilateral trade and economic ties with regional partners, optimistic leaders in business and industry and even a few in government had urged a more institutionalized and formalized structure. Former Prime Minister Hendrik Verwoerd had seen economic cooperation as a substitute for political and diplomatic ties. But now, among all but the most naive, especially in official circles, the hope for a "co-prosperity sphere" is dead.

This is a by-product of the imposed shrinkage of South Africa's hinterland. Multilateral regional cooperation has been reduced. Bilateral activities have been cut back and plans for expansion have been shelved. South Africa's hopes of the late 1960s and early 1970s have been replaced by a fragmentation of previous ties and a conscious rejection of South Africa's cooperative overtures. First came the closure of the Rhodesian-Zambian border in January 1973 (although, in fact, there was at least one train daily across the Victoria Falls bridge). Angolan and Mozambican independence, Angola's civil unrest, problems on the Benguela railway, coupled with the Portuguese exodus led to economic slumps. The heating up of the guerrilla war in Rhodesia also contributed to economic dislocations and external trading problems. Then came the closure of the Mozambique-Rhodesia border. Political factors have slowly in some cases, abruptly in others, superseded deeply etched economic patterns and attractions southward. When Zambia reopened its southern border in October 1978 it was only because of its vital need for fertilizer for its crops, not because of a basic change of policy.

Functional Cooperation

One reflection of the euphoria of the "outward policy/détente" years was an enlarged interest, in South Africa and elsewhere, in high-level functional cooperation. States became involved in bilateral projects that would significantly alter or strengthen the economic infrastructure of the region as an integrated subsystem.

Cabora Bassa

Epitomizing this outward thrust of South African leadership in regional cooperation was the Cabora Bassa hydroelectric project, on the Zambezi River in Mozambique.[7] South Africans thought in the 1960s that an electrical grid linking all of Southern Africa was possible. The jewel in this crown was to be Cabora Bassa, with a dam to be the largest in Africa and one of the largest in the world. Despite guerrilla struggle around the construction site and threats to destroy the dam, it was completed in 1975. Its very genesis is attributed to political motives—Portugal's desire to have a symbol of its commitment to stay in the region and South Africa's desire to offset the impact of the Tazara railway project and to solidify its links with Mozambique. Although South Africa eventually put up two-thirds of the $447 million capital for it, the project had been originally conceived as a way of associating European governments and businesses with the regional status quo. Yet within South Africa, the Electricity Supply Commission (ESCOM), which expected to be the chief customer of the output, would have preferred to supply South Africa from domestic energy sources. Only when pushed by the Department of Foreign Affairs and the South African Industrial Development Corporation (IDC), whose director was one of the original proponents of the plan, would ESCOM agree to participate.

However, it took longer to produce power than expected. South Africans began receiving electricity on an experimental basis in June 1976. But "technical difficulties" delayed full transmission of the contracted 680MW at the rate of R0.3 per kilowatt-hour. Through this delay the contract was being renegotiated by the Portuguese-controlled *Companhia Hidroelectrica de Cabora Bassa*. The company was understood to be seeking a price double the original rate, a rate which had been pegged to electricity production costs in RSA. Since then these costs have risen around 38 percent. Thus, the company argues that it is fair to adjust the prices upward. Despite pricing disagreements and political difficulties, by April 1977 South Africa was drawing power from Cabora Bassa at the rate of 800MW. This then represented 7 percent of South Africa's total electricity requirements. Still, for the dam to do more than pay interest charges, power generation must increase to 1500MW. The second planned stage, increasing South African consumption to 1440MW, was to be ready by early 1978. As one of Mozambique's principal assets, Cabora Bassa has prompted the Machel government to adopt a pragmatic attitude toward both Portugal and South Africa, the latter at present the only possible large-scale market for the power, since at present the only domestic user is Maputo.

The supply of power from Cabora Bassa to Maputo must go via a converting station in South Africa. Mozambique has an assured income of around $27 million per year from power sales and the opportunity to use Cabora Bassa as a focal point for the development of mineral and agricultural resources of the lower Zambezi. The Mozambican government would think carefully before it jeopardized what is currently its third-ranking source of foreign exchange. The others, remitted mine-workers' earnings and port and handling fees from Maputo, are also dependent on South Africa.

Cunene

Although the Portuguese and the South Africans agreed in 1969 to collaborate on a $259 million hydroelectric, irrigation, and economic development scheme on the Cunene River dividing Angola and Namibia, and although the facilities under construction are to be located chiefly in Angola, it is Namibia that would benefit most directly from this complex project. Some 50 percent of the water for Ovamboland (the northernmost province of Namibia) comes from the Calueque dam in Angola. An electrical generating facility at Ruacana on the Namibian side of the border was planned to provide 240MW largely for Namibia. But Ruacana cannot operate properly without cooperation from the Angolans at Calueque, where the river is regulated.

At the time when Angola had achieved a tenuous independence, South Africa had already spent $116 million on the works at Gove, Calueque, and Ruacana and another $75 million in Namibia on transmission lines. The civil war, and especially South Africa's extended intervention in Angola from 1975 to 1976 and briefer penetrations in 1977 and 1978, had left Cunene with an uncertain future. The justification for the intervention initially announced was to protect the workers and the dam at Calueque and to protect the refugees ostensibly fleeing the fighting zones. By the time the MPLA government, with Cuban military assistance, had asserted itself and the South African forces had withdrawn from Angola, work on the Angolan sections had come to a halt. This included the dam and pump station at Calueque and the diversion weir and pressure tunnels above the Ruacana Falls. The South Africans are now forced to await the pleasure of Angola before they can proceed with the construction, which was to have been completed in 1978. The South Africans publicly remain optimistic that an agreement to supply water and power can be reached with the MPLA government.

Meanwhile, South Africa has launched an alternative $9.3 million water scheme for Ovamboland to replace the supply from Calueque. They have also started a $23 million expansion program on the Windhoek power station to increase its capacity from 90 to 120MW. But there are reports of Cuban occupation and Angolan seizure of South African machinery and stores at Calueque, justified, they say, "as part of South Africa's debt to Luanda" presumably for damage done by South African forces in Angola and by South Africa's raids far across the border. Despite the short-term economic blandishments of cooperation with South Africa, the political considerations take precedence. Angola apparently has opted to await a favorable settlement in Namibia. Angola has a great deal more latitude than Mozambique for arriving at such a decision. Angola has no workers in South Africa or Namibia remitting large sums of money. It has virtually no trade or transport relations with South Africa. Economically it is relatively free to bargain hard or simply to wait and encourage SWAPO.

Kariba

For years Kariba had been an example of the only major hydroelectric facility that contributed to cooperative interaction between otherwise hostile regional states. From its inception in the 1950s Kariba was a political issue. Southern Rhodesia, over the objections of the Zambian (then northern Rhodesian) copper corporations, insisted on and secured the placement of the dam on the Zambezi between the territories, and the situation of the power station on the south (Rhodesian) bank of the river. Although Kariba was ostensibly jointly owned and operated by Rhodesia and Zambia, the Rhodesians were thereby in a position to destroy the copper-based economy of Zambia, which uses the facilities power to pump its mines dry. Despite UDI, border incursions in both directions, and formal border closures, power continued to flow to Zambia. Implied threats to switch off power were not carried out.

Nonetheless, Zambia has taken steps to free itself from this vulnerability. Zambia has developed Kariba II on the north bank. With considerable Yugoslav assistance Zambia has also brought the Kafue scheme into production. In 1967 some 81.3 percent of Zambia's electricity had been supplied by Kariba. By 1977 Zambia announced that it was now self-sufficient in electric power with a surplus to export. Nonetheless, Kariba power still flows northward. Zambia's decreased reliance on Kariba power illustrates the country's larger situation—reduced dependence on the white South but at great economic sacrifice.

Oxbow/Malibamatso

One of South Africa's pressing needs, especially since it became industrialized and urbanized, has been for a large volume of water. Hence, years ago South Africa enthusiastically entered discussions with the Lesotho government on the cooperative construction of the Oxbow dam across the Orange River in Lesotho, where it is called the Malibamatso River. Discussions between the Lesotho government's Oxbow steering committee and the World Bank and South Africa's Department of Water Affairs adjourned before they could resolve the issues of the scale of the project and the price South Africa would pay for the water.

In 1975 the Shah of Iran offered to finance at least half of the estimated costs of the scheme, and, it was rumored, under Iranian pressure South Africa agreed to offer a higher price for water. Yet misunderstanding persisted. Negotiations again broke down for "political reasons." South Africa wants a much bigger project. Lesotho, in contrast, announced that it is planning a scaled-down version of the previously discussed $350 million plan. With technical assistance supplied by Canada, the new dam is expected to be completed by 1983. But at this level neither country will maximize benefits. Lesotho wants to be independent of South African electricity. South Africa desperately needs lots of water. With the present plan Lesotho would gain electrical self-sufficiency but would not be in a position to export either power or a great deal of water. It is, in short, an import substitution option, little more. The previously cooperative character of the project has been lost for the time being, but negotiations continue (see Lesotho chapter).

South African-Mozambican Functional Cooperation

Less dramatic but no less important have been the various ad hoc efforts by South Africans to keep their links with Mozambique firm. The South Africans particularly want to keep open their access to the port at Maputo, which handles around 15 percent of South Africa's exports. Thus, it is in South Africa's interest, with Mozambique's permission, to rectify operating bottlenecks on the railway and at the port. After Mozambique's independence, the departure of thousands of skilled Portuguese led to a decline in traffic from South Africa. South African Railways has been willing to supply technical assistance on a permanent basis to both the Mozambique railways and the Maputo harbor administration. Until the port at Richards Bay (Natal) is equipped to handle bulk cargo and perhaps even afterward, South Africa must encourage its shippers to use Maputo, and so Maputo must be made more reliable. But South Africa understandably would like to see Maputo as more than an interim outlet until its own additional capacity becomes available.

The projects discussed above are major examples of functional cooperation that bridges racial divisions in the region. It is no accident that South Africa has had a hand in all but the Kariba scheme. As the richest and most industrialized state in the region, it had to find alternative sources of water, electricity, and infrastructural support. (The following section will expand on this pattern.) The trends are clear. Interest in long-term projects in tandem with South Africa has diminished among black governments. In fact, talk of joint or cooperative ventures among only black governments seems to be increasing. When a government acceptable to Zimbabwe's black neighbors achieves power, one would expect renewed interest in integrative projects in Southern Africa. This would also apply to Namibia. Already this has begun with regard to regional rail, road, and pipeline projects.

Transport Relations

Economic interrelations reflect to a large degree the regional map of transport routes. At least that is the starting point. Thenceforth, governments and businesses can make decisions on which routes to use or whether to establish new ones, on the basis of a variety of criteria—speed, reliability, efficiency, cost, and ideological and political preference.

The principal lines of rail had been established by the 1930s. The network was a product of intensive ad hoc interterritorial negotiations, compromises, and competition over railway routes and rates and of customs tariffs, especially between 1889 and 1906. Until Rhodesian UDI, the predominant flow from as far north as the Zambia-Shaba (Katanga) Copperbelt was southward and coastward toward Rhodesia, South Africa, Angola, and Mozambique. The landlocked situation of Zambia, Malawi, Rhodesia, Botswana, Lesotho, and Swaziland and the effective landlocked situation of Zaïre virtually dictated those states' continued dependence on routes and ports under control of white governments.

The single most important development in transport, with profound political meaning for Southern Africa, was the construction of a railway linking the Zambian system with the Tanzanian port at Dar es Salaam. The People's Republic of China, which constructed the project under most favorable terms for Zambia and Tanzania, completed the line in June 1975. It began operations in 1976. Despite the inadequacies of the port at Dar,[8] Tazara serves its purposes well: carrying almost all of Zambia's copper, it is a lifeline for Zambia and a boon to the exploitation of Tanzania's western provinces.

Other political factors have contributed to changing transport patterns. Rhodesia closed its border with Zambia in January 1973. Ian Smith had hoped to force President Kaunda to clamp down on Zimbabwean guerrillas operating out of Zambia. Instead, in retaliation Zambia declared the closure permanent. It was economically costly, yet it was politically important.

It will be a considerable time before Zambia can do without the services of its alternate routes, including the roads through Malawi and Tanzania and the Benguela railway. In 1973 and 1974 the Benguela route handled around 50 percent (by volume) of Zambia's foreign trade. But the railway was closed in August 1975 because of the civil war in Angola. UNITA continues to operate in the region (with South African assistance), and the wars in Shaba province in 1977 and 1978 added to difficulties. Despite the normal functioning of the line in some stretches, it remains closed to Zambian traffic. Because of President Kaunda's initial opposition to MPLA and his earlier support for UNITA, the MPLA government was long uncooperative. Political disagreements, involving all three parties—Zambia, Angola, and Zaïre—prevented a rapid reopening. Zambia has also considered building a railway extension to the Benguela route in order to bypass the unreliable Zaïrian section. As for the Benguela route, the technical and operational problems apparently are solvable. But Zaïre's relations with Angola were so strained that Zaïre sought alternate routes to the east and south. In June 1977 Zaïre shipped 24,000 tons of copper through South African ports (via Zambia and Rhodesia) and some 1,400 through Dar via Tazara. Zaïre is inclined to increase its use of Tazara, since the war in Zimbabwe makes the southern route unreliable. Moreover, the Tazara route is cheaper. For its imports Zaïre still uses the South African-Rhodesian route heavily.

But Tazara is only the most significant among several new projects that have contributed to Zambia's transport alternatives. An oil pipeline from Dar to Ndola was completed in 1968. All of Zambia's petroleum needs are supplied by this route. The Great North Road to Dar was upgraded, and road routes to Malawi and Mozambique were also improved. Zambia (with EEC assistance) is also surveying two additional railway routes, one a direct link from Lusaka to the railhead at Tete in Mozambique, the other a line from Tazara to Malawi, connecting Zambia to Nacala and Beira.

Zambia's redirection of shipping has had some effect on Mozambique as well, for income derived from transit trade with neighboring states at one time (1973) had earned for Mozambique 2.8 billion escudos (around 80 percent of invisible earnings). In pre-independence years, foreign-exchange earnings from transit facilities averaged around 30 percent of total foreign-exchange earnings. Without these earnings the economy would have been bankrupt, because visible trade regularly incurred a deficit. Mozambique had been (and still is in many respects) an economy of ports and railroads. The construction of the port at Nacala and the rail link with Malawi in 1970 (it was financed by South Africa) added to this pattern.

Maputo is the most important of Mozambique's ports and South Africa is Maputo's main customer. In 1973–74 it handled 19 percent of South Africa's seaborne exports. Of the 14.1 million tons handled in 1973, approximately 32 percent was South African and Botswanan traffic, and 21 percent came from Swaziland. The rest was local and Rhodesian traffic. But independence brought additional problems. The departure of Portuguese colonists living in Mozambique, and later those on contract to the railways, led to a fall-off in productivity of the ports and railways. The accident rate increased. Political uncertainty compounded the difficulties. South African Railways subsequently mounted a program to put the system back on its feet by loaning staff and signal equipment. Still, in 1976 total tonnage handled by Maputo had fallen by 70 percent.

In this regard Mozambique's application of sanctions against Rhodesia in March 1976 was economically risky. Mozambique severed all communications between the two countries and a state of war was declared. Before then, Mozambique's ports handled about 25 percent of Rhodesia's trade. In the early 1970s it had been as high as 80 percent. This act thereby cost Mozambique around '$120 million per year, although some international aid (about $60 million) has offset the losses. Actually Beira has never recovered from the loss of traffic caused first by UDI and then by the Zambian-Rhodesian border closure in 1973,[9] and subsequently by anti-government guerrillas.

Tazara has provided Zambia and Zaïre with options to the north. The closure of the Zambian-Rhodesian border in 1973 and the Mozambique-Rhodesia border in 1976, in addition to the severance of the Benguela route in Angola, had forced Rhodesia to operate almost exclusively through South Africa. But these actions also resulted in Zambia's increasing reliance on Tazara. The result has been the emergence of two transport systems, one with South Africa as its hub and including Rhodesia, Namibia, the BLS states, and to some extent Mozambique. The second is a black-dominated transport system that includes Tanzania, Zambia, Zaïre, Malawi, and Mozambique, with Angola relatively independent of the others.

The Rhodesian government had taken steps to mitigate the impact of this trend. At the time of UDI Rhodesia had four major railway routes—the Beira line, the line to Lourenço Marques (Maputo), the railway through Botswana to the Cape, and the route to Lobito via Zambia and Zaïre. There were also road connections to each of these territories and to South Africa as well. Ian Smith's ill-considered closure of the border with Zambia cost Rhodesia $1.2 million per month in lost revenues and fees. The establishment of the Frelimo government in August 1975 had a more direct impact and led to the March 1976 border closure. Rhodesia had been effectively reduced to just two southern routes.

Rhodesia's newly constructed rail link directly with South Africa began operations in October 1974, but brought two additional problems for the Smith government. First, South African railway and port congestion meant that although Rhodesia may have been less dependent on rail access to South Africa through Botswana, technical and operational bottlenecks remained. Second, Prime Minister Vorster used the route as additional leverage in his efforts to encourage Salisbury to arrive at an internal settlement with the "right" black or racially mixed government.

In 1974 Botswana announced its intention eventually to take over the railway running through its territory. The Botswana government began studying the proposals for taking over the 642 km line, at that time wholly owned and operated by Rhodesian Railways. The Botswana economy relies on the line, since it carries virtually all the country's exports and provides its vital communication link. President Sir Seretse Khama intended ultimately to nationalize the line and deny Rhodesia its use. Yet he realized that such a move would hurt Botswana's economy more than it would hurt Rhodesia's. Guerrilla operations and manpower shortages in Rhodesia did not force Rhodesia to abandon the line. So Botswana has called in Canadian and British consultants to help plan a transition. The Botswana government has negotiated with several European countries as well as with the Arab Bank for Economic Development in Africa (ABEDIA) to help finance the takeover. The situation was filled with uncertainty as alternatives were narrowed to those neither party particularly favored (see Botswana chapter).

An all-weather road linking Zambia and Botswana via the ferry at Kazangula was officially opened in January 1977. This road reduces Botswana's dependence on the railway, and it also has other strategic and economic importance. First, it opens a viable route to Zambia, not just for Botswana's products (such as meat) but particularly for South African goods to Zambia and Malawi. Only Zambian and Botswanan registered trucks are permitted to carry goods under contract on the highway. The road will eventually be tarred, and talks between Zambia, Botswana, and international financing agencies have been held concerning the construction of a bridge over the Zambezi at Kazangula. Second, the road was a psychological boost to Botswana, its only direct link with independent black Africa. To some it was seen as an extension of Tazara into the heart of white-ruled Africa. Much of this criticism fell away when an "acceptable" black government was established in Zimbabwe.

Swaziland, like Botswana, is concerned about the adequacy of its existing transport ties. Swaziland recently got its first rail link with South Africa. By early 1979 rails connected the present Swazi line 95 km to the border town of Golela, which is on the South African Railway line to the new port at Richards Bay. Thus, Swaziland has two convenient outlets, one to Maputo (opened in 1964) and one to Richards Bay.

Rhodesian UDI set in motion a transformation in the transport infrastructure of the region. Successive events, especially the independence of Angola, Mozambique, and Zimbabwe, with Marxist-oriented governments, have added to the efforts of black regimes to rearrange linkages in order to maximize policy alternatives and to assert their independence of white minority regimes. The picture that is emerging since the establishment of a black government in Zimbabwe is already radically different from the pre-1965 pattern. The structural links—railways, roads, air connections, pipelines, transmission lines—have yet to be reflected substantially in trading directions and alliances, largely because the economies in question are not complementary. But insofar as transport networks provide political levers or pressure points, the impact is not inconsequential. South Africa now finds its regional economic and strategic advantages less decisive than in the past, except in relation to the BLS countries, Namibia, and Mozambique.

Labor Supply and Migration

One element of South Africa's economic domination in the region and a further factor in its need to interact economically with its neighbors is its allure as an employer of foreign workers on mines and farms. Despite its diminishing commercial hinterland and the uncertainties of political relations with nearby states, South Africa continues to employ large numbers of foreign laborers in tenuous migratory existence (see Table 2).

The economic growth regions of Southern Africa have for years been a magnet to laborers. Relatively free flow of labor before the independence period augmented well-organized and well-financed private and governmental recruiting networks. Except for the attraction of Zambia's Copperbelt and rail line, most of this flow has been toward white-dominated and away from black-governed Southern Africa. Yet, this flow affects the politics and economics of both "exporters" of labor and recipient countries.

Table 2

Black Foreign Workers in South Africa

	1965	1970	1971	1972	1975	1980
Lesotho	117,000	147,400	165,000	131,749	80,526*	140,746
Mozambique	161,000	144,900	132,000	121,708	127,000	56,424
Malawi	80,000	107,180	100,000	131,291	11,000	32,319
Botswana	59,000	47,360	51,000	31,960	34,020	23,200
Swaziland	39,000	24,260	12,000	10,108	17,000	10,377
Rhodesia	27,000	11,640	N.A.	6,200	16,000	19,853
Angola	11,000	3,440	N.A.	4,466*	2,862*	291
Zambia	16,000	N.A.	N.A.	638	N.A.	918

Sources: 1965—Kenneth W. Grundy, *Confrontation and Accommodation in Southern Africa: The Limits of Independence* (Berkeley: University of California Press, 1973), Table 6, p. 60.   1970—G.M.E Leistner and W, J, Breytenbach, *The Back Workers of South Africa* (Pretoria: Africa Institute, 1975), Tables 2–5, p. 15. 1971—Francis Wilson, *Migrant Labour* (Johannesburg: The South African Council of Churches and SPRO-CAS, 1972), pp. 110–18. 1972—South Africa, House of Assembly *Debates* (Hansard), June 14, 1973. 1975—Diverse sources. 1980—House of Assembly *Debates* (Hansard), 26 February 1981, Q. col. 294–96.
* Items from South Africa Foundation News, I, no. 7 (December 1975), p. 3. These data refer only to workers employed in gold mines.

Lesotho has consistently depended on the export of its workers to South Africa. Regularly over 40 percent of the adult male population of Lesotho is employed in South Africa, but it is not simply because Lesotho is unable to create enough cash employment for its work force. Even if enough new jobs could be found, the economic blandishments of the Republic lure Basotho away, partially due to the far greater opportunities and higher pay available in South Africa. In 1971, for example, it was estimated that the average daily wage for an agricultural laborer in Lesotho was around twenty cents (South African) compared to a minimum starting cash wage in the gold mines of forty cents. That imbalance has widened markedly in recent years. Further, a substantial portion of the Lesotho economy (especially its governmental revenues) is generated by the wages, remittances, and deferred pay that are returned to Lesotho by workers and employers' organizations. In 1965–66, R4,395,000 out of a total Lesotho GNP of R39,244,200 (slightly over eleven percent) had been returned to Lesotho in this fashion. This income equaled the country's tangible exports, and when combined with recruitment fees and taxes paid the Lesotho government and revenue from customs and excise that year, it left Lesotho financially dependent on South Africa. The total earnings of Basotho in South Africa exceeded Lesotho's total GDP.

This dependence is further reflected in the events of 1975. On New Year's Day Basotho miners in the gold mines of South Africa struck in protest of Lesotho legislation requiring all miners to send 60 percent of their salaries to the Lesotho National Bank until their contracts expired. Rioting and faction fights led to eight deaths and numerous injuries. The Chamber of Mines threatened to repatriate all "troublemakers." Eventually, the Lesotho government "clarified" the legislation and Basotho workers returned to the mines. Yet, at one point around 10,000 Basotho returned home, and the Lesotho government had to approach black governments in Africa about employing the returnees. Indications are that the Lesotho government would like to (1) have a larger voice in the labor-exchange process, (2) have access to a larger share of the earnings abroad, and (3) provide organizational help to the mine workers to enable them to identify with their government and exert greater negotiating clout.

Labor-export dependence has not changed noticeably in recent years. The number of Basotho employed in the gold mines has been rising steadily from a 1965 figure of 62,576 to around 90,000 in 1975. This is roughly four times the total number of Basotho employed for wages within Lesotho. Some economists estimate the total number of Basotho employed in South Africa to be between 160,000 and 210,000. Thus, in 1973–74 approximately R52 million, compared to a total GDP of R64 million, was earned by Basotho migrants in South Africa.

Botswana and Swaziland have similar though less-pronounced patterns of labor movement. Both countries have been relatively successful at generating some new jobs and thereby mitigating the "push" factors that contribute to migration. The considerable short-term fluctuations in migrant patterns reflect the twin factors of proximity of labor to jobs in the respective countries and changing political relations between them. In 1970 one and a quarter times as many Batswana were employed in South Africa as were employed for wages in Botswana itself, and that number included about fifteen percent of the total employable labor force in Botswana. These percentages have been reduced since then and, in fact, have shrunk steadily since 1950. Swaziland is even more favorably situated. It has a larger number of persons employed in the domestic economy and fewer working in South Africa. The 1971 estimate of persons employed in South Africa equalled about 15 percent of the number of Swazis working for wages in Swaziland and only 3 percent of the total Swazi labor force.

Malawi and Mozambique which rely heavily on the export of labor to South Africa have seen their recent fortunes fluctuate appreciably. At a high point in 1974 around 106,000 Malawian workers were employed in South African gold mines. In April of that year an aircraft carrying home Malawian contract workers crashed in Botswana. Seventy-five workers died. The Malawi government immediately banned further recruitment by foreign organizations. The effect was to reduce the number of Malawian miners in South Africa to a low of 207 three years later. In the short run this created immediate labor-supply problems for South Africa that necessitated considerable readjustment. Yet by 1975 Malawi was exploring ways to reopen labor recruitment. In 1977 recruitment was resumed and by early 1978 the number of Malawians in the gold mines had risen to 20,000. It is unlikely, however, to go much beyond 40,000 in the foreseeable future.

The importance of sending labor abroad cannot be exaggerated for Malawi. In 1973 there were said to be some 300,000 Malawians working abroad; fewer than 258,000 in wage employment at home. Labor was said to be Malawi's third most important export, after tobacco and tea. It had been widely assumed that to unload on Malawi large numbers of unemployed able-bodied men accustomed to relatively lucrative employment might create conditions of social unrest. In fact, evidence of discontent spilling over to the political arena has been slight. Although Malawi has been unable to absorb all the returnees into its cash economy, the Malawi experience does serve to throw into question the dire predictions of those who saw the laborers as a political lever in the hands of South Africa.

The flow of Mozambique mine recruits to South Africa has long been a support to Mozambique's dependent economy. A 1901 agreement (updated in 1928) between the South African and Portuguese authorities enabled a private organization, the Witwatersrand Native Labour Association (WNLA), to have exclusive rights to contract up to 100,000 workers a year from southern Mozambique. In return, South Africa agreed to ship at least 47.5 percent of the exports from and imports to the Transvaal through Lourenço Marques (now Maputo). In addition, WNLA paid the Mozambique government a head fee for each recruit. This fee plus remitted taxes and wages, earned for the Portuguese government around $10–12 million per year. A portion of the miners' wages (60 percent) was deferred and remitted in Mozambique after being converted into gold at the official price of $42 per ounce. The Mozambique authorities in turn sold the gold at world-market prices and paid the miners their wages in escudos at the official exchange rates. The result after 1968 was a windfall profit for Portugal, since the free-market gold price was often two or three times the official rate.

When Mozambique became independent one immediate result was an even greater dependence on South Africa over the labor issue. The number of Mozambique gold miners increased from 80,412 in June 1974 to 127,198 in November 1975. In addition, wage increases were raised by almost one quarter. To top that off, the price of gold was soaring. With Portuguese rule ended, these premiums accrued to Mozambique, only slightly tarnished by the 17.9 percent devaluation of the rand in September 1975 and a drop in the gold market. Nonetheless, with the free price of gold at $140 early in 1976, Mozambique dreamed of inflating its foreign currency earnings handsomely. In cold cash this meant about $180 million extra for Mozambique in 1975 and about $115 million extra in 1976.

The South Africans came to realize that the Mozambique Convention worked to their disadvantage. The first increase in the number of Mozambican laborers reflected an effort to replace Malawian miners. But as mine wages increased, more South Africans have taken up mine work. As adjustments were made, the Chamber of Mines sought to cut back on Mozambican sources. Mine-labor recruitment dropped from 1,500–2,000 per week in 1975 to only 300–400 per week in 1976, an overall reduction from 100,000 to around 75,000 Mozambicans. Frelimo authorities were put in an awkward situation. They appreciated the revenue but were critical of the process on ideological grounds. So they aggravated the cutbacks by requiring workers to have passports instead of travel documents. As the price of gold fell and the mines suffered financial difficulties, the foreign workers were the first to be let go. Under pressure from the mine corporations, at the end of June 1977 the South African Reserve Bank abolished the official price so that Mozambique is no longer to benefit from windfall profits. Along with the further reduction of Mozambican miners in South Africa to around 38,000, the loss of profits has considerably reduced Mozambique's dependence on this source of income.

The social impact of migratory labor is as deep as the economic though more difficult to analyze. In effect, the export of labor serves as a safety-valve to relieve population pressures on the land, to reduce the level of domestic unemployment, and to serve as a viable economic alternative for those whose expectations cannot be satisfied at home. The hypothesized side-effect is to reduce domestic discontent and to channel it to economic pursuits abroad. But the long-range impact, it may be argued, is to remove the young, healthy, economically ambitious from the country, thereby retarding local economic activity and reducing the chances for self-generated reform or revolution.

The impact on South Africa, the major importer of foreign labor, has been less obvious though no less important. The total number of foreign black laborers in Rhodesia and South Africa in 1972 was estimated to be around 840,000. The vast majority were drawn from Malawi (33 percent), Mozambique (26 percent), and Lesotho (25 percent), with the remainder from Botswana (7 percent), Zambia (5 percent), and Swaziland (4 percent). At that time over three-quarters of them worked in South Africa. Roughly 10 percent of the black work force in South Africa are aliens. Their concentration in select industries is even more apparent. The mining industry in South Africa absorbs approximately half the foreigners. So, no less than 78 percent (in 1972) of the black labor force employed in the gold-mining industry and in the coal mines of the Transvaal were from outside the Republic. Recent developments such as the increase in wages paid and most notably the cessation or reduction of recruitment in Malawi and Mozambique have lowered the percentage of foreign migrants in the mines. But for South Africa the availability of an extensive foreign-labor pool beyond its borders has been vital. First, cheaper imported labor helps to depress the economic conditions and bargaining power of the domestic labor force. To a Basotho or Malawian, mine wages may appear to be high in relation to what he might earn at home. However, they are barely near the poverty datum line for South African residents. Second, the whole social fabric of temporary migratory labor (family-less males) enables the South African authorities to sidestep a variety of social welfare costs that otherwise might have to be faced. Third, by importing foreigners subject to on-the-job and in-the-hostel regimentation the policing and supervisory responsibilities of the authorities are lessened. The migrants are, in effect, prisoners of the compound. The promise of deferred earned pay and the liaison with their own home governments generally deter political protest and organization, all of which, in turn, facilitates the implementation of apartheid and separate-development legislation. Fourth, the South African information service gets propaganda mileage out of the presence of hundreds of thousands of foreign Africans in the RSA. Finally, in terms of foreign policy, the prospect of the return of large numbers of contract laborers (its reality has not been demonstrated) has probably provided South Africa with a useful political weapon in dealing with labor-exporting neighbors. It is, at any rate, felt to have been a contributing factor in their ostensible deference to South Africa's policies. For governments inclined to be wary of economically stronger neighbors, labor export serves to make their cautious foreign policies seem realistic and prudent. This is less true, however, for Mozambique, Botswana, and Lesotho.

Conclusions

Southern Africa has in the past fifteen years undergone traumatic political change. As a result, significant economic adjustments have been and are being made, although with a marked time lag. Redirections and conversions will, themselves, contribute to future behavioral patterns. William James once observed that "habit is the enormous fly-wheel of society, its most precious conservative agent." In fact, during cataclysmic periods of history, habits can be broken and new ways of doing things devised. The political economy of Southern Africa is presently in the midst of such an historical shake-up. But searching for historical break-points is like trying at the time to identify a low or a high on the stock market; your only validation is retrospect. Seldom does historical change arrive with fanfare and decree. Rather, it creeps up on us, a series of subtle yet significant changes that add up to new structures of behavior and power.

Crucial to such a break with the past will be the political settlements in Namibia and Rhodesia/Zimbabwe, especially the latter. Although Zimbabwe is not large or powerful, it holds the geopolitical and infrastructural keys to the future. South Africa is understandably deeply interested in the character of the new regime in Zimbabwe. Pretoria realizes that the extent to which it can relate economically to the Salisbury regime will largely determine South

Africa's fate. One might sketch a scenario of majority-ruled Zimbabwe and Namibia in which South Africa could survive for years. And such regimes would not need to be cooperative or sympathetic with apartheid. If black Southern African governments completely turned their backs on South Africa, aware that militarily they were deficient, they might seek to fashion a new Southern African subsystem while still encouraging liberation forces from and in South Africa. (Zambia, for example, redrew its trade and transport links northward, yet still remained a part of the southern political system.) Conceivably a black-ruled, sanction-free Zimbabwe would then utilize trade and transport routes through Mozambique, thereby enabling all black-governed territories except Lesotho to bypass South Africa. A new Southern African economic subsystem excluding South Africa might evolve, creating new historical "habits," as through SADCC (see below).

Another alternative might be for the black states, unwilling or unable to divert large sums of money to redesign the economic superstructure of the region, to bide their time in the hope of a revolution in South Africa that would make infrastructural renovation unnecessary. But to accept the assumption of imminent collapse would be a grievous error. Positive action must be taken before Pretoria will collapse. Thus, the temptation will be to call upon external support to unseat the apartheid regime. But not all regional governments are likely to take the same approach to white-ruled South Africa. There will probably be varying degrees of commitment and sacrifice among them while they maintain a publicly unified approach to South Africa. Each alternative has its costs, the most important of which is the reaction to a particular policy by those forces in a position to stabilize or unseat the government in each state. Thus, alternatives can be effectively evaluated only when viewed in their sociopolitical context.

Without a militant liberationist regime in Salisbury, South Africa could continue as before, increasingly isolated from its neighbors and plagued by domestic protest. Depending on the attitude of Mozambique and the extent to which European and North American governments continue to support South Africa economically, South Africa's life could be relatively unimpaired in the short run. In the long run, however, Pretoria would, like an ostracized Rhodesia before it, begin to atrophy. The apartheid system is predicated on the need to subjugate a large labor pool, which requires an unlimited source of cheap labor, unlimited markets, and virtually unlimited investment opportunities. In short, South Africa needs its hinterland. An internally oriented apartheid economy is not sufficient to assure economic growth, surpluses, and hence capitalist dominance. The homelands policy is a delicate balancing game, designed to yield superficial structural changes while assuring a continued supply of labor, markets, and investment outlets. But, like Rhodesia, an ostracized South African economy—even including the homelands, "independent" or in limbo—would still be untenable. New investments, new technologies, and the drifting away of the young, the skilled, and the professional, would progressively weaken South Africa and render it more vulnerable to internal uprising and external pressure.

Much of this speculation depends on Salisbury's future policies and its ability to reinvigorate the Zimbabwean economy. With South Africa a pariah and Zimbabwe economically vibrant, many of the "services" formerly supplied to black neighbors by South Africa (for example, agricultural and industrial exports, employment opportunities, railways and ports, investment capital) could be made available by Zimbabwe and Mozambique and by an external world willing to make points with black Africa and eager to deflect or dampen the socialist commitment of the liberation movement. Undeniably there has been a shifting center of gravity in the region. What the United States and West European powers are pushing for today in Namibia would have been inconceivable a decade ago. Their fundamental purpose has not changed, just their appraisal of what is possible in this kaleidoscopic but not patternless transition.

Among the alternatives available to black states in the region, it is apparent that their governments have opted to redesign and redirect the economic infrastructure of the area, excluding as much as practical the South African economy. The format they have created is the Southern Africa Development Coordination Conference (SADCC). SADCC has attracted massive assistance from various western governments and institutions (as much as $800 million over the next five years). Its planning and organizational activities demonstrate both the desire and the conviction on the part of black-controlled Southern African states that they can succeed in reducing the economic centrality of South Africa and freeing their economies from dependence upon South Africa.

A major guide to the bibliography of Africa listing some 3,100 bibliographies, guides, indexes, and other reference works, as well as essential serials and monographs, all annotated. The *Guide* has been supplemented by Hans E. Panofsky's *A bibliography of Africana* (Westport, Conn.: Greenwood Press, 1975. 350 p.).

Friends, Society of. American Friends Service Committee. Nonviolent Action Training Program. *Action guide on Southern Africa.* Rev. ed. Philadelphia: 1976. 59 p.

Information on U.S. and Canadian organizations concerned with Southern Africa; liberation movements; addresses; resources.

Nguyen van Chi-Bonnardel, Regine. *The atlas of Africa.* New York: Free Press, 1973. 335 p.

A comprehensive atlas of the continent which includes maps and explanatory content on such features as population, geology, climate, vegetation, languages, history, agriculture, communications, etc., followed by regional and country maps.

Bibliographies

American–Southern African relations: bibliographic essays. Edited by Mohamed A. El-Khawas and Francis A. Kornegay, Jr. (African Bibliographic Center. Special bibliographic series, n.s., v. 1) Westport, Conn.: Greenwood Press, 1975. 188 p.

Skurnik, W. A. E. *Sub-Saharan Africa: a guide to information sources.* (International relations information guide series, v. 3) Detroit: Gale Research Co., 1977. 130 p.

Bibliography on African foreign relations, with section on liberation movements; helpful for locating U.S. government documents on Africa.

Smaldone, Joseph P. *African liberation movements: an interim bibliography.* Waltham, Mass.: African Studies Association, Brandeis University, 1974. 17 p.

References to books and articles as well as a listing of periodicals issued by liberation groups and their special interest lobbies.

Continuing Bibliographies

The following bibliographies, along with such standard indexes as the *Readers' guide to periodical literature,* the *Social sciences index* and the *Public affairs information service (PAIS) bulletin,* are all published at regular intervals and thus give up-to-date information on new books and articles. Book reviews and lists of books currently received in many periodicals provide another way of keeping up with new publications.

Africana journal. 1970– . Quarterly.

Africana Publishing Co., 30 Irving Pl., New York, N.Y. 10003.

Current listings arranged by subject and country, as well as book reviews, bibliographic essays, and longer bibliographies.

"Current Africana." In: *Review of African political economy,* 1974–   .

Lists publications of relevance to the study of contemporary African political economy.

Current bibliography on African affairs. 1962–   . Quarterly.

Baywood Publishing Co. for the African Bibliographic Center, Farmingdale, N.Y.

Book reviews and bibliographies; listings under subject and country.

International African bibliography. 1971–   . Quarterly.

Mansell, 3 Bloomsbury Pl., London WC1 2QA, England.

Coverage of books, articles, conference papers, reports, etc., arranged by subject and country.

SADEX, the Southern Africa development information/documentation exchange. 1979–   . Bimonthly.

African Bibliographic Center, 1346 Connecticut Ave. N.W., Washington, D.C. 20036.

Especially useful for materials relating to SADCC.

Filmographies

Africa from real to reel: an African filmography. Compiled by Steven Ohrn and Rebecca Riley. Waltham, Mass.: African Studies Association, 1976. 144 p.

The most comprehensive list of films on Africa available; approximately 1,300 16mm films distributed in the U.S. and Canada, with the following information: title, date, producer and filmmaker, location, distributors, synopsis; bibliography.

Films on Africa: an educator's guide to 16mm films available in the Midwest. Compiled by the African Studies Program, University of Wisconsin. Madison, Wisc.: African Studies Program, University of Wisconsin, 1974. 68 p.

List of films available in the midwestern United States, with descriptions provided by distributors; also recommendations by category from other U.S. Africanists; suggested age levels of usage also included.

South African politics: a film guide. Edited by Rebecca R. Riley & Steven G. Ohrn. Bloomington, Indiana: Prepared by the African Studies Program, Indiana University, 1975, 25 p.

Periodicals and Newspapers

Periodicals and newspapers, particularly those from Africa, provide one of the best methods of keeping informed about African opinions, social, political, and economic events, and analyses of the current situation. Listed below are a number of titles which regularly feature news and information on Southern

Africa, with the date of original publication, frequency of publication, publisher, and address. Additional listings can be found under country headings.

Current Events: Periodicals
*AF press clips. 1966–   . Weekly.
    AF/P—Room 3509, Department of State, Washington, D.C. 20520.
Africa; an international business, economics and political monthly. 1971–   .
    Africa Journal Ltd., Kirkman House, 54a Tottenham Court Rd., London
    WIP OBT, England.
**Africa confidential.* 1960–   . 25 issus per yr.
    Africa Confidential, 5/33 Rutland Gate, London SW7, England.
Africa currents. 1975–   . 4 times a yr.
    Africa Publications Trust, 48 Grafton Way, London WIP 5LB, England.
**Africa news.* 1973–   . Weekly.
    Africa News Service Inc., P.O. Box 3851, Durham, N.C. 27702.
Africa research bulletin: economic, financial and technical series and *Africa
    research bulletin: political, social and cultural series.* 1964–   .
    Africa Research Ltd., 18 Lower North St., Exeter EX4 3EN, England.
Facts and reports: press cuttings on Southern Africa. 1970–   . Biweekly.
    Holland Committee on Southern Africa, Da Costastraat 88, Amsterdam,
    Netherlands.
New African. 1966–   . Monthly. (Formerly *African development; New
    African development.*) IC Magazines Ltd., 63 Long Acre, London WC2E
    9JH, England.
**Southern Africa.* 1967–   . Bimonthly.
    Southern Africa Committee, 156 Fifth Ave., New York, N.Y. 10010.
To the point international. 1971–   . Biweekly.
    P.O. Box 2000, Antwerp 20, Belgium; U.S. distributor, P.O. Box 697,
    Hightstown, N.J. 08520.
X-ray. 1970–   . Monthly.
    The Africa Bureau, 48 Grafton Way, London W1, England.

Scholarly Articles and Analysis: Periodicals
Africa Institute. *Bulletin.* 1963–   . 10 times per yr.
    Africa Institute, P.O. Box 630, Pretoria 0001, South Africa.
**Africa report.* 1956–   . Bimonthly.
    African American Institute, 833 U.N. Plaza, New York, N.Y. 10017;
    subscriptions should be sent to: Transaction Inc., Rutgers, the State University, New Brunswick, N.J. 08903. Includes "African update."
**Africa today.* 1956–   . Quarterly.
    Africa Today Association, c/o Graduate School of International Affairs,
    University of Denver, Denver, Colorado 80208.

Issue. 1971–   . Quarterly.
    African Studies Association, Epstein Service Bldg., Brandeis University, Waltham, Mass. 02154. Subscription is part of membership dues.

* *Journal of modern African studies.* 1963–   . Quarterly.
    Cambridge University Press, P.O. Box 92, London NW1 2DB, England, and 32 E. 57th St., New York, N.Y. 10022.

Journal of Southern African affairs. 1976–   . Quarterly.
    Southern African Research Association and Afro-American Studies, 4133 Art/Sociology Bldg., University of Maryland, College Park, Maryland 20742.

* *Journal of Southern African studies.* 1974–   . Biannual.
    Oxford University Press, Oxford Journals, Press Rd., Neasden, London NW 10 ODD, England.

Review of African political economy. 1974–   . 3 times a yr.
    Merlin Press, Sufferance Wharf, 2–4 West Ferry Rd., London E14, England.

A number of liberation periodicals and other titles from Southern Africa have been microfilmed by the Cooperative Africana Microform Project (CAMP), which is administered by the Center for Research Libraries. These are available for loan to CAMP and Center members and many of them for purchase to others. For information write to: Ray Boylan, Assistant Director, Center for Research Libraries, 5721 S. Cottage Grove Avenue, Chicago, Illinois 60637.

U.N. Periodicals
For the publications of the U.N. Office of Public Information: *Objective: Justice* and *United Nations and Southern Africa: bulletin,* write to United Nations Publications, Room LX-2300, New York, N.Y. 10017. *Decolonization* may be obtained from the U.N. Center against Apartheid, Dept. of Political Affairs, Trusteeship and Decolonization, New York, N.Y. 10017.

Newspapers
A substantial amount of news about Southern Africa is published in the following newspapers, many of which can be found in university/college and larger public libraries: the *Christian Science Monitor; The New York Times;* the *Guardian Weekly* (Manchester, Eng.), which regularly includes articles from *Le Monde* and the *Washington Post; The Observer* (London); and *The Economist* (London). The *Star International Airmail Weekly* (Johannesburg) provides coverage for Southern Africa. In the United States it is distributed by Argus South African Newspapers, 1501 Broadway, New York, N.Y. 10036. The *Guardian* and *Economist* also have New York addresses.

Since subscriptions to African newspapers are expensive, few libraries have extensive collections. Microfilm copies of newspapers are sometimes available

through interlibrary loan. To identify newspapers which have been microfilmed see: U.S. Library of Congress. Catalog Publications Division. *Newspapers in microfilm: foreign countries, 1948–1972* (Washington: 1973–),
and McKee, Malcolm. *African newspapers on microfilm* (London: SCOLMA,
1973). Universities and colleges which are members of the Foreign Newspaper Project of the Association of Research Libraries and/or the Center for
Research Libraries in Chicago may borrow a number of African newspapers.

The Southern African Quadrant

Suggestions for Further Reading

Africa and the United States: vital interests. Edited by Jennifer S. Whitaker.
   New York: New York University Press, 1978. 255 p.
After Angola: the war over Southern Africa. 2d. ed. New York: Africana
   Publishing Co., 1978. 85 p.
   Includes: Legum, C. "The role of the Western powers in Southern
   Africa." Legum, C. "A study of international intervention in Angola."
   Hodges, T. "How the MPLA won in Angola."
American policy in Southern Africa: the stakes and the stance. Edited by
   Rene Lemarchand. Washington, D.C.: University Press of America, 1978.
   450 p.
*Conflict and change in Southern Africa: papers from a Scandinavian confer-
   ence.* Edited by Douglas G. Anglin, et al. Washington, D.C.: University
   Press of America, 1978. 269 p.
Cooperation and conflict in Southern Africa: papers on a regional subsystem.
   Edited by Timothy M. Shaw and Kenneth A. Heard. Washington, D.C.:
   University Press of America, 1977. 419 p.
*Davidson, Basil, Joe Slovo, and Anthony R. Wilkinson. *Southern Africa: the
   new politics of revolution.* Harmondsworth: Penguin, 1976. 374 p.
*Grundy, Kenneth W. *Confrontation and accommodation in Southern Africa:
   the limits of independence.* Berkeley: University of California Press, 1973.
   360 p.
*The Kissinger study of Southern Africa: the National Security Study Memo-
   randum 39 (secret).* Edited by Mohamed A. El-Khawas and Barry Cohen.
   Westport, Conn.: Lawrence Hill, 1976. 189 p.
*Legum, Colin. *Vorster's gamble for Africa: how the search for peace failed.*
   New York: Africana Publishing Co., 1976. 127 p.
Makgetla, Neva, and Ann W. Seidman. *Outposts of monopoly capitalism:
   Southern Africa in the changing global economy.* Westport, Conn.: L. Hill,
   1980. 370 p.
The political economy of contemporary Africa. Edited by Peter C. W.
   Gutkind and Immanuel Wallerstein. Beverly Hills: Sage, 1976. 318 p.
SADCC 2-Maputo: The proceedings of the second Southern African Develop-

ment Coordination Conference. Edited by Aloysius Kgarege. London: SADCC, 1981.

Southern Africa in perspective. Edited by Christopher Potholm and Richard Dale. New York: Free Press, 1972. 418 p.

Southern Africa since the Portuguese coup. Edited by John Seiler. Boulder, Col.: Westview Press, 1980. 252 p.

Southern Africa: toward economic liberation. Edited by Amon J. Nsekela. London: Rex Collings, 1981. 274 p.

Whitaker, Jennifer S. *Conflict in Southern Africa.* (Headline series) New York: Foreign Policy Association, August, 1978. 240 p.

Zimbabwe

Bibliographies

O'Meara, Patrick, and Jean E. Meeh Gosebrink. "Bibliography on Rhodesia." *Africana journal,* pt. 1, 9/1 (1978): 5–42; pt. II, 9/2 (1978): 101–112.

Pollak, Oliver B., and Karen Pollak. *Rhodesia/Zimbabwe: an international bibliography.* Boston: G. K. Hall, 1977. 620 p.

Reference and Documentary Sources

Cary, Robert, and Diana Mitchell. *African nationalist leaders in Rhodesia: who's who.* Bulawayo, Rhodesia: Books of Rhodesia, 1977. 310 p.

From Rhodesia to Zimbabwe: behind and beyond Lancaster House. Edited by W. H. Morris-Jones. London: F. Cass, 1980. 123 p.

Nelson, Harold D. *Area handbook for Southern Rhodesia.* Washington, D.C.: Foreign Area Studies, American University, 1975. 394 p. Distributed by Government Printing Office.

*Rasmussen, R. Kent. *Historical dictionary of Rhodesia/Zimbabwe.* Metuchen, N.J.: Scarecrow Press, 1979 (African Historical Dictionaries, no. 18). 445 p.

The Rhodesian problem: a documentary record, 1923–1973, edited by Elaine Windrich. London & Boston: Routledge and Kegan Paul, 1975. 312 p.

Zimbabwe, Parliament. House of Assembly. *Parliamentary Debates.* 1980– .

Zimbabwe independence movements: select documents. Edited and selected by Christopher Nyangani and Gideon Nyandoro. London: R. Collings, 1979. 456 p.

Periodicals and Newspapers

The African times. 1966– . Biweekly.

Focus on Zimbabwe. 1976– . Biweekly. (Formerly *Rhodesian commentary*) Both publications of the Rhodesian Ministry of Information, Immigration and Tourism, P.O. Box 8122, Causeway, Salisbury, Rhodesia.

The Zimbabwe herald. 1892– · Daily newspaper.
P.O. Box 396, Salisbury, Rhodesia. Available on microfilm 1956– from the Center for Research Libraries, Chicago, and 1927– from Microfile Ltd., Johannesburg.
Zimbabwe project news bulletin. 1980– . Monthly.
Zimbabwe Project, P.O. Box 4590, Salisbury, Zimbabwe.
Zimbabwe review. 1969– .
African National Council, Lusaka, Zambia. Available from LSM Information Center, P.O. Box 2077, Oakland, Calif. 94604. Also available on microfilm from the Cooperative Africana Microform Project, Center for Research Libraries, 5721 Cottage Grove Avenue, Chicago, Illinois 60637.

Suggestions for Further Reading

*Bowman, Larry W. *Politics in Rhodesia: white power in an African state.* Cambridge, Mass.: Harvard University Press, 1973. 206 p.
Catholic Commission for Justice and Peace in Rhodesia. *Civil war in Rhodesia: abduction, torture and death in the counter-insurgency campaign: a report.* Salisbury: 1976. 96 p.
————. *The man in the middle: torture, resettlement and eviction.* London: Catholic Institute for International Relations, 1975. 22 p.
Drums of war; the continuing crisis in Rhodesia. Edited by George M. Daniels. Foreword by William H. Booth. New York: The Third Press, 1974. 190 p.
Dumbutshena, Enoch. *Zimbabwe tragedy.* Nairobi: East African Publishing House, 1975. 138 p.
*Good, Robert C. *U.D.I.; the international politics of the Rhodesian rebellion.* London: Faber & Faber, 1973. 368 p.
*International Commission of Jurists. *Racial discrimination and repression in Southern Rhodesia: a legal study.* London: Catholic Institute for International Relations, 1976. 118 p.
Joyce, Peter. *Anatomy of a rebel; Smith of Rhodesia, a biography.* Salisbury: Graham, 1974. 480 p.
*Lake, Anthony. *The "Tar Baby" option: American policy towards southern Rhodesia.* New York: Columbia University Press, 1976. 316 p.
Let's build Zimbabwe together: ZIMCORD—conference documentation, conference on reconstruction and development, Salisbury, 23–27 March, 1981. Salisbury: Ministry of Economic Planning and Development, 1981. 111 p.
*Martin, David. *The struggle for Zimbabwe: the Chimurenga war.* London: Faber & Faber, 1981. 378 p.
Maxey, Kees. *The fight for Zimbabwe: the armed conflict in Southern Rhodesia since UDI.* London: Collings, 1975. 196 p.
Nkomo, Joshua. "The principles of unity and struggle in Zimbabwe." *Black scholar,* 9/5 (1978): 21–28.

O'Callaghan, Marion. *Southern Rhodesia: the effects of a conquest society on education, culture and information.* Paris: Unesco, 1977. 293 p.

*O'Meara, Patrick. *Rhodesia: racial conflict or coexistence?* Ithaca, N.Y.: Cornell University Press, 1975. 217 p.

Palley, Claire. *The constitutional history and law of Southern Rhodesia, 1888–1965, with special reference to imperial control.* Oxford: Clarendon Press, 1966. 872 p.

*Palmer, Robin. *Land and racial domination in Rhodesia.* Berkeley: University of California Press, 1977. 400 p.

Raeburn, Michael, ed. *Black fire! accounts of the guerrilla war in Rhodesia.* London: Julian Friedmann, 1978. 256 p.

*Ranger, Terence O. *The African voice in Southern Rhodesia, 1898–1930.* Evanston, Ill.: Northwestern University Press, 1970. 252 p.

Rhodesia: economic structure and change. G. M. E. Leistner, ed. Pretoria: Africa Institute of South Africa, 1976. 239 p.

Riddell, Roger C. *Report of the Commission of Inquiry into incomes, prices, and conditions of service under the chairmanship of Roger C. Riddell, June 1981.* Salisbury: The Government Printer, 1981. 330 p.

*Shamuyarira, Nathan M. *Crisis in Rhodesia.* London: Andre Deutsch, 1965. 240 p.

Sithole, Ndabaningi. *African nationalism.* 2d. ed. London: Oxford University Press, 1968. 196 p.

————. *Letters from Salisbury prison.* Nairobi: Transafrica Publishers, 1976. 186 p.

————. *Roots of a revolution: scenes from Zimbabwe's struggle.* Oxford and New York: Oxford University Press, 1977. 142 p.
    Fictionalized account.

Strack, Hary R. *Sanctions: the case of Rhodesia.* Syracuse, N.Y.: Syracuse University Press, 1978. 296 p.

Tjabavu, K., and K. Chabavu. *Zimbabwe, Rhodesia: guidelines to national liberation.* London: 1976. 25 p.

*Todd, Judith. *The right to say no.* New York: The Third Press, 1973. 204 p.

Utete, C. Munhamu B. *The road to Zimbabwe: the political economy of settler colonialism, national liberation, and foreign intervention.* Washington, D.C.: University Press of America, 1979. 170 p.

Weinrich, A.K.H. *Mucheke: race, status, and politics in a Rhodesian community.* New York: Holmes & Meier, 1976. 278 p.

————. *Women and racial discrimination in Rhodesia.* Paris: UNESCO, 1979. 143 p.

Wilkerson, Anthony R. "Political violence, counter-insurgency and change in Rhodesia." In: *Southern African research in progress.* Edited by C. Hill and P. Warwick. York: York University, 1975: 118–138.

Windrich, Elaine. *Britain and the politics of Rhodesian independence.* New York: Africana Pub. Co., 1978. 283 p.

South Africa

Bibliographies

The South African Institute of Race Relations (68 de Korte St., P.O. Box 97, Johannesburg 2000) has issued a number of bibliographies concerned with social, political, and economic trends in South Africa. Among them are: *The African homelands of South Africa*, by Hilary Chosack (1975): *Church and state relationships in South Africa*, by Jan Edwards (1974); *Migrant labour: a select bibliography*, by Jan Edwards (1974); *A select bibliography on the question of foreign investment in South Africa*, by Jan Edwards (1975); and *A select bibliography on the poverty datum line in South Africa*, by Jan Edwards and Dudley Horner (1974).

Evalds, Victoria K. "The 'Bantu Education' system." *A Current bibliography on African affairs*, n.s. 10/3 (1977–78): 219–242.

Greyling, J. J. C., and J. Miskin. *Bibliography on Indians in South Africa*. Durban: University of Durban-Westville, Institute for Social and Economic Research, 1976. 51 p.

Hattingh, P. S. *Bophuthatswana: a select and annotated bibliography*. Pretoria: Africa Institute, 1973. 32 p.

Kalley, Jacqueline A. *The Transkei Region of Southern Africa, 1877–1978: An Annotated Bibliography*. Boston: G.K. Hall, 1980. 218 p.

South African political materials: a catalogue of the Carter–Karis collection. Compiled by Susan G. Wynne. Bloomington: Southern African Research Archives Project, 1977. 811 p. Distributed by Indiana University Press, Bloomington.

Index to a massive collection which includes correspondence, interviews, ephemera, and some published reports related to African politics. The collection has been microfilmed and with some exceptions may be purchased or borrowed from the Cooperative Africana Microform Project (CAMP) of the Center for Research Libraries, 5721 S. Cottage Grove Avenue, Chicago, Illinois 60637.

U.N. Dept. of Political and Security Council Affairs. Unit on Apartheid. "Selective bibliography on apartheid." *Notes and documents* series 10/74, May 1974. 14 p.

Covers 1970–73; supplements: *Apartheid: a selective bibliography on the racial policies of the Republic of South Africa*. (U.N. document ST/LIB/22/rev. 1) 1970.

Reference and Documentary Sources

*Black review. 1972– . Durban, South Africa: Black Community Programmes, 1973– . Annual.

"Black effort to present goings-on in the Black community . . ."; information on government action and opposition, black organizations, social and economic matters.

From protest to challenge; a documentary history of African politics in South Africa, 1882–1964. Edited by Thomas Karis and Gwendolen M. Carter. Stanford, Calif.: Hoover Institution Press, 1972–77. 4 v.

History of African political struggle, with selected documents from the Carter–Karis collection (see *South African political materials . . .*, above). Vol. 4, "Political profiles, 1882–1964," by Gail M. Gerhart and Thomas Karis, consists of 333 biographical sketches of persons of all races involved in African political activity.

Kaplan, Irving. *Area handbook for the Republic of South Africa.* Washington, D.C.: Foreign Area Studies, American University, 1971. 845 p. Distributed by Government Printing Office.

South Africa: official yearbook of the Republic of South Africa. 1974– . Pretoria: 1975– .

General reference work prepared by the South African government.

A survey of race relations in South Africa. 1953/54– . Johannesburg: South African Institute of Race Relations. Annual.

Summary review of developments and trends of the year in such areas as politics, economics, education, sports, legislation, government action, the opposition, etc.; statistical information and bibliography.

U.N. Dept. of Political Affairs, Trusteeship and Decolonization. Centre against Apartheid (formerly Dept. of Political and Security Council Affairs. Unit on Apartheid). *Notes and documents* series, 1969– .

Voluminous materials: reprints of unpublished papers, documents, and reports, biographical material, etc.

Periodicals

The African communist. 1962– . Quarterly.
Inkululeko Publications, 39 Goodge St., London W1, England.

The African nationalist. 1977– . Monthly?
African National Congress of South Africa, P.O. Box 20894, Dar es Salaam, Tanzania.

Azania news: official organ of the Pan Africanist Congress of Azania. 1966– . Irreg.
P.O. Box 2412, Dar es Salaam, Tanzania.

Ikweci: a journal of South African and Southern African political analysis. 1975– . 8–N Victoria Centre, Nottingham, England.

Optima. 1951– . Quarterly.
Anglo American Corporation Group, 44 Main St., Johannesburg 2000. Available from P.O. Box 28, Toronto—Dominion Centre, Toronto 111, Ontario M5K 1B8, Canada.

Reality: a journal of liberal and radical opinion. 1969– . Bimonthly.
P.O. Box 1104, Pietermaritzburg 2000, South Africa.

Sechaba. 1967– . Quarterly.

African National Congress of South Africa, 49 Rathbone St., London WiA 4NL, England. Available from LSM Information Center, P.O. Box 2077, Oakland, Calif. 94604.

Social dynamics. 1975– . 2 times a yr.
  Dept. of Sociology, University of Cape Town, Rondebosch 7700, South Africa.

*_South Africa/Namibia update._ 1977– . Biweekly.
  Africa Policy Information Center, African American Institute, 833 U.N. Plaza, New York, N.Y. 10017.

South African international. 1970– . Quarterly.
  South Africa Foundation, P.O. Box 7006, Johannesburg. Available from South Africa Foundation, Suite 300, 1925 K St. N.W., Washington, D.C.

South African journal of economics. 1933– . Quarterly.
  The Economic Society of South Africa, P.O. Box 929, Pretoria 0001.

*_South African outlook._ 1870– . Monthly.
  Outlook Publications (Pty.) Ltd., P.O. Box 245, Rondebosch 7700, South Africa.

*_South African pressclips._ 1978– . Weekly.
  P.O. Box 84, Houtbaai 7872, South Africa.

The following periodicals, published by the South African Dept. of Information, reflect government policies and propaganda. They may be requested from: The Deputy Consul-General (Information), South African Consulate General, 425 Park Ave., New York, N.Y. 10022.

Bantu. 1954– .
South African digest. 1954?– .
South African panorama. 1956– .

Newspapers

The Cape times. 1876– .
  77 Burg St., P.O. Box 11, Cape Town 8000.
The Daily news (Durban). 1936– .
  85 Field St., P.O. Box 1491, Durban 4001.
The nation. 1977– . Monthly newspaper of Inkatha.
  Isizwe-Sechaba (Pty.) Ltd., Box 31134, Braamfontein 2017, South Africa.
Rand daily mail. 1902– .
  171 Main St., P.O. Box 1138, Johannesburg 2000.
The Star. 1887– .
  47 Sauer St., P.O. Box 1014, Johannesburg 2000.

Suggestions for Further Reading

*Adam, Heribert. *Modernizing racial domination: South Africa's political dynamics.* Berkeley: University of California Press, 1971. 203 p.

*Adam, Heribert and Herman Giliomee. *Ethnic power mobilized*. New Haven: Yale University Press, 1979. 308 p.

African perspectives on South Africa: a collection of speeches, articles and documents. Edited by H. W. Van der Merwe, Nancy C. J. Charton, D. A. Kotze and Ake Magnusson. Cape Town: David Philip; Stanford, Calif.: Hoover Institution Press, 1978. 612 p.

The apartheid regime: political power and racial domination. Edited by Robert M. Price and Carl G. Rosberg. Berkeley: Institute of International Studies, University of California, 1980. 376 p.

*Benson, Mary. *South Africa: the struggle for a birthright*. Harmondsworth: Penguin, 1969. 314 p.

*Biko, B.S. *I write what I like*. London: Bowerdean Press, 1978. 216 p.

Black Renaissance Convention, 1974. *Black Renaissance: papers from the Black Renaissance Convention, December 1974*. Editor, Thoahlane Thoahlane. Johannesburg: Ravan Press, 1975. 75 p.

Black theology: the South African voice. Compiled by Basil Moore. London: Hurst, 1973. 156 p.

Brotz, Howard. *The politics of South Africa: democracy and racial diversity*. Oxford and New York: Oxford University Press, 1977. 164 p.

*Carter, Gwendolen M. *The politics of inequality: South Africa since 1948*. New York: Praeger, 1958–59. 535 p.

*_____. *Which way is South Africa going?* Bloomington: Indiana University Press, 1980. 162 p.

Change in contemporary South Africa. Edited by Leonard Thompson and Jeffrey Butler. Berkeley: University of California Press, 1975. 447 p.

Change, reform and economic growth in South Africa. Editors, Lawrence Schlemmer and Eddie Webster. Johannesburg: Ravan Press, 1978. 244 p.

Conference on Constitutional Models and Constitutional Change in South Africa, University of Natal, 1978. *Constitutional change in South Africa: proceedings*. Edited by John Benyon. Pietermaritzburg: University of Natal Press, 1978. 297 p.

Conflict and compromise in South Africa. Edited by Robert I. Rotberg and John Barratt. Lexington, Mass.: Lexington Books, 1980. 212 p.

Counter Information Services. *Black South Africa explodes*. Washington: Transnational Institute, 1977. 63 p.

*de Klerk, W. A. *The Puritans in Africa: a story of Afrikanerdom*. London: Collings, 1975. 376 p.

*De St. Jorre, John. *A house divided: South Africa's divided future*. New York: Carnegie Endowment for International Peace, 1977. 136 p.

Dugard, C. J. R. *Human rights and the South African legal order*. Princeton: Princeton University Press, 1978. 470 p.

*DuToit, Darcy. *Capital and labour in South Africa: class struggles in the 1970s*. London: Kegan Paul, 1981. 495 p.

Feit, Edward. *Urban revolt in South Africa, 1960–1964; a case study.* Evanston: Northwestern University Press, 1971. 365 p.

First, Ruth and Ann Scott. *Olive Schreiner.* London: Deutsch, 1980. 383 p.

*Gann, Lewis H. and Peter Duignan. *Why South Africa will survive.* New York: St. Martin's Press, 1981. 312 p.

*Gerhart, Gail M. *Black power in South Africa: the evolution of an ideology.* Berkeley: University of California Press, 1978, 364 p.

*Greenberg, Stanley B. *Race and state in capitalist development: comparative perspectives.* New Haven: Yale University Press, 1980. 489 p.

Heard, Kenneth A. *General elections in South Africa, 1943–1970.* London and New York: Oxford University Press, 1974. 269 p.

Hirson, Baruch. *Year of fire, year of ash: Soweto revolt, roots of a revolution.* London: Zed Press, 1979. 343 p.

Hoagland, Jim. *South Africa: civilizations in conflict.* Boston: Houghton Mifflin, 1972. 428 p.

*Houghton, D. Hobart. *The South African economy.* 4th ed. Cape Town and New York: Oxford University Press, 1976. 310 p.

Hugo, Pierre J. *Quislings or realists? a documentary study of "coloured" politics in South Africa.* Johannesburg: Ravan Press, 1978. 744 p.

Johnson, Richard W. *How long will South Africa survive?* London: Macmillan, 1977. 327 p.

Kane-Berman, John S. *Soweto: black revolt, white reaction.* Johannesburg: Ravan Press, 1978. 268 p.

Kuper, Leo. *An African bourgeoisie: race, class and politics in South Africa.* New Haven: Yale University Press, 1965. 452 p.

Labour perspectives on South Africa. Edited by Wolfgang H. Thomas. Cape Town: David Philip, 1974. 259 p.

Lapchick, Richard E. *The politics of race and international sport: the case of South Africa.* Westport, Conn.: Greenwood Press, 1975. 268 p.

Lever, Henry. *South African society.* Johannesburg: Jonathan Ball, 1978. 312 p. Accompanied by: *Readings in South Africa society.* Edited by Henry Lever. Johannesburg: Jonathan Ball.

Lewin, Hugh. *Bandiet:seven years in a South African prison.* London: Barrie & Jenkins, 1974. 223 p.

Luthuli, Albert. *Let my people go: an autobiography.* New York: McGraw Hill, 1962. 255 p.

Makgetla, Neva and Ann W. Seidman. *Outposts of monopoly capitalism: Southern Africa in the changing global economy.* Westport, Conn.: L. Hill, 1980. 370 p.

Moodie, T. Dunbar. *The rise of Afrikanerdom: power, apartheid, and the Afrikaner civil religion.* Berkeley: University of California Press, 1975. 328 p.

*Munger, Edwin S. *The Afrikaners.* Cape Town: Tafelburg, 1979. 183 p.

Myers, Desaix. *Labor practices of U.S. corporations in South Africa.* New York: Praeger, 1977. 123 p.

Nolutshungu, Sam C. *South Africa: a study of ideology and foreign policy.* New York: Africana Pub. Co., 1975. 329 p.

Perspectives on South Africa: a collection of working papers. T. Adler, ed. Johannesburg: African Studies Institute, University of the Witwatersrand, 1977. 366 p.

Race relations in South Africa, 1929–1979. Edited by Ellen Hellman and Henry Lever. New York: St. Martin's Press, 1980. 278 p.

Robertson, Janet M. *Liberalism in South Africa, 1948–1963.* Oxford: Clarendon Press, 1971. 252 p.

*Roux, Edward. *Time longer than rope: a history of the black man's struggle for freedom in South Africa.* 2d. ed. Madison: University of Wisconsin Press, 1964. 469 p.

Sachs, Albie. *Justice in South Africa.* Berkeley: University of California Press, 1973. 288 p.

Seidman, Ann W., and Neva Seidman. *South Africa and U.S. multinational corporations.* Westport, Conn.: Lawrence Hill, 1978. 251 p.

Shepherd, George W. *Anti-apartheid: transnational conflict and western policy in the liberation of South Africa.* Westport, Conn.: Greenwood Press, 1977. 246 p.

Sikakane, Joyce. *A window on Soweto.* London: International Defense & Aid Fund, 1977. 79 p.

*Simons, H. J., and R. E. Simons. *Class and colour in South Africa, 1850–1950.* Harmondsworth: Penguin, 1969. 702 p.

South Africa: the prospects of peaceful change. Edited by Theodor Hanf et al. Bloomington: Indiana University Press, 1981. 492 p.

South African dialogue: contrasts in South African thinking on basic race issues. Edited by N. J. Rhoodie. Johannesburg and New York: McGraw Hill, 1972. 611 p.

Student perspectives on South Africa. Edited by H. W. Van der Merwe and David Welsh. Cape Town: David Philip, 1972. 229 p.

*Study Commission on United States Policy toward Southern Africa. *South Africa: time running out.* Berkeley: University of California Press, 1981. 517 p.

Stultz, Newell M. *Afrikaner politics in South Africa, 1934–1948.* Berkeley: University of California Press, 1974. 200 p.

*Thomas, W. H., et al. *The conditions of the black worker.* London: Africa Publications Trust, 1975. 289 p. (Available from the African-American Institute, 833 U.N. Plaza, New York, N.Y., 10017)

Turfloop testimony: the dilemma of a black university in South Africa. Edited by G. M. Nkondo. Johannesburg: Ravan Press, 1976. 93 p.

*Van Zyl Slabbert, Frederick and David Welsh. *South Africa's options: strategies for sharing power.* New York: St. Martin's Press, 1979. 196 p.

*Walshe, A. P. *The rise of African nationalism in South Africa: the African National Congress, 1912–1952.* Berkeley: University of California Press, 1971. 480 p.

Wilson, Frances. *Labour in the South African gold mines, 1911–1969.* Cambridge: Cambridge University Press, 1972. 218 p.

*————. *Migrant labour: report to the South African Council of Churches.* Johannesburg: South African Council of Churches and SPRO-CAS, 1972. 281 p.

Woods, Donald. *Asking for trouble: the autobiography of a banned journalist.* New York: Atheneum, 1981. 373 p.

————. *Biko.* New York: Paddington Press, 1978. 288 p.

The Homelands

*Butler, Jeffrey, Robert I. Rotberg, and John Adams. *The black homelands of South Africa: the political and economic development of Bophuthatswana and Kwazulu.* Berkeley: University of California Press, 1977. 250 p.

*Carter, Gwendolen M., Thomas Karis, and Newell M. Stultz. *South Africa's Transkei: the politics of domestic colonialism.* Evanston: Northwestern University Press, 1967. 200 p.

Namibia

Periodicals

Namibia bulletin. 1977– . Irreg.
U.N. Commissioner for Namibia, U.N. Headquarters, Room 3264, New York, N.Y. 10017.

Namibia today. 1977–
South West Africa People's Organisation (SWAPO), P.O. Box 577, Lusaka, Zambia. Available from LSM Information Center, P.O. Box 2077, Oakland, Calif. 94604.

South Africa/Namibia update. 1977– . Biweekly.
Africa Policy Information Center, African American Institute, 833 U.N. Plaza, New York, N.Y. 10017.

Suggestions for Further Reading

Crocker, Chester A. *Namibia at the crossroads: economic and political prospects.* Washington, D.C.: Center for Strategic and International Studies, Georgetown University, 1978. 55 p.

First, Ruth. *South West Africa.* Baltimore: Penguin, 1963. 269 p.

*Fraenkel, Peter. *The Namibians of South West Africa*. London: Minority Rights Group, 1974. 48 p.

*Green, Reginald H. *Namibia: the last colony*. London: Longman's, forthcoming, 1981.

*International Defense and Aid Fund. *All options and none: the constitutional talks in Namibia*. London: 1976.

Kerina, Mburumba. *Namibia: making of a nation*. New York: Books in Focus, 1981. 314 p.

Landis, Elizabeth. "Human rights in Namibia." *Human rights journal*, 9 (1976).

Segal, Ronald, and Ruth First, eds. *South West Africa: travesty of trust*. London: Andre Deutsch, 1967. 352 p.

Serfontein, J. H. P. *Namibia?* Randburg, South Africa: Fokus Suid Publishers, 1976. 433 p.

South Africa. *Report of the Commission of enquiry into South West African affairs, 1962–63*. Pretoria: 1964. R.P. no. 12, 1964. "The Odenaal report."

The South West Africa/Namibia dispute: documents and scholarly writings on the controversy between South Africa and the United Nations. Edited by C. J. R. Dugard. Berkeley: University of California Press, 1973. 585 p.

U.N. Office of Public Information. *A trust betrayed: Namibia*. New York: 1974. 43 p.

Wellington, J. H. *South West Africa and its human issues*. London: Oxford University Press, 1967. 461 p.

Winter, Colin O. *Namibia*. Grand Rapids, Mich.: Eerdmann, 1977. 234 p.

BLS Countries

Reference

Each title in this series includes an extensive bibliography:

Grotpeter, John J. *Historical dictionary of Swaziland*. (African historical dictionaries, no. 3) Metuchen, N.J.: Scarecrow Press, 1975. 251 p. Bib.: 195–243.

Haliburton, Gordon M. *Historical dictionary of Lesotho*. (African historical dictionaries, no. 10) Metuchen, N.J.: Scarecrow Press, 1977. 223 p. Bib.: 185–223.

Stevens, Richard P. *Historical dictionary of the Republic of Botswana*. (African historical dictionaries, no. 5) Metuchen, N.J.: Scarecrow Press, 1975. 189 p. Bib.: 155–189.

Periodicals and Newspapers

Botswana notes and records. 1968– . Annual.
    Botswana Society, Private Bag 31, Gaborone, Botswana.

Daily news. 1969– . Newspaper.
    P.O. Box 51, Gaborone, Botswana.
Kutlwano. 1961– . Monthly.
    Information Services, P.O. Box 51, Gaborone, Botswana.

Suggestions for Further Reading

Cervenka, Zdenek. *Landlocked countries of Africa.* Uppsala: Scandinavian In-
    stitute of African Studies, 1973. 368 p.
*Selwyn, Percy. *Industries in the Southern African periphery: a study of in-
    dustrial development in Botswana, Lesotho and Swaziland.* Boulder, Colo.:
    Westview Pres, 1976. 156 p.
Stevens, Richard P. *Botswana, Lesotho and Swaziland: the history of the for-
    mer High Commission Territories.* London: Pall Mall, 1967. 294 p.

Botswana

*Benson, Mary. *Tshekedi Khama.* London: Faber & Faber, 1960. 318 p.
From the Front Line: speeches of Sir Seretse Khama. Edited by Gwendolen
    M. Carter and E. Philip Morgan. London: Rex Collings, 1980. 339 p.
*Hartland-Thunberg, Penelope. *Botswana: an African growth economy.*
    Boulder, Col.: Westview Press, 1978.
Sillery, Anthony. *Botswana: a short political history.* London: Methuen, 1974,
    219 p.
Smit, P. *Botswana: resources and development.* Pretoria: Africa Institute,
    1970. 256 p.
Van Rensburg, Patrick. *Report from Swaneng Hill; education and employ-
    ment in an African country.* Stockholm: Almqvist & Wiksell [for] the Dag
    Hammarskjöld Foundation, 1974. 235 p.
Vengroff, Richard. *Botswana, rural development in the shadow of apartheid.*
    Rutherford, N.J.: Fairleigh Dickinson University Press, 1977. 205 p.

Lesotho

Breytenbach, W. J. *Crocodiles and commoners in Lesotho: continuity and
    change in the rulemaking system of the Kingdom of Lesotho.* Pretoria:
    Africa Institute, 1975. 136 p.
Hamnett, Ian. *Chieftaincy and legitimacy: an anthropological study of exec-
    utive law in Lesotho.* Boston: Routledge & Kegan Paul, 1975. 163 p.
*Khaketla, B. Makalo. *Lesotho, 1970: an African coup under the microscope.*
    Berkeley: University of California Press, 1972. 350 p.
Spence, John E. *Lesotho: the politics of independence.* London and New York:
    Published for the Institute of Race Relations by Oxford University Press,
    1968. 88 p.
*Ström, Gabrielle W. *Development and dependence in Lesotho, the enclave*

of South Africa. Uppsala: Scandinavian Institute of African Studies, 1978.
186 p.
*Thompson, Leonard M. *Survival in two worlds: Moshoeshoe of Lesotho,
1786–1870.* New York: Oxford University Press, 1975. 389 p.
*Weisfelder, Richard F. *The Basuto monarchy: a spent force or a dynamic
political factor?* (Papers in international studies: African series, no. 16)
Athens, Ohio: Ohio University, Center for International Studies, 1972.
97 p.

Swaziland
*Kuper, Hilda. *Sobhuza II: Ngwenyama and the king of Swaziland.* London:
Duckworth, 1978. 500 p.
Matsebula, J. S. M. *A history of Swaziland.* 2d. ed. Cape Town: Longman
Penguin Southern Africa, 1976. 131 p.
*Potholm, Christian P. *Swaziland, the dynamics of political modernization.*
Berkeley: University of California Press, 1972. 183 p.

Lusophone Southern Africa: Angola and Mozambique

Bibliographies

Chilcote, Ronald H. *Emerging nationalism in Portuguese Africa; a bibliog-
raphy of documentary ephemera through 1965.* Stanford, Calif.: Hoover
Institution, 1969. 114 p.
Enevoldsen, Thyge. *A political, economic and social bibliography on Mo-
cambique with main emphasis on the period 1965–1978.* Copenhagen:
Centre for Development Research, 1978. 60 p.
Flores, Michel. "A bibliographic contribution to the study of Portuguese
Africa (1965–1972)." *Current bibliography on African affairs,* n.s. 7/2
(1974): 116–137.
Henderson, Robert d'A. "Portuguese Africa: materials in English and in
translation." *African research & documentation,* no. 11 (1976): 20–24; no.
12 (1977): 15–19.

Reference and Documents

Chilcote, Ronald H., comp. *Emerging nationalism in Portuguese Africa: doc-
uments.* Stanford, Calif.: Hoover Institution Press, Stanford University,
1972. 646 p.
Kaplan, Irving. *Area handbook for Mozambique.* 2d. ed. Washington, D.C.:
Foreign Area Studies, American University, 1977. 240 p. Distributed by
Government Printing Office.
————. *Angola, a country study.* Washington, D.C.: Foreign Area Studies,
American University, 1979. 286 p. Distributed by Government Printing
Office.

*Martin, Phyllis. *Historical dictionary of Angola*. Metuchen, N.J.: Scarecrow Press, 1980. 1974 p. (African historical dictionary no. 26.)

Portuguese Africa; a handbook. Edited by David M. Abshire and Michael A. Samuels. New York: Published in cooperation with the Center for Strategic and International Studies, Georgetown University, by Praeger, 1969. 480 p.

Periodicals

Angola in arms. 1967–1974. Irreg.
People's Movement for the Liberation of Angola, Dar es Salaam, Tanzania.

Agêncía de Informaçâo de Moçambique. *AIM information bulletin, 1978–* .
Monthly. Available from Mozambique Information Agency, P.O. Box 896, Maputo, Mozambique.

Mozambique revolution. 1963–1975. Irreg.
Mozambique Liberation Front (FRELIMO) Information Dept., Dar es Salaam, Tanzania.

    Back issues of the above titles are available from the LSM Information Center, P.O. Box 2077, Oakland, Calif. 94604, and on microfilm from the Cooperative Africana Microfilm Project, Center for Research Libraries, Chicago.

Peoples power in Mozambique, Angola and Guiné Bissau. 1976– .
Mozambique, Angola and Guiné Information Centre, 34 Percy St., London WP9 FG, Eng.

Earlier issues of *Facts and reports* (see above) were concerned chiefly with Portuguese Africa.

Suggestions for Further Reading

Ferreira, Eduardo de Sousa. *Portuguese colonialism in Africa: the end of an era: the effects of Portuguese colonialism on education, science, culture and information.* Paris: Unesco Press, 1967. 170 p.

Humbaraci, Arslan, and Nicole Muchnik. *Portugal's African wars: Angola, Guinea Bassao, Mozambique.* London, New York: Macmillan, 1974. 250 p.

Minter, William. *Portuguese Africa and the West.* New York: Monthly Review Press, 1974. 200 p.

Southern Africa since the Portuguese coup. Edited by John Seiler. Boulder, Col.: Westview Press, 1980.

Angola

Barnett, Don, and Roy Harvey. *The revolution in Angola: MPLA life histories and documents.* Indianapolis: Bobbs-Merrill, 1972. 312 p.

*Bender, Gerald. *Angola under the Portuguese: the myth and the reality.* London: Heinemann Educational, 1978. 256 p.

*Davidson, Basil. *In the eye of the storm; Angola's people.* New York: Doubleday, 1972. 367 p.

Gjerstad, Ole. *The people in power: an account from Angola's second war of national liberation.* Oakland, Calif.: LSM Information Center, 1975. 108 p.

Harsch, Ernest, and Tony Thomas. *Angola: the hidden history of Washington's war.* New York: Pathfinder Press, 1967. 157 p.

Heimer, Franz-Wilhelm, ed. *Social change in Angola.* München: Weltforum Verlag, 1973. 284 p.

*Henderson, Lawrence W. *Angola, five centuries of conflict.* Ithaca: Cornell University Press, 1979. 272 p.

Houser, George, et al. *No one can stop the rain: Angola and the MPLA.* New York: Africa Fund, 1976. 45 p.

Klinghoffer, Arthur J. *The Angolan war: a study in Soviet policy in the Third World.* Boulder, Col.: Westview Press, 1980. 229 p.

*Marcum, John. *The Angolan revolution.* Cambridge: MIT Press, 1969–78. 2 v. Vol. I: *The anatomy of an explosion (1950–1962).* 1969. Vol. II: *Exile politics and guerrilla warfare, 1962–1976.* 1978.

Movimento Popular de Libertacao de Angola. *Road to Liberation: MPLA documents on the founding of the People's Republic of Angola.* Richmond, B.C.: LSM Information Center, 1976. 53 p.

Stockwell, John. *In search of enemies.* New York: Norton, 1978. 285 p.

*Wheeler, Douglas, and René Pelissier. *Angola.* New York: Praeger, 1971. 296 p.

Mozambique

Alpers, Edward, Allen Isaacman, and Alan Smith. *A history of Mozambique.* London: Heinemann. Forthcoming.

*Henriksen, Thomas H. *Mozambique: a history.* London: Rex Collings, 1978. 276 p.

Houser, George M., and Herb Shore. *Mozambique; dream the size of freedom.* New York: Africa Fund, 1975. 68 p.

*Isaacman, Allen F., and Barbara Isaacman. *The tradition of resistance in Mozambique: anti-colonial activity in the Zambesi valley, 1850–1921.* London: Heinemann, 1976. 232 p.

*Machel, Samora. *Mozambique: sowing the seeds of revolution.* London: Committee for Freedom in Mozambique, Angola and Guiné, 1975. 68 p.

*Mondlane, Eduardo. *The struggle for Mozambique.* Harmondsworth: Penguin, 1969. 222 p.

*Paul, John. *Mozambique: memoirs of a revolution.* Harmondsworth: Penguin, 1975. 232 p.

*Saul, John S. *The state and revolution in Eastern Africa.* New York: Monthly Review Press, 1979. 454 p.

Vail, Leroy and Landeg White. *Capitalism and colonialism in Mozambique: a study of Quelimane District.* Minneapolis: University of Minnesota Press, 1980. 419 p.

Glossary of Acronyms
Selected African Currency Rates
Population Distribution

Glossary of Acronyms

ANGOLA
FLEC	Front for the Liberation of the Enclave of Cabinda
FNLA	National Front for the Liberation of Angola
MPLA	People's Movement for the Liberation of Angola
PRA	People's Republic of Angola
UNITA	Union for the Total Independence of Angola

BOTSWANA
BDP	Botswana Democratic Party
BIP	Botswana Independence Party
BNF	Botswana National Front
BPP	Botswana People's Party

LESOTHO
BNP	(Basotho) National Party
BCP	(Basotho) Congress Party
MFP	Marematlou Freedom Party
UDP	United Democratic Party

NAMIBIA
DTA	Democratic Turnhalle Alliance
NCN	National Convention of Namibia
NNC	Namibian National Council (successor to Namibian National Convention)
SWANU	South West African National Union
SWAPO	South West African People's Organization

SOUTH AFRICA

ANC	African National Congress of South Africa
AZAPO	Azania People's Organization
BAWU	Black Allied Workers Union
BPC	Black People's Convention
FOFATUSA	Federation of Free African Trade Unions of South Africa
NUSAS	National Union of South African Students
PAC	Pan Africanist Congress
RSA	Republic of South Africa
SACTU	South African Congress of Trade Unions
SASO	South African Students Organization
TUCSA	Trade Union Council of South Africa

SWAZILAND

DSP	Swaziland Democratic Party
NNLC	Ngwane National Liberatory Congress
SPP	Swaziland Progressive Party

ZIMBABWE

ANC	African National Congress of Rhodesia (founded in 1957)
FROLIZI	Front for the Liberation of Zimbabwe
NDP	National Democratic Party
RF	Rhodesian Front
UANC	United African National Council (founded in 1974 by Muzorewa)
UDI	Unilateral Declaration of Independence (signed Nov. 11, 1965)
ZANLA	Zimbabwean National Liberation Army
ZANU	Zimbabwean African National Union
ZAPU	Zimbabwean African People's Union
ZIPA	Zimbabwe People's Army (combined forces organization)
ZIPRA	Zimbabwe People's Army
ZLC	Zimbabwe Liberation Council
ZUPO	Zimbabwe United People's Organization

OTHER

BLS	Botswana, Lesotho, and Swaziland
EEC	European Economic Community (or Common Market)
FRELIMO	Mozambique Liberation Front
OAU	Organization of African Unity
UNIP	United National Independence Party (of Zambia)

Selected African Currency Rates*

Country	Rate per dollar	Name of Currency
Angola	.0325	Kwanza
Botswana	1.2150	Pula
Kenya	.1110	Kenya Shilling
Lesotho	1.0380	South African Rand
Mozambique	.0350	Mozambique Escudo
Nigeria	1.5770	Naira

South Africa	1.0380	Rand
Swaziland	1.0380	Lilangeni (plural: Emalengeni)
Tanzania	.1240	Shilling
Zaïre	.1850	Zaïre
Zambia	1.2300	Kwacha
Zimbabwe	1.5025	Rhodesian Dollar

* Rates quoted as of 31 December 1981 from Chase Manhattan Bank, New York.

Population Distribution

Angola 7,100,000 (est. 1980)

Botswana 791,000 (est. 31 Aug. 1979)

Lesotho 1,279,000 (est. mid-1978)

Mozambique 11,750,000 (est. 1979)

Namibia 989,100 (est. 1980 based on 1970 census)*

South Africa 24,091,000 (est. June 1979, excl. "homelands" granted "independence." Also excl. Venda.)

Swaziland 530,000 (est. 1 July 1979)

Zambia 5,834,000 (est. mid-1980)

Zimbabwe 7,360,000 (est. mid-1980)

* Office of U.N. Commissioner for Namibia—1,200,000 (est. 1974).

Source: Africa South of the Sahara 1981–82, 11th ed., Europa Publications Ltd., Martins Publishing Group, 18 Bedford Square, London WC1 3JN.

NOTES

2. Zimbabwe

1. *Zimbabwe Herald,* April 18, 1980.
2. Ibid.

3. Mozambique

1. It consisted of the members of the Frelimo Central Committee and Executive Committee, the ministers and vice-ministers of the government, the provincial governors, military leaders chosen by Frelimo, two representatives from each province chosen by Frelimo, members of Frelimo chosen by the Central Committee, and "a maximum of ten reputable citizens chosen by the Central Committee of Frelimo." The first nationwide elections were held at the end of 1977.

2. In the cities universal suffrage was used at the local level to elect delegates to city-wide electoral colleges, which then met to elect the members of the city assemblies. So, in Maputo the 71 deputies of the capital's city assembly were selected on November 27 at a meeting of the 820 locally elected delegates to the Maputo electoral college.

4. South Africa

1. *Africa News,* May 8, 1978.
2. R. W. Johnson, *How Long Will South Africa Survive?* New York, Oxford University Press, 1977, p. 31.
3. The *Star,* April 15, 1978, p. 8.
4. Ibid., June 3, 1978, p. 3.
5. *The Conditions of the Black Worker,* London, Africa Publication Trust, 1975, p. 187.
6. *The New York Times,* May 25, 1978, p. 2.
7. Among Inkatha leaders mentioned in *Africa Confidential* (February 3, 1978, pp. 6–7) are Mrs. Willel Yengwa, who is related to ANC president Nelson Mandela, a Xhosa, and David Thebehali, current mayor of Soweto, who is a southern Sotho. Among prominent and widely trusted Zulus are Bishop Zulu, Professor Bengu, and others from the University of Zululand.
8. The Arnold Bergstrasser Institute for Socio-Political Research of West Germany, which held an important conference in Germany in June 1978 on Peaceful Change in South Africa, commissioned a market-research firm to do a study of urban blacks. In 1977 the firm IMSA approached 1,000 blacks in Johannesburg,

Durban, and Pretoria and among its conclusions found that Buthelezi had not only overwhelming support among the Zulus but also approximately 40 percent support among other groups. The *Star,* international airmail weekly, June 17, 1978, p. 8, and pp. 10–11.

9. See debate between Welsh and Thula printed in *Race Relations News,* April 1978, p. 2.

10. In a speech in Holland to a body that promotes closer ties between the Afrikaner and Dutch peoples. The *Star,* May 20, 1978, p. 9.

11. David Welsh, "The Politics of Conflict Negotiation in South Africa," *Optima,* 1977, no. 3, pp. 18–33.

12. The *Star,* June 10, 1978, p. 2.

13. *Newsweek,* October 25, 1976, pp. 53–54.

14. An interesting plan for Natal is outlined in Paul N. Malherbe, *Multistan: A Way Out of the South African Dilemma* (Cape Town: David Philip, 1974).

15. *A Survey of Race Relations,* Johannesburg: South African Institute of Race Relations, 1980, p. 8.

16. Ibid.

17. London: Rex Collings, 1975.

5. Namibia

1. References to the ICJ judgment can be found in the *Human Rights Journal* issue on the Dakar International Conference, Volume IX, Sec. 2–3, 1976.

2. The British observer was Jo Herbertson, *The Observer,* April 7, 1974.

3. The General Assembly resolution declaring SWAPO the sole representative of the Namibian people is printed in the U.N. "Namibia Bulletin Special Issue."

4. The Decree of the U.N. on Namibia is printed on page 465 of the *Human Rights Journal.*

5. For the SWAPO draft constitution, see *Human Rights Journal,* pp. 392ff.

6. The constitution provided for a central government consisting of a president, a Ministers Council, a National Assembly, and a judicial authority called the Supreme Court of the Republic of SWA/Namibia. The president was to be appointed by the South African state president and, according to the constitution, would represent the governments of both the Republic of South Africa and the Republic of SWA/Namibia. He would exercise powers and functions on the advice of and with the permission of the Executive Council of the Republic of South Africa or the Ministers Council of Namibia set up under the constitution.

The Ministers Council would be composed of a leader chosen by the National Assembly as a whole, and members chosen by population groups represented in the National Assembly, one minister for each group.

The Legislative Assembly was to consist of members chosen by each of the eleven population groups. The National Assembly was to consist of sixty members, with each of eleven population groups having at least four members and the remaining sixteen to be distributed according to the figures for the 1970 census. It will be noted that no provision was made for election to the National Assembly, and the entire structure was based on the existing segregated ethnic groups and representative authorities—in effect, the existing Bantustans. South African control over the president was manifest from provisions already quoted. The National Assembly was to hold office for the duration of what was described as the "interim government," although when that government would terminate was not made explicit. Furthermore, during the term of the interim government crucial legislative and executive powers would be retained by the South African

Parliament and government, including defense, external affairs, internal security, communications, customs, and finance. The National Assembly was to control emigration, registration of companies, roads, power, energy, registration of prisons, population, education, public works, courts at the High Court level, registration of deeds, and civil defense, inter alia. Local powers, including "judicial administration of justice," were granted to representative authorities. (The representative authorities were to rule over members of their population groups rather than over the inhabitants of areas where they had jurisdiction.)

The constitution contained a chapter headed "Protection of Fundamental Rights," which significantly did not specify any of the usually recognized fundamental human and civil rights: for example, freedom from torture, freedom from arbitrary arrest, right to an impartial judiciary, right of privacy, and freedom to exercise a full and democratic franchise. The salient "fundamental right" placed first in the listing was a guarantee of the "rights of every population group, whether a minority or a majority group." This evidently was to entrench the existing ethnic and separatist system. It is evident that the protection of the white group was a paramount consideration. The right of personality was provided for but was hedged with a proviso that it would not infringe on "the rights of others or conflict with public order and morals." Similarly, physical inviolability of the person "may only be assailed by virtue of a legal directive." The right to free expression of opinion was granted, but again with a qualification that it not infringe the rights of others or harm the state. A particularly curious "fundamental right" regarded the press, whose freedom was guaranteed but was to be restricted "by general legal provisions, the protection of the State, youth and personal honor and prestige." Ownership of private property was guaranteed. The right to hold meetings and establish political parties was also explicitly provided for, with the prohibition, however, of "parties or groupings with Marxist, Leninist, or Maoist ideologies." The constitution also provided for a constitutional court with advisory powers on legislation and restricted access to a negative form of procedure.

The qualifications for members of the National Assembly significantly provided that only persons resident in Namibia for the preceding five years could be eligible, which would rule out almost all politically active exiles or members of SWAPO abroad. Under the judicial authority, the Appellate Division of South Africa was to remain as the Supreme Appellate Court until such time as the National Assembly provided otherwise.

The judges of the Supreme Court of South West Africa were to be appointed by the Ministers Council. As already indicated, the constitution did not provide for any elections whatsoever and was capable of amendment only by South Africa. Furthermore, no machinery was provided for the achievement of final "independence," and essentially the constitution would have the effect of continued white domination in a fragmented territory.

7. A detailed account of the negotiations on Namibia carried on by the contact group was provided by the secretary of state for external affairs of Canada, Don Jamieson, on April 25, 1978, to the Ninth Special Session of the General Assembly on behalf of the five governments of Canada, the United Kingdom, the United States, France, and the Federal Republic of Germany.

8. Almost simultaneous with the Mondale–Vorster meeting was a special six-day United Nations Conference in Maputo, Mozambique, that ended with an assertion that the armed struggle of Namibians, coupled with international action, had created positive conditions for settlement in Namibia. The Maputo Conference called for a special United Nations Conference to review the "Namibian

question" and also reiterated that SWAPO was the sole and authentic representative of the people of Namibia. The Turnhalle conference was denounced, and complete isolation was called for of any interim government arising from it.

6. Angola

1. Senator Dick Clark, "Angola Still Off Limits: Reaffirming the Clark Amendment," *The Nation*, August 5–12, 1978, p. 111.

2. *The New York Times*, May 31, 1961.

3. George Thomas, M.P., and the Rev. Eric L. Blakebrough in *Congo-Angola Border Enquiry* (London: Angola Action Group, 1961), p. 12.

4. United Nations, Committee on Decolonization, A/AC 109/L. 765, March 24, 1972, p. 23.

5. *The Economist*, February 26, 1972.

6. *Le Monde*, March 30, 1972.

7. United Nations, Committee on Decolonization, p. 22.

8. See text in Mohamed A. El-Khawas and Baring Cohen, *The Kissinger Study of Southern Africa* (Westport, Conn.: Lawrence Hill and Co., 1976).

9. *Izvestia*, October 10, 1976.

10. *Informação do Bureau Político Sobre a Tentativa de Golpe de Estado de 27 de Maio*. Special edition of MPLA, *Boletim do Militante*. Luanda, July 12, 1977.

11. *The Observer* (London), March 26, 1978; *The New York Times*, May 24, 1978.

12. John Stockwell, *In Search of Enemies: A CIA Story* (New York: Norton, 1978).

13. Agostinho Neto, "Who is the Enemy?" *Angola in Arms* (Richmond, B.C.), May-August, 1974.

7. Zambia

1. For an analysis of Zambia's foreign and development policies since 1964, see Douglas G. Anglin and Timothy M. Shaw, *Zambia's Foreign Policy: Studies in Diplomacy and Dependence* (Boulder: Westview, 1979).

2. On the series of declarations and documents that reflect these responses, see Timothy M. Shaw, "The Foreign Policy of Zambia: Ideology and Interests," *Journal of Modern African Studies* 14(1), March 1976, pp. 79–105.

3. Urban-rural disparities and decentralization, and class formation and centralization are discussed in later sections of this chapter.

4. A. D. Roberts, "The Lumpa Church of Alice Lenshina," in Robert I. Rotberg and Ali A. Mazuri, eds., *Protest and Power in Black Africa* (New York: Oxford University Press, 1970), pp. 513–68; *Report of the Commission of Inquiry into the Former Lumpa Church* (Lusaka: Government Printer, 1965).

5. Gerald L. Caplan, "Barotseland: The Secessionist Challenge to Zambia," *Journal of Modern African Studies* 6(3), October 1968, pp. 343–60.

6. U.N. Security Council S/PV.1944, July 27, 1976.

7. Thomas Rasmussen, "Political Competition and One-Party Dominance in Zambia," *Journal of Modern African Studies* 7(3), October 1969, pp. 407–424.

8. Robert Molteno, "Cleavage and conflict in Zambian politics: a study in sectionalism," in William Tordoff, ed., *Politics in Zambia* (Berkeley: University of California Press, 1975), pp. 62–106.

9. See Jan Pettman, "Zambia's Second Republic: The Establishment of a One-Party State," *Journal of Modern African Studies* 12(2), June 1974, pp. 231–44.

New elections are to be held before the end of 1978, though the president may postpone them for up to five years if the country is "at war." Constitution of Zambia Act, 1973, sec. 93(4).

10. William Tordoff, "Zambia: The Politics of Disengagement," *African Affairs* 76(302), January 1977, p. 69.

11. See Douglas G. Anglin, "Zambia and Southern African Liberation Movements: 1964–1974," in Timothy M. Shaw and Kenneth A. Heard, eds., *Politics of Africa: Dependence and Development* (New York: Africana, 1978).

12. "Speech on Angola by H.E. Dr. K. D. Kaunda, President of Zambia to the OAU in Addis Ababa on 12 January 1976," *Southern African Record* (Johannesburg) 10, October 1977, pp. 1, 4, 5, 6.

13. On this period, contrast Douglas G. Anglin, "Zambia and Southern African 'detente'," *International Journal* 30(3), Summer 1975, pp. 471–503, and Timothy M. Shaw and Agrippah T. Mugomba, "The Political Economy of Regional Detente: Zambia and Southern Africa," *Journal of African Studies* 4(4), Winter 1977–78, pp. 392–413.

14. "Press statement concerning the breakdown of the Smith-Nkomo constitutional talks by the President of Zambia, H.E. Dr. K. D. Kaunda on 22 March 1976," *Southern African Record* 10, October 1977, pp. 13–14.

15. "Exclusive interview: Dr. Kenneth Kaunda, President of Zambia, talks to Africa's Raph Uwechue," *Africa* 77, January 1978, p. 16.

16. On Zambia's attempts to disengage and reengage, see Douglas G. Anglin, "The Politics of Transit Routes in Land-locked Southern Africa," in Zdenek Cervenka, ed., *Land-locked Countries of Africa* (Uppsala: Scandinavian Institute of African Studies, 1973), pp. 98–133, and "Zambian Disengagement from Southern Africa and Integration with East Africa, 1964–1972: A Transaction Analysis," in Timothy M. Shaw and Kenneth A. Heard, eds., *Cooperation and Conflict in Southern Africa: Papers on a Regional Subsystem* (Washington: University Press of America, 1976), pp. 228–89.

17. *Communocracy (A Strategy for Constructing a People's Economy under Humanism).* Addresses by His Excellency the President, Dr. K. D. Kaunda to the Leadership Seminar and the Ninth UNIP National Council held at Mulungushi Rock, Kabwe, 14th–24th September, 1976.

18. See Timothy M. Shaw, "Zambia: Dependence and Underdevelopment," *Canadian Journal of African Studies* 10(1), 1976, pp. 3–22.

19. K. D. Kaunda, *Humanism in Zambia and a Guide to its Implementation,* Part II (Lusaka: Government Printer, 1974), p. 110.

20. By 1975 Zambia's debt commitments totaled $1,465m. Its debt ratio (debt service charges/export earnings) is 23-25, higher than the "supposed bell weather figure of 20." *African Business,* May 1978, p. 24.

21. "Our Only Hope to Borrow," *New African* 129, May 1978, p. 147.

8. Botswana

1. *Daily News* (Botswana), June 14, 1976. Report of speech by President Khama in New York. .

2. "Botswana," in *African Contemporary Record (ACR),* draft manuscript, May 1981, pp. 11–12.

3. *ACR,* 1976–77 edition, London: Rex Collings, 1977.

4. *Daily News,* June 23, 1977.

5. *Statistical Bulletin,* December 1980, Gaborone, p. 15.
6. Ibid.
7. *ACR,* 1981, op. cit., p. 26.
8. Ibid.
9. Department of Mines, *Annual Report, 1979,* April 1980, Gaborone.
10. Ibid.
11. Budget Speech, February 23, 1981, p. 2.
12. *ACR,* op. cit., p. 28.
13. Ibid., pp. 15–16.
14. *Report of the Salaries Review Commission, 1980,* Gaborone.
15. Budget Speech, op. cit., p. 12.
16. *Statistical Bulletin,* op. cit., p. 38.
17. Speech at Gaborone Trade Fair, July, 1976.
18. *Daily News,* July 18, 1977.
19. See Paul Mosley, "The Southern African Customs Union: A Reappraisal," *World Development,* vol. 6, no. 1, 1978, pp. 31–43.
20. See Gwendolen M. Carter and E. Philip Morgan, eds., *From the Front Line: Policy Speeches of Sir Seretse Khama,* London: Rex Collings, 1980.

9. Lesotho

1. The meanings of African terms used in this chapter are as follows: Lesotho and Botswana refer to the respective African states; Basotho and Batswana are plural forms referring to citizens of those states unless otherwise specified. Basutoland and Bechuanaland Protectorate were the colonial names.

2. For a historical survey of human rights in Lesotho, see Richard F. Weisfelder, "The Decline of Human Rights in Lesotho: An Evaluation of Domestic and External Determinants," in *Issue,* vol. VI, no. 4 (Winter 1976), pp. 22–23.

3. The composition and outlooks of Basotho political parties are discussed in Richard F. Weisfelder, *Defining National Purpose in Lesotho.* Papers in International Studies, Africa Series, no. 16 (Athens, Ohio: Ohio University Center for International Studies, 1969).

4. Chief Jonathan's political performance from 1965 to 1970 is discussed at length in Richard F. Weisfelder, "Lesotho," in Christian P. Potholm and Richard Dale, eds., *Southern Africa: Essays in Regional Politics* (New York: The Free Press, 1972), pp. 125–40.

5. See W. J. A. Macartney, "The Lesotho General Election of 1970," *Government and Opposition,* vol. 8, no. 4 (Autumn 1973), pp. 121–40.

6. The economic achievements of the BNP regime from 1965 to 1970 are summarized in Richard F. Weisfelder, "Lesotho," in Potholm and Dale, ibid.

7. Excellent analyses of migration and rural life appear in Iam Hamnett, "Land Shortage in Lesotho," *African Affairs* (London), vol. 72, no. 286 (January 1973), pp. 241–51; and Sandra Wallman, *Take Out Hunger: Two Case Studies of Rural Development in Basutoland* (New York: The Humanities Press, 1969).

8. See Francis d'A Collings, et. al., "The Rand and the Monetary Systems of Botswana, Lesotho and Swaziland," *The Journal of Modern African Studies,* vol. 16, no. 1 (1978), pp. 97–121.